From Millionaires *to* Commoners

The History of Jekyll Island State Park

NICK DOMS

authorHOUSE

AuthorHouse™
1663 Liberty Drive
Bloomington, IN 47403
www.authorhouse.com
Phone: 1 (800) 839-8640

© 2019 Nick Doms. All rights reserved.

No part of this book may be reproduced, stored in a retrieval system, or transmitted by any means without the written permission of the author.

Published by AuthorHouse   January 2019

ISBN: 978-1-5462-6916-8 (sc)
ISBN: 978-1-5462-6915-1 (hc)
ISBN: 978-1-5462-6914-4 (e)

Library of Congress Control Number: 2018913746

Printed in the United States of America.

Any people depicted in stock imagery provided by Getty Images are models, and such images are being used for illustrative purposes only.
Certain stock imagery © Getty Images.

This book is printed on acid-free paper.

Because of the dynamic nature of the Internet, any web addresses or links contained in this book may have changed since publication and may no longer be valid. The views expressed in this work are solely those of the author and do not necessarily reflect the views of the publisher, and the publisher hereby disclaims any responsibility for them.

*For my beautiful wife, Teolita,
my eternal muse ...
With love, always.*

CONTENTS

Acknowledgments ix
Preface xi
Introduction xv

PART I: 1945–1986

Chapter 1	The Search for Coastal Tourism 1
Chapter 2	From Exclusive Island to Public Park 5
Chapter 3	The Battle for the Bridge 25
Chapter 4	An Island Crippled by Political Monopoly 59
Chapter 5	The Growing Pains of an Island..................................... 83
Chapter 6	An Island Rises from the Marshes................................119
Chapter 7	The State Park-Island Resort Oxymoron...................... 143
Chapter 8	The Signs of Historic Decline 165
Chapter 9	An Island at Crossroads 193
Chapter 10	The Road to Historic Preservation 239

PART II: 1987–2015

Chapter 11	The Period of Stagnation and Hesitation 275
Chapter 12	The Financial Conundrum... 301
Chapter 13	The Cosmetic Change Hides the Ugly..........................321
Chapter 14	The New Bridge to an Old Island Resort..................... 333
Chapter 15	Setting a New Course 343
Chapter 16	The Hard Road to Reinventing Jekyll.......................... 363
Chapter 17	Jekyll Becomes Every Developer's Favored Child 393
Chapter 18	Island Development: Slower, Smaller 413
Chapter 19	The Final Cut 429

Epilogue	451
Addendum 1	453
Addendum 2	457
Addendum 3	463
Addendum 4	467
Addendum 5	471
Bibliography	473
About the Author	477
About the Book	479

ACKNOWLEDGMENTS

The task of researching and writing a history book is never the sole accomplishment of one person. It does indeed take a village to write a book of this magnitude, and in this case, as is appropriate, it took an island of loving, caring people to complete the task.

My sincere thanks to Lorraine Donohue, my proofreader and editor, for spending countless hours carefully combing through the manuscript, for sharing her knowledge and personal stories with me, and for introducing me to a multitude of residents with personal knowledge and experience. I am forever in your debt!

To all the wonderful people of Jekyll Island, I owe you my gratitude for guiding and assisting me in more ways than I can recount. They include foremost Bruce Piatek, director of historic resources; Rose Marie Kimbell, archivist; and Andrea Marroquin, curator, of the Jekyll Island State Park Authority. Without your dedicated assistance, the extensive research for this book would have been impossible.

My thanks to John Donohue, Lisa and Brett Stovall, Jackie and Bruce Becker, Christine and Ron Myers, Rita and Mike Thompson, Theresa and Jim LaPean, Pamela and Mike Mueller, Paul Tillman, Eric Moody, Aaron Carone, Pam and Vance Hughes, Mindy and David Egan, and so many other Jekyll residents for your continued support and encouragement.

My gratitude goes to Caryl and Ted Rice, Jean Poleszak, Barbara Zachry, and Dan Simpson for providing access to historic information to complement this book.

Finally, eternal gratitude is due to my wife, Teolita (Teo), who patiently and lovingly allowed me to spend months away from home to complete my research and write in solitude.

PREFACE

My first encounter with Jekyll Island occurred in October 2014. I was scheduled to attend a conference here and had planned a few days of beach relaxation at the same time. I vividly remember driving over the M. E. Thompson Bridge, looking at Jekyll Island right in front of me, and being completely awestruck that very moment.

To this day, I still cannot explain why that first glimpse and that exact moment transformed my life completely, other than to say it was love at first sight.

It is a simple way to explain a feeling that most people have experienced at least once in their lives, albeit in a different way and probably under different circumstances that would involve a man or woman. Nevertheless, it is that same inexplicable emotion that stops your heart for just a split second when rational thinking makes way for pure joy, love, and happiness.

That was the emotional exuberance I felt just as I reached the top of the bridge, and it is a feeling I experience each time I cross that same bridge that leads me into my newfound paradise and piece of heaven.

I have since returned to Jekyll Island numerous times, as often as I can. Living and working in nearby Savannah obviously does not create much of an impediment either.

On that very first visit, I explored anything and everything to see, feel, sense, and experience, and I could not get enough. I started reading anything I could find about its history, old and older at first, until I had depleted the rich arsenal of historic books; there are plenty to be read.

My professional background as a Wall Street financier and my early employment with the JP Morgan empire made my visits even more compelling and attractive. Here, I could connect with the more private and exclusive side of my former employer, as well as with all his business associates and friends of the early days.

I was stunned to discover that all the history books suddenly ended with the demise of the Millionaires Club and era, as if nothing happened after that last winter of 1942. Surely there must be more to tell. The island did not transform itself from the most exclusive and private club to a state park, open and accessible to all. The multitude of hotels, motels, picnic areas, roads, and trails certainly did not appear spontaneously, as if by the waving of a magic wand, all had been created out of thin air. So, what is the story, and who are the people who designed, constructed, and managed this enormous transformation? When did it start—and more importantly, why?

Each time I returned to the island, I made new friends—locals who had lived on the island for many decades, and others who recently moved here after spending several years visiting. I listened to their stories about how they first learned about Jekyll Island and what motivated them to move or retire here. The stories and reasons are as diverse as the residents themselves, but all of them have one thing in common: a deeply rooted love and appreciation for the unique surroundings and lifestyle on the island.

That still begged the eternal questions. Why had nobody ever documented the history of Jekyll Island since it became a state park in 1947? And why had nobody written about how or why it happened in that specific year, or who designed the initial development plans? Surely, there had to be a history book that I might have missed, and there had to be some rudimentary documentation about the inception, development, and construction of the state park and the authority.

Each time I raised the questions, the answer was always the same. Nobody had ever documented a comprehensive historic book of Jekyll Island, a state park, and if the topic so intrigued me, then I should start writing the missing link myself.

I am not exactly sure what thoughts came to mind at that specific moment, but I do remember saying that I would take on the project, research the topic and history, and try to write a comprehensive development story from the island's birth as a state park in 1947 to the present, and anything of consequence in between.

After several months of researching the authority's archives, reading the multitude of newspaper articles, digging up old documents, and interviewing several involved people, I understood why this piece of history had never been documented. It is a Herculean task, and many times I felt like Ariadne, trying to let the real story find its way out of the labyrinth of documents, press releases, board meetings, plans, alterations, and changes of direction.

The missing link is now finally here.

The reward for the lengthy days of research and writing is not simply the completion of the book. It is much deeper and far more philosophical than that. I have had the privilege of living through seventy years of history, day by day, week by week, and year by year as if I had been part of it and witnessed the transformation in real time. This writing project has given me a unique perspective and understanding of the complexity of such an endeavor as the creation of a state park out of the ruins of an exclusive era gone by. It has given me an additional layer of appreciation for my newfound love and my slice of paradise, one I hope transcends and translates to each reader as the pages of history are being turned.

If love for Jekyll Island was my catalyst, then I hope the story becomes your very own Ariadne and a thread that will lead you through the maze and labyrinth of complex and complicated decisions—some man-made, some circumstantial, others rational, and some questionable.

Nevertheless, may the comprehensive historical recantation shed light on the complexity and may it contribute to the admiration of its natural simplicity that exists today.

INTRODUCTION

The transformation of a private, secluded, and exclusive island into a state park with open and affordable access to all Georgians requires a well-thought-out plan and the meticulous implementation afterward. It also necessitates a group of people dedicated to the performance and success of such, inspired by M.E. Thompson's mandate to offer the island's amenities at the lowest rates "reasonable and possible" for the "ordinary people" of Georgia.

But plans and ideas come and go over time. They change depending on who makes the decisions and who is in charge. It doesn't come as a surprise that Jekyll Island has seen its fair share of development and land-use plans over the last seventy years. The number of plans almost equals the number of board members that came and went with the election of governors or changes in policy.

Long-term planning requires something more philosophical, like a vision for the future that can encompass and embrace all plans without interruption or change of course.

If one thing can be said about the creation of Jekyll Island State Park, it is that since early 1948, a multitude of plans surfaced, but not one vision was ever clearly defined.

The story of Jekyll Island State Park is marred with politics since the early beginning, despite Gov. Talmadge's decision to establish the Jekyll Island Authority "to create a non-political authority and to remove Jekyll Island from politics" (*Brunswick News*, February 17, 1950).

While the goal was lofty in nature, the reality was that the first appointments to the authority, and any subsequent ones in the coming years, were all fueled by politics and not necessarily inspired by qualifications, expertise, or knowledge.

Based on this approach, it is no surprise that a visionary, if such a person existed at that time, was absent from the new authority. Instead, the initial five members, relying on Mr. J.D. Compton's recommendation, opted for a development plan without regard for the need of a clearly defined mandate or vision for the island. The determination of a possible vision because of a proposed development plan was entirely left to the design company Robert & Co.

Since the Authority Act specifically mandated that Jekyll Island be self-sufficient, it is fair to assume that the motivation behind the development was to ensure that such would create the necessitated amount of revenue centers to support the low-cost facilities that had to be included. Right from the beginning, this duality of revenue generation versus public and free cost centers took precedence over any type of vision one or more of the board members may have had. That duality is best described as the perpetual Dr. Jekyll and Mr. Hyde, and the battle between the year-round resort and the state park still exists today.

It also explains the multitude of development and land-use plans over the course of seventy years. One can imagine that changing times call for flexibility and adaptation of previous master plans, but that does not explain or justify the drastic change in approach. Dramatic alterations to previous plans with the proposal of a new plan or idea always point to contradictions where the new proposal no longer complements the previous execution, which then leads to a complete overhaul.

Consider starting a puzzle with more than a thousand pieces. Unless one has a clear view (vision) of what the puzzle will look like once completed, then one can try to place several pieces in the empty spots for quite a while. The more pieces are placed, the more difficult it becomes to place the remaining pieces until ultimately the remainder no longer fits into the empty spots unless previous pieces are removed. This can become an endless and ongoing exercise if continued in the same fashion, and one that is never finished. The solution would be to simply establish a clear view (vision) of the puzzle and start identifying the perimeter pieces first, which will make placing adjacent pieces easier and will lead to the full completion of the puzzle and the achievement of a vision through the careful implementation of multiple pieces (plans).

Obviously, this can no longer be achieved with Jekyll Island, hence every ten or twenty years, a new plan is carefully written, one that can hopefully fill in the empty and remaining spots without too much damage to the existing structure.

Hence, in the case of Jekyll Island State Park, the multiple plans have caused the vision, or initial lack thereof, to adapt itself into a less-than-perfect and artificial symbiosis between two visions and their related plans—the enduring marriage between a state park and the resort side of the island.

It is remarkable though that given the strict mandate and the lack of expertise in 1948, Jekyll Island has developed into what we see today, all while maintaining its natural beauty and surroundings. The road traveled though was certainly not paved evenly, and many obstacles had to be overcome to achieve this kind of result and success, although not applauded by all.

Those who dared to travel the road laid out for them, or those who didn't really have an option other than to travel, must be commended for their perseverance, if not for anything else, and this is their story as much as Jekyll Island's.

When placed in the corresponding time, circumstances, and prevailing conditions, the story becomes more tangible and realistic. The use of the present tense while narrating aids in creating understanding and amplifies the multitude of difficulties the early authority faced. It also enforces their daily struggle with the multifaceted problems and decisions that had to be made, mostly immediately, and with little time to digest the consequences of their decisions.

In addition, the story clearly shows that a multitude of plans, as well intended as they may have been at the time, often contradicted each other, albeit not always immediately.

The intention of this book is not to question the destiny of the island but merely to expose, clarify, and narrate the road traveled so that we may see the road ahead more clearly.

Who knows? Maybe one day our vision will prevail and supersede the multiple plans, and the puzzle will guide each piece we wish to place and not interfere with the ones already present.

PART I

1945–1986

THE BIRTH OF JEKYLL ISLAND STATE PARK

CHAPTER 1

THE SEARCH FOR COASTAL TOURISM

1945

World War II is finally ending, and soldiers are coming home in droves, dreaming of a peaceful future with family and friends.

Even Jekyll Island returns to its natural habitat. The soldiers from the 104th Infantry and the 725th MP Battalion who relentlessly patrolled the island day and night since the beginning of the war are now returning home to their families or their base camp in -Brunswick. The island is left behind to fight for itself, and so are the historic buildings, cottages, and handful of houses on Pier Road.

Once the home of the famous millionaires who called the island their private playground and winter retreat, the little gem looks more like a worn-out, abused, and tired stretch of coastline.

Maintenance and upkeep of the manicured lawns and beautifully tiled swimming pool, not to mention the club golf course, ceased when the millionaires abandoned their winter resort in April 1942, never to return. The island looks more like a weeping wilderness that is crying out for some tender loving care by someone, somebody, anybody.

The Sea Island Company offers to assist with the management of Jekyll Island upon the request of Bernon Prentice, president of the Jekyll Island Club. The cooperation between Alfred Jones, cofounder of the Sea Island Company, and Mr. Prentice dates to late 1942 when the club needed to find ways to make ends meet. After all, member contributions were steadily diminishing now that the club hotel decided to remain closed for the near future, and maintenance costs kept adding up. Despite Mr. Prentice's effort to find additional revenue sources to keep the Jekyll Island Club afloat by contracting with the American Creosite Company[1] to harvest timber on the island, the club is in dire financial straits.

Mr. Jones even considers buying Jekyll Island and instructs J. D. Compton, president of his company, to prepare a feasibility study to determine whether the island is appropriate for building a small resort like the existing Cloysters. The main problem is, of course, finding enough financing, not only to restore the club hotel and its adjacent buildings and cottages but also to finance a causeway and bridge to the island, which Sea Island has benefited from since 1927.[2]

Unfortunately, the cost is estimated at $130,000, and the only club member who can afford such an investment, Frank Gould, passes away suddenly that same year.[3]

The study concludes that such an endeavor will not be profitable, at least not in the early years of existence, so the plans are canceled. It is not known with certainty how J. D. Compton came to this conclusion, given his involvement in the Jekyll Island State Park Authority four years later. What can be concluded is that he must have had the foresight that a competing luxury resort within proximity of Sea Island, and with access to ten miles of unspoiled, white, sandy beaches, would be detrimental to the Cloysters.[4]

This seemingly missed opportunity ends up being a blessing for the state of Georgia and all its people.

Prior to 1945, Georgia never thought about tourism as a state industry, let alone made any investment in it. But that is about to change if Governor Ellis Arnall gets his way.

---

[1] The American Creosite Company paid the Jekyll Island Club $44,000 for harvesting timber on the island from 1941 to 1944.

[2] The F. J. Torres Causeway and first drawbridge connecting the mainland with St. Simons and Sea Island were constructed in 1927.

[3] Frank Gould passed away suddenly on January 13, 1945, from a heart attack.

[4] J. D. Compton was instrumental in the hiring of Robert & Co. to develop a master plan for Jekyll Island that would focus on affordability and accessibility for all Georgians, an indication that he did not want Jekyll Island to become a competitor with Sea Island.

Ellis Arnall is considered one of the most progressive and liberal governors of his time, and he is one of the youngest to rise to power. His appointment to the Georgia House of Representatives at the ripe age of twenty-five was only the beginning of his stellar political career. At age twenty-nine, Governor E. D. Rivers appointed Arnall to the office of state attorney general, only to name him attorney general two years later. When in 1942, at age thirty-five, Arnall ran for governor against the popular but controversial Eugene Talmadge, he became the youngest governor in Georgia's history.

His progressive stance leads him to change Georgia's image of a tobacco road state into a progressive and liberal state—and with it the first attempt to promote Georgia as a tourist destination. Governor Arnall is also credited with creating the Georgia Teachers Retirement System, which will play an important role in the financing and construction of the first commercial motel on Jekyll Island.

Unfortunately, Georgia does not have the same white, sandy beaches of Florida or South Carolina, but that does not deter Governor Arnall. His eyes are set on all the traffic that drives through Georgia using Highway US-17, better known as the Coastal Highway, on their way to and from Daytona Beach, which is one of the most visited vacation spots.

Each year, thousands of cars pass through Georgia on their way to Florida, but few stop and spend a few days of leisure. Even Tybee Island in the north, with its stretch of north and south beach, is not inviting or enticing enough. And St. Simons Island, more specifically Sea Island, is so exclusive that it is only affordable for the rich and famous, not the average tourist or Georgian. The barrier islands in between are still privately owned, and neither is accessible by car or has infrastructure to accommodate the willing visitor.

If the passing-through tourists can be enticed to make a pit stop somewhere along their long drive to Florida, then a brand-new tourism industry in Georgia can be created—and with it a new source of income.[5]

Less than one year later, Governor Arnall pursues his dream of creating a statewide tourism industry and appoints his protegee, Melvin E.

---

[5] Georgia tourism accounted for $59 billion in 2015 revenue and generated $3 billion in local and state taxes (GDEcD-Georgia Department of Economic Development-2015).

Thompson, to chair a special state beach park committee. Charles Gowen, state representative and committee member, is credited with approaching J. D. Compton about the possible acquisition of Jekyll Island.[6]

The search for a new industry—and the first oceanfront tourist destination—has begun. The quest for acquiring Jekyll Island and turning a once private and exclusive paradise island into a popular tourist destination and a state park is launched.

The hard road from millionaires to commoners is being prepared but paving it to gain accessibility and affordability for all will prove cumbersome.

Nevertheless, no efforts or resources will be spared to achieve this goal—and to realize Governor Ellis Arnall and Governor Melvin E. Thompson's dream.

---

[6] Charles Gowen contacted J. D. Compton by phone on August 19, 1946, as a state representative, to inquire about the availability of Jekyll Island and the possible price (J. D. Compton to Alfred Jones, August 20, 1946, SICR).

CHAPTER 2

FROM EXCLUSIVE ISLAND TO PUBLIC PARK
1946–1949

The year is 1946, and Governor Ellis Arnall is serving the last year of his term. Since he has decided not to seek reelection, it promises to become an interesting and tumultuous year—or years to come.

A legislative resolution in the newly ratified and adopted 1945 state constitution allows Georgia to acquire seashore within its borders for the development of a state park. The resolution also states that the acquisition of such land may be obtained through condemnation or eminent domain, if such is in the best interest and for the betterment of the people of Georgia.

Immediately following the ratification and the general assembly's resolution to establish a seaside state park, Governor Arnall appoints his executive secretary, Melvin E. Thompson, as the new revenue commissioner and tasks him to chair the committee[7] to locate the perfect island for the development of a state park.

On September 26, 1946, the *Brunswick News* reports that the committee has chosen Jekyll Island.

> The proximity of the island to the mainland, facilities already installed there, which include a golf course, swimming pool, many miles of roadways, and a large

---

[7] State Beach Park Committee was formed by Gov. Ellis Arnall in August 1946.

clubhouse which could be converted into a hotel, as well as the natural beauty of the island were cited by the Committee as reasons for the choice of Jekyll as the most suited on the coast for a state park.

Not a lot of information can be found about the exact reasoning or analysis that led to the single choice of Jekyll Island as the most suitable place among all Georgia's barrier islands.[8] Suffice it to say, Commissioner Thompson and his team early on noticed that a single owner held the recorded deed of Jekyll Island, namely the Jekyll Island Club Inc.,[9] and could therefore easily be obtained. Secondly, and probably the most enticing reason for choosing Jekyll Island, was the fact that, per state revenue records, the Jekyll Island Club had been in arrear for state taxes since 1942. Add to this equation that the club was not in very good financial health, had not attempted to open or operate the Jekyll Island Club since 1942, and had seen its once prominent membership dwindle during the war.[10]

The combination of the dire financial straits of the Jekyll Island Club and the state's desire and resolution to acquire seashore land for a state park could not have culminated at a better time for Commissioner Thompson.

Despite the committee's recommendation and the seemingly perfect alignment of circumstances, which should have favored Governor Arnall's decision to proceed with the condemnation filing, he decides to postpone the purchase. That delay would eventually turn into a political battle between his successors and those believed to be his rightfully elected successors.

Before we examine the exact process of condemnation proceedings and the ultimate unopposed acquisition of Jekyll Island, it is important that

---

[8] Blackbeard Island, Saint Simons Island, and Ossabaw Island were also considered. State Representative Charles Gowen, also a committee member, ruled out all and proposed Jekyll Island, an island synonymous with unlimited wealth (reported phone conversation between Charles Gowen and J. D. Compton on August 19, 1946).

[9] The Jekyll Island Club was incorporated on December 9, 1885. The Club purchased Jekyll Island from Eugene DuBignon on February 17, 1886.

[10] An attempt was made in 1944 to create a syndicate to purchase all outstanding bonds issued by the Jekyll Island Club in 1933 for ten cents to the dollar. The syndicate collapsed, and by 1947, only nine club members remained.

we shed some light on the surrounding circumstances of 1946–1947 and the ensuing years so that we may better understand the early years and the subsequent political, financial, and managerial challenges our newfound state park faces.

Georgia faces interesting and challenging political campaigns. Governor Arnall is not seeking another term, while Commissioner Thompson seeks the position of lieutenant governor, which was created by the 1945 state constitution.

In addition, there is the flamboyant Eugene Talmadge, a well-known and controversial political figure seeking an unprecedented fourth term in office. Mr. Talmadge served two consecutive terms as governor from 1933 through 1937 and a third term beginning in 1941.[11] If elected, Eugene Talmadge would match Joe Brown's record of the mid-nineteenth century as the only politician to ever have been elected and serve four terms as Georgia's governor.

Given Mr. Talmadge's age and flailing health, the Democratic Party of Georgia takes their precautions to the rural counties and voting booths and makes sure their loyal followers will have the option of a write-in candidate, should Eugene pass away before he can be inaugurated.

That party-promoted write-in candidate is none other than his own son, Herman Talmadge, and one must admit that the Georgia Democratic Party had great foresight and insight, given what occurred after the election.

Eugene Talmadge, popular in the rural areas of Georgia, despite his controversial politics and his clear stance against Roosevelt's New Deal, wins the unopposed election for governor and hereby forever seals his place in state history as only the second politician to be elected four times to the highest political office in the state since Joe Brown in 1863.

During the same election, Melvin E. Thompson is elected as the very first Lt. Governor of Georgia,[12] and all seems to be perfectly fine, except

---

[11] Prior to 1942, the Georgia State Constitution limited the governor's term to two years with only two consecutive terms allowed (Georgiaencyclopedia.org/Georgia-constitution).

[12] The new 1945 State Constitution created the new position of Lt. Governor. The revised constitution was ratified in August 1945. (Georgiaencyclopedia.org/state-constitution)

Nick Doms

at that time, the proposed purchase of Jekyll Island is not on anybody's radar screen. At least not for now.

On December 21, 1946, the new governor-elect of the state of Georgia, Eugene Talmadge, dies and immediately gives rise to what is known as the "three governors controversy" between outgoing Gov. Ellis Arnall, Lt. Gov.-Elect Melvin E. Thompson, and Eugene Talmadge's son, Herman Talmadge, the popular and secret write-in candidate of the Democratic Party.

Immediately following the New Year's celebration, the general assembly decides to appoint the write-in candidate as the next governor—Herman Talmadge—as was standard protocol and in accordance with the Georgia State Constitution, except for one small detail.

The newly ratified 1945 State Constitution stipulated that in the event the governor or governor-elect dies, then the lieutenant governor or lieutenant governor-elect will automatically assume the duties ad interim until a special election can be called.[13]

Lt. Gov.-Elect Melvin E. Thompson assumes the role of governor-elect as per the 1945 State Constitution, while Gov. Arnall decides to continue to act as governor until someone has been appointed or inaugurated as the new governor.

That does not deter Herman Talmadge or his fervent supporters from breaking into the governor's office in the Capitol Building, changing the locks, and taking his seat as acting governor for sixty-seven days. The Capitol Building looks more like a warzone with the National Guard showing their loyalty to their ex-navy commander Talmadge, while the Home Guard protects the interests of outgoing Gov. Arnall.

One must assume that it is impossible to conduct business in such turmoil, but Talmadge has strong support from B. E. Thrasher, the state auditor, who pledges warrants to the banks so that bills are paid, and the government can continue to operate. The warrants are an innovative way to get around the uncooperative state treasurer George Hamilton, who is a strong supporter of Gov. Arnall and loyal friend of Lt. Gov.-Elect Melvin

---

[13] Patrick Novotny, PhD, *This Georgia Rising: Education, Civil Rights, And The Politics Of Elections In Georgia In The 1940s* (Mercer University Press, 2007).

E. Thompson and refuses to sign any checks or pay any bills, including payroll checks, without being able to affix the Seal of the State of Georgia.

The result is that three individuals claim the right to act or continue to act as governor, and the only solution is to let the state Supreme Court make a ruling on this ambivalent and dubious political case. The Supreme Court issues its ruling in March 1947 and decides that per the new state constitution, Lt. Gov.-Elect Melvin E. Thompson will and can act as governor of the state of Georgia until special elections in the fall of 1948.[14]

Herman Talmadge graciously steps aside, following the Supreme Court ruling, and outgoing Gov. Ellis Arnall vacates his office so that state business may be conducted as usual without further interference.

Herman Talmadge's gesture to step down voluntarily and vacate his self-appropriated office in the Capitol Building will win him enormous respect and support of voters in the upcoming election, despite his controversial and racial politics.

One of the great stories told many years later comes from Ben Fortson, secretary of state during those controversial times. Neither of the self-proclaimed governors could execute the office they claimed to represent because neither of them could find the great Seal of the State of Georgia. Ben Fortson carefully protected the seal that was entrusted to him by keeping it hidden under the cushion of his wheelchair until the Supreme Court could make a ruling. Nobody ever suspected Fortson of this mischievous act, and if they had, nobody at that time would have had the courage to search his wheelchair. It is, however, widely known and well documented that all parties involved searched each other's offices relentlessly to locate the great Seal of the State of Georgia.

Three months after the state Supreme Court ruling, Gov. Thompson pursues the purchase of Jekyll Island. Contrary to general belief or perception, the State did not immediately start condemnation proceedings against the Jekyll Island Club to obtain Jekyll Island and create a state park. Even during Gov. Arnall's tenure, several written communications were exchanged between the Governor's Office, the legislation, and Bernon

---

[14] The Georgia State Supreme Court ruled in favor of Lt. Gov.-Elect Melvin Thompson but called for special elections to be held in 1948 to allow the voting public to determine who would fulfill the remainder of the four-year term.

Prentice, president of the Jekyll Island Club. The written exchanges[15] between the two parties, however, were merely an attempt to test the waters of a possible friendly sale-purchase agreement and were never pursued in earnest. Prior to the gubernatorial race of 1946, all communications halted with one last letter[16] from Gov. Arnall stating that the State was no longer interested in an acquisition.

Gov. Thompson however, now clearly able to pursue his dream, picks up the conversation with the Jekyll Island Club again, this time with a proposal directed at J. D. Compton, president of the Sea Island Company, and Alfred "Bill" Jones, cofounder of the Sea Island Company and overseer of Jekyll Island during the war years.

On May 19, 1947, Gov. Thompson makes an official purchase offer for Jekyll Island and all its improvements in the amount of $600,000 as "fair compensation." The answer back is that the island is not for sale. While the answer may puzzle some, it needs to be understood that despite all the financial troubles of the Club, some members still believed that the island could be saved through the formation of a syndicate. History proves that such attempt was futile, but nevertheless, the initial refusal to sell contributed to the expeditious condemnation filings.

On June 3, 1947, Gov. Thompson instructs "Judge" Hartley[17] to draw up the condemnation proceedings, and three weeks later, on June 26, 1947, Judge Gordon Knox presides over the hearing in Glynn County Superior Court. Those who expect a furious battle over exclusive property that has been privately held for over a hundred years are very disappointed. The Club prohibits its lawyers from taking any action and instead instructs the attorneys to seek every fair and legitimate persuasion to keep the State from dismissing the condemnation. That sounds contradictory to any outsider, but understand that the Club, and specifically Bernon Prentice and Alfred "Bill" Jones, who bore the major expenses of island maintenance, could no longer afford to retain the island. Instead, they wanted the State to proceed but at the fairest price possible.

---

[15] *Brunswick News*, September 26, 1946, and *Atlanta Constitution*, September 27, 1946.

[16] Bernon Prentice Memorandum, November 14, 1947, SICR.

[17] A. J. "Judge" Hartley was a former assistant attorney general. He was given the nickname "Judge," although he never served in that official capacity.

The only two other parties, besides the Jekyll Island Club, are Mr. Lawrence Condon and Ms. Margaret Maurice. Both are defendants in the case and want the court to block the State from condemning the island.

As a reference, Mr. Condon had acquired some properties himself on Jekyll Island after settling the estate of Frank Gould,[18] who died unexpectedly in 1945. Mr. Condon, as part of his legal fee and settlement with Ms. Helen Gould, received title of the Gould house[19] and therefore became a party of interest in the court hearings. His petition for a separate hearing was denied previously.

Ms. Margaret Maurice, the title holder of the Hollybourne house, wants her home to be excluded from the sale based on the testimony that Hollybourne was never officially deeded to the Jekyll Island Club Inc. and could therefore not be considered for condemnation inclusion.[20]

With all other legal objections being settled, including a petition from State Rep. Herschel Lovett to prohibit the State from issuing bonds to purchase Jekyll Island, the only unresolved item remaining now is the actual purchase price.

The State's appraisers value Jekyll Island and its improvements at $675,000, while the Club estimates its worth to be $850,000.

Judge Knox settles the case on October 4, 1947 and allows the State of Georgia to condemn Jekyll Island for $675,000, the same appraised value as submitted by the State, and on October 7, 1947, the State takes full legal possession of Jekyll Island.

The final financial settlement of the verdict takes place in January 1948. Court records and financial statements show that Mr. Condon received $60,000 as compensation for his claim, while Ms. Maurice received $20,000 as fair compensation for the Hollybourne house. Most of the net purchase price was paid to the New York Trust Company

---

[18] Frank Gould was one of the nine remaining Jekyll Island Club members after WW II and one of the richest members. His sudden death probably prohibited the club from reviving itself due to lack of capital.

[19] The Gould house refers to Villa Marianna, which still exists today.

[20] During the war, most of the remaining club members had donated their private cottages on the island to the Jekyll Island Club through a quit claim deed. Ms. Maurice had always retained the personal title and deed of Hollybourne Cottage, hence her objection for inclusion in the condemnation proceedings.

($396,000) and Bankers Trust Company ($11,000), with only a mere $153,000 to be distributed among the remaining shareholders. It is not clear who was considered a remaining shareholder at the time of settlement and distribution. It is known, however, that the Maurices, the Goulds, and the Jenningses still held an interest in the club, as well as the Annex Association, which received $18,000 in compensation.[21]

Gov. Melvin E. Thompson has achieved his goal and has realized his dream: "A playground that now belongs to every Georgian."

The Georgia State Parks Department, under the leadership of Director Charlie Morgan, begins repair and construction work in early November 1947. Do not assume that this entails massive construction work or revitalization of any kind. Remember that the island has been sitting idle for five years, with little or no maintenance performed; so, repair work mainly consists of cutting and trimming the overgrowth in and around the club, the original roads in the Historic District, the golf course, and beach access roads.

Gov. Thompson appoints Thomas Briggs as the first manager of the newly renamed Jekyll Island Hotel[22] on February 2, 1948. A previous North Carolina beach park manager with experience in Hotel Fort Raleigh, Roanoke Island, and Manteo, Mr. Briggs receives an annual salary of $6,000 per year and 10 percent of the net profits in exchange for readying the island by spring 1948.

Even though the Causeway, although commissioned and in legislative progress, is not under construction, let alone finished, the Jekyll Island State Park opens to the public for the first time in its history on March 1, 1948.

More than three hundred eager visitors, primarily from Glynn County but also from surrounding counties and curious out of state people, board the *Robert E. Lee* steamer for the forty-five-minute boat ride to Jekyll Island. The roundtrip fare for a day of sightseeing costs $1.50, and there is room for four hundred guests in the Jekyll Island Hotel, the Annex

---

[21] The Jennings family owned what is now known as Villa Ospo. The Annex Association consisted of several club members who had initially financed the Annex building. Although the building was an integral part of the Jekyll Island Club, a separate entity fully owned it.

[22] The Jekyll Island Club was renamed the Jekyll Island Hotel in 1948.

From Millionaires to Commoners

Building, the Sans Souci, and even the Crane House. Guests are treated with dinner in the grand dining room, while a big band is playing in the background. Hotel accommodations for the grand opening are offered as an "American Plan" for five dollars, six dollars, or seven dollars, depending on the choice of room, suite, or accommodations.

The State Park Department has even organized sightseeing bus tours on the island, and for twenty-five cents, one can observe the splendid ocean view, the Club Golf Course, the Oceanside Course, later renamed Great Dunes, or the Horton House. Visitors can also rent scooters and bikes for a small fee and explore the island on their own or take a leisurely tour on horseback. The only thing missing from the attractions is golf. The original Club Golf Course built in 1898 and located on the riverside[23] is still overgrown and not playable at the time. The Oceanside Course, designed by Walter Travis in 1927, and later renamed Great Dunes, is not cleared and ready for play either.

Imagine the sight the first visitors must have experienced when stepping off the boat and onto the wharf where, once upon a time and not too long ago, only the elite millionaires could walk, stroll, dine, and entertain. Despite some early shortcomings and maybe some disappointments as well, this is a dream come true for the average Georgian, and curiosity is not in short supply.

Visitors stroll besides the millionaires' houses, and everybody calls the "humble abodes" by name. They know which one the Jennings House is, or the Gould, Baker, Pulitzer, or James House. They know it all because it has been in the papers for such a long time. Now they can see it with their own eyes, touch it, and even sleep in it. What a sight to see. So many things to do, so many places to see, and so little time.

That most of the island is still largely overgrown and not accessible does not dampen the enthusiasm of the first visitors. This is heaven and paradise as far as they are concerned, and they absorb it all with every step they take.

The following Friday, March 5, 1948, the *Robert E. Lee* steamer is kept at bay in the Brunswick harbor because of strong northeastern winds. Smaller vessels like the *Bernice* can carry one hundred passengers during an early-morning run and another hundred before noon. Overall, two

---

[23] The Club Golf Course was located at today's Jekyll Island Airport.

hundred curious visitors are transported to Jekyll Island in the morning, and by midafternoon, four hundred guests occupy every available room. Even the Boy Scouts and the Brunswick Pirates are joining the party. The Jekyll Island Hotel offers an American Plan, ranging from five to seven dollars per night, and a European Plan, for one to three dollars per night. The hotel's flexible offerings have something for everyone and can accommodate anyone's budget. That is exactly what Gov. Thompson had in mind: open, accessible, and affordable for the average Georgian.

By now, the Jekyll Island Hotel offers various dining locations, readied by the island manager, Mr. Briggs. Visitors can choose to dine in the hotel dining room or opt to enjoy a snack at the snack bar, the cafeteria,[24] or the trading post, located on the old wharf.

The snack bar was located left of the main hotel entrance and lobby and served sodas, candy, cookies, and ice cream. It would continue to serve as a popular snack bar during Barney Whitaker's tenure as hotel lessee and manager in 1949 and 1950.

Guests indulge themselves in the luxuries left behind by the millionaires. After all, with the purchase of the island also comes all the luxury furnishings, including an extensive library, with some of the books marked by the previous Jekyll Island Club owner or donor. Every guest can sleep in the same luxurious bed, place their clothes in the same ornate drawers and chests, and of course relax on the velvet lounge chairs and sofas.

Unfortunately, some guests do more than simply enjoy the luxury. They want to keep a small souvenir—and who will really miss one single plate or glass, or even a simple set of fork, knife, and spoon, all carrying the club's exclusive emblem or embossment. Several "small" inventory items disappear in the first year, either taken by guests or hotel staff.

By the end of April, more than six thousand visitors make the daytrip to the island in one single week; such is the immediate popularity of the new state park.

But not everything runs so smoothly in the background. There is still the political side of Herman Talmadge and allies who remember the Supreme

---

[24] The makeshift cafeteria was probably located in one of the small cottages on Pier Road (based on limited description from archived documents and newspaper clippings).

Court ruling and gear up early for the special election in September 1948. The Thompson opposition uses every possible opportunity to publicly declare their disagreement over the Jekyll Island purchase, which they immediately dub Thompson's "white elephant" and "a place where crooked politicians can hide and spend tax money." Insurance Commissioner Zack Gravey, a fervent Talmadge supporter, publicly calls the Jekyll Island Hotel a fire trap. The accusation features prominently in local newspapers and causes the termination of A. L. Pope, the island's first fire chief. Poor Mr. Pope is dismissed after only one full day on the job, but his name will resurface very soon.

The state legislation is not sitting still either, and B. E. Thrasher,[25] state auditor, calls for the first profit and loss statement on Jekyll Island State Park. Law requires Mr. Briggs to submit such reports within fifteen days of the end of each quarter, and on April 19, 1948, Mr. Briggs is considered four days late. The first quarterly report shows a profit of $15,930.39 and a loss of $15,895.59, resulting in a net profit of $31.32 for the state and $3.48 for Mr. Briggs. Not a bad result for the first month of operations, given that there is no road to the island from the mainland, let alone a bridge over Jekyll Creek. That is going to change soon enough if the legislation gets its way.

The general assembly approves the building of a causeway over Colonel's Island and Latham Hammock in January 1948 and files its request with the US Bureau of Public Roads for matching funds. The cost is estimated at $2 million, with 50 percent to be paid by the state of Georgia through its State Highway Department.

In May 1948, two contracts are allowed to start the causeway project. The dredging contract is let to Hendry Corp. of Florida, and the construction contract is fulfilled by W. L. Cobb Construction of Decatur, Georgia—an immense project and one that will see multiple delays because of funding and unexpected dredging and road stability problems.

The new causeway is to be seven miles long and run through marshland to the westside of Jekyll Creek. As unimaginable as this project sounds today, it was common practice to simply dredge the marshes on both sides of the proposed route to build a foundation upon which the roadbed

---

[25] B. E. Thrasher, as state auditor, was also a member of Melvin Thompson's Special State Beach Park Committee in 1946.

could be built. The fact that such a long road could or would disrupt the natural tidal movements in the surrounding marshes and have a serious ecological and environmental impact was not considered or thought of in 1948. Possible flooding during high tide or heavy thunderstorms did not deter the original plans.

At the same time, the state also allows contracts to redirect US-17 south of the F. J. Torras Causeway to connect with the new causeway to Jekyll.[26] The multitude of simultaneous projects does not deter Gov. Thompson, who announces on June 19, 1948, that the causeway will be ready by May 1, 1949. There is still no mention of a bridge over Jekyll Creek, but visitors are happy to hear that two miles of pristine ocean beach has been or will be set aside for the Boys and Girls Scouts, each of which will have public access to one mile for their own entertainment and enjoyment. In addition, thirty efficiency cabins, featuring one to three bedrooms, will be constructed on the island. Both plans are applauded in the local press, but neither one of them materializes, disappearing from the radar screen to make room for more pressing issues.

The news of a new ferry service between St. Simons Island and Jekyll Island is welcomed. Now visitors will be able to go island hopping on board the *Robert E. Lee* to Jekyll Island and on board a converted navy carrier, the *Biscayne*, to St. Simons Island. The *Biscayne* will depart the St. Simons pier at 10:00 a.m., 1:30 p.m., and 4:00 p.m.; and from the Jekyll Island wharf at 11:15 a.m., 2:45 p.m., and 6:45 p.m.

Jekyll Island State Park becomes more popular with time. The Georgia Chamber of Commerce holds its annual meeting on the island for the first time, and the state's 4-H Club holds its first rally. The spring of 1948 counts no less than four large conventions on the island with the Kiwanis Club, the State Press Association, the State County Commissioners, and the Schoolboy Safety Patrol all visiting Jekyll Island. The average attendance of the conventions is 250, and despite the lack of a large or formal meeting room, let alone a convention center, the Jekyll Island Hotel can easily accommodate the visitors.

The real attraction is of course when the newspapers announce the upcoming Miss Jekyll Island State Park pageant on August 1, 1948, and

---

[26] The old US-17, also known as Coastal Highway-Route 17, bypassed Brunswick to the west and connected to Spring Bluff to the south, slightly west of the current I-95.

the election of Miss Georgia State Park three weeks later, on August 22. Forty aspiring beauty queens between the ages of fifteen and twenty-one compete in the pageant in front of hundreds of curious onlookers, and Miss Jane Pitts becomes the first "Miss Jekyll Island State Park."

Given its increasing popularity, it is no surprise that B. E. Thrasher, state auditor, reports a net profit of $8,018 for the second quarter of 1948. Things are looking good, despite the lack of a causeway, a bridge, or even road expansion on the island itself. None of these seemingly shortcomings deter the flow of visitors that culminate in the first July Fourth weekend celebration of one hundred and fifty thousand people over a three-day period.

The number of visitors is stunning, even in today's environment with all the modern accommodations and amenities. It is even more stunning when placed in 1948 when all island transportation is by boat and overnight lodging is limited to four hundred. It does indicate the importance and the popularity of Georgia's first and only oceanfront state park.

Things are moving along nicely on the island, even though a new political battle is looming on the horizon. The Jekyll Island Golf Course, previously known as the Oceanside Course or Great Dunes in later years, is almost ready, and a new bathhouse casino is being built midway between the first and second nine holes, which will also function as the golf clubhouse. Thompson Brothers of St. Simons Island finishes the bathhouse/clubhouse in October 1948 at a cost of $60,000.

To the delight of newspaper readers, the very first marriage takes place on Jekyll Island since it became a state park. Mr. Al Schlepper, manager of the JI Laundry, marries Ms. Oneida Cook in Faith Chapel. Both spend their honeymoon in the Gould House[27] and take up residence at the Sans Souci. Although the *Brunswick News* reported the story as the very first marriage on Jekyll Island, it should be noted that the marriage of Miss Emily Maurice and Mr. Whitey Dall was the very first wedding ceremony to be performed in Faith Chapel. Nevertheless, the news is an uplifting welcome amidst the negative campaign news.

The gubernatorial race is now in full swing, and as expected, Herman Talmadge and incumbent Gov. Melvin E. Thompson go head to head with the disputed Jekyll Island purchase as the white elephant in the middle.

---

[27] Now named Villa Marianna.

Thompson is no match for the barrage that comes out of the Talmadge camp, and the "county unit system" of vote counting at the time certainly doesn't work in Thompson's favor either, given the heavy rural support for Herman Talmadge, who wins the 1948 special election by a landslide.

But even after the election dust settles, there is still this newly found state park. The irony of the story is that the strongest and most forceful opponents of the Jekyll Island purchase ultimately end up with its destiny, despite the continuous dispute and the resulting political fallout.

Before the year is over, Gov.-Elect Talmadge tells the press that he may end up selling Jekyll Island,[28] although the comment is taken with a grain of salt, given that both the State Highway Department and the US Bureau of Public Roads have contributed over $2.5 million to redirect US-17 and build the causeway, funds that are difficult to recoup with a sale to private investors. Talmadge also publicly accuses[29] outgoing Gov. Thompson of missing state property on Jekyll Island, which leads to a mandatory move-out inspection, performed by J. L. Pilcher, who also made a detailed inventory of assets when the island purchase was completed. In the end, the newspapers report that nothing is missing, and all inventory is present.

With a change of guard in the capital also comes change on the island. Mr. Briggs, who was appointed by M. E. Thompson as the first island manager, leaves Jekyll Island on December 1, 1948, and is replaced by James Page, named by Gov.-Elect Talmadge.

The beginning of 1949 brings with it not just a new governor, who has made it very clear before, during, and after the political campaign that he would rather divest Jekyll Island, but it also raises new concerns about finishing the causeway without a commitment of funds for a bridge across Jekyll Creek. The bridge issue becomes more pressing since the general assembly has omitted funds from the running budget to finance a bridge.[30] It later becomes clear that while the US Bureau of Public Roads approved a grant to finance the bridge in 1948, the state withdrew matching funds from its 1949 budget. It is unclear though whether this was a politically motivated decision on the part of the general assembly, strong favorites of

---

[28] *Brunswick News*, December 6, 1948.
[29] *Brunswick News* article, December 6, 1948.
[30] *Brunswick News*, January 11, 1949.

Herman Talmadge, or whether this decision was purely driven by budget constraints at the time.

It will, however, have rather serious repercussions and is one of the main reasons the Jekyll Creek Bridge was not completed until December 1954. But let's not get ahead of ourselves and focus on what is next on the agenda.

The winter months are taking a toll on the island as the state auditor, B. E. Thrasher, reports a net operating loss of $16,618.15 for the period of November 1948 through January 1949.

To make matters worse, a dispute breaks out between L. H. Simkins, owner and operator of the *Robert E. Lee* steamer, and the Brunswick Port Authority about docking fees. It is interesting to note here that the original ferry contract was negotiated and entered into between the Brunswick Port Authority and the Brunswick Chamber of Commerce, who subsequently sublet the contract to Mr. Simkins. The *Robert E. Lee* is grounded, awaiting settlement of the dispute, and a new contract is awarded to Capt. Ralph Chumbley of Ft. Lauderdale and part owner of the *Seven-Eleven* and *Dragon* that will resume the daily run to Jekyll Island for a roundtrip fare of $1.15, a 25 percent discount from the previous fares.

The problems are resolved only temporarily, and yet another dispute between the ferry owners breaks out in the summer of 1949. The result is that the *Seven-Eleven* halts service and is being placed in receivership on behalf of Mr. and Mrs. Bottenfield. Both claim to be part owners of the Dragon Corporation, operator of both ferry boats, and dispute their payment and employment contract with Capt. Chumbley.

To make matters worse, the only other ferry boat, the *Dragon*, breaks down before the summer and peak season begins. The smaller vessel, the *Neptune*, makes the daily runs to Jekyll Island so interested visitors and tourists can still vacation on the island without too many problems.

With all the commotion and disputes on the mainland, one would think Jekyll Island was peaceful and quiet, but things are changing, and plans and ideas are being tossed around, both on the island and the state capitol.

Early 1949, and following his defeat of M. E. Thompson, Gov. Herman Talmadge appoints a Jekyll Island Committee to determine the fate and the future of his white elephant. The committee members are Mike Benton as chair together with Carl Rhodes, Gould Barrett, and B. E. Thrasher, the state auditor. The latter will play an important role in the future development and financing of Jekyll Island.

The committee issues a request for proposal through an open bid process to manage and lease Jekyll Island for a period of two years. Mr. Whitaker, a successful hotel owner and manager, submits the winning bid. An interesting side note here is that Gov. M. E. Thompson also submitted a bid and even offered to outright purchase Jekyll Island on numerous occasions, including much later in 1955.

It is doubtful that Mr. Whitaker won the bid by merit and reputation only. Multiple personal correspondence letters between Mr. Whitaker and Gov. Talmadge in 1949 suggest that both were very good friends. One such letter, signed by Gov. Talmadge, even mentions: "I hope you get the bid."[31]

While it may not be unusual for the times that a prominent hotelier such as Mr. Whitaker has a close and personal relationship with a successful and influential politician like Gov. Talmadge, one can question the objectivity of the JI Committee in its choice and selection of the winning bid.

The lease agreement, starting on April 27, 1949, and ending January 15, 1951,[32] allows Mr. Whitaker to operate the main Jekyll Island Hotel, the Annex building, the Sans Souci, and the Crane House in exchange for 20 percent of gross receipts, payable to the State Parks Department, in addition to maintenance of all buildings and structures. Mr. Whitaker is also expected to pay all utilities needed to operate the accommodations year-round.

Things don't go very smoothly for Mr. Whitaker, and the number of visitors and occupancy rate are not enough to make this a successful enterprise, despite his creative efforts to attract and entertain his guests. In July 1949, after only three months of operation, Mr. Whitaker asks the Jekyll Island Committee for state relief. His request for a fee reduction from 20 percent to 15 percent and for the state to pay the never-ending maintenance costs is met with a resounding no. In addition, the committee

---

[31] Letter from Gov. Talmadge to Mr. Whitaker, March 1949. Jekyll Island Museum Archives.

[32] The expiration date of January 15th is not unusual as the contract had to expire on and coincide with the end of Gov. Talmadge's term.

demands its first quarterly payment of $4,681.61, which triggers the first dispute between the committee and Mr. Whitaker.

At the beginning of the lease agreement, Mr. Whitaker had deposited $2,000 as an advance toward the first quarterly payment and argues that he only owes the difference of $2,681.61, which he paid on July 29, 1949. B. E. Thrasher argues that the deposit was merely a security deposit for the duration of the lease and not to be considered a prepayment of fees due.

The *Brunswick News* and the *Atlanta Journal* report in detail about the ongoing problems and disputes and even report that Mr. Whitaker is closing the island (July 11, 1949). The following day, Mr. Whitaker reacts to the newspaper articles by clarifying that he does not intend to close the island but that he loses $150 per day due to low occupancy and that the cost of running the hotel amounts to $4,000 per month in electricity bills alone.

From the beginning, it was clear that this lease arrangement was not meant to last and was only a temporary solution to a management problem until a more definitive plan could be presented. That did not discourage Mr. Whitaker from finding very creative ways to make his business venture work.

During his tenure, Mr. Whitaker installs supersized ventilating fans in every hotel room to accommodate his guests. His aggressive advertising in the Savannah, Augusta, and Atlanta areas pays off, and he can accommodate several conventions during the summer of 1949.

The Georgia Education Association (GEA) holds its first Jekyll Island convention in August with more than five hundred attendees, and the Auto Parts Department of Georgia and the Southeastern Parks Association both organize their annual conventions in October.

He even surfaces a parking lot adjacent to the Jekyll Island Hotel and installs a miniature railroad in front of the hotel—anything to attract visitors and entertain them during their stay. He subcontracts with Mr. Nichols to operate two horse carriages and two buses for sightseeing on and around the island. Visitors and guests can also rent one of the fifty bikes or scooters that Mr. Nichols's enterprise has available should they decide to venture out on their own.

During this time, Mr. Whitaker also gets help on the island. Dudley W. Gay becomes the first state trooper to police and patrol the island to make guests feel safe and secure. Mr. and Mrs. Gay reside in the "Brown house,"[33] while Mrs. Gay also operates the Gould Playhouse,[34] which would later become their home as well.

It is also the first time that Mr. Hoke Smith appears on the island, a name that will resurface again in several capacities and functions throughout the early history. In 1949, Mr. Smith becomes the first foreman on the island, and while his duties are limited to oversee the repair and removal of debris caused by the severe storm of August 30, 1949, he is to remain on the island and take an active leadership role, as we will see in a later chapter.

The storm of 1949 causes so much damage to the buildings and grounds that it is reason enough to ignite another dispute between Mr. Whitaker and Mr. Eugene Cook, attorney general, about the maintenance costs and the payments of 20 percent of gross receipts. Even State Rep. Iris Blitch, future sponsor of the JIA Bill, together with the State Parks Department get involved. This is how serious the relationship is deteriorating.

Ultimately, Mr. Whitaker does not get a fee reduction, but the state does decide to pay for the storm damage, the repairs, and the cleanup, hence the appearance of Mr. Hoke Smith.

Mr. Whitaker declares in the fall of 1949 that Jekyll Island is a true health resort. The air on the island is so pure and crisp that it cures hay fever, per Mr. Whitaker, and he relentlessly campaigns across the state, including multiple newspaper interviews and even patient testimonials, that Jekyll Island is "the" cure for hay fever. It works! Even doctors are willing to recommend a weeklong stay on Jekyll Island to their patients, and the testimonials, strategically publicized in the newspapers, attract multiple patients looking for a cure.

By the end of the year, things are looking better for Mr. Whitaker. He can make his monthly payments to the State Parks Department: $3,879

---

[33] The original "Brown" house was located between the Jekyll Island Club and the Sans Souci. The traced outline can still be seen in the exit driveway between the croquet lawn and the Sans Souci.

[34] The Gould Playhouse, also referred to as the Gould Casino, contained an indoor tennis court, casino, bowling alley, and a greenhouse. It is still adjacent to Villa Marianna. It was later converted into the island's first Convention Center and is currently in use as a storage facility for the JIA.

for July and $3,517 for August. He even manages to install a new water purification system and a new heating system in the Crane House, despite the renewed rumors that the island is closing again. Undeterred by such newspaper rumors, Mr. Whitaker can now accommodate a thousand guests and promises to open furnished cottages by the spring of 1950, with private homes to be available for larger groups or parties. Future guests can also expect new and upcoming amusements next year, as the Jekyll Island Hotel will feature a Ferris wheel, a merry-go-round, and a skating rink and will hold stock car races on the island.

Despite a year of difficulties and the inherent child diseases that accompany any new venture, most certainly the creation of a state park, Mr. Whitaker closes out the year in a very appropriate style.

Mr. Charles M. Daniels, member of the Jekyll Island Club from 1924 through 1932, visits Jekyll Island on December 28, 1949, to ring in the new year, and local newspapers are on hand to document the visit. Not only is Mr. Daniels a past member of the exclusive Millionaires Club, he is also a national hero in his own right. He was, after all, the Olympic swimming champion in 1904, 1908, and 1912.

The new year promises to be exciting since the new highway is expected to be open by summer. But what about the bridge? There is no news about the bridge at the end of 1949, but that is about to change soon.

CHAPTER 3

THE BATTLE FOR THE BRIDGE

1950–1954

Herman Talmadge is ready to start his second year in office as governor. So is Barney Whitaker as lessee of the Jekyll Island Hotel, although his term will end January 15, 1951. The State Parks Department is still officially overseeing Jekyll Island, but the Jekyll Island Committee, formed in July 1949, is still active and in charge of finding a more permanent solution for the island's management and eventual development, whenever such may occur.

The new year starts fresh, and nobody in the general assembly is short of his or her own idea about how to manage the "White Elephant," as it is still referred to lovingly.

The total net income, since March 1948, is merely $23,511 and enough reason for the opposition to submit new and improved plans to alter the course and the future of the island. The opposition is of course the Talmadge supporters in the general assembly and other regional political offices.

The loyal M. E. Thompson supporters, however, see more than enough reason to continue to operate and develop the island into a real state park for the benefit of the average Georgian. After all, a net profit with minimal investment and without the use of taxpayers' money is a positive sign.

On January 4, 1950, two proposals are made on the general assembly floor. The state parks director Newton Moye proposes to appoint a five-man authority to manage Jekyll Island and transfer the ultimate decision-making from the State Parks Department to the newly formed authority.

State Representative Charles Gowen submits his proposal on the floor to investigate the current state of affairs on Jekyll Island through the formation of a five-man commission, who in turn will report and recommend any action to be taken with regards to the future of Jekyll Island.

But the battle for power does not end there. Two weeks later, state Rep. Iris Blitch introduces what would be known as the Jekyll Island Authority Bill or the JIA Bill.

The bill[35] stipulates:

1) Jekyll Island to be leased to the Jekyll Island Authority (JIA or also commonly referred to later as "The Authority") for a term of ninety-nine years at one dollar per year.
2) The JIA to be authorized to sublease lots for residential and/or commercial use for a term of ninety-nine years.
3) To be determined who or which entity would have the authorization to issue revenue certificates to finance and build the Jekyll Creek Bridge.

At the same time, another bill is also introduced to the House that requires all 159 Georgia counties to receive no less than half an acre of land on Jekyll Island to develop their own resort. Although the JIA Bill does not pass, it does find an audience, and Stipulation 3 will resurface again a few years later.

The first objection is made by state Rep. Charles Gowen, who questions both the legality and the constitutionality of the issuance of revenue certificates or revenue bonds by the JIA as a state agency. This objection is important to note now, as the issue will arise again on multiple occasions as development starts on the island.

The second objection comes from Senator W.B. Cochran, who introduces legislation to sell Jekyll Island and calls the JIA Bill "the wrong plan."

---

[35] The bill, as first introduced in the legislation, did not specify that Jekyll Island State Park should be self-sufficient. That mandate was added during the legislative session and became part of the 1950 Authority Act in addition to the commercial and/or residential development limit of one-third of the island.

Despite the above objections, the Jekyll Island State Park Authority Act, known as Law Number 630 and House Bill No. 604, wins Senate approval on February 8, 1950, with a 34–8 majority vote.

The JIA Act ultimately includes certain provisions, such as the term of the lease being fifty years instead of the proposed ninety-nine-year lease and the express stipulation that the governor cannot sell Jekyll Island without general assembly approval. This is clearly a political and protective move that ensures no future governor can act alone and without the approval of the legislation.

Whether state Rep. Iris Blitch, as sponsor of the original bill, or Gov. Talmadge had the foresight of what would happen a few years later remains unknown and should be left open for speculation. Needless to say, the issue of getting rid of the problem and selling Jekyll Island will resurface several times during the terms of various governors.

The original JIA Act of 1950 also stipulates that only one-third of the island can be offered for commercial and/or residential lease.

Gov. Talmadge names his first candidates to serve on the Jekyll Island State Park Authority Board on February 13, 1950. His motivation for the nominations is: "To create a non-political authority and to remove Jekyll Island from politics."[36]

All five members are confirmed that same day with terms to expire as set forth in the JIA Act and subsequent terms not to exceed ten years. All members are selected and appointed by Gov. Talmadge from the state-at-large as follows.

> Sen. Braxton Blalock (chair)—term expiration July 1, 1962
> Mike Benton (vice chair)—term expiration July 1, 1958
> J. D. Compton[37]—term expiration July 1, 1960
> state Rep. Ben Tarbutton—term expiration July 1, 1956
> Gould Barrett[38]—term expiration July 1, 1954

---

[36] *Brunswick News*, February 17, 1950.

[37] J. D. Compton, president of the Sea Island Company, was not a governor's choice. His name was included upon the request from Charles Gowen, state representative and St. Simons Island resident, in exchange for his support to reelect Gov. Talmadge in the 1950 election.

[38] Both Gould Barrett and Mike Benton were previously members of the Jekyll Island Committee, formed in 1949 by Gov. Talmadge.

The newly formed and appointed authority visits Jekyll Island for the first time on March 4, 1950, to perform a visual inspection and to determine a course of action. Although the authority is not in charge of the island until Mr. Whitaker's lease ends on January 1, 1951, there is plenty of work to be done and plans to be made.

The first action taken at the very first board meeting on March 4, 1950, is to determine the place, time, and frequency of board meetings. The authority agrees to meet on the second Saturday of each month in Atlanta and further agrees to hire John Calhoun as the authority and board secretary/treasurer at $100 per month plus travel expenses.

The hot and pressing topic is of course the status of the Jekyll Creek Bridge, how it should be built, and more importantly how the project should be financed. However, the real question is not the how but the who, as we shall see in minutes of upcoming meetings and the related newspaper articles of the time.

Back in 1949 when M. E. Thompson was governor, he requested the firm of Sverdrup & Parcel from St. Louis to prepare a design and proposal for the Jekyll Creek Bridge. The design was made and submitted but subsequently tabled, pending the completion of the causeway and the rerouting of US Hwy-17.

The same proposal now finds its way back into the mix, specifically between the authority and the Glynn County Commission. Now, the story about the battle for the bridge becomes interesting and convoluted at the same time.

But before we get into the details of the plot and how it ultimately ends, it is important to start by shedding some light on the original plan, design, and proposal, keeping in mind that the causeway project is almost completed.

Early March, the Hendry Corp. finished dredging the marshes of Colonel's Island and Latham Hammock, and the roadbed for the causeway is ready for paving.

According to the plans of Sverdrup & Parcel, the Jekyll Creek Bridge will cost $1.2 million for a bascule bridge with a twenty-five-foot clearance and a total length of 1,496 feet. The bridge design, a double-leaf bascule design, was modeled after the existing bridge to Saint Simons Island.[39] If, however, the design would be altered to accommodate a lesser clearance between 9.5 feet and 17 feet, then the cost would be $850,000. Still a considerable investment given that no funds were appropriated in the 1950 state budget despite the available funds from the US Public Roads Bureau.

Glynn County Commissioner Ray Whittle enters the picture and proposes to build the bridge on behalf of the authority with financing obtained through the issuance of revenue bonds or certificates. He even has the commitment of a Chicago firm, Ketchum & Nongard, to underwrite the certificates without a firm agreement or consent of who is ultimately willing and able to build the bridge or who will own and maintain the bridge after completion.

Commissioner Whittle is serious about building, owning, and operating the bridge, as is clear from the several meeting discussions with the authority. The question is now what motivates the Glynn County Commission to be so involved in the accessibility and potential development of Jekyll Island State Park?

The answer lies within Saint Simons Island where the double-leaf bascule bridge was built in 1927 and, more importantly, operated by Glynn County as a toll bridge. A roundtrip to Saint Simons or Sea Island was fifty cents, and the annual income was $180,000. The motivation was not necessarily the potential income, which would be removed once the toll income paid for the principal and interest on the bonds. The driving force behind Commissioner Whittle's involvement was to protect the residents and business owners of Saint Simons Island by imposing the same toll schedule on future residents and business owners of Jekyll Island, thereby equaling the playing field among the county residents. It should be noted, however, that despite Jekyll Island being physically located within the boundaries of Glynn County, it would remain a stand-alone entity as a state park for many years.

In the meantime, the authority starts its own research about possibly financing the bridge at 4 percent and par issuance. Both terms and conditions refer to the specific stipulations in the JIA Act of 1950. The

---

[39] The first drawbridge to St. Simons Island was constructed in 1927 and featured a double-leaf bascule design. This unique bridge design can still be seen today in St. Augustine where the Lions Bridge is still operational and functional.

authority requests three firms to bid on the potential underwriting, namely Roberts Humphrey & Co. with Johnson, Lane & Space; Clement Evans with Courts & Co.; and finally, J.H. Hilsman with Varnedo-Schism.

But Glynn County does not sit idle, and the county commissioners approve a plan to finance $600,000 with revenue certificates, based on a modified Sverdrup & Parcel design that changes the original double-leaf bascule bridge to a simplified vertical lift design that makes the project much less expensive and more affordable. There are still some obstacles to overcome though. The county cannot proceed with a contract unless it receives the approval of the US Public Roads Bureau, the State Highway Department, and more importantly, the authority.

The battle is now clearly taking shape, with all parties involved drawing the line in the sand and defending their own turf or best interests.

First, there is Commissioner Ray Whittle, who wants to protect the Saint Simons Island Causeway as a toll road and therefore insists that the Jekyll Creek Bridge must be a toll bridge.

The multiple conversations and corresponding newspaper articles during that time clearly outline Glynn County's intention. If Saint Simons Island residents need to pay a toll to reach their residence or business, then the same principle should apply to future Jekyll Island residents.

There is one major obstacle though. The Authority Act of 1950 does not mention any form of taxation with regards to future residents, and unless a specific clause is added that specifies the payment of certain fees to the county for services rendered, like Saint Simons Island, a toll bridge owned by the county is problematic to say the least. This "little" obstacle will find its way back into the island's history once development starts in earnest.

Sen. Braxton Blalock, as chair of the authority, is the strong opposing voice on the board who insists that the Jekyll Creek Bridge must be free of charge, lest it impacts all future visitors negatively. However, Sen. Blalock also opens the door for a toll bridge under the condition that should a free bridge not be possible, at least the authority should finance, build, and own the bridge, not the county. His motion for the authority to finance the bridge falls short, but they do decide to open bids to all engineering firms in Georgia.

From Millionaires to Commoners

And then there is of course the US Public Roads Bureau, who is willing to finance 50 percent of the bridge construction together with matching funds from the State Highway Department but with only one condition attached. It must be a free bridge, and Mr. McWorther, director of US Public Roads Bureau, threatens to withdraw $700,000 from the State Highway Federal Aid Funds if tolls should be levied.

And here we are: the lines have been drawn, the opponents have made their intentions clear, and the battle can begin in earnest. And a battle it will become all the way to the end of 1954.

There are a multitude of other problems and projects to focus on besides the bridge. After all, the Authority Act[40] stipulates that Jekyll Island State Park must be self-sufficient, a unique concept in itself as no other state park must adhere to this financial limitation, and plans and ideas need to be made to build some sort of infrastructure.

J. D. Compton, president of the Sea Island Company, seems to have the most rational approach following his first inspection of the island in March. He offers his immediate plans and ideas to the press and goes on record as stating, "First, we need easy access to Jekyll Island. Secondly, we need a master plan for development. And lastly, we need to gather all the facts about the park before we make any decisions."[41]

The mention of a development plan in 1950 sounds intriguing, given that time will tell us that a multitude of development plans have been made over several decades. Mr. Compton's reference, however, does not refer to what has become known as the first master plan developed by Robert & Co. in 1951. Instead, it refers to a little-known plan made by Mr. Clark, employee of a New York development firm and designer of Jones Beach, Long Island. He was requested to make a study of Jekyll Island in 1948 with the intention of applying the Jones Beach design and development to the island. Ultimately, the plan was never used.

An interesting note here is the public proposal by J. D. Compton, which is worthy of some historic and political perspective.

---

[40] The mandate to become self-sufficient was added during the legislative session and became part of the 1950 Authority Act.
[41] *Brunswick News*, March 6, 1950.

Imagine the existence of Sea Island as an exclusive and private beach resort, just north of our newly discovered Jekyll Island State Park. Mr. Compton must have kept in mind that to protect the exclusivity of his own Sea Island Company, Jekyll Island should be developed in such a manner that it would never become a competitor or an attraction for his upper-class guests. After all, if Jekyll Island was ever developed as an exclusive beach resort, like Sea Island, and attracted the same clientele, Jekyll Island would have the upper hand with its ten-mile stretch of unspoiled white beaches. When we view Mr. Compton's participation and guidance within that context, his advice to carefully follow and implement a development plan starts to make more sense. It does not take away from his early contributions, but Mr. Compton's advice was not merely guided by his vision to create a state park for the average Georgian. It was also discreetly motivated by his intention never to allow Jekyll Island to become a fierce competitor with his own private and gated resort.

As the battle for power continues, the island continues to operate under the management of Mr. Barney Whitaker. Few, if any, direct conversations take place between the authority, meeting in Atlanta monthly, and Mr. Whitaker, handling the day-to-day affairs of the island. Other than their first visit and inspection in March 1950, the authority doesn't return to the Island at all. It seems that the present affairs are handled on-site, while the future of Jekyll Island is being decided off-site and in Atlanta, a management concept that will become prevalent for the next seven years.

By the fall of 1950, the authority has contracted Georgia Power to install power poles and lines along the causeway and to complete submarine lines across Jekyll Creek with the installation of four above-ground conductors. The total cost is estimated at $76,000 plus three dollars per pole if Georgia Power is willing to furnish all the fixtures.

Given that the authority does not have a budget and is mandated to be self-sufficient, a loose term and open for interpretation depending on the definition used and the context within which it is placed, funds for such expenses need to be raised somewhere.

Ultimately, governor discretionary funds are used to pay for such expenses until the authority can raise funds from land leasehold options and land leasehold estates.

The authority also requests $30,000 from the Governor's Office to pay for JIA Board expenses in 1950. That amount is raised to $89,580 for the 1951 fiscal year.

In preparation of the upcoming Whitaker lease renewal, the authority unanimously votes not to renew the lease, ending January 15, 1951, and to close the island for six to nine months upon expiration so infrastructure can be built. On October 8, 1950, Mr. Whitaker is notified and ordered to vacate the premises at the end of the lease and to return all furnishings to the authority as per the move-in inspection and audit performed by Osborne & Co. in May 1949.

Although no mention is made about the result of such inventory audit, it is questionable whether all furnishings, large and small, moveable or attached, were still present at the end of 1950. Numerous small Jekyll Island Hotel "mementos" disappeared, and several newspaper articles reported on the firing of hotel personnel for "removing hotel furnishings." The disappearance of these small and probably nostalgic furnishings pales in comparison to what will happen to the inventory of the Club Hotel and the cottages in the ensuing five years.

Mr. Whitaker attempts on numerous occasions to obtain a lease renewal or extension, despite the official notification by the authority. Multiple letters and proposals to both Gov. Talmadge and State Parks Director Newton Moye cannot alter the decision made by the authority. At one point in time, late October 1950, Mr. Whitaker submits a lease proposal for a period of ten years at a guaranteed annual rent payment of $3,000 in addition to the 20 percent of gross revenue. One can assume that either business was not very bad or slow after all, or maybe Mr. Whitaker expected business to increase dramatically now that the authority was officially in charge. His proposal finds no support, and his extension request is denied by both Gov. Talmadge and the Department of State Parks.

Two house fires on the island within one week of each other shake up the authority, and Constable Dudley Gay must explain himself. After all, he is responsible for the safety on the island. But it also happens that the cottage, which was destroyed by the fire, is his rental home. The house was located between the Club Hotel and the power plant, and near the Sans Souci. The second fire destroys part of the Gould Playhouse where Mrs.

Gay operates an indoor amusement park and where the Gays are planning to reside very shortly.

Though reported in the local newspapers as dubious and suspicious, an investigation by the GBI, ordered by the authority, does not reveal any foul play, and the fires are dismissed as accidental.

The highlight of 1950 must be the dedication of the Jekyll Island Causeway on November 4, 1950. Two and a half years in the making and no less than $2 million in state and US matching funds, the dedication also comes at a very opportune time for Gov. Talmadge. Dignitaries and residents line up to take the scenic drive across Colonel's Island and Latham Hammock to get a glimpse of the marshes on the Jekyll Island side, barely 1,100 feet away and yet unreachable by car. The views on both sides of the causeway must have been spectacular as residents got a first glimpse of the natural Georgia marshland. Seven miles of new and smooth road with unobstructed views that lead to the newfound paradise. Only a small and narrow Jekyll Creek separates reality from the dream, soon to be materialized.

In addition to the power poles alongside the causeway, Georgia Power also agreed to attach light fixtures to every other pole so that the "road to paradise" could be lit at night from the entrance all the way to the future bridge.

What a sight it must have been to drive a brightly lit causeway with a gorgeous view of the marshes at dusk or nightfall, and to be able to see Jekyll Island in the distance at the end of the road. It must have increased the future visitor's appetite even more to come and vacation on the island, if only the bridge could be constructed.

With Mr. Whitaker gone and the Jekyll Island Hotel free of any lease encumbrance, the authority starts preparing for development. Tentative subdivision assignments are made for "white" subdivisions and one "Negro" subdivision on the south side, based on a preliminary and rudimentary development plan made by Vinson & Co. in late 1950.[42]

Two main obstacles still stand in the way that can only be resolved by the general assembly and the governor. An amendment of the original

---

[42] The notion of assigning a "Negro" subdivision was unique for a southern state that was still marred by racial tensions. The creation of such subdivision, however, would take another five years.

Authority Act of February 14, 1950, is therefore envisioned and does not meet much opposition from either the legislation or the governor. After all, Gov. Talmadge wins reelection in the gubernatorial race with a landslide victory of 98 percent over his Independent Party opponent Morgan Blake.

The first proposed change—found in House Bill No. 517, Law Number 490—pertains to the term of the authority. Initially granted a term of fifty years in 1950, the amendment now confirms a term of ninety-nine years, or in legal terms, in perpetuity. The reason for this proposed change is because the Federal Housing Authority, FHA, refuses to underwrite any subleases unless the authority can assign such sublease for a term no less than ninety-nine years. Obviously, the authority was handicapped by its own term limit of fifty years; hence the proposed change in Section 2 of the above House Bill and the 1951 Authority Act.

The second proposed change is the bridge financing and its ownership. After a yearlong battle with both Glynn County and the State Highway Department, not to mention the US Public Roads Bureau, it is time to stipulate in the Authority Act who and how the bridge can be financed in the best interest of all Georgians.

House Bill No. 416, known as Law No. 448 or Jekyll Island Bridge, stipulates in Section 4 the following:

> The contract shall provide that upon the payment by the Authority and receipt by the Highway Department of the final payment due under such contract, the bridge across Jekyll Creek shall become the property of the State of Georgia, and a part of the State Highway System of Georgia. Said bridge thereafter shall be maintained and operated by the State Highway Department as a free bridge and the Authority shall cease to collect tolls, taxes, or charges of any nature whatsoever for the use of said bridge, and the right, title, and interest of the Authority in the bridge shall terminate ...

This amendment eliminates the role Glynn County commissioners attempted to play and now limits the negotiations to the authority, as the contractor, and the state/US as equal financers of the bridge.

One obstacle is now resolved, but another one will soon appear. It will delay the bridge construction for another three years due to unforeseen circumstances but the result of political bickering for too long.

On March 10, 1951, the authority meets for the first time on Jekyll Island. The Gould House,[43] now equipped with a phone, becomes the new location for meetings, although the authority headquarters will remain in Atlanta for several years. The authority unanimously appoints Hoke Smith, previously acting as foreman, as Jekyll Island State Park's first superintendent.[44]

Mr. Smith makes two proposals to the authority on the immediate future of the island, pending the building of infrastructure and development and pending the reopening of the island to the public.

Proposal 1 suggests opening and leasing the Crane House, which is immediately deemed to be not profitable and therefore not pursued.

The second proposal to open bids for ferry services and sightseeing tours on the island finds more traction with the board members. One name from the past immediately comes to mind: Mr. Bottenfield, the former operator of the *Dragon* and the *Seven-Eleven* and the person who was involved in legal disputes with Capt. Chumbley.[45] A proposal for open bid is published in the local newspapers with a response deadline of April 16, 1951—presumably just in time for summer season opening when the authority, by recommendation of Superintendent Smith, plans to offer sightseeing tours on the island from April through Labor Day, six days per week.

The Dragon Corporation, owned and operated by Mr. Bottenfield and Mr. Smith, provides daily ferry services between Brunswick, Saint Simons Island, and Jekyll Island at seventy-five cents a roundtrip. They also carry passengers on guided tours on the island.

---

[43] The Gould house refers to Villa Marianna and was the designated meeting place for the authority while convening on Jekyll Island. Most of the meetings would still take place in Atlanta.

[44] The term and function of superintendent refers to the first superintendent as appointed by the Jekyll Island Authority. Historically, Mr. Ernest Grob is considered the first superintendent of the Jekyll Island Club.

[45] The legal dispute over ownership and employment compensation took place in 1948 (see chapter 2).

From Millionaires to Commoners

Following J. D. Compton's earlier advice, the authority selects the Atlanta firm of Robert & Co. to build a master plan with an immediate focus on development between Shell Road and the bridge entrance, later referred to as Phase I development. The design and blueprint cost are estimated between $7,500 and $10,000.

With things now set in motion and some construction envisioned soon, the topic of labor is brought up, and with it Mr. Blalock's earlier recommendation to bring in prisoners and open a prison camp on the island. Mr. Blalock, chair of the authority, is authorized unanimously to "Negotiate with Mr. Warren of the State Prison Commission, the placement of a convict camp on Jekyll Island in the near future."[46]

The first two employees of the authority, Mr. James Vandergriff and Mr. Booker T. Thomas, begin work on the island at sixty-five cents and seventy-five cents per hour respectively, and the superintendent is instructed to open the commissary[47] to supply the laborers, including the prisoners.

The old dairy farm,[48] once holding the millionaires' livestock, is being converted to hold the first twenty-three convicts from Reidsville, Georgia, a maximum-security prison, who arrive on the island in July 1951. Fifty more are expected in the next few months.

With convicts on the island and now also three full-time employees, including Superintendent Hoke Smith, the question becomes who can pay for all these expenses when the authority does not have a budget, except for the annual allowance from the governor to pay for board expenses, and has no source of revenue.

Here is where the development of the Jekyll Island Authority first starts to take shape, or at least sets the foundation upon which the ultimate operational and managerial framework will be built going forward.

Gov. Talmadge creates a Jekyll Island Committee with the mandate to preserve state property. The committee consists of three of the five existing authority members with some sort of financial oversight by the

---

[46] The idea to use prison labor to prepare the island for development came from Gov. Talmadge but was presented to the authority by Chair Blalock (JIA Board meeting, May 26, 1951).
[47] The original commissary was located on the corner of Pier Road and Stable Road.
[48] The dairy farm was located on the corner of Jennings Road and Riverview Drive. Only the grain silo remains standing today.

state auditor, B. E. Thrasher. Mr. Thrasher acts more in an advisory capacity to the JI Committee than firm oversight, as the immediate future will confirm.

To accommodate the separation of funds between the JI Committee and the authority, a Special Permanent Improvement Fund is established, and a bank account is opened with Fulton National Bank of Atlanta on May 26, 1951. Three weeks later, Gov. Talmadge "donates" $100,000 to the JI Committee.

Since the authority cannot spend money unless they raise their own funds, the authority approves a resolution (i.e., the same five members of which three form the JI Committee) to finance any island expenditures with 80 percent of committee funds and the remaining 20 percent to be paid for by the authority. As history will show, this separation of funding and spending, and the separation between the Jekyll Island Authority and the Jekyll Island Committee, despite the confluence of members, is the beginning of a management structure that leads to a Board-Executive Committee structure in later years.

With funding now firmly in place, Robert & Co. is instructed to focus on twenty areas on the island that are formed by the existing roads. Each division should be developed in a different way with the total to ultimately become the Island Development Plan.

Mr. Mike Benton, vice-chair, goes on record and wants all original roads to be restored and all original road names to be kept intact. He is also the person who makes a motion to designate the Horton Plantation and the DuBignon Cemetery as historic places that can never be developed. It may not be the equivalent of a modern-day National Historic Landmark designation, but it is certainly worth mentioning that one member of the authority found both sites to be important enough as to give them this development exempt status in early 1951.

Under Mr. Hoke Smith's supervision, the prisoners are put to work, and one of the first tasks is to prepare the existing roadbeds for paving. The first road to be completed is McCormick Road, which originally ran from Shell Road in a northerly direction across Capt. Wylly to connect with Beachview Drive, parallel to the Baker Road junction. Second in line are Baker Road, connecting Old Plantation Road with Beachview Drive,

From Millionaires to Commoners

Old Plantation Road, and lastly Jennings Road, which connected Old Plantation Road with Baker Road.

The second task is to demolish the Albright-Pulitzer house.[49] The house is declared beyond repair or salvation, although the bricks are later used to build the first golf clubhouse, now better known as the Red Bug Pizza.

The authority also buys a boat of its own, the *Sea Wolf*, from Mr. R. J. Reddick for $3,000 in addition to using the Dragon Corporation for ferry services and hires Mr. Reddick as guard and operator of the vessel. His starting salary is $200 per month, plus free lodging in one of the Pier Road houses. He is also responsible for hauling groceries and food to the island for the prisoners. In comparison, the superintendent's salary at the time was $315 per month plus lodging.

Given the intensity of the preparation, road building, and construction, the authority also hires a resident engineer, Mr. John Miller, at $4,500 per year plus living quarters. He will reside with his family in the Jennings house.[50] While the superintendent will oversee the convict workforce, Mr. Miller's primary responsibility is to implement the Master Development Plan. His task also includes to prepare two hundred lots for lease north of Shell Road and to assist Trent Jones in assessing and determining the fate of the millionaires' golf courses, specifically the nine holes below Shell Road. The Club Golf Course on the riverside and north of the Jekyll Island Hotel is in disrepair due to overgrowth and neglect after the 1949 storm.

The Oceanside course, an eighteen-hole links course designed by Walter Travis in 1927, is still intact, as is the 1910 Jekyll Island Club course.[51]

---

[49] The Albright-Pulitzer house was located on the corner of Stable Road and Riverview Drive. The perimeter of the house is still marked today with ground stakes.
[50] The Jennings house is now known as Villa Ospo and is the most northern of the historic cottages.
[51] The original Club Golf Course, constructed in 1898, was razed, and the topsoil was used to build road and bridge embankments. Its original location is today's JI Airport. The Oceanside Course was renamed Great Dunes, of which only nine holes remain intact. The 1910 JI Club Course was originally laid out as a nine-hole in the current location of the Oleander golf course.

The authority has its hands full trying to get the island ready as much as possible, but it still has not forgotten about the Jekyll Creek Bridge, an issue that keeps popping up.

By mid-1951, the authority has received three competitive bids to build the long-awaited bridge. Tidewater Construction Co. from Norfolk, Virginia, Scott Construction Co. from Thomasville, Georgia, and Hardaway Construction Co. are all bidding for the contract, but another unexpected obstacle must be cleared.

This time, the National Production Authority[52] puts a hold on the bridge. Any procurement request for more than twenty-five tons of steel needs priority approval, based on the necessity for military defense and importance to civilian needs. This rationing of steel throughout the US is of course the result of the Korean War, and steel production is to be used for defense purposes first. Only then can steel be appropriated for civilian use, based on the above priority approval process.

Given that the Jekyll Creek Bridge is barely meeting any of the criteria of defense or civilian necessity at the time and given that the Turtle Creek Bridge[53] needs steel to be completed first, the bridge project is delayed again.

Mr. H. McDonald of the US Bureau of Public Works immediately halts all plans for the bridge and cites the need to divert critical material as the main reason, although he also disputes the lowest bid as being too high.

Again, a year goes by, and access to Jekyll Island State Park is limited to ferry services despite the causeway being so inviting and bringing Jekyll so much closer to Georgians.

Nevertheless, both Mr. Miller and Mr. Smith have their hands full cleaning the island and clearing lots while attempting to supervise fifty convicts. In the first year alone, three escape attempts are made, but all convicts are ultimately captured in a few days.

Another year begins in the capitol and yet another request to amend the Authority Act is submitted to the legislation.

---

[52] The National Production Authority (NPA) was created on September 11, 1950, by Executive Order 10161 (September 9, 1950).
[53] State and federal authorities had already approved the Turtle Creek Bridge project in 1948. The bridge was near completion at the time of steel rationing, hence any priority approval obtained from the National Production Administration was assigned to the Turtle Creek Bridge first.

This time around, the requested change pertains to the amount of land that the authority can sublease and the number of lots any individual can lease.

The original 1950 Authority Act specified that only one-third of the highland portion of Jekyll Island could be subleased, and no more than three lots could be assigned to any one individual or corporation.[54]

House Bill No. 630, also known as Jekyll State Park Authority-Amendments, Law No. 860, states in Section 10: "The Authority is empowered to survey, subdivide, improve, and lease as subdivided and improved not more than one-half of the highland portion of Jekyll Island, the lease property described aforesaid …"

Section 11 states: "No person, partnership, or corporation, except the Authority, may, during the life of the Authority, hold under lease a total of more than three (3) lots in any of the property subdivisions made upon Jekyll Island by the Authority; provided this limitation shall not apply to any bank, insurance company, building and loan association, mortgage loan company, Federal or State lending agency, which may be holding lots under lease in excess of this number by virtue of foreclosure on loans made upon the security of improvements erected or existing on such lots …"

The change in Section 11 is important, as it will become very applicable after the first commercial leases are in effect and the underwriting for construction starts in earnest.

By April 1952, the Robert & Co. master plan has been accepted, and the first 170 acres have been identified and designed for streets, roads, and two hundred lots to be staked and assigned.

Pending the lot assignment and to keep track of ongoing expenditures, present and future, the authority hires its first bookkeeper, Robert Youngblood, at $125 per month plus free housing, and the payroll keeps increasing while no revenue source is identified yet.

Then again, remember that the JI Committee absorbs 80 percent of the development and improvement costs and that Gov. Talmadge has committed another $100,000 for fiscal year 1952 to improve and preserve state property.

Even the prisoners start to weigh on the monthly budget. At eight dollars per day, per prisoner, the total monthly cost for fifty prisoners is

---

[54] Jekyll Island State Park Authority Act, 1950, House Bill No. 604, p. 157 and 159.

now $400 per month. But their work pays off as the road network has been prepared and is ready for paving, and all the buildings[55] have been reroofed and repainted. Overall, a lot of progress has been made in a short time.

The underbrush between the wharf and the north end is removed, which is the exact location of the Club Golf Course of 1898 that was so overgrown and damaged by hogs and palmetto roots that removing the underbrush meant demolishing one of the oldest golf courses in the US.

By mid-1952, despite the steel rationing still in existence, the US Bureau of Public Roads approves the contract bidding process for Jekyll Creek Bridge, and the State Highway Department accepts open bids until late June.

Tidewater Foundation Co. of Savannah, Georgia, submits the low bid for the understructure of the bridge, excluding the lift structure, for $274,301 and is approved by the State Highway Department. The vertical lift itself is constructed by the Industrial Construction Co.

The contractor starts three test pilings for the substructure, for which the required steel is approved and secured. The total understructure will ultimately require 228 pilings, and construction is underway. No bridge workers can stay on the island during construction except for Mr. Nichols of the State Highway Department.

The authority continues to prepare the island as best as possible with a clear view toward being ready once the bridge is finished and lots can be assigned.

The existing cul-de-sac between Shell Road, Capt. Wylly Road, Howland Road, and McCormick Road is removed to make room for future golf courses.

Road extensions are proposed from Riverview Drive to Stable Road and further to Crane Road, to Jekyll Parkway, and Morgan Road. Crane Road was later converted into a bike path that still exists today.

Morgan Road is extended from Crane to Shell Road, and Howland Road extends from Shell Road to Capt. Wylly, while Lanier extends from Capt. Wylly to Baker Road. Horton Road is extended from Bourne to Riverview Drive, while Bourne extends from Baker Road to Horton Road. Most of the old roads have since either been closed, designated as fire roads, or converted to beautiful bike paths. Whatever the case may be, the road

---

[55] Buildings refers to the cottages in the Historic District.

grid and plan was extensive and well thought out with a clear vision of sightseeing and enjoyment.

Beachview Drive originally included an S-shaped curve on the north end to provide unique ocean views.

The cost of rebuilding and extending the road grids is expensive, and costs do not even include the much-needed remodeling of the old clubhouse or the Annex building, let alone the removal of the water tower, northwest of the Jekyll Island Hotel, and the installation of a sprinkler system to maintain the grounds. The total cost was estimated between $200,000 and $500,000, funds that were not available but could be requested from the state. There is no proof in any of the archived documents or state records that such funding was provided but given the inability of the authority to be self-sufficient at this time, it is fair and reasonable to assume that Gov. Talmadge provided the necessary funding through the JI Committee.

Even though the Federal Housing Authority applauds the change in lease terms from fifty to ninety-nine years, FHA approval cannot get obtained, and the lease agreements must be reworked. FHA requests that the authority relinquishes its control over future lease assignments, that lease amounts are prepaid by the lessee, and that a lease termination clause is included for breach by lessee. The FHA recommendations are all incorporated in the new lease agreements, but it will take a few years before the first residential and/or commercial mortgage is underwritten and approved.

August 1952 marks a milestone in Jekyll Island State Park history. The Robert & Co. master plan is displayed to the public for the first time during the Southeastern Fair.[56] It is considered the first promotional effort by the authority to lease individual lots for the year 1953.

A second historic milestone that same year is certainly noteworthy here.

Minutes of the Jekyll Island Committee meeting dated August 23, 1952: "Mr. S. G. Dent, Chairman, Citizens Civic League of Brunswick, and F. P Williams, M.F. Jackson, Jr. and W. P Holmes appeared and spoke before the Authority in favor of a section of Jekyll being allocated

---

[56] The Southeastern Fair was a major event held annually at Lakewood Fairgrounds in Atlanta.

to negroes. It was agreed that the Committee could inspect the south area at any time after clearing the matter with Mr. Compton …"[57]

The response is noncommittal at the time, and no further action is taken. What is interesting to note, however, is that around the same time, the authority floats the plan to change the white prison camp into a Negro camp because they feel that Negro workers are in high demand and known to be more industrious and more efficient than white prisoners. Within the context of the time and the obvious prevalent segregation, the thought of using Negro labor instead of white labor was far more acceptable than the consideration of allocating a Negro subdivision.

Maintenance on the island continues at a fast pace, and half of what would become the Jekyll Parkway is graded and ready for pavement by fall. The grading is accomplished by removing topsoil from the Oceanside golf course and razing the dunes at the end of the parkway. Two miles of natural sand dunes are removed or bulldozed between 1952 and 1953 to provide the necessary roadbeds and abutments for the parkway and the access road between the island's entrance and the island Village, once the home of the millionaires. After all, visitors will want to see the ocean when entering the island, and dunes only block the beautiful view. This development approach is stunning and inexplicable in today's world, but when viewed through the eyes of a new and inexperienced authority with a mandate to deliver results fast and cheap, it seemed like a logical choice to move "dirt" from one spot to the other to flatten the land and build a road. After all, the same principle was used a few years earlier to build the causeway through natural marshland.

House rentals are identified for future lease once the island becomes accessible, and the authority decides to possibly rent the Claflin house, Macy house, and Goodyear house on the south side, and the James house, Jennings house, and Maurice house on the north end.[58] All will be available

---

[57] Even though the Vinson & Co. Development Plan of 1950 indicated the creation of a "Negro" subdivision, no efforts were made by the authority to pursue the proposal, hence the official request in 1952.

[58] The Claflin house is now better known as Mistletoe cottage. The Macy house is now referred to as Moss cottage. The Goodyear house is now home to the Jekyll Island Arts Association. The James house is known as Cherokee. The Jennings house refers to Villa Ospo, and the Maurice house is known as Hollybourne.

for lease at $200 to $300 per month except for the Gould, Rockefeller, and Crane houses.[59] Both the Gould and Rockefeller house are reserved for the authority, and Crane may be used or leased as a hotel.

The authority does not waste any time and opens a construction account with American National Bank in Brunswick, although construction is still years away from materializing.

Phase II of the Robert & Co. master plan is being tackled, which calls for the installation of a water system for the first 250 lots, specific planning for the next five hundred lots, and a construction plan for sewage for both businesses and public recreation. The decision is made that for the immediate future, individual septic tanks should be used, a decision that again exposes the inexperience of a young but eager authority and is again a sign of the times.

If lots are to be developed, then a company needs to be found and designated to issue title insurance. The authority decides to purchase a binder agreement with Title Co. for all 250 lots, each insured for $10,000 and a total of $2.5 million at an annual cost of $300 to $500.

Since the authority is and remains the legal owner of the lots and the lessee only holds a lease land option or estate, none of the lessees would be able to obtain title insurance; hence no mortgage company would underwrite a construction loan or standard mortgage.

That is the train of thought. But obtaining construction loans will prove to be far more difficult than simply providing a blanket title insurance for the lots.

The authority spends much of 1953 working out the locations of various subdivisions, building waterlines, sewage, and sprinkler systems, and drilling additional wells for water supply throughout the island. With the old water tower, adjacent to the Jekyll Island Hotel, demolished and replaced with a new water tank, the island needs three additional wells during the first development phase, with two more to be drilled in a later stage. The water supply system, as designed in 1953, envisioned an embryo supply system drawing water from five different wells on the island. It

---

[59] The Gould house refers to current-day Villa Marianna, while the Rockefeller house is better known as Indian Mound.

would take two years before this was implemented due to cost but also due to the slower than expected leasing of available lots.

With one hundred prisoners now on the island daily, road work is being completed at a fast pace. The perimeter road on the north side, Riverview Drive, is completed between the parkway and the entrance of the prison camp at the old Jennings Road. Beachview Drive is prepared for paving between the parkway and the accessible north end of the island. Again, topsoil and dunes are used as filler for the road. The entire perimeter road connecting Riverview Drive with Beachview Drive would not be completed until late 1954, but the two main roads running north-south were graded and paved first to provide access to the intended subdivisions.

Along with the perimeter road project, Old Plantation Road, north of Capt. Wylly Road, is being graded and becomes the first accessible subdivision of Jekyll Island. Both Bond Road and Baker Road still provide access across the island to the beach but are later converted to fire roads or bike paths. The same fate awaits the old Jennings Road when the prison camp, the old dairy farm,[60] is demolished in 1961.

To accomplish all this and to absorb the cost of labor and material, the authority receives the approval of the State Highway Department and therefore the necessary funding.

Mr. Gillis, director of the State Highway Board, was instrumental in obtaining contract and funding approval for most of the road work on the island. He proved to be a loyal supporter and a man with important connections in both the state capitol and Washington; hence his name will resurface again.

With all the construction on the island, Hoke Smith recommends not allowing any sightseeing on the island during the summer, and regular ferry services are cancelled for the season.

The latter part of the year is devoted to assigning subdivisions and finalizing the lease agreements.

The Robert & Co. master plan calls for five residential subdivisions on the north side of the island; the Negro subdivision in the south is not included in the original plan.

---

[60] The silo is the only remaining structure of the dairy farm and still stands in its original location, south of Jennings Road and east of Riverview Drive.

The original Beach subdivision is located between Beachview Drive and the ocean, bordering south by what is now Borden Lane and stretching to the north to Porter Lane. This configuration will later change as new lots are added for commercial and residential use with the rerouting of Beachview Drive in the 1960s.

The other two subdivisions, Palmetto and Oakgrove, are both located on the oceanside of the island but west of Beachview Drive. Palmetto is bordered on the south by Forest Road, stretching north to Tyler Lane. Again, the northern boundary of Palmetto will be extended further north later. Oakgrove subdivision is nestled between Palmetto and Capt. Wylly to the north, and the golf course to the south.

On the riverside, Plantation subdivision runs north from Capt. Wylly toward Potter Avenue, running parallel with Riverview Drive, while Pine Grove is nestled in the Historic District between Riverview Drive and the golf course.

The intention is to open 750 lots per year with a grand total of two thousand lots to be available for residential and commercial use. The question is now how to assign the lots, what restrictions to place on such, and what recourse the authority has in case of breach.

The authority feels it is restricted in lot assignments by the verbiage used in the Authority Act, and yet again another amendment is proposed in the general assembly.

Senate Bill No. 46, known as the "Jekyll Island State Park Authority Act Amended" or Law Number 306 of 1953, Section 11 and 11 states:

> The leasing of the lots subdivided shall be for no more than 99 years under restrictive limitations as to use, style and character of the structures allowable thereon, and such other limitations as the Authority may deem wise; any and all such restrictions may be incorporated in the leases as covenants and may, at the discretion of the Authority, provide for termination or forfeiture upon breach. Such leases as the Authority shall designate may be made freely assignable subject to all the liabilities, obligations, and duties imposed upon the lessee by the Authority in its original lease. The Authority may in its

lease hold conveyances or rental contracts, create and provide for the preservation of such rights and privileges in the present or future security grantees, mortgages, or other lenders upon the security of the lessee's or tenant's rights as it may deem wise; such rights and privileges when created may also provide for their continuance or survival after termination or forfeiture of the original leasehold or rental contract.

Section 11-A reads:

The Authority may waive this limitation as regards groups of not more than 25 lots when lessees thereof shall covenant to erect or cause to be erected a shopping center or business block or housing project thereon which, when completed, shall be offered for rental or assignment, unit by unit, upon such terms and conditions as may be agreed to by the Authority prior to its construction.

Section 12:

The lots in the various subdivisions created on Jekyll island by the Authority may be leased either singly or in groups deemed appropriate by the Authority, only after publication of a complete schedule of the lease rentals applicable to the lots in the official organs of Glynn and Fulton Counties ...

A drawing shall be held to determine which of the acceptable applications and the sequence in which acceptable applications shall be accepted by the Authority for leases upon the available lots;[61]

Although it may seem that additional restrictions are being placed on the authority, the above amendments provide certain loopholes that pertain to lot offerings, restrictions, and commercial leases that may be negotiated. It opens the door for future block-leasing to construction or

---

[61] See http://neptune3.galib.uga.edu for the full and unabridged legislative text.

development companies within certain subdivisions and the building of duplexes and multifamily dwellings.

It also reflects an indirect and less visible change of vision and direction by the authority. The fear of being unable to find enough individual interest and lease all available lots must have created an impetus to insert the above specific clause that allows for multiple lots to be assigned to one single lessee or interested party, specifically pertaining to residential lots. The change and impact on commercial lots is more obvious, as the future will clearly show. It is now entirely possible for one hotel/motel owner or operator to lease multiple commercial properties without any of the previous lease agreement restrictions.

The authority also adds to its standard lease agreement the restriction that upon signing a lease option, lessee obligates itself to complete construction within thirty-six months with a "visible commencement of construction" within thirty months of execution.

The newspapers report that 1,500 applications have been filed and that two thousand lots will be available to the public, while the authority receives only 231 applications or inquiries for residential lots. If this is any indication about what the future holds and what it may mean to the expected revenue stream, then the authority faces a difficult decision. Should less lots be publicized and offered with a second offering to follow later, or should the advertising be postponed to a later date?

Rep. Ben Tarbutton in the meantime claims that his contacts or constituents have been waiting for two years and should be given priority instead of being subject to a drawing process.

Independent of whether his claim is true, the fact remains that interest is lower than expected despite the Glynn County Chamber of Commerce's folder on Jekyll Island that includes maps and pictures of what the island looks like. But who can blame the average Georgian? After all, the island is not open yet, the bridge is not finished, and nobody has even been able to see the location of the available lots. If the authority's hope was that Georgians would blindly lease land, build houses, and live in a state park without infrastructure or amenities, solely based on the promise that such will come soon, this can be marked as the first eye-opener for the authority and a first taste of the road that lays ahead.

By year-end, the authority has agreed that every applicant should be able to make a down payment upon signing the lease option plus twenty-five dollars for administrative costs and deed issuance. They also mark the location for what would become the very first service and filling station on the island: one block west of the Parkway/Beachview corner on the north side.[62]

The year ends on another remarkable note when Mr. Dinkler Sr. and Mr. Alberting, both prominent hotel owners at the time, launch the first idea of building a beachfront hotel on Jekyll Island with forty to fifty rooms. The location both gentlemen pick for their enterprise is the corner of Capt. Wylly and Beachview Drive.

Both gentlemen can be remembered as visionaries of their time for the selection of the ideal location to build a hotel since that specific corner saw the first building of the first two hotels[63] on Jekyll Island in 1958, a mere five years later.

Neither one of them became involved with any of the island hotels later, but their prospect must have inspired the authority, as the future will tell.

Another busy year passes, and so many things still need to be done and decided upon. The authority scrambles to get the island ready for the bridge opening that is tentatively scheduled for June 1954. The actual opening and dedication will be postponed twice again because of technical difficulties or installation oversight.

Mr. Pendergast from the Industrial Construction Co. is hired to finish the electrical wiring to the control house and promises the bridge will be fully operational by September 30, 1954. The authority immediately starts preparing for an impressive bridge dedication.

The list of invites and dignitaries is endless and includes of course Gov. Talmadge, Gov.-Elect Marvin Griffin, Eugene Cook as attorney general, and their wives. Add to this list all the State Department Highway Commissioners and wives plus all US senators and US congressmen and wives, and you can imagine the crowd the authority prepared to receive. It would be inappropriate though if state officials, state legislators, Glynn

---

[62] The designated site is currently home to Flash Foods and Dairy Queen.
[63] Jekyll Estates Motel and the Wanderer were built on this site a few years later.

County commissioners, and the mayor of Brunswick were omitted, so they also receive an invitation to attend.

The initial plan is to invite all to a luncheon served at the Sea Island Beach Club, after which the parade of dignitaries will drive along the causeway to dedicate the Jekyll Creek Bridge at 3:00 p.m.

Unfortunately, the elaborate plan and ceremony will have to wait just a little while longer, as the dedication is further postponed to December 11, 1954.

The good news is that the authority has a little bit more time to finish the last-minute details on the island.

First on the to-do list is to connect the bridge with the parkway. To accomplish this, the authority instructs Hoke Smith and his prison laborers to push sand from the dunes to create the required abutment.[64]

Second order of the day is to finish the north end of Beachview Drive and to "muck" three parking lots by the beach. One will be located at the end of the parkway, the others about one and a half miles north, facing the ocean. The problem is that just north of Capt. Wylly is a large beach pond that needs filling to create dry land and to build the roadbed. Ultimately, dunes and sand are used to solve that problem, one that will resurface in 2011 when the original Wanderer Motel is remodeled and renovated.[65]

It is difficult to imagine that natural sand dunes and barriers are simply removed to build roadbeds and embankments around the island, but that was simply the innocent approach of the times. Those annoying dunes didn't fit in with the vision of future tourist attractions. In the mid-fifties and even early sixties, the tourist experience was clearly defined as a visual driving/touring experience at slow speed along the shoreline, so clear and unobstructed views were considered a must, at least in the minds of the authority.

---

[64] Oceanside dunes, some as high as forty feet, were razed by bulldozers in 1954 to provide the necessary roadbed for Riverview Drive, between JI Parkway and the historic district. The remainder of the sand was used to build the bridge embankment and the roadbed for the double-lane parkway.

[65] The Wanderer Motel was completely remodeled and converted into the Holiday Inn Resort. During the demolition of the original restaurant kitchen, a large sinkhole was discovered—the remains of the original beach pond. The sinkhole was filled in permanently during renovation.

Now all is ready to hard-surface the remainder of the perimeter road, so visitors can easily drive to the subdivisions and around almost the entire island; the south end is not entirely reachable yet.

The Acme Construction Co., from Cochran, Georgia, is hired to complete the paving of the perimeter road at $207,893.46 despite the objection during a regular board meeting by J. D. Compton. Mr. Compton publicly opposes the contract award, citing "insufficient equipment or qualified personnel" to complete the contract.[66] There is no further explanation to be found for his objection other than the fact that Mr. Compton must have known something then that would only become visible once the island opened for business the next year.

The Acme Construction Co., its owner, and associated businesses[67] will play a pivotal role on the island in the next three years.

The Pure Oil Co. gets the first permit to construct and operate the very first filling station on the island. The location on the north side of the Jekyll Parkway, one block west of Beachview Drive was previously approved for such purpose. The lease agreement requires a monthly lease payment of $100 and seventy-five cents per gallon for any sales over five thousand gallons. The small print of the lease also requires the authority to purchase all its gasoline from the Pure Oil Co.

Again, this is a business name to remember as the business development story on the island starts to unfold.

With most of the labor contracts now in place and underway, the authority starts to fine-tune its leasing business. Three subcommittees are formed to handle the hotel leases and the zoning and to oversee the grand opening day.

Mr. Tarbutton and Mr. Calhoun as secretary will oversee the hotel leases; Mr. Barrett and Mr. Faircloth, the new resident engineer, will be responsible for any zoning issues; while Mr. Benton and Mr. Calhoun will orchestrate opening day.

To determine the fair value of each residential and commercial lot, and to determine the fair rental price, the authority requests lot valuations from the Brunswick-Glynn County Board of Realtors. The average lot valuation

---

[66] Authority board meeting, November 3, 1954.
[67] Sen. Dykes owned the Acme Construction Co. and had a business interest in the Oxford Construction Co. (see chapter 4).

is set at $4,500 (ranging from $3,000 to $8,000) bringing the total of 440 available lots at approximately $2,494,750 as per the final valuation report dated October 10, 1954.

The rental percentage is set at 4.8 percent, bringing the annual lease payments to about $144 to $384 per year. The authority clearly states during a July 31 meeting: "The leasing facility does not have a charitable purpose. It is a business that exists to accommodate the use of public recreational facilities on the island as per the Authority Act."

This simple statement clearly defines the direction the authority envisions once commercial and residential development commences. The notion that leasing is considered a business that should allow to pay for the creation and maintenance of public facilities in the park is the earliest indication found in archived documents that the authority clearly sees an island split into two components. On one hand, there will be the revenue-generating side, comprised of leased commercial and residential lots, while on the other hand will be the cost centers—that is, public recreational areas—that will be paid for and maintained by the first. Although such is not expressly written in any of the documents, the notion itself clearly mentions that this approach is in accordance with the Authority Act.

It is the unspoken but intended beginning of the Jekyll and Hyde conundrum, or the still-present resort-state park oxymoron.

The authority estimates it needs $40,000 per year, which amounts to $1,000 per year, per lot to become self-sustainable after the first two hundred lots have been leased.

That amount will change dramatically next year once the first lot applications are received. For now, those are the projected figures.

The only thing left to do is advertising and publicity to attract the average Georgian to come to the island on opening day, select a desirable lot, make a down payment, and live happily ever after.

The entrance of Jekyll Island, at the intersection of US Hwy-17 and the causeway, is adorned with two-sided illuminated signs, about 26' by 7' advertising: "Rental: 3 years-$100.00/Month."

Each subdivision is marked with 4' by 6' signs indicating the name of the subdivision. Island maps are to be handed out to visitors and interested lessees, and the island engineer is on hand to provide details about the lot, the subdivision, and the island in general.

The authority also hires Tom Wilson as the first golf professional to prepare and maintain the golf course with the use of prison laborers.

Everything is set and ready for the grand opening day in October, except that the engineers decide that for the next month only lightweight traffic[68] is allowed on the bridge and only between 7:30 a.m. and 6:00 p.m. The long-awaited opening ceremony and dedication is postponed again, this time until December 11, 1954.

A small oversight can now also be addressed while there is still time. Nobody thought about enclosing the control house on the bridge or installing a phone line between the control house and the bridge tender's house on the island. An extra $2,650 takes care of that little problem.

One final thing remains to be done, and that is to open a separate bank account with American National Bank in Atlanta to deposit the tolls levied on the bridge. The toll was set at that time at fifty cents, and as per the original agreement with the State Highway Department and the US Bureau of Public Works, despite the recorded objection of Chairman Blalock, who has always been a strong opponent of any tolls levied to enter a state park. Nevertheless, the authority agrees to repay the State Department for principal and interest, using the toll income.

During the last weeks of seclusion on the island, the authority instructs its laborers to remove all personal mementos, books, and papers from the Jekyll Island Hotel and place such in the vault of the Rockefeller house. Whether such was done with foresight about what was to happen only a few weeks later or not remains open for interpretation.

Independent of its motivation, the authority receives a visit from Mrs. Tallu Fish, who was editor at the *Democratic Women's Journal* of Kentucky. Mrs. Fish requests "The concession and right to occupy two rooms in the Rockefeller House to become curator of the house and furnishings as a museum. To add all old mementos and records and to be allowed to charge 50 cents admission."[69]

Mrs. Fish also offers her services and connections as a journalist to assist the authority with its publicity and advertising, given her experience

---

[68] Initial traffic on the bridge was limited to lightweight only as a test and to avoid any potential breakdown or to cause any unnecessary stress on the new structure. The weight limit was lifted prior to the inauguration ceremony in December 1954.
[69] Authority board meeting, November 22, 1954.

From Millionaires to Commoners

and vast network of weekly and monthly publications' editors. As history tells us, Mrs. Fish became instrumental in establishing the very first museum on the island and is considered the pioneer of preserving island history for generations to come. She signed her first lease in 1955 to become the first Jekyll Island Museum curator.

The days leading up to the grand opening and bridge dedication are frantic, which would explain why the authority orders that all trunks of outgoing cars be searched until after the dedication. Granted there must have been a lot of coming and going on the island to make last-minute preparations or inspections, but if the authority was so protective of its historical treasure, it probably was five years too late to confiscate any little mementos or memorabilia.

The big day has finally arrived, and no expenses are spared to make the Jekyll Island Creek Bridge dedication a memorable and historic event.

Thousands of cars line up on the causeway, creating a traffic jam, to attend the dedication and the ceremony and to be the first ones to cross the long-awaited bridge. The prospect of being able to leisurely drive alongside the ocean, slowly maneuvering the 1954 Chrysler Imperial four-door sedan must have been a dream come true. The views certainly must have been spectacular since no dune was left untouched, and one could almost touch the salty water from the slow-moving car. The roadbed and hightide waterline are so close that they almost seem to kiss and embrace one another with each incoming wave.

It looks like one big July Fourth celebration with the main clubhouse decorated with flags and buntings and a Jekyll Island plaque erected on the west bridge head in the center of the JI Parkway. Blimps are gliding in the sky overhead, boats are floating in the river, and even the Brunswick Pirates are landing on the wharf to symbolically "raid" the island.

Outgoing Gov. Talmadge has the honor of cutting the ribbon on the bridge head, recognizing Mr. Gillis, Mr. Oxford, and Mr. Quillian of the State Highway Department, and Mr. McWorther of the US Bureau of Public Works for their contributions to this historic event.

Ms. Emma Belle Roan, daughter of Chairman Blalock, unveils the Jekyll Island plaque on the parkway in the presence of the governor, governor-elect, Mrs. Iris Blitch, and the entire JIA Board. Both Gov.

Talmadge and Gov.-Elect Marvin Griffin give eloquent speeches with special recognition to those who were instrumental in the endeavor.

A special prayer and dedication are again held at the clubhouse in front of all state senators and congressmen, where Mr. J. D. Compton very appropriately speaks about the history and the future of Jekyll Island.

It is then Mr. Barrett's turn to take a more practical approach and talk in detail about the application and leasing process. After all, the audience is nearly perfect and holds the ideal candidates for leasing desirable lots, or so it seems.

The entire ceremony is concluded with an extensive guided tour along beautiful Beachview Drive where the ocean almost meets the shoulder of the road. Postcard and picture-perfect, almost, but the day ends without any promising candidates.

Thousands of curious onlookers tour the island for the next two days, but few, if any, are interested in leasing a residential lot on the island. Who can blame them? There is no infrastructure to be found except a beach house[70] and the Club Hotel, and without amenities, the prospective lessees cannot envision building a home here, let alone a second home. The island itself is beautiful, and the views are stunning, but besides spending a relaxing weekend on the beach, the average Georgian is not interested in homeownership on the island. A few interested visitors return the next day to get a second look or to view other subdivisions, but the weekend opening is not what the authority expects.

The year ends on a disappointing note when only two hundred applications are received for the five hundred lots available. Most of the applicants fail to pay the required fee, leaving the authority to rethink their approach. Before the end of the year, the authority revises its lease agreements and offers the less desirable lots, inland and without beach view, for $100 per year, while beach corner lots and apartment/multifamily lots are offered at $400 per year. Potential lessees are even informed through the local and regional newspapers that there will be no county taxes levied against the new homes on Jekyll Island—an interesting notion that requires some background explanation.

The Glynn County Commission offered to provide access to public schools, health services, and fire and police protection for ten years at a

---

[70] A beach house/concession stand was constructed in 1948.

flat annual rate per leased lot in exchange for not charging any county property taxes. Glynn County had tried unsuccessfully to levy some sort of tax or toll on future island residents. Since it was not authorized to build and finance the Jekyll Creek Bridge, it devised another plan by offering county services in exchange for a flat annual rate. The authority declined the offer, but the discussion about county services and possible taxation continued to linger for many decades.

Of all applications received, only 126 lots can be assigned, all of which are in the Beach and Oakgrove Division. The authority now prioritizes the limited water supply on the island to supply the Beach subdivision and all lots fronting Beachview Drive, Capt. Wylly, and Oakgrove subdivision. The other subdivisions will take a back seat until lots can be leased.

The final thing to do is to open another separate bank account with C&S National Bank of Atlanta to deposit rental income. Two hundred dollars of each deposit will be deposited in the account, while twenty-five dollars will be placed in a separate account to cover attorney fees (fifteen dollars) and record/credit searches (ten dollars). Mr. Calhoun as secretary/treasurer of the authority will be on hand to provide the legal services for the land lease options and the land leaseholds.

Despite the disappointment, at least it must be noted that progress is made. If the expectation was that all of Georgia would fall in love with their new state park, then it must be noted that the island looked like a wilderness. It may be beautiful to come and drive or walk around for a day, but leasing lots and building homes in a place that has no infrastructure or amenities is not exactly an enticing concept.

The progress lies in overcoming the big obstacle: building the causeway and opening the bridge to connect the mainland with the island. At least the island can have a future, and the authority is so convinced that interest in residential and commercial leases will rise rapidly in the next year that it requests the local postmaster to create a star route mail service to the island. Despite the absence of any permanent residents or even commercial hotels-motels, the very first mail route is approved and created on December 21, 1954. A permanent post office will be constructed a few years later.

The question is, Who will come and build first? The answer is that the next two years will alter the direction the authority chose to follow, and J. D Compton's original vision of a state park will forever change.

CHAPTER 4

AN ISLAND CRIPPLED BY POLITICAL MONOPOLY

1955–1956

The new year seems to start well for the authority as all fifty-four beachfront lots have been assigned. Only limited financing, maximum 67 percent, is available for those who wish to obtain construction loans, since banks are still not willing to lend without formal FHA approval or underwriting—a small problem that will persist and slow down the residential development phase.

One of the first houses on the island is constructed on Lot A-1[71] in the Beach subdivision. Mr. Norbert Overstolz presents his construction plans to the authority in February 1955 and receives approval for construction from Laurence Miller, architect and chair of the Architectural Committee.

The approval process is not something to take lightly and is certainly not a mere formality. The authority has strict rules, regulations, and mandates that need to be adhered to if one is to receive a building permit. Not only does the authority limit the height of the residential structure, and the easement between the house and street side, it also has specific requirements for the exterior and the materials that can be used. But restrictions do not stop there. The authority also issues a two-page instruction sheet about materials and finishing touches that need to be used on the interior of the house. The selection of primer, paint, and

---

[71] Lot A-1 is located on the southeast corner of Brice Lane and Beachview Drive.

trim finish must all adhere to the specific instructions as provided by the authority,[72] lest a final inspection of the premises does not receive a stamp of approval and the issuance of a certificate for occupancy.

To accommodate the future demand for building materials, the existing stable and garage buildings[73] are advertised for lease in the newspapers, and requests for proposal are being mailed to Crandall Hardware, Paulk Hardware, Builders Supply & True Hardware, James Dykes[74] of Cochran, Georgia, and Homer Starr of Atlanta, Georgia.

Charlie Davison from the Davison Granite Co. in Lithonia, Georgia, wants to rent the Jennings house[75] for ten years at $200 per month with an option to renew for another ten years, while Mr. Albert Crews submits a lease request for the Crane house at $150 per month or 10 percent of the gross revenue plus maintenance. Both are placed on hold pending Gov. Griffin's decision on which of the millionaires' houses he selects as a governor's mansion[76] on Jekyll Island.

Albert Crews is a very well-known restaurateur and founder/owner of Crews Restaurants. Although his initial lease request is denied, he will play an important role in the food services industry on the island in the late 1950s.

A work inventory shows that by now the entire perimeter road is completed, as is the initial water system, pending the completion of a new well for the Beach, Palmetto, and Oakgrove subdivisions with adjacent pump house and reservoir.

---

[72] The original blueprint of Mr. Overstolz's house is accompanied by a two-page list of instructions for interior finishes, including the specific selection of primers, wall, and trim colors, and even the type of trim wood or flooring to be used. (Original blueprints and building permit. Courtesy of Mr. and Mrs. Michael Thompson.)

[73] The historic stables and garage, located on Stable Road, is now home to the Jekyll Island Museum. Plans are in progress to renovate the historic building that will become the new home of "The Mosaic," the new JI Museum.

[74] James Dykes was a state senator and had no direct experience in building supplies. His inclusion in the RFP is probably related to his ownership of the Acme Construction Co. and his business interest in the Oxford Construction Co.

[75] Jennings house is now referred to as Villa Ospo.

[76] This marks the first time that a historic house on Jekyll Island is being considered as the governor's mansion. Gov. Griffin ultimately declines the offer. No Georgia state governor has ever selected Jekyll Island as the location for a governor's mansion.

A Negro bathhouse still needs to be commissioned and completed on the south side where thirty acres of land are set aside as a preliminary Negro subdivision. The original Vinson & Co. Development Plan of 1950 provisioned a Negro subdivision, followed by an official request from Mr. Dent and his delegation to assign a designated area. Both recommendation and request were duly noted but never acted upon until 1955.

Since no more beach lots are available, the authority focuses on leasing the other lots first and prepares the commercial lots because it is in dire need of funding and revenue.

The idea is to build two beach motels, one with twenty-four units on the beach and the other a twenty-unit court on the west side of Beachview Drive—an excellent idea but one that will take two years to materialize, and even then, under unique circumstances.

Two potential candidates appear at a February board meeting, both submitting a proposal to build a motel and annex restaurant on the west side of Beachview Drive, between Shell Road and JI Parkway. Mr. Webb wants to lease the 400' by 400' lot at 10 percent of gross rental revenue and 5 percent of restaurant revenue with a minimum monthly payment of $125. Mr. Lee, who submitted his proposal late the previous year, is interested in the same lot under the same conditions but with a minimum monthly guarantee of $200. It doesn't seem that the authority is short of interest, but interest and concrete realization of plans and proposals are two different things, as the authority learns over time. That same month also marks the first time a proposal is made to the authority to build a Negro motel on the south side.[77] That proposal is ignored, as there currently is still no bathhouse, let alone a water supply line.

But the authority dreams big and already envisions plans to construct a shopping center on the northwest corner of JI Parkway and Beachview Drive, even though no applicant has begun construction, and no motel plans have been approved.

It is a sign of the time and inherent to the eagerness of the authority to desperately try to find a way, any way possible, to attract residents to the

---

[77] The proposal is made by Mr. Rolleston on February 11, 1955, requesting a lot assignment of 300 feet by 300 feet with a minimum monthly guarantee of $200, identical to the proposals of Mr. Lee.

island. It sounds like the equivalent of putting the cart in front of the horse. Constructing a shopping center in the absence of any potential customers is not an attractive proposal for any business owner to then lease commercial space. The authority wants to find a solution for the Catch-22 game and will consider any proposal that may ignite the revenue engine. In the meantime, the Historic District and its buildings sit idle and unoccupied.

Remember that since Barney Whitaker left the island in January 1951, the Jekyll Island Hotel, the Annex building, and the Sans Souci have been closed to the public. Besides the occasional repair, maintenance, cleaning, or painting, if any, the buildings have not been occupied for the last four years and are in bad shape. Moreover, none of these historic buildings have generated any revenue over the last four years, although the authority insists it will become self-sufficient.

Hope is on the way as two proposals are made to the authority to lease the Jekyll Island Hotel and other properties in the Historic District.

The first proposal is made by a group of businesspeople, Mr. Walter Green, Mr. Jack Anderson, Mr. George Thomas, and Mr. William McCaskill, but no agreement can be reached. It is not documented anywhere what the proposal was or why no agreement could be reached other than that negotiations ended late February 1955.

Two months later and out of nowhere comes another proposal for the hotel properties. This time it is made by Mr. Leo L. Phillips, president of State Bank of Cochran, Georgia, who submits a detailed plan for restoration and repair of the Jekyll Island Hotel properties and the existing bathhouses. Even the press is aware of this latest offer, as the *Brunswick News* reports on April 29, 1955, on the JI Hotel Corporation, as the legal entity is known. The company has $250K in capital and is issuing five hundred stock certificates at a par value of $100 to the public in an initial public offering. What is not known yet by the newspapers or the public is who the actual owners/directors are, but that little piece of knowledge will soon be revealed.

Mr. Phillips's proposal, as submitted on April 9, 1955, must have been very detailed since the authority completes a list of specific expenses, most of which pertain to repairs and maintenance to be done on hotel property, at the same time.

One month later, it becomes clear that Mr. Leo L. Phillips & Associates offered a thirty-two-year lease agreement at $15,000 rent per year. In addition, they are willing to pay 20 percent of gross room rentals, 6 percent of food sales, and 10 percent of the concession sales. In exchange, the authority must invest no less than $150K in repair on hotel property and build a Negro bathhouse on the south side that can be operated as part of the lease.[78]

Minutes of the Jekyll Island Authority Board Meeting of the same day include a detailed plan of expenses that match the JI Hotel Corp.'s requirements:

> Expected Expenses:
> Building, repairing, and painting: $161,500.00
> $10K: Crane house
> $25K: negro bathhouse
> $6.5K: white bathhouse
> $85K: Clubhouse and Annex
> $35K: Sans Souci
> Other Expenses: $46,000.00
> $20K: A/C James house
> $19K: Golf course
> $15K: negro water system
> $1.6K: termite control
> Regular expenses: $41,900.00
> Reserve: $30,000.00 to $40,000.00

The authority needs $250K for immediate investment in the Jekyll Island Hotel and to build a Negro bathhouse with a new water supply line and on April 5, 1955, requests $489K from the governor. The required hotel funding is made available immediately, not to the authority itself

---

[78] It is not clear why the JI Hotel Corporation would have an interest in the construction of the Negro bathhouse, other than their intent to operate all bathhouses and concession stands on the island without the possibility of unwanted competition.

but rather donated to the Jekyll Island Committee for preservation and protection of state assets.[79]

It is not a coincidence that a detailed proposal from a Cochran financier, Mr. Phillips & Associates, and a matching fund request all find immediate governor approval at the same time.

Mr. Phillips is not only a well-established banker and financier in Cochran and Bleckley County. He is also a close friend of Herman Talmadge and therefore a strong campaign supporter of Gov. Griffin[80] the year before. His proposal finds even more support with the authority when personally endorsed by Sen. James Dykes. Sen. Dykes is no stranger to the political arena either as a fervent Talmadge supporter; nor is he a stranger to Cochran. He is a successful real estate agent, businessman, and owner of the Acme Construction Co. that obtained the exclusive paving contract for the JI Parkway and portions of the perimeter road in 1954. The fact that Cochran, as seat of Bleckley County, was founded by B. B. Dykes in 1850 and known as Dykesboro until 1869 only confirms the influence Sen. Dykes has professionally and politically.

But let's not get ahead of the game. Let the story unfold and the chapter become worthy of its title.

In May 1955, a lease agreement is signed between the JI Hotel Corp. and the authority that defines the roles and responsibilities of the new lessee. Besides the main Club Hotel, the Annex building, and the Sans Souci, in addition to full use of the Crane house, the corporation also gets the exclusive operation of the beach concession stands, both white and Negro, which must be open and have adequate lifeguards during the day. Room rates are set at four dollars and up per night and are modeled after a European Plan.[81] Coca Cola is served in paper cups at five cents each, but if a customer prefers a bottle, such can be purchased for an additional five cents. The consumption and sale of alcohol is prohibited anywhere—an

---

[79] All funding and donations are made through "Governor discretionary spending accounts" up until 1964 as per the archived general assembly minutes. Starting in 1965, funding will be obtained through the issuance of revenue bonds.

[80] Gov. Griffin was lieutenant governor under Gov. Talmadge and a personal protegee. He was personally selected by Gov. Talmadge as his successor in 1954 and won the primary by majority vote despite eight opponents.

[81] A European Plan (EP) pertains to lodging only and does not include any meals.

interesting concept that will return when the first motels are opening for business. For the time being, Jekyll Island is dry land amidst the water.

The lessee promises to keep the hotel, restaurants, and concession stands open year-round and agrees to pay all rental payments after ninety days of lease execution and all fee payments monthly thereafter.

Things are moving along quite nicely in the first five months of operation. The Jekyll Island Hotel is rented and in good and capable hands. The beach concession stands are all open and operational. Even the filling station is coming along just fine, and Pure Oil Co. is building its own septic tank and water lines.

That leaves the cottages, but before long, Acme Construction Co., the contractor that paved most of the perimeter roads and the parkway the year before, is interested in leasing the Claflin Cottage[82] "as is" at $100 a month for the first five years, with rent to be increased with every lease renewal. The company promises to put the cottage in "excellent state of repair" in exchange for the reduced rent.

The Oxford Construction Co. from Albany, Georgia, owned and operated by Sen. Dixon Oxford, rents the Goodyear Cottage at the same time and at the same price.

The James house[83] is selected to become the governor's mansion in the meantime, with property rights to be extended to the low tide waterline so that a private fishing and boat dock can be constructed.

The lease for the Jennings house is amended to include Mr. Scarboro as a co-lessee, and the terms and conditions are changed to match the new leases for the Claflin and Goodyear Cottages.

Earlier in the year, the authority requested open bid proposals from several companies and hardware stores for the existing stable and garage buildings, and a contract is awarded to the Bonded Supply and Building Co. of Cochran, Georgia.[84]

---

[82] Currently known as Mistletoe Cottage.
[83] Now better known as "Cherokee" and operated by the Jekyll Island Club Resort.
[84] The company was not included in the original RFP. Its owner and operator, Sen. James Dykes, did receive the authority's request and subsequently formed the Bonded Supply & Building Co. to submit his winning bid.

That leaves the authority with four more island leases up for bid. One is for an oceanfront amusement park; the others for a nursery, a trailer park, and a fishing dock/marina at the old wharf.

There is no further news on the earlier motel plans, despite the lease requests and proposals, because no actual construction plans or concrete financing plans are being presented to the authority.

A third request for lot and lease assignment is received from Mr. John Ambler, this time to build the Jekyll Island Inn on the first 600 feet facing the ocean on the corner of Capt. Wylly and Beachview Drive. Mr. Ambler's proposal is for twenty years at 10 percent of gross receipts with a minimum annual guarantee of $2,500 for the first year, $3,000 in the second year, $3,500 in the third year, and $4,500 for any subsequent year thereafter. So far, that is the best financial proposal of the three the authority has received. Mr. Ambler also discloses the names of his business partners in his lease application, the first full disclosure of its kind but one that will be demanded very soon going forward. The owners/investors are, besides Mr. and Mrs. John Ambler, Georgia Hayes and Clyde Bryan, both from Virginia, and William Ambler Jr. from Philadelphia.

Earnest money in the amount of $2,500 is included in the application on April 30 but returned on May 14 without any documented reason or explanation.[85]

The lot lease options and assignments for residential lots do not fare so well, and the authority adopts strict rules for lease cancellations and for unsigned leases. A full refund will be given only if the cancellation is received within the first thirty days. Any other cancellation is subject to liquidation damage or a penalty equal to the rent for the period plus the closing costs. Unsigned leases face $100 in liquidation costs plus closing costs.

Despite that temporary setback, plans are made to build a shopping center on the island, and the first design is made and presented by Prof. D.J. Edwards and Prof. D. A. Polychrone of Georgia Tech, with the help of their students Fount Smathers, Richard Mixon, Hasso Olbrick, and Walter Smith Jr.

---

[85] Archived minutes of the authority board meeting dated April 30, 1955, simply state that a decision has been made to return the earnest money to Mr. Ambler without further discussion or explanation.

But things are taking a strange turn as a series of newspaper articles is published about the current lessees on Jekyll Island. Previously, the authority had decided not to release the names of any lessee, and such could be found only in the Glynn County records, but the *Brunswick News* reports on May 25 that five legislators, three former lawmakers, two state officials, and three well-connected businesspeople have all signed leases on the island out of 104 names listed in the county records. A second article points out that Sen. James Dykes is not only connected to the Acme Construction Co. but that his brother-in-law is the owner of the Coffee Construction Co. Both companies have shared in the paving contract of the perimeter road and the parkway at the end of 1954. The press also alludes to their close friendship with Herman Talmadge and Gov. Marvin Griffin, not to mention their close ties with Sen. Braxton Blalock, chair of the authority. Speculation is made that contracts and leases are awarded based on political favoritism, which at the time is not quite substantiated, but it will only take a few more months before the real picture will emerge.

The example used at the time was that the Seaboard Construction Co. had the same paving machines as Acme Construction Co. but a lot more experience and better qualified laborers. Yet the contracts were somehow awarded to the lesser qualified of the two. Something that J. D. Compton had pointed out previously in a board meeting now suddenly becomes public knowledge and certainly catches the attention of the public.

To throw more oil on the fire of distrust, the *Brunswick News* reports on June 9, 1955, that the authority "donated" Jekyll Island furniture to the governor to furnish his Atlanta home. It is true that the authority sold furniture and inventoried items from the Club Hotel, the Annex building, and the Sans Souci to collectors and antique dealers, but whether some of the Jekyll Island Hotel inventory found its way to the governor's home or mansion is not documented or proven anywhere. The donated furniture refers to inventory of the James house that was previously reserved as the governor's mansion. Gov. Griffin, affected by all the negative publicity surrounding him and his political friends and allies, decides not to occupy the James house but instead removes most of the historic furniture, paintings, and mementos to his personal mansion in Atlanta.

The rumor mill has been started and continues to be in full swing with one storyline after another, the most prominent one being Sen. Dykes's involvement with most of the active businesses on Jekyll Island. The pressure for full public disclosure finally results in Sen. Dykes admitting his ownership interest in Jekyll Hotels Inc., the entity that operates the Club Hotel, its adjoining buildings, and all the beach concessions stands.

The public quickly adds two and two together and draws the conclusion that Sen. Dykes now runs Jekyll Island single-handedly. He owns and/or operates Jekyll Hotels Inc., Acme Construction Co. that rents the Claflin house, and Bonded Supply & Building Co. that leases the old stables and garage buildings.

Jekyll Island is renamed "Dykes Island" in the popular vernacular, but the story gets another twist and makes things even worse for the authority.

The media insinuate that Sen. Blalock has received orders for machine parts from the authority without any open bid, as required by law. The senator owns Blalock Machinery Co., which, according to public records, received orders for machine parts for $101,000 out of a total order in the same period of $127K. Sen. Blalock denies any wrongdoing but does confirm that his company delivered most of the parts to the authority, not because of favoritism but because of the price and quality of the parts in comparison to his competitors.

Gov. Griffin must step in and prohibits the authority from making any purchase from a company that represents a conflict of interest because of owners or part owners also being in the employment of the state. This new rule does not only apply to Blalock Machinery Co. It also applies to Bonded Supply & Building Co., where Sen. Dykes is part owner with Mr. McMath, who recently was hired as the new island engineer.

The story is so twisted, and the lines become so blurry that J. D. Compton abruptly resigns from the authority. The one rational voice in the authority who has served loyally on the board and the committees from its early beginnings and who could conceptualize his long-term vision and goals to the average Georgian is now gone.

If one can pick a single hero in the various time periods of the Jekyll Island State Park Authority, then J. D. Compton is the first one who should be remembered. While his motivation to preserve the island may have been suspicious or questionable, and while it was certainly influenced by his own desire to protect Sea Island from any future competition, his contributions ultimately led to the creation and preservation of Jekyll Island as it exists today.

But life must go on, despite the accusations and the intricate web of connections, contracts, and favoritism.

By late summer, the Negro bathhouse is finally finished by Thompson & Davis at a low cost of $8,658 compared to the $60K white bathhouse[86] on the ocean. All that is left to do before officially opening the Negro subdivision on the south end is to connect the southern well to the first street in the subdivision and to connect the same to the bathhouse.

The official opening is planned for September 24, 1955, five years after the first request for a "separate but equal" subdivision.

The authority is certainly not going to miss this opportunity for publicity and advertises the availability of "Negro lots" in Glynn and Fulton County, in *Atlanta World*, and Pittsburgh Negro newspapers. The price for the lots is the same as in other island subdivisions, despite the lack of comparable amenities. Besides the bathhouse, referred to as the pavilion, there were simple picnic tables, a snack bar, and restrooms.[87]

All the prominent local Negroes are invited to conduct and attend the ceremony on that day, and they certainly make it a memorable one.

Dedication Program
Jekyll Island State Park Beach House
J.M. Atkinson, presiding
3:00 pm

National Anthem	Risley Band
Invocation	Rev. Julius James
Music	Risley School
Recognition out of town guests	J.P Atkinson & J. Wilkerson
Presentation of City, County & State Officials	J.L. Carmousche
Introduction of speaker	Rev. R.W. Moore
Address	Rev. J.P. Mann

---

[86] The white bathhouse was constructed in October 1948.

[87] A replica of the original pavilion can be seen today at Jekyll Camp.

Presentation of Park	Hon. D.B. Blalock
Acceptance	Pres. Luscious Bacote
	State Teachers Association

Joe Malone from Albany, Georgia, is the first to apply for a residential lease in the brand-new subdivision, although he is not the first one to construct a home there. That memorable and historic event is reserved for someone we shall meet later.

J. M. Atkinson, who presided over the dedication ceremony, applies for the first motel and restaurant lease in the Negro subdivision. He offers $1,200 in annual rent for the motel lot and $600 per year for the restaurant lot, plus 5 percent of gross receipt as monthly payment.[88]

With the sudden departure of J. D. Compton, Gov. Griffin appoints Mr. W. F. Aldred of Summerville to join the authority, but the problems continue.

Early September and right after all the negative publicity, the State Economy Committee summons the authority to testify about the current policies, specifically the ones pertaining to purchasing and acquisition. During the hearing, it becomes known that not only did Sen. Blalock benefit from no-bid contracts, but that more than a thousand gallons of paint are missing from the official inventory. The paint in question was ordered from Bonded Supply & Building Co. and was to be used to paint the Jekyll Island Hotel as part of the agreed-upon maintenance. It is now clear to everybody that a conflict of interest among numerous interested parties is the rule of thumb and that such must be stopped immediately. The same committee launches a second investigation about the daily wheeling and dealings after they speak with Mr. Miller, the previous island engineer.

The irony of the *Brunswick News* articles, the change in purchase legislation, and the subsequent investigation is that Mr. Miller, who was hired and fired as resident engineer, ends up being part owner/operator of the island marina at the old wharf, together with Mr. Scarboro and Mr.

---

[88] J. M. Atkinson ended up leasing both lots for four years before the motel was constructed in 1959. Both lots, together with the future site of the St. Andrews Club and Auditorium, are now part of Jekyll Camp.

Davison. The latter are the two gentlemen that renegotiated their lease agreement for the Jennings house after Sen. Dykes negotiated his deal for the Jekyll Island Hotel, the stables, and the Claflin house.

Trying to put these issues to bed and to let transparency prevail, the authority invites the press to its next board meeting on October 18, 1955.

Present are the *Atlanta Journal*, *Atlanta Constitution*, and *United Press*. By now, everybody gets a sense of wrongdoing on the island but seeks clarification on how to avoid the prevailing conflicts of interest. Sen. Dykes is also present and confirms the disputed purchase of paint and promises to rectify the situation. Overall, the authority and Sen. Dykes save face for the time being, but other than a public reprimand, nothing really changes, and the next day is business as usual.

Toward the end of the year, another name pops up suddenly, one that will become part of the intricate island web yet again.

Mr. Overstolz, who now lives in his new home on Beachview Drive, complains about the prisoners that are still on the island and work for Mr. McMath and Mr. Hoke Smith. The latter is no longer the island superintendent. He is now the island's first manager. The authority promises to remove all prisoners from the island by year-end and to release Mr. McMath. We will elaborate on Mr. Overstolz's role and his connection with Sen. Dykes a little bit later.

Before the year ends, Sen. Dykes has some other requests that pertain to the Jekyll Island Hotel. Despite the $250K investment by the authority, he also wants air-conditioning units installed in the Crane house and for the authority to open the road in front of the hotel as a two-way street to increase the hotel's visibility. That portion of the historic road would later be changed and referred to as Jekyll Boulevard[89] as it did resemble some grandiose drive-by boulevard all lit on both sides with streetlights. The request is granted, but the speed limit is set at 15 mph.

The capitol, still trying to digest the accusations, the investigation, and the purchasing scandal, demands the abolishment of the Jekyll Island Authority mid-December. The current business conduct is quoted as being unethical and too lax, with not enough oversight and too much power in the hands of the secretary/treasurer, Mr. Calhoun. Five million dollars has

---

[89] What was commonly referred to as Jekyll Boulevard is now known as Stable Road.

been spent in tax money,[90] and the island continues to drain on the budget while nothing has been developed and only 136 leases have been signed.

The "Solons," as the press refers to them, recommend that no further state funds be used, that lots be sold instead of leased, that the island is returned to the authority of the State Parks Department, or that the island be sold completely.

The second recommendation seems to find some traction, at least with some individuals but particularly with Gov. Griffin, who wants to sell residential lots but would prefer to keep all commercial lots and beaches in addition to the parks and recreation areas.

A tumultuous year, yet again, and the new year will not be that much different.

The holidays are barely over when Gov. Griffin announces to the press that he is willing to sell Jekyll Island for $3.5 million but changes his mind two days later when he indicates that he favors the sale of individual residential lots rather than a sale of the entire island. The governor is, after all, a good student of the Talmadge administration and does not hesitate to publicly refer to Jekyll Island as the White Elephant, like his predecessor. And so, the saga and seesaw adventure of dismantling the authority, selling the island outright, or portions thereof, continues.

Sen. Blalock certainly must have had some influence on this rapid change of mind. He estimates that the island should at least be worth $5 million and questions the legality of an outright sale because of the "Dykes lease." That is the now common term used for the thirty-two-year lease agreement for the Club Hotel and surrounding buildings and indicates how entrenched Sen. Dykes was at the time. The investigative reporting by the *Brunswick News* and *Atlanta Journal*, combined with the well-publicized probe of the Legislative Economy Committee a year earlier, brought full disclosure and some sort of transparency to the business deals that were struck and the intricate web of interconnections between seemingly separate legal entities on the island.

The fact that Sen. Blalock believes that the hotel's lease can be an obstacle in any future sale of the island certainly indicates who holds the power and trump card at the time. That trump card will ultimately

---

[90] The amount referred to includes the construction cost of the causeway, the bridge, and governor's discretionary spending.

be played out well and very subtly when the time is right, as we shall see shortly.

In the end, a compromise is reached, and Gov. Griffin appoints yet another Legislative Committee to decide on the future of Jekyll Island. This now marks the fourth time in only ten years that a committee is tasked with assessing the destiny of Jekyll Island.

The first one was formed in 1946 to determine the condemnation and purchase. A second committee, formed in 1948 to protect the state assets, was followed by number three in 1951 to improve the infrastructure and to develop the island.

The average Georgian must have quietly shaken their combined heads about the constant battle over their new state park. To them it was supposed to be a simple vacation and relaxation spot by the ocean, where families can spend time together during a beach picnic, or where ordinary citizens can drive or bike around the island while enjoying the peace and tranquility of this little beach jewel. Although Gov. Talmadge specifically created the authority in 1950 "To create a non-political authority and to remove Jekyll Island from politics,"[91] it seems that the island is destined to remain a political battleground, without end in sight.

House Resolution No. 260, known as "Jekyll Island Study Committee" or Law No. 152 states:

> Whereas the Legislative Economy Committee has made certain recommendations relative to Jekyll Island and the Jekyll Island Authority, and
>
> Whereas, the General Assembly has determined that additional study should be made relative thereto, before the passage of any legislation affecting the Authority or Jekyll Island, and
>
> Whereas, there has been a divergence of opinion as to the best possible method of solving the problems connected with Jekyll Island.
>
> Now, therefore, be it resolved by the General Assembly of Georgia that there is hereby created a committee to be composed of five members of the House, to be appointed

---

[91] *Brunswick News*, February 17, 1950.

by the Speaker, and four members of the Senate, to be appointed by the President. Said committee shall make a thorough study on all matters concerning Jekyll Island and the Jekyll Island Authority so as to determine whether legislation should be enacted relative thereto, and to determine whether it would be to the best interests of the citizens of this State to make any changes in the present method of operation relative thereto, or whether some method should be used for the disposition of the island or portions thereof ...

The resolution is approved on March 17, 1956, and again leaves the door open for a potential sale, should such be in the best interest of the citizens.

What is interesting about the committee is that it marks the first time that the governor delegates his appointment powers to both the Speaker of the House and the president of the Senate. All previous committees have always been appointed by the governor alone.

During all this renewed political upheaval, business on the island continues as usual. Sen. Dykes, now officially representing the Hotel Corp., requests additional improvements on the hotel property with funds that have already been committed. The improvements consist of all the necessary wiring and plumbing, plus additions to the heating system and air-conditioning units in 168 rooms. The cost so far is estimated between $320K and $400K and well above the promised investment at the time of lease signing in May 1955,[92] a trend that will continue for at least one more year. Sen. Dykes also wants to lease 1,200 feet of beachfront property, adjacent to the white beach house. His intention is to provide entertainment and amusement to the beachgoers and customers of his beach concession stands. The authority, growing weary of his continued demands for more lots and exclusive leases, places his request on hold and never commits to approve or execute his application.

It should be clear by now why the average Georgian calls the island "Dykes island" and why these two years in the island's history are

---

[92] The total amount committed in the original lease agreement was $150K.

remembered as the "Dykes years," although not necessarily with fondness or respect. At least not by everybody.

The Whittle Furniture Co, from Brunswick, Georgia, operated by Ray Whittle, the Glynn County commissioner whose involvement with the battle for the bridge is documented in the previous chapter, leases the Maurice house[93] to display model homes. He is not authorized to sell furniture but can use the cottage as a model home display for future residents.

The commercial side of the island seems to draw some attention as well, and the authority announces that A. B. Newton & Co. from Vidalia, Georgia, will build the first motel/restaurant on the island. The selected lot is half a mile north of the white beach house and will consist of thirty units. The company receives a twenty-year lease for $2,000 per year plus 5 percent of all gross revenue, both motel rentals and restaurant sales. This would ultimately become the very first motel on Jekyll Island and known as the Jekyll Estates Motel, better known in recent times as the Beachview Club,[94] but construction would take another year.

J. M. Atkinson, whose lease in the Negro subdivision was approved earlier, also announces he will build the first Negro motel on the south side with twenty units to be ready by June. It would take a little longer before construction was finished, and the hotel finally opened as the Dolphin Motor Lodge.[95]

Things are moving along quite well, and at least the prospect of motel units opening soon is positive news, which contributes to the new committee's recommendation not to sell Jekyll Island. With this dark cloud out of the way, other infrastructure and development projects can now be tackled.

Four business ventures, the marina at the old wharf, an amusement park, a nursery, and a trailer park, were placed for open bid the year before, and two receive applications.

The Jekyll Island Marina Inc., owned by Mr. Miller, Mr. Scarboro, and Mr. Davison, opens the old wharf as a fishing, tackle, and bait operation

---

[93] Hollybourne was previously referred to as the Maurice house.

[94] The Beachview Club was included in the Holiday Inn Resort lease in 2017.

[95] The 4-H Center later used the motel until it was demolished in 2015. A commemorative plaque is placed in its original location at what is now Jekyll Camp.

in the spring of 1956. All three gentlemen are already well known on the island since Mr. Miller is also the resident engineer and in charge of the large and expensive renovations of the Jekyll Island Hotel. Mr. Scarboro and Mr. Davison both hold a lease on the Jennings house.

When an outsider, the Southern Miniature Railroad Co., finally bids on the amusement park request, Mr. Harvey Smith's proposal is first verbally approved and then rejected by Mr. Mike Benton, vice-chair of the authority, who reminds his colleagues that Sen. Dykes submitted a lease request earlier for the same location, namely the 1,200 feet oceanfront. Nobody seems to remember that the lease in question was awarded, and the minutes of the meeting do not show that the authority approved Sen. Dykes's request. Nevertheless, the meeting turns into an intense argument between the authority and Sen. Dykes, who appears in person to make his case. He goes on record as stating: "I was promised beachfront by the Authority one year earlier and would install rides ..."[96]

The discussion ends with Mr. Smith withdrawing his proposal and the authority, upon recommendation from Mr. Aldred, deciding to reopen the bids. Mr. Harvey Smith resubmits his original bid of $1,200 for 200 feet of oceanfront property with a maximum extension to 800 feet, and 5 percent on after-tax revenue for income below $50K and 10 percent for revenue above. Peppermint Amusement Park would open shortly thereafter and was located just south of the old beach house and concessions stands that later converted into the first beach restaurant, the Charcoal House Restaurant, and is currently the location of Tortuga Jack's.

The showdown of power at the meeting is not the end but merely the beginning of a new tension building up inside the authority that will again cause a change of direction.

The first stage of failure for this authority starts with the sudden resignation of Sen. Blalock as chair. Mr. Blalock senses that, with the ongoing disputes and the appointment of Mr. Aldred, his days are numbered, and the governor would prefer his personal appointee to be in charge. His instincts are intuitive, as before long, Mr. Aldred suggests that the chair should rotate on an annual basis.

---

[96] Authority board meeting, March 21, 1956.

Pending governor instructions, Mr. Benton becomes the acting chair, and Mr. Barrett is selected to the Executive Committee to replace outgoing Sen. Blalock.[97]

In April 1956, Gov. Griffin appoints Mr. Deke Giles of Warner Robbins and Mr. Earl Edwards from West Point as the two new authority members, and suddenly there are now six members instead of the original five seats, as has been standard since its inception in 1950.

The number of authority members will change again over time, not in declining numbers but by adding more governor appointees.

The attention is back to the Jekyll Island Hotel where this time Sen. Dykes wants twenty-four more bathrooms for the hotel and an additional lease for five acres of land around the old servants' quarters. His intention is to build a trailer park, one of the unanswered open bids the authority had requested one year ago, and he is willing to pay $600 per year for the land lease. The idea may seem awkward or unusual, certainly considering the presence of trailers around historic servants' quarters, but the purpose was identical to the current situation. Today, two large parking lots surround the original servants' quarters, so the proposal at the time does not seem as outrageous as it sounds.

He also gets a little break from the authority when he is authorized to tap into the authority's water well and supply lines for the next five years on the condition that the water is used only for cooling of the air-conditioning units in the hotel and for filling the pool. This of course will become another dispute between the two parties, but for now, all seems to go smoothly.

A sudden and unexpected resolution is issued on June 15 by the State Highway Department to free the Jekyll Creek Bridge from any toll, effective June 20, 1956, at noon. All toll passes need to be refunded by the authority, when submitted. The resolution is the result of the opening of the Sydney Lanier Bridge, which now becomes a toll bridge, hence the decision to make the Jekyll Creek Bridge toll-free. Mrs. Neill, the

---

[97] The authority created an Executive Committee, consisting of the chair, vice-chair, and secretary/treasurer of the authority, to address and examine any policy issues. The committee did not have any voting or decision-making powers and reported its recommendations to the entire board.

current treasurer of the authority and a new permanent presence at board meetings, is charged with the refunds and instructed to retain a small amount in the designated bank account for future expenses.

The news calls for an elaborate celebration at the Jekyll Island Hotel, including a beauty contest at the swimming pool where Kathryn Ruark from Bostwick, Georgia, is crowned Miss Jekyll Island.

Not long after, the *Brunswick News* breaks the story that the Jekyll Island Hotel and the beach houses are serving beer and liquor to the guests, despite Jekyll Island being dry and the specific instructions from the governor, plus the clause in the hotel lease, prohibiting alcohol sales anywhere.

The little spat is again enough reason to bring back the old ideas of abolishing the Jekyll Island Authority or of shutting down the Jekyll Island Hotel altogether. Neither of these happen at the time, but there are a few ideas that linger and ultimately end with another transformation.

The first idea to abolish the current authority is proposed by Sen. Dixon Oxford, who instead suggests that a new authority should be formed with state officials as its members—an idea that was implemented in 1957, as we shall see later. It is important to note here that Sen. Oxford is none other than the owner of Oxford Construction Co., who not only received part of the paving contract for the parkway and the perimeter road in 1954 but also leases the Goodyear house and is embedded in the day-to-day wheeling and dealing on the island.

The second proposal and idea worth noting here comes from none other than Sen. Dykes himself and his JI Hotel Corp. He defiantly proposes to offer his current lease agreement for sale at $175K to recoup his investment. He must have known that big changes were coming and that the current state of affairs was no longer tenable. His instincts were proven correct when in August the Joint Legislature Committee decides to attend a regular authority board meeting on the island.

The Joint Legislature Committee consists of Robert L. Scoggin, chair; Senator W. B. Steis, Twenty-Sixth District; Senator E. D. Clary, Twenty-Ninth District; Senator Brinson Jones, Eighteenth District; Representative John Drinkard, Lincoln County; Representative Steve Cocke, Terrell County; Representative Ebb Duncan, Carroll County; and Representative Harold Willingham, Cobb County.

From Millionaires to Commoners

Quite an impressive representation to discuss the hotel improvements and the status of repair, progress, and cost involved.

A full and detailed report is provided by Mr. Miller, architect/engineer, Mr. Asher, the new island manager, and Mr. Morris, the building inspector. It seems that all exterior painting, interior floor and tiling, and electrical work are completed or near completion. The only large outstanding contract is the interior painting and of course the installation of an elevator in the hotel lobby.[98] The latter is said to arrive mid-September with installation to be completed within four to eight weeks afterward.

The overall sentiment is that the work completion has been "fairly satisfactory," and the "only delays were caused by lack of scheduling between the individual contractors, a problem which both the architect and the inspector had worked hard to minimize."[99]

With the remaining work to be completed by month-end, and the second annual rent payment due shortly, Sen. Dykes submits a lease adjustment request, prepared by Mr. L. L. Phillips, president of the JI Hotel Corp.

The proposal is to rebate the first year's rent by 75 percent to become 25 percent of the normal and prepaid amount of $15K. The argument used in the letter is that since the beginning of the lease, the only unrestricted access and use have been the Crane house and the beach concession stands. The main club building and the Annex have not been improved as per the joint committee agreement until just recently. Furthermore, the Sans Souci still lacks central heat and cannot be fully used.

The authority finally agrees on a 50 percent rent rebate and uses half of the prepaid $15K as rent payment for the first year (May 1955–April 1956) and the remainder to be applied to the following year. In the end, only $3,364,66 is deemed due for the first year, and the remainder can be used again as prepayment for the next year, which is not to be due until August 1957. Another nice amendment negotiated carefully by Sen. Dykes.

The trouble is still not over, despite a smooth negotiation and full report to the joint committee. At a press conference on October 18, 1956,

---

[98] The original lobby staircase was removed to install the elevator, and a new enclosed staircase was constructed next to the hotel's tower. The elevator was removed during the 1986 restoration project, and the staircase was placed back in its original location.
[99] Authority board meeting, August 11, 1956.

the authority provides a full status report on the Club Hotel. Present are Charles Pou of the *Atlanta Journal*, Nick Chris of the *United Press*, and Carlton Morrison, who owns several local radio stations. The authority promises that all repair and improvement work will be completed by November 1.

Robert Scoggin, chair of the joint committee, reconfirms his expectation that the Jekyll Island Hotel should be open and occupied by the above date. He also sets an official dedication date for November 10, with the joint committee to stay at the hotel as guests and ceremony attendees.

But before the year is over, the authority still waits for the new lease amendment to be signed and ratified. To make things worse, the JI Hotel Corp. fails to pay its electric and water bills, and the authority is ready to cut all services to the hotel unless payment is received in full by year-end. Not a very promising way to end the year, or maybe it is a foreboding of what is to come.

But not all is bad, in the sense that Berger & Co. submits a proposal to lease 875 feet of oceanfront property, south of the parkway. During the negotiations of the base annual rate and the percentage of gross revenue, Mr. Berger and Mr. Bergman, co-owners of the company, offer their insight that will inspire the authority in the next few years.

According to Berger & Co., the cost of building a small motel amounts to $180K in mortgage plus an additional self-financed $400K investment. No lessee so far has been able to begin construction because the rental amounts as a percentage of gross revenue are too high and reduce the future revenue stream to such an extent that mortgage companies or banks are not willing to lend the funds. A 5 percent of gross rental and sales revenue means an actual loss for any investor, according to Mr. Berger. If, however, the authority would reduce the rental payments to 1 percent of gross revenue, then funding would become available, and construction could start.

The authority ends up agreeing to the Berger & Co. argument and proposal but not until Mr. Thrasher, state auditor, provides another innovative idea during an authority meeting (October 18, 1956):

> Mr. Thrasher believed that despite efforts to preserve the most beautiful beaches in the State for the people and to forever preserve a truly public beach for Georgians, that the average person could never afford a second home and that what Jekyll most needed was a whole range of accommodations comparable to the motel accommodations at Daytona ...[100]

To achieve the above vision, Mr. Thrasher suggests that the authority use its power to borrow funds through the issuance of revenue certificates. Although credit markets are tight, and investors are hesitant to purchase such certificates unless similar projects are already operational and successful, the suggestion is made to pursue the current motel offers at the best possible rate.

A board resolution to that extent is approved unanimously on October 18, 1956:

> That John Calhoun be authorized ... to negotiate with all motel lessees and applicants to ward securing the best agreement possible for the best rental and rate ceiling possible, making for commencement of construction of not less than 100 motel units ...

A most interesting chapter in the history of Jekyll Island and Mr. Thrasher's suggestions and recommendations would find its practical application soon enough, although not in their entirety. Gov. Griffin is 100 percent in agreement with the plan and supports the issuance of revenue certificates to fund up to fifty low-rent vacation units.

In between all the ideas and suggestions about the future financing and construction of rental units or motels is the little-known fact that the authority suddenly decides in a closed executive meeting to set up its own purchasing department. State approval is no longer needed for any purchase or acquisition of material or inventory, and it marks the first time that the state no longer has authority over future purchases on the island. What it means is that the authority is trying to separate itself

---

[100] Minutes of the authority board meeting, October 19, 1956.

from the State Parks Department, which is contradictory to what the legislature ultimately wants. The small detail and sense of separation is never mentioned again in any document and is not reported by the press or newspapers.

At least the JI Hotel Corp. lives up to part of its deal and agreement, and by the end of the year, the Jekyll Island Hotel has seventy-eight rooms available with nineteen more in the Crane house. The Sans Souci is closed for the winter.

CHAPTER 5

THE GROWING PAINS OF AN ISLAND

1957–1961

The new year, as most of the preceding years, starts again with a full vengeance, and State Auditor B. E. Thrasher completes a full audit of the Jekyll Island Hotel and the entire island.

It is noted that the lease amendment for the Jekyll Island Hotel has not been signed and ratified, including the rent increases that are due because of extra funds that have been made available for repairs and improvements. The audit also reveals that sixty residential leases remain unpaid.

The authority has its hands full, it seems, and in addition to addressing the audit issues, the board members also prepare an annual 1957 report for the Glynn County Commission and the Joint Legislature Committee.

In essence, the authority is trying to address the recommendation from the county after the turbulence of last year.

The county commission recommends:

1) An advisory committee be appointed consisting of the state auditor, the president of the Brunswick Chamber of Commerce, and the president of the Georgia Press Association.
2) No residential lots are to be sold outright.
3) No more than 5 percent of the available commercial lots are to be sold.
4) County to furnish police and fire protection on Jekyll Island through the authority and county to negotiate for educational services.

It needs to be noted that this is the second time the county attempts to get somehow involved in the operation of the island. The first time was during the battle for the bridge, which the county ultimately lost, and now again with the offering of oversight and county services. What is not mentioned very often in the newspapers is the fact that Glynn County requested a Georgia State Supreme Court ruling in 1955 on whether the county could tax Jekyll Island homes. The Supreme Court ruled on September 15, 1955, that Glynn County can tax Jekyll Island homes but must provide county services to the residents in exchange for such tax levy,[101] an interesting fact that would become pivotal in the tax and services discussion in later years.

By February, the Georgia House of Representatives votes 180 to 9 to:

1) Add the director of state parks to the Jekyll Island Authority.
2) Authorize the lease-purchase of residential lots.
3) Authorize the sale of commercial lots.
4) Prohibit the sale of beach areas.
5) Authorize the State Parks Department to spend state funds.

The new law brings with it an avalanche of drastic changes to the authority and how business is conducted on the island. In one of its last meetings, the existing authority manages to ratify the amended hotel lease and grants a construction extension of sixty days to Berger & Co. and a 120-day extension to J. M. Atkinson on his south-end lease option.

When the newspapers hit the stands on February 20, 1957, the news spreads like wildfire. "The Jekyll Island Authority is out, and Dykes is still in." That is the word on the street, but B. E. Thrasher leaves the door open for Sen. Dykes and his associates and/or business partners to leave as well. The new law will not be officially enacted and signed by the governor until March 15.

Both Mr. Aldred, authority chair, and Mr. Calhoun, secretary/attorney for the authority, sensing that their days are numbered, resign ahead of the official announcement. Mr. Benton will act as chair while Mr. Barrett acts as vice-chair until the change becomes effective.

---

[101] Despite the Supreme Court ruling, Jekyll Island remained free of county taxes for several more years.

From Millionaires to Commoners

March 20, 1957, rings in the new beginning for the Jekyll Island State Park Authority and another chapter in its history. Maybe Sen. Dixon Oxford was right in his assumption that the authority should be comprised of elected state officials, or maybe it was simply time to try another approach. Whichever the case may be, the change of guard marks the third such drastic change of plans, and who knows how long this configuration will last.

The island started under the supervision of the State Parks Department with a private lease of the island that lasted only two years.[102] The next approach was an appointed board of at-large citizens that ultimately was complemented with one or two elected officials.[103] Now, we have a new slate of officers, and all of them are state officials.

The new board holds its first official meeting on Jekyll Island[104] and is comprised of the following individuals:

> Mr. Eugene Cook (attorney general)
> Mr. B. E. Thrasher (state auditor) and secretary/treasurer
> Mr. Matt McWorther (Public Service Commission director) and vice-chair
> Mr. John Brinson (state parks director)
> Mr. Ben Fortson (secretary of state) and chair

It may not be a surprise that Mr. Thrasher is part of the board, although when placed into historic perspective, it does seem a little odd. When the Joint Legislature Committee was appointed the previous year, a *Brunswick News* reporter asked Mr. Thrasher whether he would take a seat on the new board given his involvement with the financial audits of Jekyll Island, to which he replied that he would prefer not to partake in the board and that if the governor would ask him to accept a seat on the board, he would probably decline politely.

---

[102] The private lease agreement with Mr. Whitaker started April 27, 1949 and ended on January 15, 1951.
[103] First Jekyll Island Authority, as formed in March 1951.
[104] The first official meeting was held at the Gould house, better known as Villa Marianna.

It seemed that Mr. Thrasher wanted to distance himself from any direct involvement and preferred to play his role of advisor behind the scenes and out of the limelight, but he was already deeply involved, and he would continue to play a pivotal role for several years, only this time in plain sight.

Ben Fortson may be new to the authority and his role as chair, but he is certainly very familiar with Jekyll Island and has been involved since its early beginnings in 1946, albeit from a distance. Fortson had already served six years as a state senator[105] when Gov. Ellis Arnall appointed him secretary of state in 1946. Bound by wheelchair since his car accident in 1928 at the young age of twenty-four, his paralysis did not deter him from mingling with the average Georgians and becoming the longest-serving secretary of state. His jovial demeanor and his relentless efforts to share state history with teachers and children made him one of the most popular and well-liked politicians in state history. He is credited with building the Georgia Archives Building[106] in 1965 and relocating the Georgia Archives to Capitol Avenue. Ben Fortson was also responsible for maintenance and ground keeping of the capitol buildings and Confederate cemeteries, an unusual responsibility for any secretary of state but one that will be used wisely in the beautification of Jekyll Island a few years later.

The new authority, under the competent leadership of Ben Fortson, wastes no time putting things in order. Mrs. Neill is retained as the assistant secretary, and Mr. Asher continues as island manager,[107] as are the laborers on the payroll.

Three Atlanta banks are approved or confirmed as designated depositors for the authority: Citizens and Southern Bank, Fulton National Bank, and First National Bank, all based in Atlanta. In addition, only one local Brunswick bank is authorized to act as depository for the authority: American National Bank.

With the formalities out of the way, the authority tackles the problems with existing leases and places most or all of them on notice with a request

---

[105] Ben Fortson served as a state senator from 1938 to February 1946. He was appointed secretary of state by Gov. Arnall to fill the unexpired term of John B. Wilson.

[106] The building on Capitol Avenue was named after Ben Fortson in 1982.

[107] Mr. Asher succeeded Mr. Hoke Smith as the new island manager in 1956.

to either comply or vacate the premises. The Jekyll Island Hotel Corp., the Acme Construction Co., and the Bonded Supply & Building Co., all owned or part-owned by Sen. Dykes, are in arrears and are placed on official notice. So are the owners of the JI Marina Inc. (Miller, Scarboro, and Davison), Oxford Construction Co. as lessee of the Goodyear house, and Lewis T. Bean, the operator of the Great Dunes golf course. Mr. Whittle, owner/operator of the Whittle furniture store and lessee of the Maurice house,[108] is not placed on notice. He is ordered to vacate Hollybourne as the authority outright rescinds his lease, signed only two months earlier.

Such is the stern approach the new authority brings to the island toward anyone who has conducted business on the island for the past two years. The rules are being enforced, and the authority wants everybody to know they are serious. The rules can no longer be bent by favoritism or politics.

Next on the agenda are the commercial leaseholders that are either past due or whose construction extensions have expired. Coastal Estates Inc., owned by A. B. Newton and H. K. Rushton, who received the first lease option and a building extension, is called upon to submit their annual payment. The same fate awaits Mr. Atkinson's St. Andrews Beach Club, whose extension has expired and whose annual payment is past due.

Ben Fortson guides his new board along the same path that his earlier predecessor J. D. Compton tried to carve out in the beginning years. He wants to adopt the original master plan, the 1951 Robert & Co. master plan that took a back seat once the island opened for business, and he wants to employ an architect/engineer to study any encumbrances and to proceed with the development of the picnic areas as designated.

That Ben Fortson attempts to return to the vision and policies of J. D. Compton does not come as a surprise, given his political background and affiliation. After all, he served under Gov. Arnall and was very much aware of the plan and vision of Gov. M. E. Thompson.

A new breeze blows across the island, but Mr. Fortson and his board do not stop there. All non-executed residential leases are immediately placed on hold, and no new leases are to be assigned until further notice. The authority receives multiple letters from individuals claiming they were

---

[108] The Maurice house is now better known as Hollybourne.

promised lots or had already been assigned lots. Further investigation into the claims finds that no such documents are on file, hence the dismissal and the decision to halt new lot leases. If this means that a refund must be issued to the leaseholder, then the authority will possibly issue such if warranted. Traffic rules are adopted on the island, like the existing traffic rules in any other state park, and the current police presence, one full-time officer (Mr. Dudley Gay) must be changed by securing a contract with the state highway patrol.

By late April, there are so many changes that one can hardly believe that more ideas and suggestions are in the works. What is very clear at this point is that most of the contracts or leases and, in general, most of the past decisions, are being unraveled, undone, and outright cancelled at a very fast pace.

The first unexpected victim of this spring cleaning by the authority is Sen. Dykes himself, although it is not caused by his own doing.

Mr. Overstolz, the island resident who previously complained about the prisoners becoming a nuisance and danger on the island, now appears before the board and requests permission to continue to function as the authority's leasing agent. The request stuns the board members, as neither one of them even knew that such a function existed. Mr. Overstolz works for the Jekyll Island Insurance Corp., which is co-owned by Sen. Dykes, who is also a licensed insurance broker in Cochran, Georgia. During the years when the popular vernacular for Jekyll Island was Dykes Island,[109] he had arranged with the previous authority for his company to act as agent on behalf of the authority. Mr. Robinson was the assigned rental agent, while Mr. Overstolz was the leasing agent. This was a revelation to the new authority, who until now always assumed that the island manager performed rental and leasing functions. The "working arrangement" is cancelled, and permission is not granted to Sen. Dykes's insurance company to continue to operate on the island.

Mr. Lewis Bean and Mrs. Tallu Fish are approached to voluntarily rescind their leases for the golf course and the Rockefeller house respectively and instead be placed on salary. The intention here is clearly to shift the potential revenue stream from leaseholders directly toward the authority and is in sharp contrast with the previous board, who believed in

---

[109] Jekyll Island was commonly referred to as Dykes Island from 1955 through 1956.

outsourcing to third parties in exchange for a monthly revenue percentage. This current authority sees more benefit in owning and managing as much as possible in-house and hiring contractors as employees. This shift from outsourcing to self-management will be seen again many times over the ensuing years and will become a constant variable in the decision-making and ultimately the future of the island.

Mr. Bean is the first one to give up his lease through a quit claim deed to the authority but continues to operate the golf course. A list of equipment and inventory is made, the value of which is to be paid to Mr. Bean as compensation. In the end, Mr. Bean's lease agreement is kept intact despite his willingness to deed his lease back to the authority. The same occurs with Mrs. Tallu Fish, who continues as the museum curator in the Rockefeller house.

There is no indication why the authority changes its mind and allows the lease agreements to continue. A probable explanation is that so many problems need to be tackled and need attention, primarily the ones that have been causing frustration, that agreements with individuals such as Mr. Bean and Mrs. Tallu Fish, which seem to be working perfectly fine, are better left alone for the time being.

The year also marks the first time that a request is made to establish an educational and cultural center on the island to hold summer courses in history, art, and theatre. The request is made by the Georgia Federation of Women's Clubs, represented by quite a delegation of ladies under the leadership of Mrs. Mamie Taylor, president.[110] No commitment is made other than the request by the authority to formulate and submit a plan for consideration. It would take a few more years before Jekyll Island welcomed its first music theatre, but the birth of the original idea should be mentioned here, as it took place in 1957.

A multitude of various projects are underway, and loose ends are being tied up neatly, and that also includes the new white elephant, the JI Hotel Corp. with its sister companies Bonded Supply & Building Co. and Pure Oil Co. The latter may not be mentioned frequently, but let's not forget that the sole filling station on the island is also still in the same hands as the hotel, namely Sen. Dykes.

---

[110] Mrs. R. E. Dunn, Mrs. J. C. Hayes, Mrs. Charles Inman, Mrs. George Doughtie, and Mrs. H. B. Ritchie all appear before the board on May 13, 1957.

Documents confirm that both the JI Hotel Corp. and Bonded Supply & Building Co. are in arears for $4,497.66 and $150.72 respectively, and Judge Hartley is instructed to investigate what, if any, legal action can be brought against both companies for noncompliance. The process will prove more difficult than anticipated, and for the next two years, both companies will be in and out of compliance multiple times.

With two commercial leases signed, Coastal Estates Inc., with the desire to begin construction of a twenty-unit motel north of Capt. Wylly, and Berger & Co., who envisions building a motel south of the parkway, the idea is proposed to connect both future motel sites with an oceanfront boardwalk that stretches about 1.75 miles and features two beach houses, one north and one south.[111] A fabulous idea but one that will need funding from the governor.

Gov. Griffin approves the boardwalk idea, and $65K is appropriated to pay for the construction cost.

Little is known about how this project was completed, but constructing a boardwalk between the existing Beachview Drive and the beach is no small task, with or without funding. A solid roadbed must be created again, this time almost two miles long and at least twelve feet wide, and there are still these remaining annoying dunes that always seem to stand in the way of modern progress. Heavy equipment and bulldozers can of course take care of the natural impediments. The boardwalk runs parallel with Beachview Drive and stretches from Capt. Wylly Road, past Shell Road and JI Parkway, to end south of the Corsair (currently the Days Inn & Suites). When the roadbed is finished, the inland side is lined with palm trees that are removed from elsewhere on the island and placed in perfect alignment between the two future motel sites. At several intervals, in front of the old beach house and the concession stand/cafeteria, concrete steps[112] provide easy access to the white sandy beaches everybody has been dreaming about.

By June, Mr. Mann, our island manager, reports big crowds on the weekends and holidays. Snacks are available at the beach houses, and meals

---

[111] The boardwalk connected the Jekyll Estates Motel (Beachview Club) to the north with the Corsair (Days Inn & Suites) to the south.

[112] One of the original concrete steps can still be seen between Tortuga Jack's and the nearest beach access, both the south and north.

are being served at the Crane house. What is needed now are streetlights and water fountains along the boardwalk.

The authority wastes no time and authorizes the construction of two new beach houses, the North Beach house, located south of Capt. Wylly, and the South Beach house, just slightly north of where the Corsair motel would be constructed.[113] The old beach house is converted into a concession stand/cafeteria and later a full restaurant. Toilet facilities with the requested water fountains are also constructed, and streetlights adorn the island side of the popular boardwalk.

Just imagine the sight daily visitors encounter when arriving on the island. An enticing view of the boardwalk and the ocean greet every visitor when crossing the Jekyll Creek Bridge.

It is no surprise that the new feature becomes a major attraction. With plenty of parking nearby, an unobstructed view of the ocean, and concession stands strategically placed alongside, the boardwalk becomes a favorite pastime for late-evening strolls on a beautiful summer evening when waves crash in the background and an ocean breeze cools down the air. It even creates a romantic ambiance when the dim streetlights provide subdued but ample light for late-night enjoyment.

Daily visitors embrace the opportunity to stroll alongside the white sandy beach and the rolling waves that are only a few steps away. The multiple benches and water fountains invite tourists to sit down, relax, and enjoy the magic view, while beach houses offer affordable snacks and drinks. The bathrooms along the walkway allow visitors to change clothing and relax on the beach or take a dip in the ocean. No effort is spared to turn this splendid innovation into the most memorable of experiences.

With the first beach attraction in place and the accommodations ready for large summer crowds, the authority also constructs a new police station headquarters right off the bridge and near the island entrance. But construction does not stop there. The original master plan also recommends several picnic areas, and six roadside parks are created with six table and two grills each, just for starters.

---

[113] The North Beach house was located at the parking lot south of the Holiday Inn Resort. The South Beach house was located just south of the future site of the Aquarama (current location of Jekyll Ocean Club) and north of the Days Inn.

The north picnic area[114] is still easily accessible by car since Beachview Drive is adjacent. Roadside parking is not a problem, and the picnic area is only a few steps way. The south picnic area[115] was originally located just south of the Corsair, now the Days Inn & Suites. A third one was and is still known as St. Andrews Beach area, and picnic area number four is now known as Clam Creek. Originally, there were two more picnic areas, which have since disappeared. One was located on the river side of Baker Road and Riverview Drive, and the last one was in front and adjacent to the beach concession stands across the street from the first golf clubhouse.

The original picnic equipment is purchased from surplus inventory of the State Parks Department, but as the picnic areas grow in popularity, the authority orders five hundred premade picnic units from Augusta Concrete Products. A few years later, the authority would go into the concrete business itself and use its own cement factory on the island to produce the tables and benches that are still visible today in the remaining areas.[116]

To complete the demand for infrastructure, Mr. Miller, the former island engineer and architect, is hired to furnish the legal land description on the island, finish staking the lot markers, and inspect the current wells on the island. It is recommended that six new wells are needed since only one operational well remains intact. Bailey Drilling Co. is contracted to drill three new wells for the time being until funds are available to drill the remaining three when demand increases.

Plans for a business or shopping center start to resurface again now that there is a steady flow of visitors. The original plan for a shopping center dates to early 1956 when the original site was first identified and staked on the northwest corner of Beachview Drive and the parkway. By the time the new authority takes control of the island, eleven applications are already on file. Two drugstores, one snack and dairy bar, one bakery and delicatessen store, one bingo hall, one electrical store, one snack bar, and four other businesses had responded to the original request for proposal but were never acted upon.

---

[114] The north picnic area is now better known as Driftwood Beach.
[115] The south picnic area is now known as South Dunes picnic area.
[116] Original cement tables and benches made on Jekyll Island can be found at Clam Creek and South Dunes picnic area.

It is envisioned that the business center will accommodate administrative offices for the authority, in addition to a drugstore, grocery store, and a cafeteria that can serve up to five thousand meals per day, a slight difference from the original plan but nevertheless a possible great addition to the island. An open bid request will be published before yearend.

The story of construction, building, and financing now takes an interesting turn, and takes us back to the original advice State Auditor B. E. Thrasher gave to the previous authority back in late 1956,[117] "The issuance of revenue certificates and to use its power to issue bonds to finance the construction of low-income units ..." Although the authority can issue such certificates as provisioned under the Authority Act of 1950, there is a legal problem within the Georgia State Constitution that prohibits a state agency from issuing certificates or bonds while collateralizing the underlying assets and future revenue stream of said assets, if and when such assets are located on land that is state owned and leased for a predetermined and limited time. The legal issue will later be resolved by establishing leasehold estates for commercial property, which can be transferred in the open market and by amending the Jekyll Island State Park Authority Act in 1960 with a revision of the Revenue Anticipation Certificate and Bond provisions, also known as Act No. 447.

When Coastal Estates Inc. suggests to immediately construct twenty units with ten more to be completed the next year, the authority signs the lease agreement in exchange for a minimum annual payment of $2,000 and 3 percent of gross receipts. Construction of the first motel, the Jekyll Estates Motel,[118] begins immediately, and the initial funding of $100K is provided by the Georgia Teachers Retirement System.

The question now is how and why would a public pension plan finance the construction of a private motel on Jekyll Island?

The answer can be found with State Auditor B.E. Thrasher. Besides being the state auditor and a member of the authority, Mr. Thrasher is also a director of the Georgia Teachers Retirement System and the perfect connection to bring private borrower and public lender together to construct the very first motel. So instead of the authority violating state

---

[117] Jekyll Island Authority Board meeting, October 18, 1956.
[118] Jekyll Estates Motel was later renamed the Beachview Club and was purchased by the Holiday Inn Resort in the spring of 2017.

law by attempting to issue revenue certificates directly and placing such with an underwriting agent or agency, Mr. Thrasher cuts out the middle man, avoids a potential conflict, and arranges for his Georgia Teachers Retirement System board members to directly finance the endeavor with a $100K loan at 6 percent. His hope is that once the Jekyll Estates Motel opens, other investors will follow. And they do. Not only that, they will follow the same financing route as Coastal Estates Inc.

In September of that year, Mr. Walter Williams of the Seaside Investment Co. receives a lease option to build ninety-six oceanfront units just south of the JI Estates Motel and north of the boardwalk. The hotel will be known as the Wanderer, "Georgia's largest resort motel," and opens its doors in the summer of 1958. The construction cost of $704,000 is financed and underwritten by the Georgia Teachers Retirement System at an annual rate of 6 percent.

The public pension plan now holds a lien on the only two commercial properties on the island, soon to be joined by a third. While one may question the financing approach and whether the direct investment of a public pension plan in a private and risky endeavor is an intelligent or acceptable choice, or even legal, one must admit that without this type of financing, it would have taken several years before any construction would have started on Jekyll Island.

Mr. Thrasher's advice, influence, and connections certainly paved the way for future private investment and most definitely were the spark that led to the creation of GIDA (Georgia Industrial Development Agency) in 1959 that would oversee and regulate the loans issued by state pension systems.

By the end of the summer, the island now proudly features its first motel, the Jekyll Estates Motel, with twenty efficiency units and flanked by a palm tree-lined boardwalk that features beach houses, water fountains, public restrooms, concession stands, and its first full-service restaurant, the Charcoal House Restaurant,[119] which is operated by John Crooms, Sen. Dykes's father-in-law. The Big Dip Dairy Bar, in the parking lot of the white beach house, is also operational. The owners, Mr. and Mrs. Millican, will ultimately operate the Charcoal House Restaurant after their food

---

[119] The same location now features Tortuga Jack's but has been home to a long list of restaurant names and owners over the years.

stand is demolished. The Charcoal House would be renamed the Jekyll Sandwich Hut, one of many names in its history.

It certainly is not bad progress made by a new authority that has only been in charge for a few months and has bigger plans for the immediate future.

To make sure that visitors can enjoy the entire island, the authority purchases a train to transport them from the Old Village to the beach and back for twenty-five cents, ten cents for children, and to take them on a sightseeing tour around the island for a mere ninety cents for adults and forty cents for children. Extra parking[120] is added by the operators of the JI Marina (the old wharf) to facilitate visitors.

Continuing repairs on the main clubhouse and Annex building are coming along with the new lobby elevator now installed and inspected and the reroofing almost complete. Although the cottages remain closed, except for the Rockefeller house, now dubbed the JI Museum under the curatorship of Mrs. Tallu Fish, and the Claflin house that is still occupied by the Acme Construction Co., visitors have ample opportunities to enjoy their newly invigorated state park.

Before the end of the year, the authority will complete its outright purchase of the filling station from Pure Oil Co. and continue its quest of self-management and ownership. Sen. Dykes receives $22,500 as compensation for the buildings and improvements, plus an additional $3,400 for equipment and inventory. That transaction takes away one source of revenue from Sen. Dykes, but his battle for the hotel will continue as the JI Hotel Corp. continues to be in arears.

Not a lot of attention is being given to the available residential lots, and it is clear that the authority focuses on the implementation of the master plan first before it considers lifting the ban on new residential leases. The only two exceptions are made for Mr. Lang, a private developer who receives permission to stake three blocks of twenty-five lots in the Palmetto and Oakgrove subdivisions with the purpose of building homes for sale. Mr. Lang relies on the fact that the Federal Housing Authority has just announced it is willing to make loans on Jekyll Island, and buyers

---

[120] The current parking lot next to the wharf was constructed in 1957 to allow overflow parking for day visitors who wished to be transported to the beach or hop on the island sightseeing tour.

will come to the island very soon. The second exemption is given to Mr. Camp from Rome, Georgia, who already owns two rental units and wants an extra lot in the Oakgrove Division to construct six to eight multifamily units adjacent to his existing properties. He is the first owner to receive a zoning variance on the island for the construction of duplexes and/or multifamily units in the inland subdivisions. Prior to this variance, all residential lots were designated as single-family dwellings only.

The south side of the island remains in status quo with no expectation of immediate construction, and Mr. Atkinson requests the authority to write off his back rent for 1956 in the amount of $2,400, and to allow him to pay $500 immediately and another $500 at the end of 1957. He promises that twenty units will be constructed in 1957 with the addition of a dance hall and a restaurant the year after. The authority allows him to pay half of the rent for the first six months but demands full rental payment for the other six months and expects construction to be completed within twelve months (i.e., by the end of 1958). It will take more than two years before the motel, the Dolphin Motor Lodge, is completed.

To complete the initial phase of development, the authority accepts a proposal to open a family campground. Mr. Wayne Morrow from Thomaston, Georgia, submits his proposal and awaits final approval of what will become the Cherokee Campground on the north side of the island.

The only notable improvement made in the Historic District, besides the Jekyll Island Hotel of course, is the renovation of the Gould Casino or Playhouse. Sitting idle since the Whitaker years when it was used as an entertainment and playhouse, the authority renovates the building so it can be used as an auditorium. The original greenhouse and bowling alleys had burned down in 1950, so the only structure left standing is the indoor tennis court with upstairs lounging rooms. By late 1957, the building becomes known as the Gould Auditorium and is advertised as the first convention center on the island that can accommodate up to six hundred people.

The National Convention of Public Utilities Workers will be held here in 1959 and is the very first convention held on Jekyll Island.

The year 1958 starts vigorously, and all cylinders are fired on several fronts. Now that the oceanfront development is in full swing, it is time to pursue other infrastructure projects and proposals.

The authority realizes that with so many new recreation areas and an increasing number of visitors coming to the island, a dedicated person must oversee the beautification and maintenance of the island. Ben Fortson, who is responsible for maintenance of all capitol grounds and the Confederate cemeteries, is the perfect man for the job. He recruits Mr. Hoffman[121] in late 1957 to beautify the JI Parkway between the bridge ramp and the beach with shrubs and flowers. For the first month, Mr. Hoffman, who resides in Forsyth, Georgia, offers his services for free except for lodging, transportation of plants and shrubs, and his meals. By January 1958, he is authorized to hire a gardener at fifty dollars per week and a supervisor at $500 per month, in addition to getting reimbursed for the cost of plants and shrubs totaling $3,233. Mr. George Newberry joins Mr. Hoffman to supervise the landscaping and becomes the island's first horticulturalist. During the early years, plants and shrubs are grown in the Gould greenhouse,[122] but by 1959, ten acres of land are developed as a nursery that will further expand, and by 1964 includes five greenhouses under the careful supervision of George Newberry and his son Bill.[123]

Mr. Morrow, the applicant for a campground, and Mr. Bostwick, his business partner, sign a twenty-year lease at $1,750 per year plus 3 percent of gross revenue. A specific clause is included that stipulates the duration of the lease based on completed improvements. The lease is granted for ten years with $40K of capital improvements and reverts to a twenty-year agreement if $65K or more is invested and completed—a clause that will later become significant when the authority decides to terminate the lease with cause.

The Cherokee Campground Inc. must construct one bathhouse per fifty camping lots and three bathhouses for one hundred lots. It must also build a commissary, not to be smaller than 25 feet by 40 feet. Why the authority was very specific in the exact dimensions of the bathhouses and

---

[121] Mr. Hoffman was the groundskeeper for the capitol buildings and cemeteries and reported to Ben Fortson.

[122] A temporary greenhouse was constructed next to the Gould Auditorium, approximately in the same location as the original greenhouse that was destroyed by fire in 1950.

[123] Both Mr. Newberry and his son are duly credited for making remarkable flower arrangements in the greenhouses that would beautify the median of the JI Parkway year-round.

the commissary is not known. The specific language, however, is later used against the lessee as cause for termination, so one can assume the authority had the intention of operating the campground from the start but couldn't make the investment.

It also allows the campground to install a gasoline tank, the second filling station after the Pure Oil Co. but only accessible to campers, in exchange for 3 percent of the gross sales. To allow water supply to what was then the most northern accessible point of the island, a water supply line is drawn from the Plantation subdivision and along Old Plantation Road to the entrance of the campground. This requires the drilling of another well on the island, the fourth one of its kind and probably still two short of what is required. Let's also remember that each residential development and each of the commercial developments, including the campground, two motels, the Jekyll Island Hotel, and the public bathhouses, must have its own septic tanks, as a public water/sewage system was not available. That will change soon, and it is no coincidence that Mr. Thrasher lobbies the general assembly to allow the authority to issue revenue certificates for the construction of a water and sewage system on the island in the amount of $1 million. This first plan would later be known as JISPA-Phase 1. As mentioned before, the obstacle is of course the Revenue Certificate Law of 1937 that places limitations on such issuance.

A bid is received for the first shopping center by A. B. Newton, the same builder/developer as the Jekyll Estates Motel, for $425K. Again, the problem of financing arises, and the authority, with the help of Mr. Thrasher, turns to the Georgia Teachers Retirement System to obtain a loan with the same terms and conditions as the two previous motels.[124] Construction begins in September of that same year at around the same time that the entrance towers on the causeway are under construction.

The idea to erect an "archway type" sign with two towers on each side was conceived earlier in the year, and the original design was made by Mr. Laurence S. Miller. Two towers are constructed on the south and north of the causeway entrance. The south tower originally houses an info booth, while the north tower features public restrooms. The archway in between is supposed to read "Year-Round Family Resort," per the original design,

---

[124] The Jekyll Estates Motel and the Wanderer Motel.

but is changed to read "Year-Round Beach Resort" in the end.[125] Note that even this early, the emphasis is placed on Jekyll Island being a resort and no longer as a simple state park. The motivation for this can be found by going back in time.

In the 1950s, state parks nationwide were known to operate seasonally only. Jekyll Island, however, being a hybrid of some sorts and having the exclusive mandate to become self-sufficient, wanted to be known as a resort rather than a seasonal state park, hence the change of emphasis. However, it is remarkable that the archway design is changed from "family" to "beach" resort, and it indicates that this early in the history of the island, the authority envisioned something much bigger and more diversified than just a simple family resort / state park. Knowing that it can now compete with other beach destinations nearby, such as Daytona Beach, and aware that its ocean development and boardwalk with its bathhouses and concession stands attract drones of day visitors, it is only logical that the advertising emphasis targets the preferred bypassing crowd.

With the Wanderer Motel now complete and open for business, Mr. Williams, the operator of "Georgia's largest resort motel" and owner of the Seaside Investment Co., seeks a joint venture with Mr. Albert Crews,[126] owner of the Crews Restaurant chain, to operate the restaurant in his new hotel. It is heavily advertised as a joint venture as the ads read: "The Wanderer Restaurant. Another Crews restaurant." The joint venture between the two businesspeople will bear its fruits later with similar business operations elsewhere on the island.

At around the same time, Mr. Williams also proposes a joint advertising campaign between the motel owners/operators and the authority and to place signage on the causeway and Hwy. 17. The cooperation will later lead to the creation of the Jekyll Island Motel Association that will coordinate all advertising for Jekyll Island.

---

[125] The original towers still adorn the entrance of the causeway, although the cast-iron banner has since been removed. Public bathrooms and the info booth have since been closed and relocated to the Welcome Center.

[126] Mr. Crews had previously submitted a lease application for the Crane house in 1950 but was denied by the authority. The joint venture with Mr. Williams would get him a foothold on Jekyll Island for several years.

Two new beach concession stands are in the process of construction, between the two ocean bathhouses, and a new road is being constructed and paved, leading south from the parkway to the Negro subdivision. The 2.4-mile road is constructed by Seaboard Construction Co. at a cost of $148K.

One must now wonder where the funds are coming from with all this new construction going on and no visible revenue increase, although some projects are obviously financed.

The general assembly appropriated $1,378,000 for fiscal year 1957 and an additional $1,678,000 for FY 1958. All state funding is still done through the JI Committee, as the authority itself can only use island revenue to pay for operating expenses, and that even excludes material, inventory, or purchases thereof.

The island itself is running smoothly, with Mr. T. Bean running the golf course and miniature golf for the authority. A new clubhouse is constructed, using the old bricks of the Pulitzer house,[127] and is inaugurated in May 1958, together with an eighteen-hole miniature golf course. Use of the driving range costs fifty cents, and a round of miniature golf can be played for thirty-five cents.

Mr. Harvey Smith, the operator of Peppermint Amusement Park, is still in business, and the authority amends the lease to a standard 3 percent of gross revenue plus the agreed-upon annual rent. There are no restrictions on the number of rides, and Mr. Smith can expand his operation within his 800-feet oceanfront park. The only problem is Sen. Dykes, who despite not having an oceanfront lease, except his beach concession stands, decides to operate beach rides nevertheless. He places his rides right next to his concession stands, in direct competition with Peppermint Amusement Park, without any concern or scruples.

He was known to be a man of great business talent and a "smooth operator," but he was also ruthless in his island business dealing and had little or no respect for his competitors. His political connections, both with the authority and certainly in Atlanta, allowed him to continue his monopoly freely without too much objection.

---

[127] The original Pulitzer house in the Historic District was demolished after extensive fire damage. The bricks were later used to build the new golf clubhouse at the current location of Red Bug Motors Pizza.

Harvey Smith runs a very successful business on the island and attracts crowds with his fancy rides daily, especially on the weekends and holidays. Unbeknownst to him, he also attracts some natural and local visitors during late spring and early summer.

Attracted and confused by the bright lights of the miniature railroad and the Ferris wheel, loggerheads make their annual pilgrimage to their favorite island in search of the perfect nesting spot, preferably the same one from last year, only to find that someone or something has taken permanent residence. Utterly confused and still drawn by the bright lights, the loggerheads slowly and carefully climb over the railroad tracks and onto the paved amusement park, only to get lost or tangled up in between the machinery and cables. Mr. Smith, unaware of the annual ritual, finds them more a nuisance than anything else when each morning he finds one or more stuck between his equipment. He simply tries to remove them and place them back on the beach that is only a few feet away. It will take several more years for Mr. Smith to realize that the nesting of loggerheads is crucial and important to the island and finally report the repeating event to the authority. By then, Peppermint Amusement Park is slowly preparing to leave the island. One could call it the first victory for the loggerheads and a demise for beach amusement, but that would be an exaggeration.

Otherwise, the authority becomes innovative about generating revenue with so many beachgoers on the island. During peak season, lifeguards are posted every 1,000 feet with clear signage for the public, and beach chairs and umbrellas can now be rented for the day for a mere seventy-five cents. Those who wish to use the locker rooms can do so for twenty-five cents, and why rent a beach towel when you can take home a commemorative one, beautifully embroidered with "Jekyll Island—Year-Round Beach Resort"? Postcards are for sale at any beach house or concession stand for the first time, and two can be purchased for the price of five cents. Business is brisk during the summer, with 32,000 cars recorded during the month of July alone.

Visitors who wish to stay on the island but do not want to rent a motel room and prefer to sleep in their own trailer can now simply park overnight for one dollar per day for the first fifteen days. After that, the daily fees go up to $1.50 or $2 per day, depending on the length of their stay.

It may be inconceivable today, but the trailers were parked around the old servants' quarters in those days, right in the middle of the Historic District, although some were also allowed to be placed on any of the three available parking lots.[128]

Monthly charges for garbage pickup are also implemented. Motels are paying $1.50 per month with a maximum of nine garbage cans, and residents, the few who live on the island, are charged seventeen cents per can. Any debris, other than regular garbage, is picked by the load at three dollars each. This notes the first time the authority starts the implementation of a municipal service and charge system, like other municipalities and yet unique for a state park; hence it will lead to multiple discussions and disputes once the sewage system is completed.

With business booming and development taking shape, it is not surprising that the authority is approached to reserve lots for religious centers. Until now, only Faith Chapel is available, and there are no longer any services or masses allowed, certainly not of any specific denomination.

Mr. Searcy Garrison is the first one to request a lot and build a Baptist church. Judge F. M. Scarlett, US District Court, files the same application soon thereafter to establish a Presbyterian church. He is later joined in support of his petition by Rev. Robert McBath, Mr. A. M. Morris, Mr. Charlie Gowen,[129] and Mr. J. D. Compton, past authority member. Other denominations (i.e., Methodist and Catholic congregations) will file the same petition in later years, but it is the Presbyterian congregation that selects its preferred lot first—a triangle-sized lot on Riverview Drive, bordered by Old Plantation Road. It will ultimately become the sites of three churches that will cause Old Plantation Road to be split into two roads,[130] with the religious centers in the middle.

---

[128] Two parking lots were available oceanside, one at the corner of North Beachview Drive and JI Parkway, and another by the Charcoal House Restaurant. The riverside parking lot was next to the JI Marina (the old wharf).

[129] Refers to State. Rep. Gowen who is also a resident of Saint Simons and instrumental in getting J. D. Compton appointed to the first JIA Board.

[130] Originally Old Plantation Road connected the Historic District (Stable Road) with Potter Avenue. The lot assignment for religious centers caused the road to be split into two parts. One part now connects Stable Road with Capt. Wylly Road. The second part runs parallel to North Riverview Drive and is a dead-end street, both north and south.

After one of the most successful summers on the island and even a respectable number of visitors in the fall, at nine thousand cars per month, two new applications are filed for motels, one on the south side of the parkway and another across from the Wanderer.

Mr. Pierre Howard of Decatur, Georgia, represents American Motels Inc. and proposes to build a 222-unit motel, just south of the South Beach House. The motel will face 1,100 feet on the ocean. The request is for a forty-year lease with an option to renew for another ten years, and the offer is to pay seven dollars per linear oceanfront foot plus 3 percent of gross revenue. Note that this is the first time that annual rent is not expressed as a fixed amount based on a return percentage of the total lot value but is calculated as a fixed price per linear footage. Berger & Co. previously identified the same location as the site for their motel. The motel will be known at opening in February 1959 as the Corsair.

The second application comes from Mr. James Whaley and Mr. John Minter, doing business as W & M Enterprises, who seek to construct nineteen apartment units on the northwest corner of Capt. Wylly and Beachview Drive, across the street from the Wanderer Motel. The new motel units will be known as the Seafarer Apartments.[131]

What makes the Seafarer so unique, besides being the first apartment motel being built on the westside of Beachview Drive, is that the six buildings that comprise nineteen apartments are constructed with old and salvaged bricks from the original Oglethorpe Hotel[132] in Brunswick. The famous hotel once accommodated the millionaires upon their arrival by train and prior to them boarding their private ferry to Jekyll Island.

The concept is slightly different from the other motels, in the sense that the Seafarer Apartment Motel adheres more to the initial idea of offering family-oriented efficiencies, with one- and two-bedroom apartments that also feature kitchenettes in addition to a small but comfortable living and dining room. The intention is obviously to attract small families seeking to stay several days while still enjoying a home-away-from-home atmosphere instead of the typical motel room experience. Ruth and Ed Goodis are hired as managers upon opening and will continue to operate the Seafarer as a family-style motel until 1984.

---

[131] Currently known as the Quality Inn & Suites.
[132] The Oglethorpe Hotel was constructed in 1888 and demolished in 1958.

The Seaside Investment Co. has enjoyed such good business that it also submits new plans, this time for an extension of the Wanderer Motel by adding eighty-four more units, bringing the total to 180 rooms. They also wish to extend three beach walks, each to be six feet wide. The existing downstairs restaurant gets a second-story addition with a combined seating of five hundred seats. The new upstairs restaurant, Sky Top Room, is designed for upscale and elegant dining while overlooking the ocean and dancing to the tunes of a big band. The Georgia Teachers Retirement System again finances the entire expansion, bringing the total cost to $1.2 million. Rooms can be rented for seven to nine dollars per day during the summer and eight to twelve dollars per day during the winter months.[133]

But private investors are not the only ones who dream of expansion or construction. The authority discusses plans to build a sports coliseum on the island that will feature an indoor pool, a skating rink, bowling alleys, and a dance hall. The first seed is planted for what will ultimately become the convention center and the Aquarama, although not all the ideas will be incorporated.

The authority's decision to begin rerouting the northern portion of Beachview Drive must have been triggered by the new demand for commercial development since there is no prior indication of such a plan, nor is there any proof of a request for commercial lots north of the Beachview subdivision and south of the north picnic area.

Whatever the reason may have been, 1.1 miles of the original 1954 Beachview Drive and the portion closest to the ocean is rerouted more inland, thereby creating a large piece of land that will prove to become very valuable soon.

The original road was designed in 1954 to run alongside the ocean from Ellis Lane toward the north picnic area (Driftwood Beach). It provided beautiful and unobstructed ocean sights as far as the northern perimeter of the Beachview subdivision at the time. Portions of the old Beachview Drive can still be seen today at the entrance of Driftwood Beach, or on the southern end at the most northern border of The Cottages. The remaining road is still accessible by foot or bike but no longer by motorized vehicles.

---

[133] Even as early as 1958, seasonal rates varied with winter rates being higher than summer rates. Back then, "snowbirds" were already attracted by the mild climate and the year-round availability of accommodations and entertainment.

The island slowly becomes a sophisticated place to live. It gets its very first telephone exchange. Southern Bell proposes several names to the authority, who chooses Neptune as the new switchboard name. Phone numbers on the island now all start with NE-1 followed by a four-digit number.

It also features its own ice dispenser after Glynn Ice & Coal Co. is authorized to install such at the filling station. Prior to this, ice had to be transported from Brunswick to the island daily. The authority even implements an occupancy permit for motels and restaurants that will later evolve into monthly health inspection certificates. The first permits are issued to the Jekyll Island Hotel, Jekyll Island Annex, Jekyll Island Auditorium, Jekyll Estates Motel, Wanderer Motel, and the Wanderer Motel Restaurant.

The year could not end on a better note, or could it?

The newspaper headlines of that year describe in detail the mining accident in Nova Scotia, and while readers cannot figure out at the time why this becomes a feature article in the *Brunswick News* and *Atlanta Journal* or what this has to do with Jekyll Island, the story unravels in strange ways and one that will become bittersweet in the end.

Earlier in the year, Gov. Griffin was on an official visit to Canada when the news broke that twelve Nova Scotia miners were trapped after an explosion. After several days, the miners were rescued, and the governor invited all of them to a free vacation on Jekyll Island. A nice gesture, probably politically motivated but nevertheless compassionate and good and free advertising abroad for the island. It is doubtful that anybody in Canada had ever heard of Jekyll Island, but the way the state park / beach resort was described, it must have sounded wonderful.

Twelve miners accept Gov. Griffin's invitation and plan to arrive early November. Several businesspeople and clergy of Brunswick sponsor their stay and entertainment while on Jekyll Island, and the Wanderer Motel offers rooms for the rescued miners. There is only one minor problem: one of the miners, Mr. Ruddick, is black. Since the island is still segregated, he cannot possibly stay at the Wanderer. The Negro subdivision is staked, and the access road is paved, but no motel has been built yet, which begs the question where Mr. Ruddick will be housed.

Ultimately, a trailer is placed in the Negro Beach House parking lot to accommodate him, but unfortunately the Negro Beach House is closed for the winter season as well. One of the Brunswick businessmen arranges to place a second trailer so that Dr. W. K. Payne, president of Savannah State College, can vacation side by side with Mr. Ruddick. Together they go sightseeing and fishing, while his fellow workers enjoy the island's amenities reserved for whites only. It must have been a wondrous experience for Mr. Ruddick, who was not used to segregation at all.

It is remarkable that despite the numerous newspaper articles, not one word is mentioned of this incident in any of the authority minutes or meetings. It is even more noteworthy that Mr. Ruddick accepted a job on Jekyll Island after the Civil Rights Act and desegregation of the island in 1964. He would move his family to Jekyll Island to become a shrimper.

The only downside to an otherwise successful year is the new dispute that brews again between the JI Hotel Corp. and the authority. The nonadherence to the lease agreement and the frequent nonpayment of rent, water, and sewage are taking their toll. The constant friction between the authority and Sen. Dykes leads to a final resolution of the conflict the following year but not without a negotiated buyout.

The change of guard in the governor's mansion when Ernest Vandiver succeeds Marvin Griffin brings some changes while some policies are being reaffirmed early in the new year. The *Brunswick News* reports on January 1, 1959, Gov. Vandiver as stating, "… no State license to sell alcohol on Jekyll Island as long as I am Governor …"

Not exactly a new stance but one that is contradictory to the previous issuance of state liquor licenses by Dixon Oxford, the new state revenue commissioner, to the Wanderer Motel and the Jekyll Island Hotel. As per Gov. Vandiver's instructions, the preliminary liquor licenses are revoked, and the alcohol prohibition on Jekyll Island remains in effect. The battle over liquor licenses and eventually ordinances will continue well into the sixties.

The first major task of the year is to finally settle the long-lasting dispute between the Club Hotel operators, Sen. Dykes and Leo L. Phillips, and the authority.

For the past four years, the authority has financed most of the major improvements and has spent well over $500K in total. Yet it has never been paid the full rental amount, let alone timely payments for use of water, sewage, and the agreed-upon percentage of gross revenue. It is time for a different approach, and on February 13, the authority takes control of the main Club House, the Annex, the Sans Souci, the Crane house, and the beach houses and restaurant.

Minutes of the Jekyll Island State Park Authority Board meeting, February 13, 1959, state:

> Based on the appraisal of the Brunswick Real Estate Board as to the value of the lease, plus the actual cost of additional equipment added since the Lessee came into possession of the lease, less depreciated value, and taking into consideration the cancellation of any rent due to the Authority, Mr. Thrasher moved that the Authority terminate the Jekyll Island Hotel Corporation lease, by payment to the Corporation $175,000.00 in cash and a note executed by the Authority payable to the Corporation in the amount of $25,000.00 payable three years in the future (no interest) provided that all properties and equipment be turned over to the Authority free of any liens or encumbrances and lease surrendered ...

There were claims for back pay, which were never resolved, and creditors claimed nonpayment at the time of the takeover. Records show that Whittle Furniture, still owned and operated by Ray Whittle, Glynn County commissioner, received payments in the amount of $10,000 and $34,000 from the authority. The scheduled cash payment and subsequent note, as per the resolution, remained unchanged despite the clear encumbrances on inventory.

The Seaside Investment Co., owner/operator of the Wanderer Motel, and Albert Crews of Crews Restaurants come to the rescue and offer to operate the JI Hotel as well as the beach houses and the restaurant, Charcoal House.

The authority doesn't really have much choice other than to accept the offer, lest available accommodations and food services decline, which would seriously hamper tourism and lead to a possible decline. Better to protect the current assets and revenue stream than to face a crisis.

It is interesting to note that the four-year monopoly Sen. Dykes held on the island—after all, he was directly and indirectly involved in all the revenue generating locations—is being dismantled, only to be replaced by Walter Williams, who now controls most of the available motel rooms[134] and the island's food service locations. Mr. Crews's name will appear again very soon as well.

The other two motels on the island experience some changes, some positive and some causing more delays. The Jekyll Estates Motel keeps its promise and starts construction on eighteen more units, bringing the total to thirty-eight. The envisioned Negro motel doesn't fare so well, and a new lease is proposed by Mr. Joe Harmon and Mr. Bill Boyd, this time in the name of St. Andrews Beach Corp.

However, by February, the possible delay seems to be resolved as plans are proposed for a forty-six-unit motel, which will become the long-awaited Dolphin Motor Lodge Inn.

The first Negro motel, built on the current site of Jekyll Camp, previously known as the 4-H Center, will open its doors in August 1959. The lack of financing causes the initial delay, but that is easily resolved once Mr. Thrasher steps into the picture and arranges once again for the Georgia Teachers Retirement System to finance the required $385K construction cost.

Out of the five motels that now operate on the island, only two have been financed by other banks or mortgage companies: the Seafarer Apartments and the Corsair. All others have been made possible with financing from the public pension plan.

American Motels Inc., in the meantime, changes its initial plan for a 220-unit oceanfront motel to 164 units, still to be constructed in the same location, directly south of the parkway on S. Beachview Drive.

The Corsair design features a crescent design with a restaurant and lobby in the middle, two swimming pools, a wading pool, and a hot tub,

---

[134] The total number of available rooms in 1959 was 229. Mr. Williams's motel, the Wanderer, offered 180 rooms.

plus a boardwalk to the beach. Before construction can begin though, 800 feet of the boardwalk need to be removed between the south side of the southern beach house[135] and the southern end of the 1957 boardwalk that provides access to the south picnic area. That same picnic area, built in 1955, will later in the year be moved farther south to make room for yet another large motel development. What is now known as the South Dunes picnic area, adjacent to the Hampton Inn & Suites, was originally located immediately south of the Corsair, now the Days Inn & Suites. It was not the last time that drastic changes were made to public recreation areas to allow further commercial development, but it certainly was the first time.

It feels as if all the stars align for the authority in the summer of 1959. The opening of the new shopping center on the corner of Beachview Drive and JI Parkway coincides with the opening of the Dolphin Motor Lodge and the Corsair. The shopping center with its unique modern design[136] that will become the architectural signature of Jekyll Island until the 1980s features the authority's administrative offices, Maxwell's general store, a grocery store, cafeteria, and a drugstore.

The first drugstore is owned and operated by James W. Ferguson from Thomaston, Georgia, and has a pharmacist present from 8:00 a.m. to 6:00 p.m., seven days a week. He agrees to a ten-year lease with a reduced payment of 0.5 percent of gross revenue for the first five years and 3 percent afterward.

The first grocery store or supermarket on the island is owned and operated by Carl Dykes and Roscoe Denmark and known as D & D Supermarket. Both will later also construct and operate a second filling station on the JI Causeway.

The earlier idea to construct a sports complex on the island also starts to become more realistic as the authority requests the firm of Coite-Summers to submit a design proposal. The estimated cost is $1,159,600 but is later reduced by simplifying the design and limiting the amenities inside. It will take more than a year for the complex to be finished, and the Aquarama, as it becomes known, opens its doors in the summer of 1961.

---

[135] Current location of Ocean Views Club and the old location of the Aquarama.
[136] The half-moon shaped roof was considered unique at the time and would be replicated in 1969 with the construction of the fishing pier at Clam Creek. The design also matched the architecture of the new beach houses.

All this new construction requires the authority to expand its water supply infrastructure, and two water towers[137] are erected, each with a capacity to hold 100,000 gallons of water. One is constructed on the north side of the island, the other on the south side. Simultaneously, the island has a need for an incinerator, given the increasing amount of garbage and debris, and the first one is constructed on the south end, just north of the St. Andrews Beach subdivision.

But not everything works out well for the authority, and by the end of 1959, after only being open for a few months, the St. Andrews Beach Club dissolves because of disputes among shareholders, and the Dolphin Motor Lodge ceases operation.

Arrangements are made with the lender, the Georgia Teachers Retirement System, and the authority assumes ownership of the first and only Negro motel and restaurant on the island. Both facilities and the adjacent bathhouse will reopen in the new year under Dave Jackson and his sisters Annabell Robinson and Betty Chandler.

The very first sewage plan is being proposed for Jekyll Island at an estimated cost of $1.62 million with Phase I to be completed for $675K. It is obvious that such an undertaking will have to be financed by the issuance of revenue certificates or bonds. Given that the Georgia Teachers Retirement System is already heavily invested in commercial properties on the island, the general assembly, under the advice and guidance of B. E. Thrasher, creates GIDA (Georgia Industrial Development Authority) that will oversee all loans issued by state pension systems and limit such loans to a maximum of two-thirds of the appraised value. It also recommends higher interest rates than the prevailing market rates to discourage borrowing.

The JISPA-Plan, as the island's sewage plan becomes known, will take several years to be completed and at a much higher cost than estimated.

It is also noteworthy that during the year, the Brunswick Transit Co. starts to provide daily bus services to and from the island, courtesy of

---

[137] Both water towers are shaped in the form of a golf tee (green) with a golf ball (white) on top. Both are still in use today.

Mr. Ray Whittle's influence. The county service will later create the ideal environment to open heated discussions about taxation on the island.[138]

Now that the northern portion of Beachview Drive has been successfully rerouted with appropriated state funds, creating additional commercial and residential lots, a new proposal is submitted to build forty-eight apartments around a swimming pool with additional cabanas facing the ocean. The proposal is made by Mr. Charles Gowen, state representative, and his business partners, Mr. A. M. Harris and Jack Torbett.

Mr. Gowen is a familiar name, as he was very involved in the state legislation pertaining to the island.[139]

The proposal is unique, since it is the first time a request is made to construct a cooperative building with forty-eight units that can be owned individually yet operated jointly. Until now, the authority has granted the construction of motel rooms and efficiencies that are owned and operated by one company, but the concept of co-ops or condominiums is new, and the authority will fight to prohibit such from being built for several years.[140]

Nevertheless, Charles Gowen is considered the pioneer of cooperatives and condominium-style construction that exists today.

The year of 1960 will become a construction boom for Jekyll Island. By the end of 1959, the island features 275 motel rooms. That number will more than double to 575 in 1960. Such is the speed of motel construction.

Previously, the authority had envisioned the southern oceanside of the island to be reserved for motel and hotel development, specifically between the existing Corsair and the St. Andrews Beach division.

---

[138] The 1955 Supreme Court ruling allowed the County to levy property taxes on Jekyll Island if the County provided relevant services to the island's residents. Public transportation was deemed to be relevant and therefore became the catalyst to levy property taxes.

[139] State Representative Charles Gowen resided on St. Simons Island and was instrumental in J. D. Compton's appointment to the first authority in 1950. He pledged his loyalty to Gov. Herman Talmadge during his reelection campaign in 1951.

[140] Co-ops and condominiums were prohibited on Jekyll Island until the mid-1970s. Archived documents do not specify why the authority objected to the construction of such vacation facilities, but the possible answer can be found in the verbiage of the land lease and leasehold agreements that require a single entity to own and operate the facilities placed on such leased land.

When the San-Ten Development Corporation submits their proposal to build the Buccaneer Motor Lodge just south of the existing Corsair and requests 1,100 feet of oceanfront property, the south picnic area is obviously in the way. The authority decides to move the picnic area further south to where it is currently located and still known today as the South Dunes picnic area.[141] By June, the relocation is complete, and the new area is expanded with amenities such as covered picnic shelters and benches. Walkways are added, as well as a dune crosswalk to provide beach access. Nevertheless, there is protest from visitors and permanent residents[142] about destroying one of the original recreation areas to make way for commercial development.

The new Buccaneer Motor Lodge consists of eight buildings, four facing the ocean and four facing the swimming pool, each housing twelve units. The total cost is $916K, which is borrowed from the Georgia Teachers Retirement System. The pension fund now owns four out of the six motels on the island.

One unique concept in the building of the Buccaneer is that, despite causing the relocation of the recreational area, the eight buildings are constructed and placed in such a way as to fit into the natural landscape of oak trees and dunes. While all other motels proudly advertise their ocean views and oceanfront rooms, the Buccaneer attracts visitors with their natural landscape and surroundings. It is a new vacation experience, set in nature, peace, and tranquility.

Less than one year later, pro golfer Sam Snead attaches his name to the hotel, and it becomes known as the "Sam Snead Buccaneer Motor Lodge." This promotional stunt lasts only one year, but it pays off, and visitors love the new natural surroundings together with the opportunity to buy golf passes at a reduced rate or as an all-inclusive golf vacation package.

Immediately following the completion of the Buccaneer, A. J. Bloom Inc. requests an option on the empty lot that is now nestled between the new Buccaneer and the new and improved South Dunes picnic area, to

---

[141] South Dunes picnic area was originally located just south of the Days Inn & Suites (originally known as the Corsair). It was moved further south in 1960 to its present location, adjacent to the Hampton Inn & Suites.

[142] It is estimated that the number of permanent residents totaled twenty-one adults and approximately fifteen to twenty school children at the time.

construct the Holiday Inn.[143] The first plans call for a three-story structure with 206 units on the upper floors and a restaurant, convention room, cocktail lounge, and office on the ground floor. The plans will later change to the construction of 108 units on the designated lot but with a lease option for an additional 96 feet of land that faces South Beachview Drive to add another hundred units in the future.

What will make the Holiday Inn popular and memorable is probably the hotel's swimming pool that is shaped like the state of Georgia. It is also the first fifty-year lease at 3 percent of gross revenue, with an expiration date of 2010.

With the increasing popularity of golf and Jekyll Island promoting itself as a golf destination, the authority gives permission to design and build a new eighteen-hole golf course between Capt. Wylly and Shell Road, immediately west of the Great Dunes course, or at least the nine holes that remain. Convicts still on the island are used to do most of the labor to clear the land and make way for the Oleander course.

The bus service that was implemented last year by the Brunswick Transport Authority is suddenly halted, even though between fifteen and twenty school-aged children now reside on the island. The move is initiated by the board of education, who wants to levy taxes on Jekyll Island but is not authorized to do so without the approval of Glynn County.

Jekyll Island has been exempted from any county tax since 1947, and the exemption serves as an incentive to build personal residences on the island. There was however the State Supreme Court ruling of September 1955 that allowed Glynn County to tax island residents if county services were provided in exchange.

Initially, the county rejects the board of education's request for a school tax and instead looks for ways to apply a "fair tax." Rather than find ways to tax the twenty-one permanent residents on the island, the county targets the motels instead.

Whether the possibility of levying a county tax on motels is his ultimate motivation, Walter Williams and his Seaside Investment Co.

---

[143] This is the first presence of the Holiday Inn on the island. After its name disappeared in 1963, a second Holiday Inn was built in 1972 at the current location of the Hampton Inn & Suites. The current Holiday Inn Resort is the third hotel in as many locations during the fifty-seven-year relationship with Jekyll Island.

decide to sell the Wanderer Motel to International Motels Inc. for $1.7 million. The new owner immediately finishes the second-floor restaurant addition so it can open for business.

Coincidentally, Albert Crews receives the exclusive operating rights for food services of the JI Hotel, the Crane house, the Annex building, and the cafeteria. Since Mr. Crews also operates the Wanderer restaurant, he has a newfound monopoly of all the food services on the island, very much like the role Sen. Dykes played between 1955 and 1957.

The only subdivision that seems to lack any progress is St. Andrews on the south end, but even that is about to change before long, given that the political climate in the state of Georgia is shifting toward desegregation, and the island is not exempt from political influences.

When Ernest Vandiver became governor in 1959, *Brown vs. the Board of Education* was already a distant past, but it took almost six years for the first public schools to become integrated, or to better state it, to become desegregated. The general assembly opposed any such integration and threatened to withhold all state funding from any school that sought or pursued desegregation. Gov. Vandiver was instrumental to disassociate the state of Georgia from the stance the governors of Mississippi and Alabama took, which was to forcefully maintain segregation. By allowing Hamilton Holmes and Charlayne Hunter to attend the University of Georgia, as ordered by the US District Court, Gov. Vandiver convinces the general assembly to repeal its previous decision and allow public schools to desegregate.

The question now is why the above political change is so important to the upcoming changes on Jekyll Island and specifically St. Andrews Beach subdivision.

The change in political climate and stance, although there was still plenty of opposition to be found, spurs and inspires Dr. J. Clinton Wilkes to make Jekyll Island "equal but separate" for all.

He approaches the authority in March 1960 with the idea to hold the annual convention of the Black Dental Association of Georgia on Jekyll Island. Since the island is still segregated and the association will have to meet in the St. Andrews Beach subdivision, Dr. Wilkes requests that a convention hall be built adjacent to the Dolphin Motor Lodge to accommodate the annual gathering of professionals. Dr. Wilkes does not demand to use the existing facilities. He merely follows Gov. Vandiver's approach so as not to ruffle any feathers on the board and yet accomplish what the law provides: separate but equal.

The authority cannot refuse Dr. Wilkes's requests and rapidly constructs the St. Andrews Auditorium that can seat six hundred people. The auditorium does not have the bells and whistles to it as the Gould Auditorium in the Historic District. It is cheaply built for $37K and features no air-conditioning or bathrooms, but the purpose and the goal are accomplished. The local newspapers, with the help of members of the general assembly, proudly boast that Georgia is the first and only southern state that provides beach access to "colored people" and has even reserved an entire subdivision for that purpose, including a motel, a beach pavilion with concession stands and covered picnic area, a dance hall, and now a newly constructed auditorium.

A small and little-known anecdote accompanies the construction of the St. Andrews Auditorium. The rapid construction also led to the paving of the last portion of Beachview Drive from the south picnic area to St. Andrews subdivision. The authority had authorized the construction at a cost of $150K and with it obviously came a large sign that indicated the entrance to "St. Andrews Subdivision—Colored People of Georgia."

The maintenance crew inadvertently placed the sign on the "white" side of the border, and the mistake was noted during the regular board meeting with the clear instruction to "move the sign immediately to the colored side of the border." The principle of equal but separate was not taken lightly, and some board members strictly enforced it.

Dr. Wilkes will later become a resident of Jekyll Island, and his house can still be seen today between the St. Andrews small subdivision and the entrance to St. Andrews Beach picnic area. His house still stands on Lots 7 and 10, the original lot markers.

But not everybody is happy with the turn of events and with the NAACP's plan to request integration of all Jekyll Island beaches. Mr. Eugene Cook, attorney general and authority member, publicly declares in the *Brunswick News* of May 20, 1960, "I will close Jekyll Island if negroes want integration!"

It would take another four years before Jekyll Island would be integrated and all state-operated facilities, including beaches, pools, and convention centers, would be accessible to all. Surprisingly enough, or maybe not, "Judge" A. J. Hartley, the executive secretary-treasurer of the authority, would be instrumental in the integration process. After all, "Judge" Hartley had a long-standing relationship and personal affiliation with Jekyll Island as the author of the state's condemnation suit in 1947.[144] After thirteen years, he also became the first board member to reside on the island and would continue to be involved in the future and development of Jekyll Island.

Sky Lanes Inc. receives permission later in the year to develop an airstrip where once the oldest golf course[145] was located. The airstrip is nothing more than a short and flattened grassy area, north of the Historic District and between Jekyll Creek and Riverview Drive. The proposed lease is for ten years at 10 percent of gross revenue.

Meanwhile, Laurence S. Miller, part owner and operator of the JI Marina, starts a new venture with other business partners and receives a permit to operate deep-sea fishing charter boats with his new company, Sea Island Charters Inc.

With the convicts no longer being housed in the old dairy farm because of frequent complaints about safety and security on the island, and the building sitting idle, the authority instructs W. B. Johns of Tifton, Georgia, to build a metal garage shop that can house equipment and can serve as a repair and maintenance building. The project is finished at a cost of $96,316 only to be torn down the next year together with the historic dairy farm and adjacent smaller buildings.[146]

The year ends with major bridge repair and maintenance issues, although the structure is only five years old. Nobody could have foreseen that the vertical lift was not built to open ten thousand times per year, mostly because of the daily activity of the shrimping boats. During that time, a fleet of ten shrimping boats operated very successfully on and around the island, which caused frequent daily traffic on Jekyll Creek and

---

[144] "Judge" A.J. Hartley authored the original condemnation procedure in 1947 that was used by the state of Georgia to acquire Jekyll Island.

[145] The 1898 club course.

[146] The original dairy farm building was in such state of disrepair that it had to be demolished. The new metal garage was demolished at the same time. Today, only the silo can still be seen, just slightly east of Riverview Drive and south of Jennings Road.

congestion on the JI Marina because of limited docking space. That too would eventually be addressed by the authority.

With major improvement plans in the making or already under construction, the authority turns once more to the governor for funding. Gov. Vandiver "donates" $1,218,000 to the Jekyll Island Committee at the beginning of 1961.

Phase 1 of the sewage project receives $450K, while the remainder is intended for the completion of the eighteen-hole Oleander golf course and the Aquarama. The authority appropriates the remaining $768K to begin construction of the Aquarama and swimming pool, while the golf course is placed on the back burner, causing the Oleander golf course to open in 1963, two years behind schedule.

The new Aquarama with the first indoor swimming pool on Jekyll Island is intended to become a major tourist attraction, and therefore the design must be accordingly. The slick and modern building features a tent-shaped roof with wide and high windows on both sides, allowing for plenty of natural light to penetrate the Olympic-sized pool.[147] The open and airy design creates the feeling of swimming in the ocean but indoors.

The authority's choice pays off when the Aquarama opens to the public on June 30, 1961, right on time for the big July Fourth crowds.

Brenda Lee, the teenage singing sensation of those days, performs her show in front of thousands of attendees and to everybody's delight. Adults can use the indoor swimming pool for one dollar per day, and children are admitted for fifty cents.

Before the start of the summer season, the authority also lets a contract to convert the barn and stables in Jekyll Village, the Historic District, to a "supper club" where visitors and hotel guests can dine.

Charles Gowen, who didn't receive approval for his forty-eight-unit cooperative idea the previous year, now returns to the authority with a proposal to build eight apartments just north of and adjacent to the Jekyll Estates Motel. Together with his business partners Dalton Hayes and Marvin Bluestein, he constructs the Ocean Terrace Apartments that still exist today.

---

[147] The Aquarama pool was supposed to be Olympic sized but was a few meters short of Olympic standards. That did not stop several swimming meets to be held in the Aquarama during its short-lived existence.

Each of the eight apartments was 1,400 square feet and quite large for the time, considering the only rentals on Jekyll were small motel rooms or efficiencies.

Nevertheless, Mr. Gowen's concept paid off, and Ocean Terrace Apartments stood the test of time better than some of the motels. His idea also becomes an inspiration for Ray Whittle, a name that by now must be very familiar, and Mr. Threadgill.

Both propose to lease 145 acres, about 800 feet west of Beachview Drive, to construct co-op houses that are divided into three hundred apartments. The idea is to fill the existing marshland in that location and to create a central lake around which the houses will be constructed,[148] an innovative idea but one that never materializes. Instead, Mr. Threadgill will acquire several residential leases in the next few years that will be transferred to other business ventures after each lot is rezoned for multifamily or duplexes. Most of the duplexes are still present today and located in the Palmetto and Oakgrove subdivisions.

With $450K still available to start the new sewage project and a federal grant of $250K, work begins on Phase 1, which consists of constructing main sewage lines to connect the motels and hotels, and a municipal sewage and water pump is to be constructed. The project will take two years to complete after the authority receives another $105K grant, this time from the US Public Health Service.

The island is ready for its next big chapter of expansion, and the ensuing years will see an influx of residents willing to lease available lots and start construction. The much-needed infrastructure is underway, and the hotel/motel business is stabilized, so it is time for growth in the recreation and residential part of the island.

---

[148] The idea of luxury homes around a lake or golf course dates to 1960–1961. Although it never materialized, the idea persists even today when plans are dusted off and resurface every so often, as recent as 2017.

CHAPTER 6

AN ISLAND RISES FROM THE MARSHES

1962–1966

The new year seems to start as usual, with a minor change in the authority. Outgoing chair of the Public Service Commission, Mr. McWorther, is replaced by Crawford Pilcher, and it is business as usual, or so it seems.

There are so many projects ongoing and under construction that the next four years are the equivalent of a whirlwind passing through the island. Maybe it is not a coincidence that Hurricane Dora does its natural part to aid the authority in those same years of hyperactivity and seeming chaos.

Jules Dykes receives permission to open a second filling station on the causeway, approximately one mile west of the Jekyll Creek Bridge on the north side of the causeway.[149] It seems ironic that such permission is granted since it has only been seven years since Sen. Dykes was forced to deed his Pure Oil station on the Jekyll Island Parkway to the authority as part of their attempt to self-manage all business ventures. The new filling station seems in direct competition with the authority's Pure Oil station on the island.

As a result, Mr. Wimberly, who represents the Pure Oil Co., renegotiates his terms and conditions with the authority. It marks the first time that a calculation method is being formulated to determine the exact base upon

---

[149] The filling station is the current location of the Welcome Center and the Georgia State Patrol.

which the authority calculates its monthly percentage of gross sales and the definition of what is considered "gross sales."

Prior to 1962, "gross sales" were determined as the total of all pretax sales. The authority now agrees that the definition of "gross sales" is the equivalent amount after deduction of all applicable federal and state taxes, thereby leveling the playing field between island businesses and those conducting business off-island. The permits are granted, and the station will play another important but unexpected role during the following years.

It is also important to note that Carl Dykes[150] is part owner of the D&D Supermarket on the island. Their role in 1962 and beyond may not be as impressive or controlling as the role Sen. Dykes played between 1955 and 1957, but their presence and participation in the development of the island is noted, in a complimentary way.

On the island itself, several residential lots are being leased at a fast pace. Mr. Threadgill, the business partner of Mr. Ray Whittle whose proposal to build multiple apartment houses inland was rejected the previous year, pursues several lease agreements in Pinegrove, Palmetto, and Beachview subdivisions. Notable is also Mrs. Tallu Fish's first residential lease of Lot 3/C in the Beachview subdivision, signed and approved on September 24, 1962.

The Corsair, popular with vacationers and enjoying a steady flow of business, submits plans to the authority to construct a second floor on its existing crescent-shaped ground-floor design. It also requests permission to build a nine-hole par-three golf course by removing its two wading pools. The idea of building a golf course in this location is reminiscent of history.

Prior to the construction of the Corsair, this same location once featured part of the old golf course, so bringing back a new par three would be a tribute to the original Ocean Course or Great Dunes. No permission is granted, presumably because swimming pools are the main attraction for hotel guests, and therefore revenue, but also because all the hotels are selling golf tickets and golf packages to their guests. The hotels buy the tickets at a discount from the authority and resell them to their guests. The authority refunds any excess and unsold tickets at the end of the season or at year-end. Allowing one or more hotels to design and build a golf course, even one as small as a par-three nine-hole course, in their backyard would

---

[150] Carl Dykes also leases a beachfront lot in the Beachview subdivision.

be in direct competition with the authority. Golf rates at the time were $1.50 per round on a weekday or $2 on the weekend and a main source of income even though one could only choose to play between the old and the new nine-hole courses.

It should also be mentioned that at the time, the authority set the hotel rates not only for the hotels that were financed by the Georgia Teachers Retirement System but for all the island's hotel rooms, including the Corsair.

The lots that have been set aside for religious purposes now also start to see some construction. The Presbyterian Church is the first one to hold its services outside of Faith Chapel and in its own church in 1962. It will be a few more years before the congregation is joined next door by the Methodist church that will break ground in 1965 and ultimately share its church with the Episcopal and Roman Catholic worshippers. The Jekyll Island Baptist Chapel, although founded in 1963, would join the other congregations in 1973 when their building was finally finished.

The good news for both the authority and island visitors comes on May 7, 1962, when the general assembly approves a resolution to lift the toll on the Sydney Lanier Bridge. The new resolution brings relief for the visitors, who paid seventy cents per round-trip, but is even better news for the residents of Jekyll Island, whose annual pass of forty dollars is now being waived.

Before the year ends, the authority also negotiates a service contract with Georgia Power to operate the new sewage and water supply pumping station that is now operational and services the existing hotels/motels.[151]

That doesn't mean that all motels are already tapped in the new sewage and main waterlines, but the pumping stations are fully operational, and a new water storage tank is being built by R. D. Cole Manufacturing Co. at a cost of $72,610. It will take several months for the motels to agree on applicable water and sewage rates before the system replaces the existing septic tanks and private wells on the island.

---

[151] Georgia Power entered into an exclusive service contract with the authority in 1954 when the first high-voltage cables were installed across Jekyll Creek. The service contracts initially included a 3 percent rebate on all residential and commercial electricity bills. The rebate was and still is payable to the authority and similar to the monthly revenue charge for island businesses.

By June 1963, the authority has set its first water rates. Private residences are charged fifty dollars to tap into the water/sewage system and are charged a flat monthly rate based on the number of toilets in the residence.

- one toilet: $1.50/month
- two toilets: $2.00/month
- three toilets: $2.50/month
- four toilets: $2.75/month

It seems odd that water and sewage rates are based on the number of toilets rather than actual usage measured by meter. Water meters were available at the time since the first one was invented and patented in 1890.[152] They were probably not installed to reduce cost, but that may explain why some of the oldest and original houses on the island initially featured only one bathroom.

The hotels/motels are billed $1.50 per month for housekeeping units (i.e., efficiency units with kitchen) and a monthly charge of one dollar for simple rooms with one bath only.

If one wonders how the authority can afford these ongoing infrastructure projects and expansion of water and sewage grid around and across the island, do not assume that the revenue intake can cover the project cost. For the fiscal year of 1963, the authority receives $745K from the general assembly and another $475K in 1964 to cover the costs.[153]

But the authority does envision further expansion and therefore an increase in annual revenue and offers additional lots for lease in the Beachview and Palmetto subdivisions.

This is the first time since residential expansion was temporarily halted in 1958 and until existing lots were assigned. The new lots fetch the highest price yet: $400 per year in the Beachview division and $300 annually for the Palmetto lots.

---

[152] The Worthington duplex piston was invented in 1890 and was the first American design (*Atlantic Daily*, April 14, 2011).

[153] Annual project funding through the general assembly would continue until 1964, when direct funding was replaced with regular bond issuances.

It is interesting and noteworthy that all the lots in the Plantation subdivision are being designated as Class C, meaning exclusively residential and noncommercial. To this day, the Plantation subdivision remains as only one of two divisions[154] that are entirely residential and single-family only, while other divisions are mixed use, either multifamily, partially commercial, or a mixture thereof.

The St. Andrews Beach division, and primarily the Dolphin Motel & Club, doesn't fare as well and doesn't seem to follow the same growth pattern as the other subdivisions.

With the motel, club, beach pavilion, and auditorium now fully owned by the authority and operated by Dave Jackson and his sisters, new improvements and upgrades are again needed. This time, Mr. Jackson requests to enclose the pool, like the Aquarama, at an estimated cost of $50K, and to add new and additional picnic tables and benches. He also requests that any past due rents be waived.

It may be hard to imagine that the Dolphin Motor Lodge Inn and its adjacent club fell on hard times, given that a multitude of black performers descended on Jekyll Island and performed regularly at the Dolphin Club as part of the Chitlin Circuit.[155] Even as late as 1963, and at the latter part of segregation, the club features well-attended performances by famous names such as Percy Sledge, Tyrone Davis, Millie Jackson, and Clarence Carter. Even Otis Redding performs here in 1964.

Despite the popularity of the motel and the club, revenue is hard to get, as most of the St. Andrews Beach division is used for family gatherings and day visits rather than overnight stays. Even the beach pavilion with its concession stands doesn't attract a lot of paying customers, as the facility is primarily used to organize large dance parties that move to the tunes of jukebox music.

The proposed improvements, including the pool enclosure and the promise to build a shopping center and miniature golf course in St. Andrews, never materialize. Maybe because the authority senses the

---

[154] The other exclusive residential subdivision is Pinegrove, between Capt. Wylly and Stable Road.

[155] The Chitlin Circuit was the common name given to dance halls and clubs, primarily in the South, where black musicians could safely perform during segregation. The Circuit was known for its R&B, jazz, and blues.

changing times and the end of segregation on the island or maybe because St. Andrews subdivision has never really been important to begin with. Who knows? One thing is certain though, and that is that despite the reluctance to improve the south end, two residential lots are leased for the first time that same year.

Genoa and Mamie Martin are the first couple to lease a residential lot in St. Andrews and build a permanent home there, followed shortly thereafter by Joseph and Lilian Armstrong, the second St. Andrews Beach residents in early 1964. Mr. Armstrong once worked for the Jekyll Island Club in 1928 as the caretaker for Indian Mound, the Rockefeller house.

Even a visit by W. W. Law, president of the NAACP, Savannah Chapter, and Rev. Julius Hope, president of the Brunswick Chapter, cannot alter the destination, but they can surely alter the future of the island.

Both visit Jekyll Island in March 1963 and attempt to use the island's public facilities, such as the Aquarama, the Peppermint Amusement Park, the golf course, and the existing motels, all of which are still segregated. They are turned away and refused access, upon which W. W. Law files a lawsuit against the authority.

The premise of the lawsuit is based on voluntary desegregation of public buildings and facilities that are state owned, like the decision made by the University of Georgia in 1960 and other public educational institutions that receive state funding.

Mr. Law claims that all the public facilities on Jekyll Island are state owned and operated by the authority, a state agency as appointed by the governor, and should therefore be desegregated. It would take another two years before Jekyll Island would fully integrate, but the lawsuit got the authority's attention.

On the other side of the island, things progress as envisioned, except that the Golden Isle Tennis Courts, operator of the indoor and outdoor tennis facilities in the Historic District, is in foreclosure. The authority reluctantly takes back control and management of the tennis facilities on the island—reluctantly because the Historic District is no longer the attraction on the island now that the beachside has been developed. Most of the oceanside amenities, recreational areas, the boardwalk, and the motels have become the main magnet for tourists and visitors.

Even the Jekyll Island Hotel, now managed by Walter Williams, previously owner and operator of the Wanderer Motel, and Albert Crews, is no longer the main focal point. The hotel slowly starts to function as a second choice and facilitates tourists in search of hotel accommodations when all oceanside motel rooms are fully occupied. This trend continues for several more years and ultimately results in its closure in 1971.

The only noteworthy highlight in the Historic District is Villa Ospo, or the Jennings house, that has been rented by Dewey Scarboro for some time now. He requests permission to open his house to the public, at a small entrance fee, to display his private collection of antique furniture and art. Mr. and Mrs. Scarboro were well-known collectors of international furniture, antiques, and artworks, and Villa Ospo would become a tourist attraction for several years despite the continued decline of other historic buildings.

The beach motels are doing so well that they decide to organize themselves as the Jekyll Island Motel Association. They apply with the Department of Industry and Trade for a grant to fund their own independent marketing and advertising campaign, a departing strategy from the joint effort with the authority and spearheaded by Walter Williams.

Since business in the first shopping center is brisk and there is a need for more retail space, the authority decides to grant a lease agreement for what is known as Parcel #160, adjacent to the existing shopping center, to Mr. Wright Parker[156] and Mr. Cecil Mason. Both gentlemen are entering the Jekyll Island expansion phase for the first time but will play a crucial role going forward. They construct and operate the second shopping center under the name MaPar Investments Inc. and will acquire several residential leases afterward.

At the end of the year, the Aquarama building receives a new addition to accommodate the ever-increasing flow of visitors. A new kitchen and storage area are constructed next to the indoor swimming pool at a cost of $351,221 and is being completed by A. J. Kellos Construction Co. of Augusta, Georgia.

The new year begins in dramatic fashion. Longtime supporter and advisor to the authority and a valued member of the board after the major

---

[156] Wright Parker joined Parker-Kaufman Realty in 1941 and opened the Jekyll Island office in 1964.

upheaval in 1957, Mr. B. E. Thrasher, state auditor since 1941, suddenly and unexpectedly dies in January 1964.

It is impossible to gauge the exact importance of Mr. Thrasher's role in the development and the future of Jekyll Island, but it is fair to say that without his knowledge, vision, and connections to the state's financial world, commercial development on the island would have stood idle for many more years than has been the case. It is more than accurate to bestow upon Mr. Thrasher the role of financial visionary and deal maker that has spurred the island's development, even though one can question the objectivity of his decision-making to link the economic future of Jekyll Island to the Georgia Teachers Retirement System, of which he was an influential and prominent board member.

Whatever the interpretation or conclusion of his role may be, his creative financial plan led to the relaxation of tight money markets and opened the doors for other developers to obtain the necessary construction loans that would fuel commercial development on the island and henceforth residential development.[157]

Mr. Thrasher is replaced on the Board of the Jekyll Island Authority by Ernest Davis, the new state auditor, who is joined by Horace Caldwell as the new director of state parks, replacing longtime member John Brinson.

The beginning of 1964 also marks another new and important change. This time it pertains to the noticeable erosion in certain parts of the island's beach and waterfront lines. Remember that many dunes were removed in 1953–1954 and subsequent years to build roadbeds or to make room for development. Eleven years later, the authority is alarmed for the first time by the rapid beach erosion, so much so that they order the Seaboard Construction Co. to immediately install a "riprap" at a cost of $58K to protect the island's "vital areas." Although such are not clearly defined in any of the authority's meeting minutes, one can only guess that "vital" meant the oceanside of the island.

Less than one month later, the same company is instructed to place additional rocks on the north and south end of the island. By the end of January, 200 feet of riprap is placed on the north side of the oceanfront,

---

[157] Mr. Thrasher is credited with applying the modern-day principle of quantitative easing on a state level that created much-needed liquidity in the capital and lending markets.

400 feet on the south end, and 500 feet at Clam Creek. Such seems to be the emergency at the time.

Despite another $475K in funding approved by the general assembly to cover the operating costs, this marks the first year that the authority is seriously considering seeking alternative and long-term funding through the issuance of bonds or revenue certificates. The board, in its meeting of February 10, 1964, officially authorizes the authority's chair, Ben Fortson, and its secretary/treasurer, Ernest Davis, to issue bonds on behalf of the Jekyll Island State Park Authority and to "affix their names to the bonds." Horace Caldwell acts as agent for the authority and must approve all new construction plans for projects financed by the bond issue.

Never in state history has it happened that a state agency, operating under a lease agreement and by authority of the governor for a limited and predefined time as set forth by the Authority Act of 1950, could approve and determine to affix their names to public bonds without a state guarantee or without the Seal of the State of Georgia being attached to such ordinary bonds.

Without state approval and financial guarantee, it would seem impossible to receive the required AAA-rating that most if not all state or municipal bonds enjoy in the secondary market. The bonds are issued nevertheless and will become a point of contention.

Coincidentally, the authority approves an amendment to the existing lease agreements on January 13, 1964:

> In the event that the Party of the Second Part makes a bona fide loan with an established bank ...
>
> ... and conveys title to the real property described above to such lender by a deed to secure debt or other security instrument ...
>
> ... in such event the Part of the First Part will recognize an assignment of this Land Lease Option Contract to such lender. Further, the Party of the First Part covenants and agrees that if the Party of the Second Part defaults in the payment of the note ...
>
> ... will execute and deliver to the lender, as attorney-in-fact for the Second Party, the permanent lease described

> in paragraph one above for the purpose of enabling the exercise of the power of sale contained in the loan deed (security deed) held by the lender (unless the Party of the First Part shall have previously prepared and delivered said lease to the Party of the Second Part) ...

The above amendment clarifies for all parties involved who is entitled to the land lease option contract if and when the lessee (Party of the Second Part) has secured a construction loan and defaults on the loan payments. It also defines the responsibility of the authority (Party of the First Part) when default occurs prior to completion of the construction. If construction is not completed as per the submitted construction plans, then the authority has no obligation to transfer the lease to the lender in question. It does however have an obligation to deliver the permanent lease to the lender if the lessee defaults on its payments and the building has been completed.

The authority realizes that unless the permanent leases become transferable and can be assigned based on loan default, lenders cannot proceed with foreclosure proceedings, hence the amendment to the lease agreements, which changes the land lease option and the permanent leases into a leasehold estate, which is transferable in the open market and not subject to the authority's or its legal counsel's (attorney general's) approval.

That is a major game changer, and it opens the door for the authority to finance incomplete construction projects directly while having the certainty of placing a lien on both the property and the leasehold estate in case of default or nonpayment and nonadherence to said leases.

The amendment is certainly not a coincidence but a well-planned change in preparation of self-financing commercial construction projects on Jekyll Island and its plan to issue ordinary bonds or revenue anticipation certificates that same year.

In April 1964, the authority issues its first ordinary bonds, known as "Bond Issue-Series 1964, dated April 1, 1964," and are placed for underwriting and sale with the firm of Blyth, Robinson & Humphrey. The minutes of the same meeting also contain the following motion, made by Eugene Cook, attorney general, and approved unanimously:

… Subject to the approval of Ernest Davis, Secretary-Treasurer, of a program and Schedule of Construction and Expenditures, Horace G. Caldwell shall be authorized to act as Agent of the Jekyll Island Authority in the planning, taking bids and supervising the construction on contracts for projects under the Bond Issue, Series 1964, dated April 1, 1964, provided that all expenditures and transfer of funds shall be cleared through the Jekyll Island-State Park Authority office of the Secretary-treasurer and provided that all bids shall be opened and approved by the Secretary-Treasurer, Ernest Davis.

It will take several months before a comprehensive list is produced and approved by the authority, but business continues as usual.

A new bathhouse and bathrooms are approved for the Cherokee Campground, and bids are opened for the requested improvements in St. Andrews Beach subdivision. Multiple residential lots in the Oakgrove division are rezoned to allow apartments or duplexes to be constructed. The lease agreements are assigned to Jekyll Cottages Inc. and leased at $400 per year plus 3 percent of the gross revenue.

Before the summer is over, the authority has approved the design and construction of a new eighteen-hole golf course and has added an additional 1,200 feet of rock revetment at the north picnic area[158] and Clam Creek. Wright Parker and Cecil Mason, dba MaPar Investments, sign a lease for the construction of their new shopping center, adjacent to the existing one. And as the St. Andrews Auditorium finally gets its air-conditioning system and a new adequate floor, Dr. Clinton Wilkes signs his lease agreement as the third permanent resident[159] in the subdivision.

It also marks the first time in island history that the US Brewers Association descends on the island and is granted permission to excavate and restore the "Gen. Oglethorpe Brewery" on the Horton Plantation. Several other attempts to excavate the site will follow in the years to come, but a restoration has never been attempted. It is also the only time that

---

[158] Currently referred to as Driftwood Beach.

[159] Genoa and Mamie Martin became the first St. Andrews residents late 1963, followed by Joseph and Lilian Armstrong in early 1964.

the ruins are referred to as the Oglethorpe Brewery.[160] Despite recognition by the US Brewers Association, the authority never officially assigned the designation of "Georgia's Oldest Brewery" to the tabby ruins. Several excavations have not provided enough proof that the building in question was really a functioning brewery. The result is that even today the ruins are referred to as barn and storage buildings used by Maj. Horton and Christophe DuBignon.

That summer of 1964 can best be described as a whirlwind of projects as if everything must be finished before the storm hits. Little does the authority know that this is exactly what happens on September 10, 1964, when Hurricane Dora makes landfall about six miles north of St. Augustine.

Jekyll Island sustains major wind damage and beach erosion despite the riprap and additional rock revetments. Two motel roofs are seriously damaged by the hurricane-force winds, and Peppermint Amusement Park, unprotected from the southeastern winds blowing at 110 mph, loses its Ferris wheel and sustains permanent damage to most of the rides. It will become the first stage of failure for Mr. Harvey Smith, not because the damaged rides cannot be replaced but because the authority rejects Mr. Smith's request for a long-term lease so that he can rebuild his successful business on the island.[161] The ongoing dispute about lease terms, conditions, and specifically the duration will ultimately result in the closure of the amusement park in 1966.

Coinciding with the authority's stance regarding the amusement park also comes the idea of ending Mr. Morrow's and Mr. Bostwick's lease agreement for the Cherokee Campground. The authority wants to terminate the lease and purchase all improvements made so that it can operate the campground independently, like the golf courses. For the time being, it is just an idea but one that will be pursued soon.

Following the devastation of Hurricane Dora, the material damage on Jekyll Island is estimated to be $1 million and does not include the cost

---

[160] Early historic documents first mention the Oglethorpe Brewery as being built by Major Horton. The tabby ruins can still be seen on the northern riverside of the Horton Plantation.

[161] Mr. Smith enjoyed a renewable annual lease at very favorable conditions (3 percent of gross revenue plus $1,200/year for 200 feet of oceanfront property).

of beach repair. The authority passes a resolution to apply for financial assistance:

> Be it Resolved by the Jekyll Island Authority of the State of Georgia, that Hon. Ben W. Fortson, Jr., Chairman of the Jekyll Island Authority, be and he is hereby authorized to execute for and on behalf of the Jekyll Island Authority, an agency of the State of Georgia, any and all applications and other documents for the purpose of obtaining certain Federal financial assistance under the Federal Disaster Act (Public Law 875, 81st Congress, as amended.

It also finalizes its itemized project list as substantiation for the Bond Issue-Series 1964:

> Sewer System-Phase III 250K
> New Marina 950K
> Teenage Center 600K
> Additional 18-hole golf course 500K
> Restoration Village Area 950K
> Beach Repair 700K
> Fishing Pier 150K
> Contingency 50K

It should be noted that the above list is merely an addendum to the issuance documents of the 1964-Bond Issue and is not enforceable. Nonadherence to the above project list by the issuer, the authority, is not in violation of the terms and conditions of said bond series if the public funds are used to improve, maintain, and beautify Jekyll Island and are in accordance with the Authority Act of 1950.

This concept is nothing new per se. Governor discretionary spending or "donations" could be spent at the discretion of the authority and independent of whether the actual spending matched the list of projects that accompanied the request for funding. The issuance of general obligation bonds does require a comprehensive list of projects for which the raised funds are to be used. However, there is no binding obligation that such projects must be completed, nor is there a specific clause that would prohibit the authority to use the funds for purposes other than the ones submitted. The authority has free reign over the funds raised by the public offering and is authorized the use such as it sees fit. The only restriction is of course that said funds must be used to improve, maintain, or beautify Jekyll Island State Park. That is the equivalent of a carte blanche, and the authority will frequently redirect funds as it deems fit and appropriate without further consulting the general assembly.

Some of the funds are used to repave the outdoor tennis courts and upgrade the indoor tennis center, now both under authority management since the demise and foreclosure of the Golden Isles Tennis Club. Other funds are used as a matching contribution to improve and upgrade the existing airstrip according to new standards issued by the Federal Aviation Authority. The FAA provides $186K in grants with the matching component paid by the authority.

With the new kitchen and storage area at the Aquarama finished, Albert Crews, operator of the Jekyll Island Hotel, the Crane house, and the cafeteria in the shopping center, is recommended by Fred Zapico, chair of the Jekyll Island Resort Motel Association, to become the new lessee for the food services at the Aquarama. The recommendation comes just days after Mr. Crews secures a new three-year lease for the cafeteria with a possible extension through the end of 1969.

Mr. Crews is not the only one to position himself carefully and to ensure that he becomes an integral part of the future growth on Jekyll Island. After all, the first bond issue is underwritten, and funds are available to finance any project and foreseeable expansion on the island.

The Jekyll Cottages Inc., which requested and received rezoning of several residential lots in the Oakgrove subdivision, is also aligning its business model and is now transferring the original lease agreements into the name of W&M Enterprises. Mr. Whaley and Mr. Minter own the new company, and both have been actively involved in island development since 1958 but always behind the scenes, until now.

Another new or not so new name appears at around the same time. Mr. Stanley Friedman acquires several vacant lots in the same Oakgrove subdivision, adjacent to the recently rezoned lots, and can construct multifamily dwellings or duplex apartments on said lots, identical to the approach of W&M Enterprises.

Mr. Stanley Friedman's name may not sound familiar, but his company Seaboard Construction Co. is no stranger to Jekyll Island. After all, the major road extensions, paving, or installation of riprap and rock revetment contracts have all been awarded to his company. He is not the first or the only person to invest directly in residential lots after having established himself and his reputation with the authority through his company.

Mr. Parker and Mr. Mason precede him through MaPar Investments and their subsequent lease acquisitions in Beachview subdivision and elsewhere.[162]

It may not be as questionable as it seems, if it were not that the premise of offering residential lot by open bid, a requirement set forth in the Authority Act of 1950, seems like a distant memory, as no required publication or offering can be found at that time. The method of operation seems to be that existing professional relationships between the authority and corporations doing business on the island now result in random residential lot assignments to the owners or partners of said corporations. That stands in sharp contrast with the requirement for the envisioned and mandated "open-bid policy" of the mid-fifties, but the practice does not draw the same amount of public scrutiny as seen and read about in 1955. On the contrary, the press and local newspapers are surprisingly quiet about lot assignments and rezoning decisions.

The only ones that are exempt from the open-bid policy are the religious organizations. The authority grants a land lease option to the Methodist Church, the Baptist Church, and the Catholic Diocese of Savannah at the same time it approves the construction plans that are submitted by the Presbyterian Church. The latter would become the first denominational church on the island to open its doors and perform services.

While businesses seem to flourish with Seaboard Construction Co. receiving two more contracts to pave the airstrip, according to FAA requirements and the necessary grants, and to asphalt Beachview Drive,

---

[162] The expansion years are indicative of professional relationships between companies or corporations to result in personal favors to or preferential treatment of their owners, hence the granting of rezoning or specific residential lot assignments.

and Bailey Drilling Co. drilling an additional well on the island, one business owner doesn't fare so well.

Mr. Harvey Smith, operator of the Peppermint Amusement Park, sustained severe damage from Hurricane Dora and is seeking a long-term lease renewal to rebuild his business. The authority has other plans with the oceanfront property the park currently occupies. Instead of renewing Mr. Smith's lease or simply denying his request, the authority offers a month-to-month lease. In addition, the authority demands 15 percent of gross revenue on all rides instead of the previous monthly revenue payments of 3 percent.

Peppermint Amusement Park will continue to operate for another year and closes its operations in the spring of 1966 due to the inability to obtain a long-term lease under more favorable conditions. Mr. Harvey Smith would later state that the uncertainty of the short-term lease made it impossible for his company to make continuous investments in new rides and that the high percentage of profit sharing caused him to cease operations altogether.

What was once an oceanfront icon, and reminiscent of the early days of beach and boardwalk entertainment, now becomes a memory of the past. It is an early sign of changing times on Jekyll Island as other tourist development slowly replaces the nostalgic years of the romantic fifties.

The high percentage of gross revenue was not solely applicable to the amusement park. At the time, the authority had realized that individual businesses, other than the hotel/motel businesses, made large profits and paid low annual lease amounts for the parcels they occupied. The previous average rate of 3 percent or 5 percent of gross revenue quickly changes to 15 percent and becomes applicable to other business ventures such as Atlantic Helicopter, who provided sightseeing tours of the island and operated just south of the south picnic area.

The change in contracts or approach does not deter the growth and popularity of Jekyll Island. On the contrary, business is so brisk that the Jekyll Island Resort Motel Association, through their attorneys, Shoob & McLain, present a proposal to build a "Jekyll Island Welcome Station" on US-17 at the entrance of Jekyll Island. The project is a joint venture between the association and radio station WGIG and consists of a welcome center, an observation tower, and a remote radio studio. The construction cost is estimated at $100K and will be paid for by the joint venture. The annual operating cost of the facilities, managed by the Motel Association, is $29,400, and the proposal requests that the authority absorbs 50 percent of the cost for the first two years with a possibility to renew for two additional years.

The authority agrees to the proposal and the participation in operating costs but in exchange decides to discontinue its direct participation in all billboard advertising, a venture that began in 1958 with Walter Williams and the Seaside Investment Co.

Construction work continues on the water and sewage plan (JISPA-Phase 2 and 3), financed by another round of bond issuance: "Jekyll Island-State Park Authority Bonds, Series 1965" also referred to as "Series 1965 Bonds." The total amount borrowed this time is $5,150,000 and is underwritten by First National City Bank, Atlanta, and Chase Bank.

The interesting difference between this issuance and the Series 1964 is that the agreement requires the placement of an indenture agreement with an appointed trustee, in this case the Citizens and Southern National Bank of Atlanta.

The excerpt of the minutes of the authority meeting held on August 30, 1965:

> ... the Jekyll Island-State Park Authority (hereinafter sometimes referred to as the "Authority") is authorized and empowered to acquire real property, construct, furnish and equip public buildings, cottages, and other park and recreational facilities including tennis courts and golf courses at the various parks of the State of Georgia, and to lease the same and to enter into contracts pertaining thereto for the use of such facilities and to borrow money for any of its corporate purposes and to issue its negotiable bonds; and ...

This first paragraph refers to the original Authority Act of 1950 except for the last sentence. The "Act" does not specifically provide for the borrowing of funds or the issuance of negotiable bonds. That little detail is quickly resolved by paragraph 2 of the same excerpt.

> ... the Authority has agreed to acquire, construct and equip at various State Parks, within the limits of money hereinafter made available for that purpose certain projects certified by the Department of State Parks (hereinafter referred to as the "Department") as being of the most importance, said projects being listed in the lease hereinafter authorized to be executed; and ...

The mentioning of "various State Parks" is the key to understanding the intricacy of bond issuance without being in violation of state law, and the following paragraphs clarify the legal relationships between the authority, the State Parks Department, and the governor.

> ... in order to finance the construction and equipping of foresaid projects, the Authority proposes to borrow money in the amount of $5,150,000 and to issue its bonds evidencing the sum so borrowed, said bonds to be retired from the rentals received by it from the aforesaid lease; and ...
>
> ... the Authority has the right at this time to issue bonds in the principal amount of $5,150,000 to provide funds with which to pay the cost of constructing and equipping the aforesaid projects;

In essence, the above refers to the authority entering into a lease agreement with the state of Georgia for all public assets (i.e., land, recreational areas, and public buildings) through the Department of State Parks and the governor as commissioner of conservation. The rentals received refers to the annual payment by the state of Georgia in accordance with the lease agreement.

It is a convoluted way to finance infrastructure projects without specifically and directly using state funds for the development of Jekyll Island as a state park, but it is very innovative nevertheless. The state simply pays the authority rent for the use of public land and the public infrastructure as provided by the authority through its own financing.

To "legalize" this agreement, and to ensure proper payment of principal and interest, all parties agree to establish a trust indenture with Citizens and Southern National Bank, Atlanta, Georgia:

> ... The Secretary of the Authority is hereby directed to deliver forthwith to the said Trustee named in said Trust Indenture and executed counterpart of the lease and of the operating contract covering the Jekyll island projects to be constructed out of the proceeds of said Series 1965 Bonds ...

The agreements together with the trust indenture documents are forwarded to the solicitor general of the Atlanta Judicial Circuit for confirmation and validation of the Series 1965 Bonds.[163]

The resolution, as an integral part of the minutes of the authority meeting on August 30, 1965, is approved unanimously and certified by witness and hand of Mr. E. B. Davis and official Seal of the Jekyll Island-State Park Authority.

The issuance of negotiable bonds in two consecutive years, in 1964 for $4,500,000 and again in 1965 for $5,150,000, is a remarkable deviation from the early development years when financing for commercial properties was obtained directly from the Georgia Teachers Retirement System. Obviously, the large expansion of much-needed public infrastructure projects cannot be financed solely by a public pension plan, hence the innovative and creative approach of bond issuance.

One can question the integrity or even the legality of such issuance, based on the notion that a state agency, acting on behalf of the governor, the general assembly, and the Department of State Parks, can affix its seal and witness its signature on the bonds. Given that the bond issues are covered and guaranteed by a trust indenture, a lease agreement, and an operating contract, the issuance of said bonds and the subsequent series in 1968 and 1971 are within the legal framework of state law. The questionability of the seal and signature will be addressed by the authority and the state of Georgia through a change of the financing methodology.

---

[163] Series 1965 Bonds, addendum to the minutes of the authority board meeting August 30, 1965.

The interesting fact here is that it clearly shapes a professional relationship between the state of Georgia and the Jekyll Island Authority. Gone are the days of the authority leasing Jekyll Island for the nominal value of one dollar per year and becoming self-sufficient while operating as a state park.

The authority becomes increasingly an independent entity that renders professional, municipal, and management services to the owner of a public state park. In return, the owner makes all the capital investments, including municipal infrastructure, while the authority pledges the net revenue stream as payment of principal and interest.

It is the beginning of a municipal model/entity, like the surrounding municipalities such as St. Simons but created out of a state agency. Both bond issues and financing method in 1964 and 1965 are the start of such hybrid model and certainly mold the foundation upon which the current municipal management model exists today.

It is obvious that both the state and the authority feel the need to complete the water and sewage project based on the rapid increase in residential lot construction and given that without a complete perimeter and subdivision system, the existing private shallow wells and the septic tanks with drainage fields present a danger to the preservation of the island. The damage that Hurricane Dora left behind in its wake can also be viewed as a contributing factor to pursue the public infrastructure project sooner rather than later.

One can imagine the impact of the hurricane on the island with open drainage fields and multiple septic tanks, not to mention the risk of compromising the multiple shallow wells that still exist on the island.

It is also not a surprise that the authority revises its water and sewage rates that same year. After all, some of the installation and maintenance cost will have to be recovered from the users of the new municipal services. Add to this that Georgia Power is the sole provider for the three operating lifts and pump stations on the island, and although the authority negotiates a full 3 percent rebate on all electric bills, the cost is passed on to the resident consumer.

The new rates go in effect in August 1965, and instead of charging a flat rate per toilet, as initiated in 1963, the authority charges a flat rate of

$2.50 per single residency and per apartment unit. The commercial rates remain the same, at least for now.

Amidst all the rapid expansion years and the multitude of infrastructure projects, it almost seems that the slow but steady desegregation of Jekyll Island is a nonevent, at least according to the archival documents and newspaper publications. One of the reasons can be that integration or desegregation of public facilities on the island are far more peaceful than elsewhere in the state of Georgia or the south in general.

That "peaceful and quiet" integration is largely contributed to "Judge" A. J. Hartley, according to Rev. Julius Hope.[164] This is not the first time Judge Hartley writes history on Jekyll Island. He was also instrumental in drafting the first condemnation papers in 1947 so that the state could acquire the island from the millionaires without too much trouble, and he will continue to play a crucial role in the daily operation of the island in later years.

With integration comes the slow demise of what once was the only subdivision for colored people, or the "Negro subdivision" as it was originally known in 1955. St. Andrews Beach with its well-known Dolphin Motor Lodge and Club, its beach pavilion, and auditorium attracts less and less visitors. No more line dancing to the tune of the jukebox under the covers of the picnic area; no more dancing in the club to the sounds of Otis Redding or Percy Sledge. Those days rapidly become a distant memory. The consequences for David Jackson and his two sisters, Annabell Robinson and Betty Chandler, are obvious, and on June 1, 1966, they surrender their lease to the authority.

The Jekyll Island Resort Motel Association, under the leadership of Mr. Shoob, offers to use the facilities as a day camp for teenagers. The agreement is to compensate the authority 15 percent of gross revenue for any income derived from outside activities (i.e., without the use of the existing buildings) and 3 percent for use of any of the indoor facilities. At that time, the only teenage recreation facility was by the old bathhouse on the corner of Shell Road and Beachview Drive. Since the authority had ordered the

---

[164] Rev. Julius Hope was a Baptist minister and a very active member of the NAACP. He was later named president of the Georgia State Conference of the NAACP in 1966 and became director of religious affairs of the NAACP in 1978 (Civil Rights Digital Library).

old building to be demolished, this was the perfect opportunity to create a teenage recreational area that would ultimately become the 4-H Center.

The old bathhouse and concession stands were marked for demolition at the same time Mr. Harvey Smith lost his lease and operating license of the Peppermint Amusement Park. The minutes of the authority meeting on March 16, 1966 state:

> ... and it was reported that the contract expired on March 1, 1966. Mr. Davis moved that Harvey R. Smith be notified by the Executive Secretary to vacate the premises now occupied by him within the period provided by statute in order to terminate the tenancy of said premises and to demand the filing with the Authority the past due monthly reports and payment by Mr. Smith of the past due fifteen per cent of his gross sales since July, 1965 and the Executive Secretary is further directed to take whatever action is necessary to have Harvey R. Smith vacate said premises known as the South Concession Stand and the Amusement Area set forth in the month-to-month agreement dated March 1, 1964 and expiring March 1, 1965 ...

One can consider the simultaneous removal of the Peppermint Amusement Park and oceanfront teenage recreation facility as the beginning of separating public recreation areas from the revenue-generating resort side of the island. It certainly changes the landscape, and it diminishes the purpose and value of the long boardwalk between the Wanderer and the Aquarama. The authority must have envisioned using the available oceanfront property for future commercial development, an idea that persists even today.[165]

Elsewhere on the island, and with sufficient funds available, the authority approves the construction of a new golf clubhouse,[166] later also the home of Morgan's Grill and renamed McCormick's. It also approves

---

[165] http://www.savejekyllisland.org/BeachManagementInformationPage.html.
[166] The new clubhouse was inaugurated on December 9, 1967, by Gov. Lester Maddox.

the drilling of a new well for golf course irrigation[167] and the installation of an additional water pump to be operated by Georgia Power under the same contract agreement (i.e., a 3 percent rebate to the authority). Seaboard Construction Co., a now very familiar name, is contracted to pave the parking lot around the new clubhouse.

The airstrip, recently upgraded with a grant from the Federal Aviation Authority, receives another request from the FAA to extend the current landing strip by 1,100 feet and to clear the land between Jekyll Creek and the runway of any trees and bushes that impede visibility. The cost of the project is partially funded by the FAA, with matching funds from the authority.

The vulnerable oceanside of the island is continuously being protected with additional riprap by the north picnic area and Clam Creek. Seaboard Construction Co. constructs the additional revetments at a cost of $525,524.56 so that the popular shores can be protected, at least temporarily.

That leaves the Historic District, which by now has slowly fallen in disrepair, with only a minimal number of guests seeking accommodations. The Crane house, under the management of Mr. Albert Crews, still functions, but little or no attention is being given to the once famous Millionaires' Club Hotel.

That is until Mr. Everett Fauber of the American Institute of Architects expresses his interest in the restoration of the Historic District, or "The Village" as it is popularly known. He also wants to excavate the Oglethorpe Brewery and the Horton house and receives a $10,000 grant from the authority to start his excavation.[168] For his interest in the "Village" restoration, the authority wants Mr. Fauber to establish a project study staff and present a comprehensive project plan.

In October 1966, Mr. Albert Jones, a representative of the Jekyll Island Citizens Association (JICA), appears before the board and requests the use of the Gould Auditorium to hold meetings. His request is denied, and Mr. Jones is referred to using the Jekyll Island Club Hotel instead for any citizen meetings. JICA members will return frequently to the open board meetings a few years later but will not be allowed to attend the Executive Committee meetings.

---

[167] The well served the Oleander course, now expanded to eighteen holes.
[168] Mr. Fauber is the second one to excavate the Oglethorpe Brewery and the first one to excavate the Horton house.

CHAPTER 7

THE STATE PARK-ISLAND RESORT OXYMORON

1966–1971

The rapid expansion of Jekyll Island brings more than just visible change to the island. Slowly but steadily, it becomes obvious that the authority is trying to blend two ideas and opportunities into one, and it marks the beginning of what can be called "the duality of Jekyll," or maybe more appropriate "the Jekyll and Hyde" battle for success and survival.

Back in 1957, when the new authority took the reins of Jekyll Island, it certainly was no coincidence that the wrought iron banner between the two welcome towers at the US-17 and the causeway junction read "Year-round Resort," while the island was primarily known as a state park. Nor is it a coincidence that during one of the board meetings, the motion was made to drop the name "State Park" altogether from the Jekyll Island State Park Authority and to simply be known as the Jekyll Island Authority. Even then, the authority seemed to go through an identity crisis of who it really wanted to become, once grown-up.

The same struggle for identity manifests itself again following a successful and rapid expansion that covers both a municipal infrastructure and a resort-style development, designed to attract tourism year-round and unique in comparison with competing states such as Florida or nearby resorts such as Sea Island.

This battle is subtle and not easily recognizable, but it is there nevertheless and in between the transcripts of the board meetings. Blank spaces in between sometimes reveal more than the actual sentences.

One such intriguing decision is the announcement that "Judge" A. J. Hartley, executive secretary of the authority, is retiring on September 30, 1967. The decision itself doesn't seem to matter much, were it not for the fact that he doesn't retire but rather is terminated by the authority, who abolishes the position of executive secretary altogether. Mr. Hartley is retained as a consultant for one year at $800 per month.

The next decision raises more eyebrows and brings us closer to this sense of duality. Mr. Horace Caldwell, director, State Parks Department, is appointed director of Jekyll Island. Previously, the authority operated under a structure of board/island manager or superintendent since 1950, but this new position of island director is the first deviation of such and the beginning of a separation of duties between the authority, as an oversight board, and the director, who intends to manage the day-to-day island operations.

Later years will show that this is indeed the first step toward a typical municipal management style for all matters pertaining to the state park side of affairs, while the authority acts as a policy maker and advisory body for matters affecting the commercial development (i.e., the resort side of the island).

The structure is the equivalent of a small municipal management style of city council and city manager. The problem here is that Jekyll Island is not really a municipality in the strictest sense of the word but merely a state park, managed by an authority that itself is governor-appointed. This is an interesting deviation and separation of duties and responsibilities, and one that is the beginning of the State Park vs. The Resort battle that lingers even today.

The change does not affect the continuing development on the island, at least not yet, but it is clear the totality of focus and primary responsibilities has been split in two, with each component running its own course over time.

It is doubtful that the authority made this decision intentionally and based on a clear long-term strategy that would require a separation of responsibilities. It is more realistic to assume that development occurred at such a fast pace and on so many different levels and fronts that delegating the day-to-day to an island director would allow the authority to focus on funding, strategy, and large commercial development without being distracted by smaller agenda items.

The authority approves the plans to renovate the now defunct and empty Dolphin Motel and Club in St. Andrews so that it may be converted into a recreation area as proposed by the Jekyll Island Resort Motel Association. That will ensure extra revenue, but it also creates a new public recreation area on the south end of the island where once stood private commercial development. One year later, the area is expanded with athletic fields to complement the recreation area and is now known as the Jekyll Island Soccer Complex.

The north end receives the same kind of attention with preliminary plans being approved to build a fishing pier at Clam Creek. The original plans are drawn up by Bahr, Wilson & Associates.

An interesting note is that the original idea called for two piers to be constructed. The second one was intended to become an ocean pier, to be constructed between the Corsair, now the Days Inn, and the Buccaneer further south. The pier would have been 1,000 feet long and was meant to offer concession stands, seating areas, and fishing. The idea for an ocean pier shouldn't come as a surprise. Similar structures were popular at the time in the northeast and attracted many tourists. Since Jekyll Island already featured a boardwalk, why not add a pier? The suggestion disappeared as fast as it originated, primarily due to exorbitant construction cost and the fact it would forever ruin the unobstructed ocean and beach views enjoyed by so many visitors.

Since the authority has major construction plans, it hears again the plea from the Georgia Federation of Women's Clubs to provide an outdoor theater on the island. Mrs. Nix, president of the federation, is the second one to make such a request,[169] and this time the proposal is considered in earnest. The persistence will ultimately payoff when the authority approves plans to build the amphitheater in 1972.

Mr. Morrow, operator of the Cherokee Campground, receives a ten-year lease extension, thereby securing another public recreation area on

---

[169] The first request was made by Mrs. Taylor, then president of the Georgia Federation of Women's Clubs, on March 10, 1958.

the island, although be it that such is managed and operated by a private party, a concept that will again change in the ensuing years. For now, the campground is not only stable but is also limited to its current land lease, despite an additional sixteen acres of land having been cleared on the east side and despite a formal request from Mr. Albert Fendig to open a second camping ground on the vacant lot.

Since the authority is busy stabilizing the existing recreational areas, other than the motel/hotel sites, it also secures a lease extension for Olson Yacht Yards Inc., dba JI Marina, and agrees to purchase the remainder of the Golf Club inventory, including golf carts, pull carts, and store merchandise from Mr. Bean, making the operation of the golf courses, the miniature golf course, and the golf clubhouse now a state park business with Mr. Bean as a full-time employee of the authority and without any further vested interest in the daily operations.[170] The original eighteen-hole miniature golf course, built in 1958 together with the first golf clubhouse, is being redesigned by Mr. Buford Dean of Dean Golf Supply Co. Mr. Bean himself will later get the opportunity to start his own island business again when he receives permission from the authority to open and operate a sightseeing and air taxi service from the island's newly refurbished airport.

A few months later, Mr. C. W. Woolard becomes the first concession holder of the snack bar, located on the second floor of the golf clubhouse.[171]

Mr. Caldwell also hires Mr. Johnny Paulk as the head golf professional soon afterward, and it is clear that the authority is serious about self-management and providing its visitors and golf enthusiasts with the best golf experience possible.

Mr. Paulk[172] is very familiar with Jekyll Island. He vacationed and honeymooned here with his wife when the island was still only accessible by boat. He was also offered the job five years earlier but politely declined

---

[170] The authority purchased inventory and merchandise from Mr. Bean in 1957 and even accepted a quit claim deed to cancel the lease agreement and self-manage the golf course and miniature golf. Full execution of the deed did not pass until ten years later, during which Mr. Bean continued to operate as a lessee.

[171] The snack bar would later be converted by the authority into a full-size restaurant known as Morgan's Grill, later renamed McCormick's Grill.

[172] Mr. Paulk is credited with bringing the annual Georgia-Florida Classic Invitational to the island in 1979 in addition to the US Kids World Championship, the Georgia PGA, and the Georgia Women's Golf Association Championship.

the offer since island golf was still in its infancy back in 1963. He joins the authority staff at the most opportune time: the grand opening of the new golf clubhouse and the new Pine Lakes Golf Course. His previous experience as an assistant golf pro at Atlanta's East Lake Country Club, his memorable stories of Bobby Jones, and his southern flair make him the perfect man for the job. His tenure as director of golf and his island career that spans thirty-seven years are certainly proof, not to mention the major upgrades and redesigns under his watch.

With more projects being proposed and the continuation of a municipal water and sewage system across the island, it doesn't come as a surprise that in 1968, the authority reverts to the issuance of another bond series to raise the funds needed to finance or continue to finance infrastructure projects. This time, as the previous two times in 1964 and 1965, the authority issues $7 million in general obligation bonds, known as Series 1968 Bonds, with one minor difference. The new bonds, despite being general obligation bonds and issued "on par" with previous bonds and series, are issued as "subordinate bonds" as provided for in the following board resolution dated February 12, 1968:

> … WHEREAS, the Authority has heretofore issued, from time to time, bonds having as security therefor leases with the said Department of State Parks executed prior to January 1, 1965. The obligation of the said Department of State Parks with respect to the lease securing the bonds of this Series and bonds heretofore or hereafter issued on a parity therewith is subordinate to the obligations of said Department of State Parks created by the leases executed prior to January 1, 1965, with the Authority and the Stone Mountain Memorial Association, but no additional obligations may hereafter be incurred which will create a lien or charge on the revenues of the said Department of State Parks superior to the obligations created by the lease securing the bonds of this Series or additional bonds heretofore or hereafter issued standing on a parity therewith; …

It is obvious that, for the first time, limitations are set and that the previously issued general obligation bonds, Series 1964 and Series 1965, take precedent over the new Series 1968, despite being secured by the same leases and therefore the same revenue stream. It is also remarkable that while previous issuance documents, specifically Series 1964 and 1965, mention leases with other state parks being pledged as collateral against the bonds, this Series 1968 specifically mentions the leases with Stone Mountain Memorial Association. One must conclude that for the authority to issue bonds, based on future revenue as collateral against such issuance, the limited revenue stream on Jekyll Island cannot possibly serve as enough collateral within an indenture agreement. The "blanket" lease agreement with the Department of State Parks allows the authority to borrow far more than it would have been able to do if it were limited to its own assets and the revenue stream thereof. It is not considered unlawful or a violation of any state law, but the fact that it is unknown to the public that other state park assets are being pledged against bond issues that solely finance Jekyll Island infrastructure and commercial development projects may be questionable in nature, based on a potential conflict of interest and future liability to the average Georgian or the average taxpayer.

The big project the authority has in mind this time is not the restoration of the Island Village, the Historic District, but the creation of a new luxury marina[173] and boat basin just south of the old wharf, and a new 300K gallon water tank and well on the south end of the island, adjacent to the new recreation center. Remember that the old Dolphin Motel and Club and so many other hotel/motel facilities are still using their own shallow wells and have not even tapped into the new water and sewage system just yet. At least not all of them.

No time is wasted on starting work on the new luxury marina. Fifty thousand cubic feet of oyster shells are placed in marsh land, south of the bridge, as riprap for the new marina,[174] and an initial $50K is spent on the first round of dredging. The total cost is $400K, and no clear design

---

[173] The new luxury marina never materialized. Parts of the land were later used to build Summer Waves and the adjacent Tidelands Nature Center. The empty lot north of Summer Waves is now referred to as Shark Tooth Beach.

[174] The riprap was placed by Houdaille-Duval-Wright Co. of Jacksonville, Florida, at a cost of $362,500.

or development plan is being presented yet. The idea is to create docking slips for 450 luxury yachts, dry-docking space, restaurants and shopping facilities, and fuel stations. The project is heavily supported by Phillips 66 that envisions a major intracoastal waterway fuel and pit stop for luxury boats passing through on their way to Florida during the fall, or their return home up north during spring. A few months later, Oceanic Construction Co. begins to construct and place test pilings at the new marina site.

Out of the $7 million that is raised by Bond Series 1968, $2,137,500 is placed in reserve for a new convention center ($1.2 million), an amphitheater ($500K), and a potential and future restoration of the Historic Village ($437,500). While the true restoration of the Historic District will take several years to accomplish, part of the funds is used to restore the Rockefeller house[175] and Faith Chapel, except for the installation of air-conditioning units.

The commercial development is ongoing with John Minter and A. M. Harris receiving permission to lease additional lots in Oakgrove and expand the Seafarer Motel[176] to forty-five units. The same expansion is also underway for the Buccaneer Motel, now under the management of Motel Properties Inc., who wants additional land to construct fifty more units, bringing their total number of guest rooms to 206. The adjacent Stuckey's Carriage Inn is also eyeing expansion and receives permission to build an additional hundred units to its original capacity of 108, almost doubling its guest rooms. The rooms are constructed on the additional land that was set aside in 1960 for such a purpose.

While the authority is primarily busy investing in municipal projects, including a luxury marina, the commercial developers also sense it is time to prepare for future growth and expansion, hence the construction activity at the Buccaneer Motel and Stuckey's Carriage Inn. Both will approximate the room capacity of the Wanderer and the Corsair once finished.

It seems that the authority is not only focusing on expansion and renegotiating lease agreements. It also focuses on business ventures on the island and specifically the food services that are currently being provided by

---

[175] Currently Indian Mound.
[176] The Seafarer Motel further expanded again in 1971 and is now known as the Quality Inn & Suites.

Mr. Millican as operator of the Jekyll Sandwich Hut,[177] previously known as the Charcoal House Restaurant, and by Mr. Albert Crews, who has an exclusive contract for the JI Club Hotel, the Crane house, the cafeteria in the shopping center, and the kitchen and storage area of the Aquarama. Mr. Crews's contracts with the authority are quite extensive and exclusive, so it is not a surprise that he seeks a more long-term commitment to secure his position on the island. However, his request to extend his current lease for another ten years with an additional five-year renewal option is denied by the authority at the end of 1968. Instead, the authority wants to the lease to lapse so that bids at-large can be reopened. In the meantime, Ogden Enterprises, a name that will resurface again, wishes to take over Mr. Crews's lease at more favorable terms, but the authority wants the open-bid process to run its course.

The game of business lease renewals and/or open bids continues well into the new year, and it seems that the authority is seeking some sort of industry standard that can be applied to all commercial business leases across the board, rather than the individualized concept of the past.

For that purpose, the authority hires the firm of Harris, Kerr, Forster & Co. to conduct a lease study and make recommendations. The firm suggests and recommends that a minimum annual revenue stream of 8 percent of the actual land value is achieved or 3.5 percent of gross sales, whichever is greater.

This is the first time that annual revenue or the lease amount is correlated to the appraised land value. Previously, the annual lease amount was a fixed amount, while the monthly revenue was set as a percentage of gross sales, pre- or post-taxes.[178] The same principle will later be applied to residential leases as well, but that will not occur until lease expiration dates are getting closer.

Whatever the study may have recommended, Mr. Crews manages to transfer his new lease and the possible extensions, first to Savarin Inc.

---

[177] Mr. Millican's request for lease renewal was denied on January 13, 1969. The Jekyll Sandwich Hut was located on North Beachview Drive. Tortuga Jack's currently occupies the same location.

[178] Motel operators typically paid 3 percent of gross revenue after taxes. Small business owners paid as much as 15 percent of gross revenue, depending on the type of services offered.

(February 1969) and later to the American News Agency or AnCorp Inc. (May 1969). The transfer includes both the Aquarama and the cafeteria in the shopping center.

Other lessees in the shopping center opt for a more straightforward approach. Mr. Tarratus, who previously acquired D&D Supermarket from Carl Dykes and changed its name to IGA Supermarket, seeks and receives a lease extension for ten years. The first five years, IGA pays 2.5 percent of gross sales and 3 percent the following five years, with a minimum annual guarantee of $10K.

R. B. Maxwell, as owner and operator of Maxwell's Variety Store, also receives a ten-year lease renewal but at slightly different terms and conditions. His lease requires payment of 6 percent of gross sales for the first year, 7 percent for the next four years, and 8 percent for the last five years of the lease agreement, with a guaranteed minimum annual payment of $8K.

The Pure Oil Co., which operates the filling station on the causeway and is owned by Jules Dykes, is outright purchased by the authority. A similar fate as the first filling station on the JI Parkway that was purchased by the authority in September 1957.

It seems that the authority's approach to business leases is haphazard, and no consistent business model is being used. Such is probably the result of the transition phase between island businesses that are deemed crucial and functional for a state park and daily visitors, and other commercial businesses that are more geared toward the development of a conceptual resort.

Other infrastructure projects though seem to run smoothly and don't encounter the same scrutiny or difficulty in obtaining permissions. WHAB, builder of the first CATV (Community Antenna Television) tower on Jekyll Island's south end is a perfect example. The contract, first granted at the end of 1966, is still intact when Mr. Weldon Stamps submits a second request to erect another cable TV tower on the north side of the island. Both will ultimately be integrated into Jekyll Island TV Cable Inc. that installs and operates the Marine Public Correspondence Radio & Telephone Service and uses the existing two towers and adjacent buildings to expand services on the island.

The authority is not short on new ideas and concepts, and while it sometimes seems that any proposal deserves attention or is at least worth trying, somewhere amid a chaotic approach, there is an adherence to one or the other master plan or land-use plan. The interpretation or the use of the designated areas in any master plan, both recreational and commercial, may be wide open for interpretation as far as the authority goes, but the loose adherence is the main driver behind the multitude of decisions, changes, amendments, or alterations.

Some of the decisions made are not always as clear as expected, but when placed in time and viewed in hindsight, it is obvious that some of the decisions are made without any clear proof that another project was already proposed or even discussed at board meetings. The conclusion must be that some projects are being discussed behind closed doors and off the records. Otherwise, the decisions do not have any clear purpose or intent.

One such example is the rerouting of Beachview Drive in 1961 to create extra land lots with ocean view, while none of the lots are staked or even zoned for either residential or commercial use. That designation is now made in 1969, eight years after redirecting 1.1 miles of ocean-view driving between the north picnic area and Ellis Lane. At that time, the interpretation was that plans were being made to develop the extra land, either commercially or residentially, but no formal requests or lease applications were presented to the authority.

Now eight years later, the authority decides to change the northern boundaries of the Beachview subdivision and to extend the residential zoning northward to the current Tallu Fish Lane. The same is done with Oakgrove subdivision, facing Beachview Drive, thereby creating extra residential lots for lease.

The lots between Tallu Fish Lane and the north picnic area are zoned commercial with the clear stipulation that said lots cannot be altered or rezoned. An interesting decision since no official records exist that indicate how many commercial lots are available, nor is there any proposal on file for development. The first such proposal will be submitted one year later in mid-1970, which indicates that the authority anticipated interest in northern oceanside development and made a preemptive decision to reserve the land ahead of time.

The lots are known as Lot 350-351, Lot 352-353, and Lot 353-354. The designation here is important, not only because each of the lots appears to be available for lease as two single lots that can be combined for construction purposes but also because two of the lots have overlapping numbers. The specific designation and the lot combinations will play an important and interesting role a few years later. Suffice it to say that the authority must have envisioned large commercial development for this side of the island, hence the size of each available lot, or combination thereof.

Further north, the fishing pier[179] is finished, and the final plans for a parking lot are being approved and implemented. When the pier opens to the public in late 1969, the daily charge is set at one dollar for adults and fifty cents for children. The rates are revised a few months later to fifty cents for adults and twenty-five cents for children. The rates are not just for fishing. Even spectators who wish to walk on the pier are charged thirty-five cents just for the use of the recreation area.[180] For that purpose, the authority constructs a small kiosk where daily passes can be purchased for either fishing or sightseeing.[181]

Public bathrooms and a small concession stand are constructed at the end of the pier ramp. The spectator fee is later abolished, and only fishing requires payment of the daily fee, and even that becomes questionable. What is supposed to be a new recreational attraction for the average fishing enthusiast becomes a problem when the pier proves to make fishing impossible because of the strong current underneath and around the pier. It will take another two years for the authority, after careful examination by a study committee, to recommend a solution.[182] For now, the pier is the least popular attraction, except for the surrounding picnic area and beach access.

The Historic District, although being assigned funds to begin renovation and repair, sees its budget slashed and rerouted to fund the dredging of what is to become the new luxury marina and yacht basin of Jekyll Island. The only two projects that are approved are the restoration

---

[179] Clam Creek fishing pier.

[180] Other existing recreational areas were free of charge. The pier at Clam Creek was the first and only public recreational space that levied a charge for visiting. The fee was used to pay for some of the construction cost and later changed to a daily fishing fee.

[181] The small kiosk was located at the entrance of the pier and has since been removed. A similar kiosk can still be seen today between the ladies' and men's bathrooms entrances.

[182] George Bagby, director of the Department of State Parks and the newest board member, would be charged with finding a solution.

of Faith Chapel and the installation of air-conditioning in the Rockefeller house. Faith Chapel is closed to the public, and the authority does not allow any services to be held in the historic building despite that fact that no religious center or church is completed or even open to the public.

The Rockefeller house, operating as the Island Museum since 1954, is closed as well, and all data, documents, and historic mementos are moved to the Club Hotel until further notice.

Ms. Tallu Fish, who is considered the founder of the Jekyll Island Museum in 1954 and who is credited with documenting the history of the island during the gilded age of the millionaires, retires on December 31, 1969. For fifteen years, she faithfully shared the island's historical treasure with numerous visitors. Upon her retirement, Ms. Fish becomes the first museum archivist,[183] diligently preserving and cataloguing the historic documents from her new office space on the first floor of the Jekyll Island Hotel.

All other projects in the Village are placed on hold or are diverted to the absolute minimum, such as reroofing each of the cottages one at a time and only if needed.

But now that the old Beachview Drive is being closed to the public and commercial lots are staked and ready for development, it only takes a few months for the first initial proposal to be presented to the authority. Mr. Larry Morris expresses an interest in leasing Lot 350-351 to construct apartments. The details of what Mr. Morris has in mind are not clear yet, but his vision will result in the Sand Dollar Apartments[184] in 1971 and will cause a major change in the land lease agreements and ultimately the concept of individually owned apartments within a jointly owned building that is constructed on land leased by a corporation or financial institution.

Remember that Mr. Charlie Gowen was the first person to propose constructing co-ops on the island, a concept that was rejected in 1961 and ultimately approved as the Ocean Terrace Apartments but without individual ownership. This time, Mr. Morris has the same idea and concept, but it will require a few changes in the current land lease agreements that are in effect to make this happen.

---

[183] Chairman Ben Fortson and Island Director Horace Caldwell honored Ms. Fish with the title "Curator Emeritus of the Jekyll Island Museum, Archivist and Historian for Jekyll Island." Ms. Fish died August 26, 1971.

[184] Current site of The Cottages at Jekyll Island.

Not coincidentally and probably because of where the authority envisions the future of Jekyll Island as a resort destination to develop, combined with Mr. Morris's concept of what will become a 263-apartment complex, the land lease agreements of both the Seafarer Apartments and the Wanderer Motel are changed into a "leasehold estate." No official or archived documents confirm this assumption, but it is fair and accurate to suggest that future commercial developments between the northern boundary of the residential Beachview subdivision and the northern picnic area triggered a necessary legal change to some of the commercial land lease agreements to accommodate co-ops and condominiums. However, the authority will fight a long and hard battle to stop or slow down the development.

W&M Enterprises, the joint venture of John Minter and James Whaley, has been operating the Seafarer Apartments since 1959 and has expanded its complex by adding several new adjacent lots and by rezoning such lots from residential to multifamily to allow for apartment units to be constructed. By 1969, the company operates forty-five apartments and grows into seventy-one units by 1971. While all units are essentially part of one corporation and one complex, the lots have been accumulated a few at a time with each land lease agreement assigned, as requested and approved by the authority. The total complex, however, now holds multiple leases for what is essentially one single structure of multiple individual apartments. If the owners were to offer the Seafarer Apartments for sale, the multitude of individual leases would not only encumber such transaction but also restrict the transfer of the land lease agreements to a third party, investor, or a financial institution acting as lender or financier.

In April 1970, W&M Enterprises requests to convert its land lease agreements into a leasehold estate or, according to Georgia law, into an "estate for years" (i.e., perpetual). This is the first of its kind on Jekyll Island, and while its immediate impact seems negligible, it does have repercussions on how future commercial development is being treated. It also opens the doors, very hesitantly, to a brand-new market of co-ops and condominium developments despite the authority's mild objections. Two months later, Motel Properties Inc., owner-operator of the Wanderer Motel, files for the same lease conversion. The authority approves the request without objection.

It is important to note here that when Walter Williams and his Seaside Investment Co. sold the Wanderer Motel to International Motels Inc. in 1961, the land lease agreement was held by the Georgia Teachers Retirement System, who financed the initial construction. By converting the land lease agreement into a leasehold estate, the new lease becomes part of the assets pledged and collateralized against the outstanding loan. This fact will become important when business takes a turn for the worse in the coming years.

For now, it seems that the groundwork has been completed and that future development, in whichever capacity such may be heading, is secured.

The authority now focuses its attention back to the general development of the island (i.e., recreation and other public buildings). With funds available, the architectural firm Bull & Kenney submits a design for the construction of a new convention center, adjacent to the Aquarama. The cost is estimated at $1,385,720, and the project will not be finished until mid-1973. Building a new and costly convention center next to the Aquarama and within the same vicinity as the two shopping centers to create a central location or the concept of an island community center that integrates both commercial and public use is accompanied by a little irony. By the time the design and location are proposed, it is already known that the Aquarama roof is leaking and needs resealing, after having only been in operation for ten years.[185] When construction on the new convention center finally starts in 1972, the adjacent Aquarama is already in disrepair, thereby defying the integrational concept of the island's first beach village. Construction will nevertheless take place, and the convention center will open in 1973 while the authority tries to decide what to do with the Aquarama.

Therefore, the idea in 2012 to create a beach village in the same location was certainly not new, and several other plans and ideas have been proposed in between the first attempt in 1973 and the existing island community today.

The next big project and investment occurs on the south side of the island.

---

[185] The proximity of the beach and the salty ocean air took its toll on the Aquarama roof and caused serious leaks.

Sea World Inc., represented by Mr. B. Taylor and Mr. Furman Ricks, proposes to lease parcel 150, next to the south picnic area. The lease provides for an annual payment of 6 percent of the prevailing land value plus 5 percent of gross sales for the first three years and 10 percent for the remainder of the lease. The authority must have thought it was a great idea since the lease request is approved by Horace Caldwell, but the thought of a Florida-like aquarium and sea world with live animals never materializes despite efforts to issue stock in the new company and probably because of protests by residents and tourists alike. Due to lack of subscriptions, the idea is abandoned soon thereafter and meets the same fate as the authority's Super Slide project further north.[186]

In 1969, the authority invested $50,000 to purchase a giant slide, which was placed in the parking lot next to the Jekyll Sandwich Hut. It operated for less than two years and was dismantled because of dangerous conditions due to salt water damage.

While some existing small businesses continue to flourish and receive lease extensions, such as Mr. Ferguson, the island's pharmacist, others are not so lucky. The Jekyll Island Marina, operated by Olson Yacht Yards, does not receive a lease renewal, and the authority takes control again of the old wharf.

Little by little, the authority pushes out small business owners and lessees when the opportunity arises, preferably at the time of lease renewal, to take control of whatever revenue stream they can get to slowly continue the process of self-management and control rather than outsourcing business opportunities to third parties.

The small upside for the permanent residents, besides the continued implementation of a municipal water and sewage system that will soon replace all personal wells and septic tanks, is that the island now features two milk companies, one of which, the Pet Milk Co., makes house deliveries.

---

[186] Sea Circus Inc. was originally known as Marineland of Georgia Inc. and founded by Brunswick residents. The company changed its name to Sea World Inc. in September 1970, and again in March 1971 to Sea Circus Inc. The company offered 100,000 shares of common stock to the public at $7.50 per share. The idea to build an aquarium on Jekyll Island, like Marineland, Florida, was abandoned in 1972 due to lack of subscription and protests from residents and visitors.

Overall, the state park side of the island does have some conveniences, with two shopping centers, an ice storage facility, and a dairy company.

What is still mysteriously missing is a beer and wine or liquor store, obviously because the island is still considered dry land amidst the sea of water, but that will change very soon too.

Off the island and more specifically on the causeway, a few things change. The idea of building a boat ramp with docking space for boats and yachts near the causeway is rejected. The authority envisions its luxury marina to be the only new marina and does not allow any possible competition in such proximity. It is interesting that another Glynn County commissioner, Mr. Alton Wooten, is the person to submit the proposal.

Mr. Ralph Moore, on the other hand, is more successful when he receives permission to use the old Pure Oil Co. filling station on the causeway to open an art and ceramic store. After all, the building has been sitting empty and idle since the authority purchased the lease from Jules Dykes several months ago.

With construction of the Sand Dollar Motel underway, the old Beachview Drive is finally closed to the public, although remains of 1.1-mile scenic road with its unique S-curve that allowed optimal viewing of the ocean remains intact today and is walkable between the south end of Villas by the Sea and northern border of The Cottages.

The new motel features 263 rooms and small apartments spread out over several individual buildings, some of which face the ocean. The clubhouse and office building in the center of the property also features a restaurant and lobby lounge for the guests.

There is also a sudden interest in the two lots north of the Sand Dollar Motel construction site. The Sheraton Inn seeks a six-month option for Lot 352 at $3,000, while simultaneously a group of investors, comprised of Howard Atherton, Arthur Crowe Jr., and David Rambo under the guidance of Sen. J. H. Henderson, apply for a lease option on Lot 352-353.

The two applications for Lot 352 present a conflict of interest, which the authority resolves by letter to J. H. Henderson on October 1, 1971:

> ... and acted to approve a twelve-month right-of-refusal to you on the two lots 353 and 354.

> This right-of-refusal commits the Authority to reserve these two areas pending your submission of a plan for development which is acceptable to the Authority. The Authority is presently in the process of an overall review of its long-range plans for the island and you should not enter into any commitments for planning beyond the preliminary stage of design until your concept for development has been specifically approved by the Authority ...

Archived documents and minutes of the board meetings do not show any previous commitment for Lot 354 as stated in the letter. Instead, the minutes of the August 16, 1971, board meeting do mention the approval of a six-month option for Lot 352. The same minutes also show that the same six-month option is provided to Mr. Henderson for Lot 353-354 at $5,000.00.

Whatever the intentions of the authority were at the time, it is notable that the disputed Lot 352 is never developed and is still unoccupied today, nestled between Villas by the Sea and The Cottages. [187]

The ongoing municipal water and sewage project requires another set of financing, and the authority issues Bond Series 1971 as subordinate general obligations in the amount of $2,320,000. Note that this is the second series that is marked as being subordinate to the series issued prior to or in 1965. While all outstanding bonds are issued at par, Series 1968 and 1971 are subordinate to Series 1964 and 1965, and no additional assets in the form of future revenue can be pledged as collateral. The series are underwritten by First National City Bank and Chase Manhattan Bank, the same underwriters of previous issues, and a trust indenture, like the previous ones, is again placed with the Citizens and Southern National Bank.

The remainder of 1971 is largely overshadowed by a seemingly unimportant issue, or maybe not.

---

[187] Lot 352 is currently empty and has never been developed for unknown reasons. It is still the site of the old Beachview Drive and can be accessed by foot or bike from the most southern boundary of Villas by the Sea, behind the Conference Center.

In April 1971, Jekyll Island residents file a petition with the authority to hold a referendum to allow the sale of alcoholic beverages on Jekyll Island. The island has been dry since it became a state park, and despite the sporadic sale of liquor or beer in certain hotel/motel lounges or restaurants, official permission has never been sought or granted.

> ... Pursuant to the provisions of the "Revenue Tax Act to Legalize and Control Alcoholic Beverages and Liquors", as amended, particularly by Ga. Laws 1964, p. 771, (Ga. Code Ann. 58-1083), you are hereby petitioned to hold and conduct a special referendum election for the purpose of submitting to the qualified voters of Jekyll Island the question of whether or not the sale and regulation of distilled spirits or alcoholic beverages for beverage purposes by the drink for consumption on the premises shall be authorized within the boundaries of Jekyll Island ...[188]

The authority grants the petition and is willing to hold a special election on Jekyll Island when such petition is signed by more than 15 percent of the registered island voters. Adhering to that minimum requirement certainly does not pose a problem, as the authority announces on April 15 that a special election is called for May 18, 1971, with Mr. Frederick Griffith Jr. appointed as the election superintendent. The authority also appoints three election clerks to facilitate the special election: Roger Beedle, Louise Tennent, and Charles Rockwood.

Not everyone on the island is in favor of allowing alcohol sales, and Rep. "Gene" Leggett joins Rev. James W. Adkins in his opposition to both the referendum and the sales of alcohol on the island. The referendum passes almost unanimously, and alcohol sales are now permitted, pending regulation and licensing, which is being handled by a special committee formed by Ben Fortson, Arthur Bolton, and Ernest Davis.[189]

---

[188] The petition was signed by Mr. and Mrs. Stanton, Mr. and Mrs. Walker, Mr. and Mrs. Rosekraus, Mr. and Mrs. Jacob, and Mr. and Mrs. Woolard.

[189] The authority established an Alcohol and Beer License Committee on May 21, 1971, during its regular board meeting.

The Meyercord Corp. and American Decal Co. are assigned to issue liquor tax stamps, and by June 1971, the first liquor licenses are issued to the Wanderer Motel, Buccaneer Motor Lodge, Atlantic Carriage Inn[190] (formerly Stuckey's Carriage Inn), and Atlantic Corsair Motel.

The licenses only apply to on-premise consumption and do not include any off-premise consumption or sale, such as package stores. Another and second "inconvenience" is that according to the new regulation, licenses can only be issued to Jekyll Island residents and does not include business owners or operators whose primary residence is off-island. The ordinance also does not provide for any future or potential sale of alcohol off-island (i.e., the causeway), which would then be regulated by Glynn County. Less than one week later, the ordinance is amended accordingly, and not surprisingly, the first application to open a package store on the island is submitted to the authority.

If there was ever any doubt about whether residents and business owners have endured the "drought" long enough and have waited patiently for the opportune time to force the authority into holding a referendum, the overwhelming approval easily puts these doubts to bed.

Several wholesale companies also receive their first permit to distribute wine, beer, and liquor to Jekyll Island hotels and motels. Among them are Savannah Distributing Co., General Wholesale Co., Glynn Distributors Inc., Liberty Distributing Co., Goethe Distributing Co., and Standard Distributing Co.

Motel operators are taking full advantage of the new ordinance by immediately offering beer and wine with their lunch and dinner menus, and the motels that feature a designated lobby bar see their business grow and flourish.

The island prohibition era has ended. Finally!

While plans are being made for future development on the north end of the island, given the interest in several large lots and the potential to expand the resort side of the island with apartments, co-ops, condominiums, or any combination thereof, the south, and primarily the vicinity close to South Dunes picnic area, is being appraised for future lease.

The empty lot between the Atlantic Carriage Inn, previously known as Stuckey's Carriage Inn and originally designed and constructed as the

---

[190] Stuckey's Carriage Inn was renamed in 1970.

Holiday Inn in 1960, and the displaced South Dunes picnic area, is leased to Penmoco, a company owned by Myd Harris, Carley Zell, and Tom Pierce, to construct a new Holiday Inn Beach Resort. The South Dunes picnic area is not displaced or moved this time around, as was done in 1960 to make room for the Buccaneer Motor Lodge and the old Holiday Inn; it is merely reduced in size to allow construction on Parcel 253.

The new Holiday Inn Beach Resort will open in 1975 with 205 guest rooms. In less than ten years, Jekyll Island's guest room total has more than tripled. In 1959, the island counted approximately 275 guestrooms and efficiencies. Two years later, that amount had doubled to 500-plus, and by 1971, there are more than 1,200 guest rooms available with an additional three hundred under construction or soon to be constructed. Given that only thirty-five years earlier, at the birth of Jekyll Island State Park in 1947, only the Club Hotel, the Annex building, and the Sans Souci could accommodate overnight guests, this is an enormous explosion and growth of commercial development for an island so small, and the "progress" is not finished quite yet. There is more to come, and there are more elaborate and daring plans to be developed.

It should not come as a surprise that given the construction boom on the island, legislation is again introduced to amend the Jekyll Island State Park Authority Act. Law Number 427, known as House Bill No. 473 states:

> Section 1. An Act known as the "Jekyll Island State Park Authority Act," approved February 13, 1950 (Ga. L. 1950, p. 152), as amended, particularly by an Act approved March 15, 1957 (Ga. L. 1957, p. 608), is hereby amended by striking from section 10 the following:
>
> "one-half" and inserting in lieu thereof the following:
>
> "thirty-five percent (35%), so that when so amended section 10 shall read as follows:
>
> "Section 10. The Authority is empowered to survey, subdivide, improve, and lease or sell to the extent and in the manner herein provided, as subdivided, and improved not more than thirty-five percent (35%) of the land area of Jekyll island which lies above water at mean high tide.

The new 35 percent development limit is considered one of the most contributing pieces of legislation ever enacted in state history. The general assembly must have considered that the rapid commercial development had to be contained or slowed down somehow and that the best and most effective remedy would be to limit the available land area.

It is unclear whether a new environmental sense of responsibility can be attributed to the sudden amendment, although the timing does coincide with the purchase of Cumberland Island by the state of Georgia and its ongoing negotiations to establish Cumberland as a national seashore.[191]

With this in mind, the authority establishes again a committee to prepare a new land-use plan that includes the new marina[192] and the addition of a new eighteen-hole golf course. Mr. Davis, Mr. Bolton, and Mr. Bagby are charged to work with Robert & Co., the original designer of the first development plan in 1951, and to amend such to become a land-use plan based on current developments and infrastructure. The mandate also specifically states to exclude any possible and envisioned road closings from the land-use plan. No reason is given for this specific request in any of the archival documents or minutes of the meetings.

The remainder of 1971 passes by without any major events other than tying up some loose ends and setting things in motion for the new year.

Seaboard Construction Co. receives a new contract for another 800-foot runway extension at the airport, financed with a 50 percent grant from the Federal Aviation Authority, and A. J. Kellos finally gets contract approval to construct the amphitheater.

Liquor license renewal rates are approved and published. Retail for liquor sales off and on premises are set at $2,500 per year, while malt and beer licenses cost $2,500 for off-premise sale and $500 for sale and consumption on the premises.

---

[191] The bill to recognize Cumberland Island as a national seashore was signed by President Nixon in 1972.
[192] Preparation for the new marina is already underway. Riprap has been installed, and limited dredging of the site has started. The required funding for the project was not in place yet.

CHAPTER 8

THE SIGNS OF HISTORIC DECLINE

1972–1978

The new year starts with a surprise move and a shake-up in the composition of the authority with the sudden resignation of Ben Fortson as chairman of the authority. His letter dated January 3, 1972, states his reasons for relinquishing the chairmanship:

Honorable Ernest B. Davis
Dear Ernest,

The Chairmanship of the Jekyll Island Authority is a very important position. I have been honored to be allowed to serve as Chairman for nearly fifteen years. The last few years, I have been unable to spend the necessary time on Jekyll Island that is required of a Chairman. I have expressed this feeling to the Jekyll Authority in 1970 and 1971. I expressed a desire then that someone else take over the Chairmanship. The Authority insisted that I remain as Chairman. I appreciate this confidence, but it is necessary for me to write you and state that as of now, I am resigning as Chairman …

… I no longer will serve as Chairman of the Jekyll Island Authority …

...Thank you for your friendship, your support, and your confidence. I shall support the new Chairman in every respect.

Happy New Year, and best wishes!

Sincerely your friend,

Ben Fortson
Secretary of State

Mr. Fortson's decision to step down as chair is understandable considering the multitude of projects that are ongoing on the island and the complexity and difficulties that some pose to the authority. On the other hand, the daily presence of Island Director Horace Caldwell, who is responsible for overseeing the day-to-day operations of the island, should have taken most of the burden off the shoulders of the authority.

Whether Mr. Fortson foresaw some other untold and undocumented problems or possible unsurmountable difficulties will forever remain unknown. It is possible that he felt that the daily multitasking of projects, financing, and exponential growth became out of control and that the burden was too great to carry after an intense tenure of fifteen years.

Ben Fortson played a crucial role in the protection of Jekyll Island as a state park. His popularity as secretary of state with the average Georgian, and his social demeanor when reaching out to school children and teachers, certainly made him the perfect chair of the authority. He adhered to the principle set forth by Gov. M. E. Thompson to create a state park for the benefit of all Georgians—a state park that would be accessible and affordable to all.

Despite the authority's focus on commercial development and the creation of a revenue-generating resort side, Ben Fortson tried to balance commercial growth with residential development and the protection of recreational areas. His voice of reason and compromise served as a buffer within the authority to retain the best possible balance between resort and state park.

He should be largely considered as the last musketeer, who spoke for and defended the average Georgian for whom the island was largely and initially intended to be their public playground. He commendably stepped into the footsteps of his predecessor J. D. Compton and continued his work to protect the best interest of all people.

His gracious resignation leaves behind an authority that will continue to sail but without the confidence and stewardship of a seasoned captain with a vision of and trust in the future.

Life and business on the island must continue with Mr. Ben Wiggins, chairman of the Public Service Commission, assuming the role of interim-chair until elections are held in the spring. An interesting move and selection, given that Mr. Wiggins only joined the authority last year and was not previously involved in any capacity.

The beginning of the decline is not visible in the residential or state park area of the island. Major construction on the extensive municipal water and sewer system is ongoing, and despite the disruptions this causes in some subdivisions, empty and available lots continue to be offered to new future residents.

In fact, it seems that the authority is trying very hard to fill in the empty spaces in subdivisions such as Plantation and St. Andrews, the latter of which has certainly not reached its full potential and capacity yet. The rule of public announcements and open bid seem to be something from the past, and "first come, first serve" is becoming the new standard.[193] Interested parties are often offered multiple empty lots and parcels, after which they decide on-site which one is more suitable to them, and more lots are leased in the period of 1971–1972 than in any other preceding year. The aggressive lease approach in the residential areas is understandable, given that somehow a critical mass must be obtained for the new water and sewer system to become financially justifiable and affordable. The more users are obligated to connect to the new system and forego the use of their individual shallow wells and septic tanks with drainage fields, the higher the overall revenue stream and the faster the construction cost can be amortized. That the authority chooses to relax the land lease options or

---

[193] Although originally the authority had agreed to publish each available lot and assign such by open bid, the practice was never really implemented, except in late 1954. Since then, the policy was used haphazardly depending on supply and demand. During the first twenty-five years, demand never exceeded the supply.

the application process at this junction seems logical and warranted, but it will backfire once the plan is being implemented.

By early 1972, water and sewage rates are changed again to be more in line with the current monthly charges on St. Simons Island and in Brunswick, and a tap-in fee is being introduced for the first time. The rate is set at $100 but would change dramatically in 1978 amidst heavy protests from the Jekyll Island Citizens Association. The same applies to sanitation fees that are now set at four dollars per month. There are still about 150 septic tanks on the island, and the authority "advises" all owners to connect to the new sewage system by January 1973. It will take several years before all residential and individual septic tanks disappear from the island, and some private shallow wells still exist today. It must be noted that the old Dolphin Motor Lodge and Club continued to operate its own water well and septic tank until the University of Georgia leased the properties in 1981.

It seems ironic that all residents are mandated to connect to the available water and sewage system, while the authority's property continues to use its own septic system. A reason can of course be attributed to the lack of funds to dismantle and remove the septic tanks and large drainage fields at the Dolphin Motor Lodge and Club, given that the property sits idle most of the time and does not generate much revenue. Another reason can be that the authority, while imposing rules and ordinances on its residents and commercial lessees, does not always feel the need to adhere to its own rules and feels exempt from such when convenient.

Such is the result of a management style that is prevalent then, and if the authority had chosen to lead by example rather than imposing its ordinances, the acceptance of and adherence to by its residents might have been more positive.

In the end, the relationship between the authority and the permanent residents was not very constructive, to put it mildly, and the authority ruled mostly without much input from its residents. Hence there was not much need to lead by example either.

The residential area continues its development toward a municipal model, and while progress is made toward that end, things are not going as smoothly on the resort or commercial side of the island.

From Millionaires to Commoners

Remember that in the previous year, several large commercial lots were staked and assigned for hotel/motel development between the north picnic area and the Beachview subdivision. Lots 350 and 351 were assigned to Larry Morris to construct the Sand Dollar Apartments, while Lots 353–354, were assigned to a group of investors led by Sen. Henderson to build what would become the By-the-Sea Hotel. That left Lot 352 empty in the middle but apparently not for long.

Coastal Resorts of America signs a forty-year lease for said parcel, and the terms and conditions stipulate an annual payment of 8 percent of the land value or 3.5 percent of gross revenue, whichever is greater. Based on this new lease agreement, the existing leases of the Sand Dollar Apartments and By-the-Sea Hotel are amended to reflect similar terms and durations. Simultaneously, the existing lease of the Seafarer Motel, one of the original three lease agreements[194] in effect on Jekyll Island, is suddenly adapted as well. The individual lot leases were previously combined into a leasehold estate but is now being reassigned to W&M Enterprises at 8 percent of the combined land value plus 3 percent of gross sales for a period of forty years to coincide with the above new lease agreements. No such similar change seems to have been made for the Wanderer, the Corsair, the Buccaneer Motor Lodge, or the Atlantic Carriage Inn.[195]

With the Sand Dollar Apartments already under construction and work on Mr. Henderson's By-the-Sea hotel soon to begin, the large commercial development seems to become very promising for the resort side of the island. After all, when all three hotels open their doors, the number of available guest rooms or apartments will increase by at least six hundred units, and that is just on the north side of the island. Add the additional 205 rooms of the Holiday Inn Beach Resort on the south of the island, and the island's capacity is almost doubled when all is said and done. That is, of course, if all goes according to plan.

The authority has always looked kindly toward building guest rooms and efficiencies but has never been interested in the construction of condominiums or cooperative buildings. During a regular authority

---

[194] The Wanderer and the Corsair leases together with the Seafarer Motel make up the first three original commercial leases on Jekyll Island.
[195] The four existing hotels do not require a lease amendment since all are constructed on a single commercial lot and all are owned by a single company or corporation.

meeting,[196] it is made again very clear that the authority does not want any condominiums on the island, a determined and rather unpopular stance that will be discussed repeatedly in the next few years when the tide turns.

Despite this rapid boom of guest accommodations, the Jekyll Island Hotel has been quietly suffering for many years and is barely being used except maybe for some small overflow of visitors that need last-minute accommodations. The once-thriving and exclusive hotel has lost all its allure and extravagance in the eyes of the average Georgian or tourist and is in serious decline by the early 1970s. The decline is not simply limited to the exterior, due to a lack of maintenance, but is also visible on the inside. The attendance of front desk personnel and staff is so sporadic and minimalistic that one can hardly recognize the historic landmark. Service is quasi nonexistent in comparison to the beachfront hotels, and the outdated accommodations at the Jekyll Island Hotel certainly do not represent any competition to the modern and slick service offerings elsewhere on the island.

The island's emblem of the gilded age and once the envy of all Georgians is now slowly becoming nothing more than a distant memory, just like the millionaires and their exclusive Jekyll Island Club. Did the authority not anticipate that the rapid development of the oceanside and the aggressive commercialization of the resort side of the island would take its toll on the Historic District?

Granted that the Old Village with its collection of twentieth-century cottages, its boulevard, and the old wharf never received much attention, let alone funding, in comparison with the oceanside of the island. Nevertheless, 1971 rings in the end of history, and it seems as if the adage "out with the old, in with the new" has found roots on the once "most luxurious and most exclusive island."

The authority finally closes the doors of the Club Hotel in 1972, and an attempt is made to renovate the exterior and thirty guest rooms with the $200K that is reserved and earmarked for the project. The survey for renovation is conducted by Bull & Kenney, architects of the new convention center and the amphitheater. The buildings will sit idle, unprotected from weather conditions and the occasional curious passerby, who has easy and unsupervised access to the interior. Such is the state and fate of the Club

---

[196] February 14, 1972, Jekyll Island Authority Board meeting.

From Millionaires to Commoners

Hotel, as it will be for the next fifteen years. The guest rooms and grand dining room are often used by volunteer lifeguards that will use the facility as their free overnight accommodations during the peak summer season, but other than that and probably the occasional homeless person, the historic landmark sits unprotected from natural and human wear and tear.

The makeshift fence around the historic property certainly does not prohibit visitors or locals from entering and leaving the building as they see fit. Since security is not present 24/7, the buildings are not locked, and windows are a plenty to gain access, it is easy to imagine the rapid state of deterioration and the loss of historic integrity.

The non-hotel businesses see a few minor changes when Mr. Tarratus, owner and operator of the IGA Supermarket, receives permission to operate the old marina at the wharf. No liquor license is issued though, since all public recreational areas still fall under the state parks' rule of alcohol sales and use.[197] Soon afterward though, Robert and Elizabeth Tarratus transfer their IGA-lease to James and Lamar Fender. The timing seems coincidental, as there is no indication that the new lease assignment for the JI Marina represents a conflict of interest and therefore demands that Mr. Tarratus relinquish his IGA-lease instead.

Sailboats, floats, and umbrellas can now be rented for the day from a new beach concession stand operated by Edward Carwile, and the island's first bank opens in the shopping center as American National Bank.[198]

While one business opens, another one seems to struggle, a story that will continue to plague the island for several years. AnCorp, who assumed the lease for the shopping center's cafeteria and the Aquarama kitchen from Albert Crews two years ago, is delinquent on its payments for the second time in less than six months. It is obvious that the company struggles, and such may be due to the stringent regulations the authority places on most of its small business owners. In the case of AnCorp, as was the case with Albert Crews, the problem is the mandatory opening hours the authority

---

[197] The new liquor, beer, and wine ordinance allowed for the sale and consumption of alcoholic beverages on and off the premises but prohibited consumption in any of the state park's public areas, such as the picnic areas, the beach, the old wharf, or in any other public areas in general.

[198] American National Bank currently operates as Ameris Bank.

has set forth in its lease agreement. A letter dated two years earlier gives an indication:

> Subject: Crews Jekyll Island Cafeteria
> Dear Sirs,
>
> ... Due to increased cost of labor, food material and general overhead expenses, it is impossible to operate efficiently and profitably by continuing to serve breakfast ...
> ... The operation would be much more efficient by opening for lunch and dinner only; ...
> ... We urge you to give this request very serious consideration.
>
> Sincerely,
>
> AnCorp National Services, Inc

The same letter[199] is sent to the authority on behalf of the Seafood House[200] with a request to only open for dinner.

Both requests are ignored, as no response from the authority is documented in the archives, nor is the topic discussed in any of the board meetings, except for acknowledgment of receipt of such letters.

It is very common for the authority to dictate operating hours, service, pricing of items sold, and specific services to be rendered at the time. The Cafeteria and the Seafood House are not the only businesses that are subject to strict rules and mandates as issued by the authority and pertaining to what can be perceived as interference with small business owners, their operating plan, or their product offering altogether. The island's only pharmacy, owned by Mr. Ferguson, is subject to the same scrutiny and

---

[199] Letter to the authority dated November 4, 1970.
[200] The Seafood House was in the shopping center (corner of Ben Fortson Memorial Parkway and Beachview Drive).

inflexibility of the authority, leading to a price-comparison study[201] of the pharmacy with prevailing prices for drugstore items and medication in Brunswick and Saint Simons Island. The study would ultimately lead to the nonrenewal of the pharmacy lease and its subsequent closing.

The Jekyll Island Package Store, in the meantime, gets assigned to the Promotional Association. The store, located on the causeway, has undergone several changes since its first opening but is being reassigned to Robert Morris, who would also receive a new lease agreement for the main clubhouse at the golf course. It is not a coincidence that these lease agreements change hands quickly and happen to coincide with changes that occur simultaneously that could ultimately change the future revenue stream of such leases. For example, the fact that a new contract is awarded to install a new sprinkler system on the existing thirty-six-hole golf course obviously impacts the potential of the clubhouse. Since Mr. Robert Morris, as representative of the Jekyll Island Promotional Association, is now operating a package store on the causeway, it is easy to conclude that certain strings are being pulled between parties to position themselves to the best of their ability to secure themselves a place to profit from any future revenue that can possibly be derived from Jekyll Island, the state park, and the close ties one may be able to establish with the authority in charge.

It is not an entirely new concept. It goes back to the early days of the 1950s when influence and connections were the rule. Twenty years later, things may have changed slightly, but influence is still important.

Amidst all the turmoil and uncertainty, a long-awaited public venue for outdoor performances opens on the island without much fanfare or publicity. The amphitheater, constructed in one of the least desirable spots[202] on the island but flanked nevertheless by a beautiful artificial

---

[201] Horace Caldwell, island director, ordered several price-comparison studies to ensure that island prices were similar or identical to those charged on the mainland. The pharmacy and the foodservice industry were but two examples of the study. IGA Supermarket was also instructed to align its prices. The practice of price comparison was abandoned after Mr. Caldwell's departure in 1974.
[202] The amphitheater is located south of the entrance road to the nursery and greenhouses. It is accessible from Stable Road through a dirt road just north of the fire station.

pond, opens its doors to the public and is ready to perform its first musical theater production: *Drumbeats in Georgia*.[203]

The production has quietly been composed for the last two years and is based on the history of the thirteenth colony and its founder, Gen. James Oglethorpe. The amphitheater will not open until the summer of 1973, but the construction is finished, and the last touches are being put in place, namely the ornamental handrails, designed by the Artistic Ornamental Iron Works Co.

When considering the surrounding development, both commercial and residential, albeit the latter being minimal in comparison to the former, one can only question why an outdoor amphitheater is the choice for creating a cultural arts performance venue amidst so many other modern-day options available at the time. One would think that an indoor theater or even a movie theater that can seasonally be adapted to a small performing arts theater would be the more rational choice. After all, with design plans for a new convention center in an advanced state and the knowledge that the Gould Auditorium will become obsolete or at least vacant once the new plans are materialized, one would think that the existing indoor facility that can seat up to eight hundred people can easily become the much sought-after arts venue. Add to this that alternative plans are submitted to use the future vacant Gould Auditorium as a Jekyll Island Cinema, and that the St. Andrews Auditorium is sitting vacant and unused since the days of integration, then why design and construct an outdoor amphitheater with 1,500 seats or more? The amphitheater is not only constructed with ample seating; it also includes dressing rooms, public restrooms, a ticket office, a concession stand, and light towers. This leads to the conclusion that the authority must have had a serious plan in mind for its long-term use.

While no archival documents point toward elaborate discussions about the amphitheater or the size of the finished product, somehow the feeling is that the inspiration must have come from the very first development plan as designed by Mr. Clark, whose firm is considered the architect of Jones Beach, Long Island. The similarities and the presence of a central open-air amphitheater are too obvious to be ignored or denied. Today,

---

[203] Paul Green wrote the drama *Drumbeats in Georgia*. The amphitheater production was produced by William Workman upon request from the authority.

Jones Beach's main attraction is its amphitheater, which is renowned for its musical performances by music's own superstars, and its well-advertised summer concerts are sold out months in advance. The only difference is that the shell-shaped stage is built on the oceanside, and the attending audience has a mesmerizing view while listening to live music and enjoying snacks from the adjacent concession stands. Jones Beach, being a state park, has free access and ample parking within easy walking distance of the band shell—things that add to the continued success even after sixty-four years[204] of continuous operation.

The amphitheater enjoys its new success for the first few years, although none of the musical performances ever succeed in filling all available seats, not even during its inaugural opening in June 1973, which attracts a total of 24,500 people. The annual income of tickets sales does not begin to cover the operating expenses, and the authority subsidizes the endeavor by paying all electricity bills and providing free housing and lodging for the actors at the Gould Auditorium and the servants' quarters.[205]

By 1974 and barely in its second season, attendance has fallen by 30 percent to 17,300, and the budget deficit grows to $112,000 per annum—a shortfall that needs to be covered by the authority. The location, the climate, the ever-present gnat problem, or a combination of any of these circumstances may be considered the first stage of failure for the amphitheater before its presence and its diverse offerings of musicals can take shape.

It is obvious that some things start to unravel, while others do not seem to work out as well as planned, but there is no indication that the prevailing circumstances are reason for the authority to pause and regroup. It may be, however, an unconfirmed reason for Horace Caldwell to resign as the island's first executive director. Robert Anderson takes on the role as the island's operations manager with the intent to also hire a business manager later.

In less than one year, the authority loses its chairman and its executive director, and it is fair to state that the authority loses some of its guidance

---

[204] Jones Beach was created on August 4, 1929, by Robert Moses, chairman of the Long Island State Park Commission.

[205] The servants' quarters are currently used as the offices of the Jekyll Island Authority and are located on James Street, behind the Jekyll Island Club Resort.

and experience in the process. Neither one comes at a time of stability and assurance of continued growth, nor do they come at a time of prosperity.

The early sign of decline, besides the closing of the Club Hotel, is the announcement that Larry Morris wants to sell the Sand Dollar Apartments. Robert Morris, who is managing the apartment complex in addition to managing the golf clubhouse, is also announcing his departure and leaves Jekyll Island altogether to become the operations manager for Big Canoe Co., a resort facility in the Blue Ridge Mountains. While it may seem insignificant to most, the willingness to outright sell the Sand Dollar Apartments soon after opening and the departure of yet another experienced island resource is a sign on the wall of what will come in the next two years. Mr. Robert Morris was instrumental in promoting Jekyll Island as a year-round resort and for several years led the first Jekyll Island Promotional Association, besides being instrumental in a variety of resort suggestions and business ventures. Ultimately, the Sand Dollar Apartments are not sold, but Mr. Larry Morris will return with other plans one year later, and it is obvious that he is looking for ways to divest the complex.

While the future of the Sand Dollar may be in jeopardy, Sea Cove Inc. continues its construction of By-the-Sea Hotel and what would later become Villas by the Sea. Arthur Crowe, who oversees the construction project, strikes a deal with the authority to move 4,000 cubic feet of dirt from the Sand Dollar property to his own construction site and to purchase the additional dirt needed to level and backfill his own parcel from the island's "borrow pit" inland. The pit primarily contains dirt, sand, and silt from the continuous dredging on the riverside of Jekyll with the hopes of creating the long-awaited luxury boat basin. The basin itself and the construction of a new luxury and multifunctional marina is still ongoing, but the plans themselves have been reduced to a minimal and limited basis. The project's total cost so far is approximately $1,175,000, and there is still no sign of construction or useable docking space. The expensive project would finally be abandoned in 1974 and sit idle for the next ten years, but not after another $500K is spent on reviving the idea on a smaller scale in 1979.

The same cannot be said about the island's infrastructure project that is still ongoing. A new water and sewage extension requires an additional $1.5 million, funds that are made available by the general assembly.

From Millionaires to Commoners

The situation at the end of 1973 should really be an eye-opener for the authority, or at least an early warning sign. Some hotels/motels have changed their leasehold assignments (i.e., W&M Enterprises changes to Seafarer Motel), the Wanderer amended its lease assignment to Motel Properties Inc. two years earlier, and Larry Morris is eager to change the structure of his own Sand Dollar Apartments. Sea Cove Inc. is in the process of doing the same and will submit its request to the authority in February 1974 to reassign its existing leasehold estate in the name of By-the-Sea Hotel. What is driving the sudden change in commercial lease structures and assignments, and what triggers these similar events?

The obvious answer can be found in the change from a simple land lease to a leasehold estate as discussed before. The second reason, and probably a not-so-noticeable one, is that since leasehold estates can be transferred in the secondary market, mortgage companies can now also use said leasehold estate as collateral for the outstanding loans. Suddenly, it becomes important who holds the leasehold and who will ultimately be financially responsible in case of default—hence the above reassignments of existing leases, the transfers to new company names or owners, and the desire to sell, entirely or partially, the interest in a hotel/motel.

The authority, however, does not see or seem to acknowledge the existence of an upcoming problem, at least not as can be derived from the board meeting minutes. In the end, not all is negative, and some things do get the attention they deserve.

The convention center is still under construction but is almost finished and ready to be used the next year, and the Cherokee camping ground is flourishing so that a new ten-year lease extension is offered without much debate or controversy. The auditorium of the convention center will be named after the late "Judge" A. J. Hartley, who passed away in August 1973. Eight original murals painted by Mrs. Esther Lippincott Stewart[206] will adorn the convention center after the dedication in the spring of 1974.

The Jekyll Island Arts Association, in existence since late 1966, finally gets a permanent home in the Goodyear Cottage, although Mr. E. R. Fryer would have preferred renting the Mistletoe Cottage when renovation was completed. That specific cottage is presumably reserved for the Jekyll

---

[206] Esther Lippincott was a Jekyll Island resident and well-known American artist. She was instrumental in founding the Jekyll Island Arts Association in 1966.

Island Promotional Association, who will move its offices from the Club Hotel, where they rented rooms. The JIPA will move to the Mistletoe Cottage in the summer of 1974.

It seems that the Village restoration work under the supervision of Roger Beedle and according to the renovation plans of Ken DeBellis bears some fruits, be it limited to the absolute necessities since other cottages remain untouched. But when it seems small progress is made on one part of the island, another part doesn't fare so well and requires attention and changes.

Mr. Ferguson sells his pharmacy to Dr. D. E. Billman and Jekyll Island Pharmacy Inc. transfer its lease assignment to Hamilton-Waters Inc. with the approval of the authority and with the intention to "… open a good drugstore."[207] Whether this change is the result of Mr. Caldwell's price-comparison study with the Brunswick and Saint Simons market prices earlier is unknown, but one can accurately assume that the authority was not pleased with the current state of affairs and therefore did not object to the lease change. It is a curious approach that can be found back on several occasions where one small business suddenly disappears (Peppermint Amusement Park in 1966) without any rational or substantiated reason, while others continue to operate undisturbed. If sustainable and affordable pricing on the island is really the underpinning of the authority's decision in these cases, then such approach is certainly not applied or used as a general guideline for all existing businesses.

This has been the story since inception, and one can imagine that when Jekyll Island State Park finally opened to the public in 1954,[208] decisions were erratic, and the result of a lack of vision and a comprehensive plan for the long-term future. Twenty years later, and with the use of a development plan (Robert & Co.'s 1950 plan) and the subsequent land-use plans, one would think that the business or development approach would have found solid footing in a vision that developed over time and is based on experience of trial and error that results in long-term strategies and allows for short-term flexibility and adaptation.

---

[207] Quote from the authority board meeting on March 4, 1974.
[208] Jekyll island State Park officially opened in March 1948 but became accessible by car with the opening of the Jekyll Creek Bridge in 1954.

When the island faces changing times, the decisions continue to be instantaneous and without concern. Such immediate change seems to be merely a band-aid for today rather than a cure for tomorrow. One such "small" decision can be found in the assignment of food services for the new convention center that opens to the public in the spring of 1974.

AnCorp, Mr. Crews's business venture that has provided continuous food services on Jekyll Island since the Wanderer Motel opened its first restaurant and has operated the cafeteria and the Island Seafood Restaurant in addition to the Aquarama kitchen and storage facilities, is notified of its lease termination effective February 1974. Granted that AnCorp is delinquent on its monthly lease payments, it is more realistic and truthful to point out that the company was at odds with the authority about opening hours for a few years. The difficult relationship and the fact that the authority seemingly has control over operating hours and business strategy ends in a lease termination. It does not take very long for the authority to find a new partner in Morrison Food Services, who takes over the responsibilities for the cafeteria, the new convention center, and the Aquarama annex.

Another "impulsive" decision is to continue to explore options for the new luxury marina despite the lack of funds and the decision of the previous year to limit any development of the site given the ongoing silting problems. Nevertheless, the authority orders MAPCOtec Inc. to provide an aerial topographic plan of the marina and instructs Hartland Bartholomew & Associates to prepare a conceptual master plan for the site. The studies would lead to another capital injection of $500K in 1977.

The new marina has now been in the making since 1967. Whatever effort is made with the dredging of the saltwater and freshwater boat basins is immediately countered by Mother Nature with the deposit of silt. Seven years later, and without any visible progress, a new study and topographical mapping of the area seems futile, certainly when the total project cost is running well over $1 million. The entire endeavor seems like a bottomless pit, at least financially, but maybe not from a silting perspective.

Amid such sporadic decision-making, it goes by unnoticed that the Wanderer Motel closes one of its two pools without any given reason. Granted that municipal water supply is no longer free, including the commercial sprinkler systems at the motels, water cost seems hardly a reason to close a popular guest attraction.

A more reasonable explanation is that the economic tide is turning, and Jekyll Island's resort side is not immune. Hotel owners and operators must have seen the change coming, hence Larry Morris once again approaches the authority with his proposal to change the ownership of the Sand Dollar to create 130 separate legal partnerships. Add to the equation that Coastal Resorts, the lease holder of Parcel 352 since 1972, still has not commenced construction, and the lot between the Sand Dollar and By-the-Sea Hotel has been vacant for two years.

Even the new amphitheater, in only its second season of *Drumbeats in Georgia*, which is now the official state play, sees its attendance dwindle by 30 percent. Another small sign of changing conditions?

That does not deter the authority from continuing its expensive riprap project. In addition to placing riprap under and around the fishing pier in Clam Creek to slow the rapid tide and improve fishing off the pier,[209] and the revetments placed on the oceanside, the project is expanded to include riprap between the north picnic area and the north end of the beach at a cost of $500K, thereby protecting the commercial development from any future erosion, or so it seems.

The island also gets a new eighteen-hole golf course, Indian Mound, in accordance with the latest version of the development plan. For the course to be built within budget limits, the authority approves a plan to bring back convict labor to the island.[210] Once Indian Mound is finished in record time and opens in January 1975, the old Championship Course is renamed Oleander.

By the end of 1974, the warning signs of trouble ahead are clear as W&M Enterprises receives its first notice of default. The company owns the Seafarer Motel, although the leasehold estate is now assigned to

---

[209] Mr. Bagby oversaw finding a solution for the fishing problem on the pier. It was finely decided that placing riprap under and around the pier would be the only solution and would slow down the rapid tide. The riprap would ultimately cause increased beach erosion between Clam Creek and the north end of Driftwood Beach, resulting in more rock revetments around the parking lot and the picnic area.

[210] The convicts that were brought to the island in 1951 left in the early sixties after several complaints from residents.

Seafarer Motel as a separate legal entity. That is just the beginning of the decline, which will deepen in the next two years.

The decline is not unique to Jekyll Island but is the result of the prevailing economic and financial circumstances of the times. When placed in the context of two major historic events, it is easy to understand the change that is about to happen.

The oil embargo of 1973–1974 obviously has a ripple effect on the general population of the US and its spending habits. The combination of an oil crisis with a crash of the financial markets and the rise of oil and gas prices, because the gold standard had been abolished two years earlier, automatically result in high inflation and financial/economic insecurity. The average gas price in 1973 is 38.5 cents, but by the summer of 1974, such has risen to 55.1 cents a gallon, the equivalent of a 40 percent increase and one that has a severe impact on consumer spending. Driving habits change dramatically, and so does discretionary spending, such as vacationing.

It is not a surprise to see that hotel/motel owners and even financiers see the danger much sooner than the authority does. Though there is no statistical information available that would show the change in occupancy rates at that time, it is accurate to conclude that discretionary spending on Jekyll Island declines dramatically, and if the attendance at the amphitheater in 1974 as compared to the opening year is any indication, then the conclusion is fair.

How this will eventually cause the resort side of the island to collapse slowly but steadily can only be attributed to the longer than expected duration of the economic inflationary period, although it must be said that the US economy suffered from a hybrid inflationary-deflationary period simultaneously until the mid-1980s. Nevertheless, this is the first test of the financial foundation upon which Jekyll Island as a year-round resort destination is built and whether such is stable and secure enough to weather the storm. After all, a single public pension plan finances several hotels, namely the Georgia Teachers Retirement System, and it is unpredictable what repercussions such financing methodology will have going forward, if any.

It does not take very long for some of the answers to become visible as Coastal Resorts is placed on notice in January 1975 for lease termination due to a breach of contract for not commencing construction on Parcel

352.²¹¹ Given that the company has so far paid all its annual dues for a total of $68,000 and given that the parcel will continue to sit empty based on current circumstances, it is questionable why the authority terminates the lease rather than offer a lease extension in exchange for continued payment. After all, revenue income is key. There is no indication that the authority has another party in mind that is interested in said parcel, so one can only guess what the motivation is.

Drumbeats in Georgia is also cancelled for the season due to lack of revenue and the budget shortfall of $112K in 1974 that must be subsidized by the authority.

The only good news early in the year probably comes from the Church of God, which is again holding its annual convention on the island. The congregation has been a loyal visitor to the island since 1962, and attendance has grown to over eight thousand, a welcome crowd of visitors in an otherwise depleted tourist market.

Before the beginning of summer, three hotels/motels are in arrear for water and sewage bills or are in default of rent payments. The Holiday Inn Beach Resort, which just opened its doors, is in default of rent payments, as is the Atlantic Carriage Inn. Jekyll Estates Motel, the oldest motel on the island, in operation since 1958, is found in arrear of water and sewage bills. All will ultimately continue to operate, but again, this is certainly not a sign of prosperous times. The Jekyll Estates Motel also announces it has been sold to a group of investors, the Citizens & Southern Realty Investors, a name that will be involved with other island hotels.

It only takes four more months before it is publicly announced that the Atlantic Carriage Inn is found to be in default and that Glynn County is offering the property for sale for thirty days.²¹² The public sale is a standard county tax sale, offered publicly to the highest bidder to fulfill all outstanding and delinquent property taxes. The Georgia Teachers Retirement System, however, holds a lien on the property, and now things

---

²¹¹ Coastal Resorts initially signed a six-month lease agreement, which was automatically renewed although no design or construction plans were ever presented to the authority. After three years, the lease is terminated. Parcel 352 is still sitting idle today but can be developed according to the land-use plan.

²¹² The Atlantic Carriage Inn was publicly offered for sale by Glynn County as a "tax sale" on September 8, 1975. (Brunswick News. September 8, 1975).

start to become a little bit more complicated. Should the authority step in, purchase the outstanding tax lien, and acquire the outstanding notes from the public pension plan? The thought may seem farfetched, but it crossed their mind.

Instead, the authority prepares itself for what else may come their way. They make sure that the Jekyll Estates, despite new ownership or maybe because of it, receives a ten-year lease extension, although the current twenty-year lease does not lapse until 1978. The reasoning for this preemptive move is dual. First, it ensures that should the Jekyll Estates follow in the footsteps of the Atlantic Carriage Inn and be sold for outstanding tax liens, the authority, in cooperation with the mortgage holder (i.e., the Georgia Teachers Retirement System), could offer to purchase the outstanding notes and own the property outright.

Secondly, a lease extension makes the property more attractive for potential buyers.

There are too many other things on the authority's mind, and the course of action is not pursued, at least not immediately.

The new marina keeps the authority busy, even though it is clear by now that the earmarked or unspent $750K can be used better elsewhere. The funds are still placed in reserve in case the tide turns and a new and soon-to-be-ordered third development study is underway.

Between all the problems and urgencies, there is still some positive news, although it probably gets lost amidst the other turmoil. A new proposal is submitted to lease a portion of the old wharf to open a seafood market. Robert and Barbara Zachry will open their first fish market this year. A doctor's office is being prepared by restoring one of the old cottages on the corner of Pier Road and Old Village Boulevard, later renamed Stable Road. The effort to provide room for a doctor's office on the island is not the first one. Earlier in 1970, the authority proposed to rezone a small portion on the west side of Beachview Drive to allow residential homes to be used as doctors' offices. The rezoning was never officially approved.

The highway patrol occupies the building on the northeast corner of Riverview Drive and Jekyll Parkway. And if such is not enough for good news in bad times, the Counsel of the Arts donates $200K to renovate and restore the Maurice house, which spurs the authority to further allocate $375K to match a federal grant, received to continue the Old Village restoration project. The pier at Clam Creek also gets a welcome addition when the authority authorizes W. M. Smith to open a tackle and bait shop. After all, now that fishing off the pier seems to be picking up since riprap has been installed underneath to dramatically slow down the current, it makes sense to open a small store. Little did the authority realize that the placement of riprap would increase the current between the pier and the northern shoreline, thereby resulting in increased erosion that would later have to be addressed accordingly.

Overall, it seems that because of complicated times on the resort side of the island, the state park side seems to get much-needed attention, as if the authority is trying to compensate the loss of revenue on one side with investments on the other, while hoping that in the end all things will equal out perfectly.

It is wishful thinking, and a new ordinance proposal the next year will be counterintuitive to that end.

On January 12, 1976, Glynn County imposes a 3 percent hotel/motel tax, and the authority issues an ordinance for the collection of such:

> An Ordinance providing for the Imposition, Levy and Collection of a tax upon the furnishing for value to the public of any room or rooms, lodging, or accommodations on Jekyll Island; and for other purposes, was presented and discussed. Mr. Tanner moved that the Ordinance be approved and adopted as presented and that it become effective on April 1, 1976 …
>
> … that the Ordinance be approved and adopted as presented …

The island has always been fairly excluded and exempt from any county taxes up until now. The collection of the 3 percent hotel/motel tax was made possible by a change in state legislation that allowed individual counties or government entities to impose and collect such excise tax to fund specific county or local projects. Several hotel/motel owners and operators disagree with the new tax imposition, claiming that the extra cost will hurt their business financially.

Whether the new tax had a direct or indirect impact on an already difficult tourist climate remains unknown. If there was an impact, it was certainly minimal in comparison to the other financial difficulties the hotels experienced.

In 1976, the amphitheater attracts a new lessee as Florida State University is willing to hold summer programs. The authority agrees to subsidize the Jekyll Island Musical Theatre, as it is known, with a $10K annual grant to offset production costs.

The authority also issues an ordinance pertaining to the organization of all festivals, shows, and flea markets on the island. Only the authority can organize and hold such events on the island. Whether this ordinance has a financial revenue motivation behind it is doubtful. The need to control events such as the Annual Beach Music Festival[213] is probably the motivation behind the decision. Events that attract large crowds often get out of control and result in frequent complaints from residents and tourists alike. Another train of thought may obviously be that it sets the stage for future permitting by the authority to hold or organize any event that generates revenue for the organizers, thereby controlling some of the income.

The old marina that now features a seafood market needs renovation, and while new pilings are installed,[214] the old wharf is closed to the public, except for the market. The new marina, on the other hand, continues to draw attention. Another new study is ordered, this time to review the economic analysis. While the fourth consecutive study is ongoing, Aquaculture Systems Inc. receives a lease on the saltwater basin of the new marina.

It is not documented anywhere what the purpose is of the new company or why it receives a permit to lease the saltwater basin other than it can install a 560-foot-long bulkhead that is twelve inches wide. The company specializes in treatment of wastewater, and since a portion of the new marina site was used as a wastewater depository prior to the installation of a water treatment plant on the island, it is believed that the company was

---

[213] The Annual Beach Music Festival drew 25,000 people to the beaches of Jekyll Island. It was held at Great Dunes adjacent to the old Convention Center.
[214] New pilings were installed in April 1976 at a cost of $60,000.

hired to clean up and prepare the basin for future usage other than the intended luxury marina and boat basin.

It was very common for wastewater to be disposed of in certain areas of the island. When the Holiday Inn Beach Resort was constructed, it received permission from the authority to build a wastewater drain pipe underneath Beachview Drive to the middle of the island for disposal. Whatever the reason or specific function of the contract may be, the authority is more focused on the whirlwind of requests and changes to hotel properties, and it all happens at a very fast pace.

The owner of the Holiday Inn Beach Resort, Penmoco Inc., sells a 50 percent stake to Servico Inc. Such is concerning news, if it were not that again a hotel owner reduces its financial exposure on Jekyll Island and follows in the footsteps of the Seafarer Motel and Jekyll Estates Motel.

By-the-Sea Hotel is already delinquent on its security deposit, and the authority is forced to accept escrow from the Atlanta Title Company to offset the risk and to prevent the owners from being in default of the lease agreement.

If the above is not enough to raise eyebrows or increase the concern about the financial health of the Jekyll Island hotels in general, add into the mix that both the Corsair Motel and the Atlantic Carriage Inn change ownership. The Corsair Motel becomes the property of Corsair Properties, clearly a new separate legal entity to transfer financial risk from owners to a third-party entity with limited liability, and Golden Isles Innkeepers become the new owners of the Atlantic Carriage Inn.

To make matters worse, both hotels are also in default on payments of their promissory notes and face possible foreclosure in September 1976. The fact that the Georgia Teachers Retirement System originally financed both hotels makes things even more complex and complicated.

The trend of changing ownerships and transferring the financial liability and risk of motels to subsidiaries or other legal entities with limited liability status (i.e., limited liability companies or partnerships) is prevalent during these last few years. It was and still is a common practice to limit potential exposure, but the fact that most of the motels on the island resort to the same tactic and approach should have been worrisome. The authority simply approves the change in ownership and transfer of leasehold estates without much discussion.

From Millionaires to Commoners

Instead, the authority now seriously considers other options that may be available to stem the tide or to take advantage of an opportunity.

Those discussions bring up the question about whether the authority should purchase the outstanding mortgage from the public pension plan and issue general obligation bonds or notes of its own to finance the purchase. The idea seems farfetched for any state authority to even consider, but the proposal is discussed seriously and at length during regular board meetings[215].

A first attempt is made to allow the owners to correct the payment deficiencies, which only serves as a temporary band-aid and is never considered to be a permanent solution. Ultimately, the authority decides to withdraw any offer of postponement or waivers to allow both hotels to go into foreclosure.

Jekyll Estates Motel is not faring any better when the new owners, Citizens & Southern Realty Investors, transfer the leasehold estate to First Boston Jekyll Inc.

And things don't stop there; a fourth hotel and leasehold estate, this time By-the-Sea Hotel, is transferred to First Boston by the Sea Inc.

The fact that two out of the four troubled hotel properties are now in the hands of First Boston gives the authority some breathing room and time to handle the complex issues that surround the Corsair and the Atlantic Carriage Inn. A special committee is formed to make proposals on how to manage and operate both hotels, pending a public sale or foreclosure, and consists of Mr. Wiggins, Mr. Tanner, and Mr. Nixon, the new state auditor who replaces Mr. Ernest Davis after his resignation.[216]

The tax lien on the Atlantic Carriage Inn is the easiest problem to tackle, and the authority agrees to pay half of the tax liability, with other half paid by the Georgia Teachers Retirement System. This now allows the authority to operate the motel and negotiate terms and conditions with any party interested in managing the property until a buyer can be found. The title of the property is cleared for such purpose, but the authority is not considered the rightful owner. Full ownership now rests with the public

---

[215] Board meeting of July 20, 1976.
[216] Ernest Davis resigned as state auditor on May 28, 1976. William Nixon succeeds Ernest Davis as state auditor, while Joe Tanner assumes the responsibilities as secretary/treasurer of the authority.

pension plan, while the authority retains rights as lessor. Motel Properties Inc., already owner and operator of the Buccaneer Motor Lodge and Jekyll Estates,[217] proposes to manage the Atlantic Carriage Inn. This will give the company control of more than a third of the available guest rooms on the island, and while the proposition is frowned upon, it seems the authority has no choice but to accept the offer, at least for the immediate future.

The Atlantic Carriage Inn would become a title case in Glynn County Superior Court a year later and would not be resolved until the end of 1978. The encumbered title does not prohibit the authority from assigning a management company, but it does prohibit any sale or new leasehold estate assignment, thereby creating an uncertain future from a long-term revenue perspective.

The Corsair, officially owned by Corsair Properties, is handled slightly different by the authority. The hotel assigned the deed to secure debt, a requirement of the leasehold estate, Article XIII, paragraph 7, and Article V, Section 5.02, from its mortgage company to the Georgia Teachers Retirement System. The authority outright purchases the deed, cancels such so that it can reissue a new deed to secure debt with Sea Oats Inc., who is to become the new owner/operator of the hotel. A complex transaction that obviously involves the purchase of outstanding notes from the public retirement system and in effect makes the authority the legal owner of the property, albeit for a very short time.

Ultimately, the proposed deal with Sea Oats Inc. does not materialize, and negotiations with any interested party resume shortly afterward.[218]

While it seems that at least three out of the four hotels have been stabilized to a certain extent, another issue pops up with Mr. Larry Morris and the Sand Dollar Apartments. This time the authority takes the ongoing matter so seriously that an entire board meeting is needed to clarify the chain of events, the motions, and the proposed resolutions required to end the long-standing disagreement.

---

[217] First Boston Jekyll Inc., as the new leasehold estate owner, transferred management responsibility of Jekyll Estates to Motel properties Inc.

[218] Harold Zell represented Sea Oats Inc. during the negotiations. The terms indicated a forty-year lease of the Corsair with a $10,000 earnest money payment. Negotiations were halted on June 30, 1977, for both the Corsair and the Atlantic Carriage Inn (authority board meeting minutes, June 30, 1977).

Board meeting October 3, 1977:

> The member discussed Mr. Larry Morris' request to convert the Sand Dollar Motel to condominiums. Mr. Bolton made the following motions:
> Move that the Authority reject the August 3, 1977 proposal by Larry C. Morris for the staged condominium conversion of the Sand Dollar Motel property and further move to reject said August 3, 1977 proposal as supplemented by letter of September 28, 1977 from Larry C. Morris to the members of the Jekyll Island-State Park Authority.
> Move that the Authority reaffirm its position with respect to the October 22, 1976 assignment by Larry C. Morris to Sand Dollar Ltd., a limited partnership, of all his rights, title and interest in that certain April 27, 1971 Lease Agreement, as amended, by and between the Authority and Larry C. Morris ...

Mr. Morris has attempted on several occasions to either sell the Sand Dollar Motel outright or to sell individual portions of the property to multiple limited liability partnerships, neither one of which received written and express consent from the authority. Now that other hotels are in perilous or insecure financial situations, it is not a surprise that the authority takes this matter very seriously and enforces the terms and conditions of the original 1971 lease agreement.

But the meeting continues with several very specific motions:

> Move that the Authority declare the following defaults of the April 27, 1971 Lease Agreement between the Jekyll Island-State Park Authority, Lessor, and Larry C. Morris, Lessee ...
> ... Default by reason of failure to pay installment of ground rental due August 27, 1977 in the amount of $3,077.43 ...

> ... Default by reason of failure to report gross income for the calendar months of July 1977 and August 1977 ...
>
> ... Default by reason of failure to pay percentage rental due with respect to the lessee's gross income for the months of July 1977 and August 1977 ...
>
> ... Failure to report and to pay the hotel-motel tax collected for the months of July 1977 and August 1977 ...
>
> ... Default by reason of failure to pay late charges with respect to payments due in the months of March, May and June 1977 ...

The most interesting part of the meeting is yet to begin, and this portion explains in detail what the exact relationship is between the lessor, the authority, the lessee, in this case Larry C. Morris, and the mortgage holder, the Georgia Teachers Retirement System.

> ...Move to confirm the election of the Authority made at a duly called meeting on June 30, 1977 to decline to exercise its option to purchase the note and to receive assignment of the deed to secure debt and security agreement given by the lessee to the Teachers Retirement System of Georgia ...
>
> Move that the Authority hereby decline to exercise the aforesaid option, which option currently vests in the Authority as a result of the notification by the Teachers Retirement System of Georgia of the lessee's default in the performance of the terms and conditions of the aforesaid note and deed to secure debt and security agreement ...

The authority clearly has the right to exercise the option to purchase the outstanding notes if and when the lessee defaults on its mortgage payments. It has no obligation to do so, but it can exercise its right, upon which the authority receives the deed to secure debt and security agreement of the property in question.

In the case of Larry C. Morris and the Sand Dollar Motel, this option is not exercised, without any specific reason, but such option was indeed exercised in the case of the Corsair. There is no indication why the authority's decision and strategy differ from one property to another, unless the authority envisioned that part of the island would ultimately become condominium apartments over time. After all, First National Bank of Boston now owns the By- the-Sea Motel, recently franchised with Sheraton Hotels, and is planning expansion and additions to the property. It would still take a few more years before the condominium-hotel concept found solid footing on the island, but the authority's guess and decision to stay out of the condominium market may have been the correct one.

Immediately following the lengthy board meeting, Sand Dollar Ltd., theoretically the owner of the Sand Dollar Motel, files for bankruptcy protection under Chapter VII of the Bankruptcy Act, and by year-end, the Teachers Retirement System of Georgia has commenced foreclosure proceedings on the Sand Dollar Motel. All the past due rents, percentage of gross income, and hotel-motel taxes remain unpaid and past due.

It is a turbulent year for the resort community of the island and one that will continue for the near future, but that is not all that bothers and worries the authority. The Environmental Protection Department, nowadays simply called the EPA, orders the authority to begin an Environmental Protection Improvement Plan that will cost approximately $5 million.

It is no coincidence that the Department of Natural Resources takes over the operation and management of Jekyll Island at around the same time, despite that fact that the appropriate legislation was enacted in 1972 (Ga. L. 1972, p. 1015-Act No. 1489) but is only confirmed in 1977 after a study conducted by the authority.

The sudden EPD intervention may come as a surprise to the authority, but it also presents an opportunity, albeit not immediately visible to outsiders. Giving management control to the DNR accomplishes two things for the authority. It ensures that the Environmental Protection Improvement Plan is completely managed by the DNR, giving the authority the time and resources to focus on other important issues. Secondly, it now allows the authority to borrow funds from the DNR that can be used for other purposes, as we shall see later.

The $1 million appropriation will play an important role in the acquisition of two island motels and the subsequent restoration of the Historic District in 1986 (see chapter 10).

Sen. Ballard requests the general assembly for supplemental funding since the fiscal year 1978 budget was already $1MM over budget.[219]

---

[219] The General Assembly Supplemental Appropriations Act of 1979, page 270, Section 33 (Department of Natural Resources) states: "Payments from the Department of Natural Resources to Jekyll Island: $1,290,000.00. Provided further, it is the intent of this General Assembly that of the above appropriation related to Payments to Jekyll Island - State Park Authority, said Authority shall repay the State $1,000,000 in principal over a period of no more than 20 years, said payments to begin in Fiscal 1981."

CHAPTER 9

AN ISLAND AT CROSSROADS

1978–1984

The last two years have been chaotic to say the least, but the rapid expansion and development of the 1960s is taking its toll on the island. Barely twenty years after the first hotel was constructed on the island, followed by rapid growth in the hotel and motel industry, we now see a continued decline and deterioration of financial conditions with all the consequences that ensue.

It is not necessarily the speed by which hotel accommodations were built during the short period; maybe it is the financial foundation and the securitization of future revenue that causes the slow but undeniable collapse of the resort side of the island. The entire commercial infrastructure is built and subsidized to a certain extent by a public pension plan or by the issuance of either revenue certificates or general obligation bonds, both of which are collateralized by the identical future revenue stream. That is a risky investment that is subject to even the smallest economic downturn and not financially sustainable when the tide turns, be it even for a short period of time.

But that is not the case here. The prevailing economic circumstances are not of short duration, yet neither the authority nor the mortgagee or financing institutions are making efforts to rebuild the foundation and secure longevity once the inflationary/deflationary pressures ease, whenever such may be. It seems that every effort is made to try to keep the pieces together as best as possible by using the same approach that failed previously. Hotel properties fail financially, change title, get reassigned through leasehold estates, in and outside of the courtrooms, change owners and operators, yet nothing changes that will ultimately secure the initial investment and subsequent revenue stream.

The approach in general is one of applying multiple band-aids to stop the hemorrhaging, while everyone knows the patient is dying not because of multiple bleeds but because no one is able or willing to recognize and accept the diagnosis.

The result is that the authority, and hence Jekyll Island, continues to peddle through the crisis at hand to safeguard as much revenue as possible but without a vision to secure the stability of the island's future. There is certainly no lack of plans and ideas, but neither one is sparked and inspired by an overall long-term vision, even though over the prior twenty-year period two large-scale development plans and land-use plans have been in existence.

The problem with both development plans, besides the lack of vision, is the focus on the invisible barrier between resort and state park, and the protective approach of the 65/35 development rule. While neither one is deemed detrimental or unimportant, the narrow focus excludes the financial foundation that is necessary to derive enough revenue from the minority commercial development to finance the maintenance of the other. After all, if Jekyll Island State Park is mandated to be or become self-sufficient, then one would expect each development plan to also focus on and include a financial plan that would ultimately become part of the long-term vision and strategy.

Given that the island, and the authority, is at a clear crossroad in its short existence, one would have expected such a plan to be considered or submitted.[220] At no time is such an idea or proposal brought forward, and every decision is made as a stand-alone solution to the problem at hand without consideration of the overall picture or situation.

An economic downturn does require immediate and drastic action, but it also provides an opportunity to rethink the existing long-term strategy so

---

[220] A clear example can be found in the continued deterioration of the Jekyll Island Hotel that has been sitting idle, empty, and boarded up since late 1971 because of the oceanside resort construction boom. Now that the resort side faces economic and financial challenges, an integrated plan or vision continues to be missing.

that the financial landscape is better protected with a solid foundation that can more easily weather another storm and can create flexibility for the financial investment that is built on top. This can be compared to a shock absorber that allows the building to sway but never breaks and crumbles during an earthquake.

The authority missed the opportunity during this crisis and simply chose to sit out the storm, hoping that new owners/operators and in some cases new financiers would be the new and improved permanent solution.

The first order of business is to secure the continued operation of the Sand Dollar Motel. With the owner, Sand Dollar Ltd., under Chapter 7 of its bankruptcy filing, the Teachers Retirement System of Georgia, as mortgagee, appoints the Otter Corp. to temporarily manage the motel. Since the authority did not exercise its option to purchase the outstanding notes, any decision pertaining to the property is the sole responsibility of the mortgage holder, and the authority can only enforce lease payments and determine the percentage of gross income as provided by the lease agreement.

To that effect, the Teachers Retirement System of Georgia offers to pay all outstanding lease payments for a total of $16,066.84 to the authority in exchange for approval of its design and construction plans. The plans, as submitted by Mr. W. R. Heflin, mortgage supervisor, propose to convert the forty-eight three-bedroom apartments into 192 one-bedroom motel rooms, to renovate the administrative building, and to add a building for youth activities. The plans are approved, and the Sand Dollar receives a seven-year lease extension until 2018[221] in return, with an additional ten-year renewal until 2028.

The reason for the simultaneous lease extension and additional renewal option is important. The property has only twenty-three years left on its original lease, which is not sufficiently long for any potential buyer to secure financing, hence the odd number of years added to the lease extension for a total of thirty years. That duration is adequate and in line with the standard requirement of any mortgage company. The lease renewal option for another ten years adds another layer of security. One year later, the Sand Dollar Motel would become the Jekyll Hilton Inn for that exact reason.

---

[221] The original lease agreement of 1971 was set to expire in 2011.

The Corsair is a different case. Since the authority cleared the deed to secure debt and security agreement the previous year, it is authorized to lease the property to any interested party. Two proposals are received in February 1978. One is submitted by Mr. Wayne Morrow, owner of Morrow Leisure-time Investments Inc., and a second by Mr. Mark Smith of Our Place at the Beach. Mr. Morrow is certainly no stranger to Jekyll Island. After all, he has been in business since 1957 when he opened the first camping ground, Cherokee Campground, on the island. The lease is ultimately assigned to Mark Smith in March 1978 but only temporarily, as the property will change owners again in 1980.

There is no accurate reason given in any of the archived documents for not considering Mr. Morrow's proposal. One would think that with his expertise and familiarity of the island, he would be a suitable candidate to own or operate the Corsair. An explanation can probably be found in Mr. Morrow's involvement in multiple business ventures besides the Cherokee Campground. He also operates the liquor store on the island and presides over the Jekyll Island Promotional Association, the new and improved JI Resort Motel Association from the early days. His association is partially funded by its hotel-motel members but also subsidized by the authority. A possible conflict of interest or his multiple business interests on the island may have been the reason for the authority to select the other proposal.

The other hotel on the brink is the Atlantic Carriage Inn, which is still in litigation, and the title case will not be resolved until the end of the year.

With the most urgent business issues taken care of, at least for the time being, the authority focuses on managing the other side of the island to try to stabilize the state park.

The amphitheater, now under the leadership of Richard Fallon of Florida State University since 1976, continues to struggle with attendance despite an annual diverse offering of musicals. Like previous years, the authority decides to keep the annual grants intact for the 1978 season. The cost of keeping the musical program alive is now rising to $21K per year, with little or no revenue to offset the cost, but at least the Jekyll Island Music Theatre is secure for the next two years.

The Old Village, also referred to as the Jekyll Club Village, once the underdog in development plans and certainly lacking attention, given that the main Club Hotel has been closed and partially boarded up since late

1971, gets renewed attention. The restoration efforts of the cottages in the previous year get the attention of Ms. Carolyn Pitts, architectural historian for the National Register and Historic Landmark Division of the National Park Service. The hope is that the Club Village can be recognized as a national landmark, like the Club Hotel that was included in the National Register of Historic Landmarks in 1972. The village receives its Historic Landmark designation in July 1978.

Not everything on the island goes as smoothly, and just as one problem is solved, another takes its place. This time, the problems pertain to both the old and the new marina. The old wharf, which now houses a seafood restaurant, needs further repair of the old pilings to sustain the continued operation of the restaurant and the foot traffic it brings with it. The previous $110K piling project requires another $25K investment, and with it comes a new three-year lease for the Marina Seafood Market and the approval to expand once construction is finished.

David and Barbara Zachry operate the restaurant and later expand their operations to include a shrimp-packaging business next door.[222]

The new marina that has so far absorbed $1,175,000 without any clear progress or practical use continues to draw someone's attention every so often. This time it is Mr. Anderson, the island's operations manager, who presents a preliminary conceptual plan for the development of a new marina in a different location and smaller in size.

"The first phase will have facilities to berth 60 boats, a store, laundry and restrooms, fuel pier, small boat facilities, ramp and docks and dry storage area. Approximately 100,000 cubic yards of silt will have to be removed from the present basin ..." (board meeting minutes, May 22, 1978). No motion is made to approve the plan, but a cost analysis of annual siltation rates is ordered instead.

While the conceptual new marina may not be at the preferred location and may not be as luxurious as the authority had envisioned eleven years earlier, at least the island can have a functional marina near the old wharf but on the south side of the drawbridge. The intent is to direct some of the boat traffic away from the wharf so that the historic boat ramp can be used for other tourist-friendly attractions.

---

[222] Latitude 31 and the Rah Bar would occupy this space. It is currently the new home of the Wharf Restaurant.

Amid all the turmoil and projects, one would think that one stabilizing factor would be the authority itself. How else can stability be achieved on an island that is undergoing so many changes and faces so many uncertainties? That is not to be the case, as George Busbee, in his second term as Georgia governor, appoints Mr. Whitfield Forrester, Mr. Sam A. Williams, and Mr. J. William Weltch to join the authority as board members, bringing the total to seven members. The face of the authority has now changed dramatically midyear, with only two familiar names remaining in August 1978 and five new members joining the new authority. This does not mark the first time the composition of the authority changes, but it marks the first time since 1957 that the governor appoints nonpoliticians[223]. Ben Fortson, in his capacity as secretary of state, and Joe Tanner as DNR commissioner are the only two that remain. Mr. Zell Miller, lieutenant governor, and Mr. Donald Gammon now also join the authority in addition to the three governor appointees.

The regular meetings are now also attended by Mr. Anderson, as island operations manager, and Mrs. Neill as the authority's assistant secretary-treasurer, in addition to legal counsel as represented by the new attorney general, Mr. Verley Spivey, and his assistant Daniel Formby.

The change in format and formality, specifically the presence of the island's manager, is notable given the change that will happen at the next meeting.

In September 1978, the authority approves the appointment of an executive director for Jekyll Island and expresses the need for an Executive Committee that will consist of the chair, vice-chair, and secretary-treasurer. The first task of the new committee is to study the existing bylaws and make recommendations for changes, updates, or inclusions. The authority also selects Korn-Ferry Int'l, an Atlanta-based management consulting firm, to search and recruit an executive director within sixty to ninety days.

It seems clear that the new authority envisions a different management approach for Jekyll Island, which is not surprising given the continued but mostly invisible struggle between the resort concept and development,

---

[223] The first authority board members were selected at-large and did not hold political office in the state of Georgia. The second authority, selected in 1957, was composed of state politicians, whose term on the board was directly linked to their terms in office.

and the state park environment. To that effect, a separation of duties between the authority or the board itself and the soon-to-be Executive Committee seems logical. The former can handle any policy issues and provide advisory functions overall, while the latter can be tasked with the day-to-day operational issues at hand. It is not the first time that concrete steps are being taken to modify the management structure and morph it into a typical municipal structure of council-manager model, a popular government structure typically found in smaller municipalities or cities.[224]

By November, Mr. Robert S. Case[225] is appointed as the island's first executive director and as anticipated attends the Executive Committee meetings. New bylaws stipulate the specific powers vested in the executive director and the Executive Committee, clearing the way for a new management model for the island.

While Mr. Case is not the first director or operational manager that oversees and coordinates the day-to-day island operations, he is the first to be appointed as an executive director.[226]

An interesting side note, and based on personal stories from island residents, is that each new director or manager brings with him a personal preference for a specific color that is to be used on all the authority's equipment, including vehicles, benches, and even public garbage bins.

Mr. Horace Caldwell introduced the island to pastel colors, while Mr. Anderson preferred sky blue all over the island. Mr. Robert Case is certainly no exception to this "executive" tradition. He orders all island equipment to be painted white.

Just imagine that every few years, all the equipment and public benches or garbage bins across the island are repainted in a different color scheme based on the personal preference of the executive director. Not only does it require an unimaginable amount of man-hours to complete this task, but the financial impact on the budget cannot be underestimated either.

---

[224] A similar approach was implemented in 1967 with the appointment of Hoke Smith as island director.
[225] Mr. Case previously worked on Hilton Head Island and had been instrumental in the development and marketing of Sea Pines Plantation.
[226] Mr. Horace Caldwell was the island director, while Mr. Robert Anderson took on the role of operations manager.

The first order of business for Mr. Case is to review the lease agreement with Morrison Food Services. The company was placed on notice earlier in the year, and its lease was renewed on a month-to-month basis due to a dispute about percentage payments due to the authority. The lease agreement is now terminated, and the cafeteria and the kitchen at the convention center are temporarily closed until a new provider can be contracted. The JI Promotion Association, and Wayne Morrow, does not hesitate to fill the void in the convention center and offers to serve alcoholic beverages until a new food and beverage provider can be found and the liquor license can be transferred. The move seems logical since Mr. Morrow, through the Promotion Association, already owns the island's liquor store, so the offer to temporarily fill a void seems innocent.

Mr. Case also ensures that the required Environmental Improvement Project, as mandated by the EPD in 1977, gets underway before the end of the year. For that purpose, Bonds-Series 1975, as appropriated from the general assembly in the same manner as the 1971 and 1973 Series, is being used together with remaining funds from Bonds-Series 1972 and a federal grant of $1,126,000. Funding oversight of the project is now placed in the hands of the Georgia Finance and Investment Commission, which acts as an intermediary between the general assembly and the authority and secures future funding for the JISPA-project as well as the Environmental Improvement Plan.

As per an April 16, 1979, memo to Robert Case, the total project is estimated at $3,746,372.56 for the construction cost alone. An additional $650,456.80 is needed to cover engineering and service expenses, $209,154 for equipment purchases, and $186,198 for incinerator repairs, bringing the total estimate at $4,792,181.56.

The construction contracts are awarded to Lynch Construction Company of Savannah, Georgia; John Taylor Inc. of Statham, Georgia; Eastern Tank Service of Lannett, Alabama; with the largest contract of almost $3 million being awarded to Ethridge Construction Company of Gray, Georgia.

For that purpose, and with the authority's request to reorganize the JIA staff, Mr. Case wastes no time to recruit Ray McCadden as director of development services and Charles Skypek as director of finances. The first step toward the long-envisioned and desired municipal structure is now clearly made. Before the year ends, the Executive Committee will add another member to the structure by creating a position as director of Tourist and Convention Development Department, for which Robert Henry is hired in October 1979. That raises the question of what Mr. Robert Anderson, operations manager, will do and where he fits into the new structure. He is not the only one whose job is subject to change. There is also Mr. W. T. Sanders, who oversees all the authority's food and beverage business on the island after Morrison Food Services is placed on notice, or rather terminated, pending a new and improved plan.

Robert Anderson resigns in March 1979, around the same time Mr. Sanders retires as director of food services. Like the several shake-ups within the authority over the past twenty years, a shake-up within the brand-new municipal structure does not come as a surprise, but the rapid overhaul of an executive structure that is barely in existence for six months is certainly notable and maybe questionable.

Mr. Sanders's "retirement" happens to coincide with the appointment of Domco Food Services Inc. to manage and oversee all food operations on Jekyll Island, including all beach and picnic concession stands, the cafeteria in the shopping center, the convention center, the Sandwich Hut, previously the Charcoal House Restaurant, the golf club, and the marina snack areas. Domco Food Services may be a new face on the island, but placing all food services with one service provider is certainly not new to Jekyll Island. After all, the same monopoly existed in the mid-1950s when the JI Hotel Corporation and Sen. Dykes operated all the food stands on the island. It is also reminiscent of the Albert Crews years in the sixties and early seventies, and the recently terminated Morrison Food Services.

The restructuring does not stop there. Despite the addition of three directors, all of whom report directly to Robert Case, Mr. Donald Cheeks is hired as planning consultant to outline a plan for the use of the Old Village, now recognized as a National Historic Landmark. This is not the first attempt to revitalize the Historic District, but maybe this time the focus and intent are more geared toward the future of the Club Hotel and its adjacent properties, such as the Annex and the Sans Souci that have been sitting idle for the past eight years. Whatever the intent may have been, any daily use of any of the cottages or useable historic buildings is a plus at this juncture.

So far, only Villa Ospo has been put to good use—first with the Scarboro family, who opened their home to the public and displayed their extensive art collection, and now recently since 1976 with Mrs. Mary Miller, who operates the Doll Museum and attracts more than just a few curious visitors and tourists. Mistletoe Cottage has been well maintained since the 1950s and has been occupied for a few years by the JI Promotional Association, but that will change soon, as they are being asked to move their operations to the convention center instead.

Somehow the authority or maybe Robert Case himself sees a future use for the Historic District in the way of creating attractions for visitors. That would explain why Mr. Stauffer receives permission to open an antique car museum in the old power plant building, now the Georgia State Turtle Center.

Mr. Stauffer is an avid antique car collector and known for his restoration work. One of his most famous restorations was a 1933 Chevrolet Tourer, which is still in existence today and is the only one known to exist in the US.[227] Besides his restoration work, Glenn Stauffer displays Cadillacs and Roadsters in his car museum for all to see. And many do, as the museum becomes a tourist attraction once it opens its doors with great fanfare in March 1980.

It also creates an opportunity for Mrs. D. L. Hampel, director of Tamaloa Communion Center and a resident at St. Andrews Beach, to request the use of a building in the Historic District to create a performing arts center. The response from Mr. Case is less than accommodating, as he clearly sees no use for such activity in the old village and instead offers the use of the Hartley Auditorium at the convention center, much to the dislike of Mrs. Hampel, as her response on May 1, 1979 shows:

---

[227] Bill Staley owns the 1933 Chevrolet Tourer (Egyptianantiqueautomobileclub.com).

Tamaloa Communion Center
17 Saint Andrews Drive
Jekyll island, Georgia 31520

Dear Mr. Case,

As you very well know, we did not request use of the Hartley Auditorium. We requested facilities in the village but as a means of hinderance, you dictated the Hartley Auditorium as you knew it is not suitable for our needs …

… the Authority should jump at the opportunity to encourage young talented persons.

We should like to be respectfully submit this proposition:

Build a performing arts center.

Support (with money) the arts and people who are devoted to the pursuit of creative excellence.

Support with dedication and admiration those who strive to bring grace and harmony into our lives.

Very truly,

D.L. Hampel
Director

It is obvious that neither Mr. Case nor the authority has an interest in allowing the use of the Historic District for the performing arts, probably because the JI Music Theatre does not have the desired attendance at the amphitheater. Neither correspondence mentions the Gould Auditorium as a desired or available venue, although the actors and crew of Florida State University use such occasionally.

One idea that seems to fit and warrants the use of the Historic District is the location of the Jekyll Island Authority, its increasing staff, and certainly its executive members. Mr. Case relocates the existing authority staff from Villa Marianna to the Crane cottage.

One of the local stories of that time is that Mr. Case was known to adorn his personal car with two Jekyll Island flags on each side of the front of his luxurious car, similar to the presidential limousine, and would park his car right in front of the main entrance to Crane cottage for all to see, as if to announce that the island director was in the building and presiding over his staff. His sense for flair isn't really a surprise to any of the residents, given his earlier background as a stage performer in Las Vegas. It is also this attribute that leads to the creation of the *Jekyll Island Gazette,* the official publication of the Jekyll Island State Park Authority.[228] The other side of the coin is that it lands the authority in some troubled waters later that leads to several lawsuits being filed for discrimination and sexual harassment.[229]

But the new wave of future development is not just limited to the Historic District, as the island seems to go through yet another phase of rethinking the previous land-use and development plans for the entire island.

Mr. Lowell Evjen, director of the Office of Planning and Budget, orders a new request for proposal for the development study of Jekyll Island, the fourth of its kind in barely thirty years. The RFP is comprised of four major focal points:

- the local services provided to residents
- the internal organization of the JIA
- the internal management reporting
- the marketing and promotion of Jekyll Island

It seems that this time around, the sole focus is really on the authority itself, its structure and management, rather than true development plans.

The interesting notion here is that there is a first attempt to define the responsibilities of the authority and its Executive Committee toward the state park with its permanent residents and the municipal services rendered thereto, and the island as a resort community. It further solidifies the attempt to separate typical municipal responsibilities, to be placed within the executive structure, from the advisory capacity of the authority that pertains to promotion, marketing, and development.

---

[228] The *Jekyll Island Gazette* was first issued in April 1979.

[229] All lawsuits filed were settled out of court through mediation or settlement. No case was ever brought to trial.

Pending the outcome, the authority ensures that some commercial leases are secured and offers a twenty-year lease extension to the owners of both IGA Supermarket and Maxwell's Variety Store. The terms and conditions have changed of course, and both pay an annual base rate of $15K and $14K respectively in addition to their 3 percent of gross sales in the case of IGA, and 8 percent for Maxwell's.

But not everyone receives the same treatment. Mr. Wayne Morrow, a well-known figure for many years who has accumulated a multitude of business interests on the island, comes under board scrutiny when he requests permission to rent mopeds, bikes, and scooters through his company Intermarket, which also happens to operate the island's package store. While the request is tabled, the authority looks at how the JI Promotion Association operates, where they receive the funding from, and how expenses are being paid. At the time, all the hotels/motels and the campground pay their annual dues to the association, except for the Sheraton that has started its own advertising campaign since its name change the previous year. The authority itself paid $16K per year as a form of subsidy, but since it has hired Mr. Henry to fulfill that role, the subsidy is terminated. That is not really a surprise.

What is surprising though is that most of the annual expenses, as incurred by the JI Promotion Association, represent payment to Intermarket, the same company Wayne Morrow co-owns. A conflict of interest would almost seem an understatement. The authority takes matters a little bit further and instead of securing the lease agreement for operating the package store, it decides to open the lease for bids. Less than two months later, Wayne Morrow and his JI Promotion Association lose the package store lease to Mr. Bill Bonamie and Mr. Ken Tollison. The new lease guarantees an annual income of $15K for the first year and $24K for the second year in addition to three cents per gallon for alcoholic beverages and six cents for nonalcoholic sales.

Interstate Recreation Co. makes its first appearance at the board meeting in the summer of 1979 with a proposal to build a water-fun park. No specifics are provided, but the idea catches the interest of the authority sufficiently to pursue a proposal in more detail.

Something needs to be done to attract tourists, given the sharp drop in revenue during the summer months. Although 1979 is certainly not the first warning sign of an economic crisis that began almost six years ago, it is the first time the authority is concerned and attributes the drop in visitors to the prevailing gas prices, the weather conditions, and the persistent inflation,[230] although the true economic indicators point toward the complex and new collision of a deflationary-inflationary pressure caused by simultaneous national policies, including the oil embargo, the decoupling of the dollar with the gold standard, and the unexpected consequence of a price-fixing policy.[231]

The good news at the end of the year is that the hotel industry is finding itself in calmer waters, and some of the outstanding issues are being addressed, albeit slowly.

The Atlantic Carriage Inn finally has a free and clear title and therefore can be leased by the authority. A specific investor-operator has not been found yet, but there are at least some prospects. The new JI Hilton[232] is reopening its doors in October, after renovation and adding new buildings. The bad news is that the Corsair is again in trouble, and lease termination for default looms again.

Another difficult and tumultuous year for the authority and the island in general ends in mourning with the passing of longtime authority member Ben Fortson. He passed away on May 19, 1979, and to this day is remembered as the longest-serving secretary of state in Georgia state history. The authority decides by resolution[233] to change the name of the JI Parkway to the Ben Fortson Jr. Memorial Parkway—a fitting tribute to a man who was instrumental in the development of the island while preserving the integrity of Gov. Thompson's vision to create a state park for all Georgians.

Since the Office of Planning and Budget has ordered an in-depth study of the day-to-day management and reporting issues of the authority,

---

[230] Report from Mr. Robert Case to the authority (board meeting, September 24, 1979).

[231] President Nixon's price and wage control, first issued in 1971 by executive order and later extended in 1973, proved to have dire free market consequences by artificially reducing inflation and resulted in uncontrollable price hikes after the 1973 oil embargo.

[232] The Sand Dollar Motel was franchised into the Jekyll Island Hilton Inn in January 1979.

[233] Board resolution dated June 25, 1979.

and the services provided to permanent residents, it seems only appropriate that the authority launches its own request for another comprehensive development plan. The firm of Hammer, Siler, George Associates from Virginia is hired to develop such, based on its experience in urban downtown and waterfront development. The focus of the new study this time around is to provide guidance about the physical development of the island and to recommend opportunities to increase marketing. To complement the development plan and to make the study comprehensive, Mr. Case requests an additional $24K from the authority to conduct a topographical study of the island under the pretext that such study was never done or completed since the inception of Jekyll Island State Park. Historical archives, however, show that two topographical studies were conducted in the fifties and completed by Mr. Miller, resident engineer at the time, in 1955. Nevertheless, a new study is ordered to assist Hammer, Siler, George Associates with their final recommendations.

Pending the outcome and recommendations, Mr. Lowell Evjen presents the findings of the Office of Planning and Budget study,[234] and the results seem to come as a surprise to the authority.

1) If the current service/revenue model is to be continued, the reserve fund will be depleted by 1983. Each residential home costs $284 per year to the authority for municipal services rendered. Each Jekyll Island resident saves $848 per year versus Brunswick residents that receive similar and comparable municipal services.
2) The fire and ambulance service on Jekyll Island, operated by the authority, amounts to an annual cost of $223K. The recommendation is to turn the services over to Glynn County, whereby the authority pays $41,400, commercial businesses pay $79,200, and residents contribute $59,400. The contributions would represent approximately six per mill in county taxes.
3) Water services cause a $219K shortfall per year for the authority. The cost of operating the new municipal water and sewage system is $318,000, while the collected revenue is only $99,000. If the operating costs must be covered, then such can only be achieved by increasing the current service charge by 320 percent.

---

[234] Presented to the authority at a board meeting on July 28, 1980.

4) The municipal sewage system operates at an annual loss of $317,000. The cost to the authority is $371,000 per year, while the revenue is only $54,000. Should the authority wish to break even for this service, then rates will have to be increased by 690 percent. The study proposes a monthly water rate of $10 instead of the current $8.80 every two months, and a monthly sewage charge of $12.50 to replace the current charge of $5 per month.
5) The annual cost for refuse services is estimated at $252,000. Rates will have to be raised from $4 per month to $7, and trash collection will cost $6.85 per month instead of the current $3 monthly charge to recover the operating cost. The rates are applicable for residential services only. Commercial rates will have to increase to $158 per dumpster.

If all the proposed rate changes are implemented, the expected deficit will disappear. That is the conclusion of the Office of Planning and Budget. The approach, the recommendations, and the conclusion of the study are noteworthy here for multiple reasons.

The study assumes that all municipal services must be rendered at a cost that is fully reimbursable by its users, an approach that is logical for any stand-alone municipality but seems out of context and not applicable to an island that both services a small municipality while at the same time operates as an income-generating resort. The explanation for this approach can only be found in the original mandate given to the authority that Jekyll Island State Park must be self-sufficient. If such is the case, then the recommendations do not consider the use of resort revenue to supplement the cost of operating the state park, unless the residential municipality (i.e., the permanent residents) are not considered to be part of the state park and are viewed as a stand-alone entity that receives neither the benefit of supplemental revenue nor access to income-generating business ventures on the same island.

Secondly, the study views the authority and all its buildings and operating ventures as an entity that should receive free services from its own municipal infrastructure. If the residential communities are to pay for services rendered, the authority itself would be considered a user and entity of its own and therefore pay its fair share of said services.

Neither one of these comments can be found in the final recommendations of the report, and implementation of the proposed approach to simply fix the budget shortfall will prove to be a difficult task.

Things are changing, and the looming budget deficit for the upcoming fiscal years results in the announcement that the authority will hold its very first town hall meeting that will later lead to open board meetings, although residents will continue to be prohibited from attending any Executive Committee meetings. When the authority announces that it is amending its 1972 resolution that imposes a tap-in fee for all residents to use the municipal water system from $100 to $600, the opposition is heard during the town hall meeting.

Joe Kaylor, president of the Jekyll Island Citizens Association, protests the newly imposed tap-in fee and instead proposes that the project cost be amortized over a reasonable period of time rather than being passed on to its customers at once. He further states that the taxpayers (i.e., the island's residents) are already paying for the bond amortizations since the water and sewage project was financed through several subordinate bond issues, namely 1971, 1973, and 1975. The authority's defense at the meeting is that additional state funds are no longer available due to the imposition of self-sustainability and that the construction cost must be recovered through service fees such as the one-time tap-in fee.

But the authority also has other ideas, besides the service fee hikes, to raise additional revenue. When Chairman Weltch introduces state Representative John W. Greer to the authority during a regular board meeting, this is what he recommends:

> Mr. Greer urged the Authority to request funds from the Legislature to provide more amenities on Jekyll Island to make it more enjoyable for the people of the State of Georgia. He stated that he saw a strong need for an entrance fee to Jekyll Island and suggested that the fee be kept to a minimum of 50 cents so that it would be a source of revenue for Jekyll Island, but would not hinder people from visiting the island. Mr. Greer also stated that the decision to put the Jekyll Island Fire Department under Glynn County control should be studied very closely

> before any action is taken. He felt that higher taxes for the residents of Jekyll would result from this action ...

If the above statement is any indication, it is clear that the authority still has access to state funds if they so desire. Mr. Greer is also the first one to go on record as referring to some sort of entrance fee[235] for the island and the use thereof as additional revenue for the authority. Previously, all efforts were made to lift all tolls on both the Sydney Lanier Bridge and the Jekyll Creek Bridge to allow free access to all Georgians and tourists, but such may change soon. For the time being, no decision on entrance fees or any other fee imposition can be made without the consent and approval of the general assembly.

While the authority struggles through major upcoming changes in policy and reporting, it is faced with another new problem. Two ex-employees, Mrs. Renew and Mrs. Bleakley, file separate discrimination lawsuits against the Jekyll Island State Park Authority, the first of its kind. The change in management from a simple authority that oversees all issues pertaining to the island into a municipal-like model comes with growing pains, probably due to a lack of policies and procedures that are needed to streamline and clarify its role as a state employer. It is not surprising that with the implementation of a hierarchical structure, an employee manual or the creation of a human resources department is the last thing on their mind, given the multitude of tasks that need attention. There are no specific details about the two lawsuits other than both linger in court for several years before they are either settled out of court or dismissed altogether.

Mr. Case comes under heavy fire and criticism during a public meeting with the State Senate Industry, Labor and Tourism Committee.[236] Residents and business owners publicly blame Mr. Case for the negative publicity surrounding the island and for the lack of communication between the executive director and the residents. The fact that a state senate committee even descends on Brunswick to hear the complaints in person is more

---

[235] The initial Jekyll Island drawbridge toll of fifty cents was discontinued on June 20, 1956. Since then, no toll or entry fee had been imposed.

[236] "Jekyll protesters rap services, authority, director" (*Florida Times Union*, October 11, 1979).

proof that the island's image is tarnished and surrounded by negative press articles. It seems that the blame is placed with Mr. Case rather than the authority.

But not everything is gloom and doom on the island. The shopping center receives several new lessee proposals midyear. Ken Tollison, who now operates the package store, receives approval to open a mini-mall, while Mr. and Mrs. Rollinson are approved for a boutique and gift shop in the shopping center. C. R. Maxwell is to open a Tru-Value hardware store, and Frank King and J. H. Boatwright want to open a full-service restaurant. This is good news overall for the small business community and for Jekyll Pharmacy, which receives a ten-year lease extension. At least some parts of the island are stable, and the hotel/motel industry that has been fragile for the last two years receives some welcoming news as well.

A new investor, J.I. Investments, Inc., a company organized under Panama law and legally recognized in the state of Georgia, proposes a lease amendment to purchase the defunct Corsair. Mr. Shafik Ladha, president of J.I. Investments, proposes the following amendment on April 28, 1980:

> The Authority was advised by Mr. Formby, Legal Counsel, regarding a proposed amendment to the J.I. Investments, Inc. lease which would allow junior security interests to be placed upon the leased premises, provided that upon the placing of any junior security interests upon the premises on and after January 1, 1986, the lessee must either invest in the leased premises at least 25% of the net increase in aggregate junior mortgage debt, or in lieu thereof the applicable rental shall increase to 4% of the monthly gross income or shall in accordance with a defined formula established according to the yield rate of certain corporate bonds ...

The Corsair, whose outstanding debt security deeds were purchased by the authority in 1978[237] and subsequently leased to Mark Smith, now gets an offer from a foreign company but with strings attached.

The issuance of junior debt and the requested time line of 1986, still six years away, becomes a point of contention in later board meetings. The new debt must be junior or subordinate to protect the authority in case of default or bankruptcy—a very realistic threat given the current circumstances and the less than healthy state of other island hotels. The combination of junior debt and the mandatory capital reinvestment or higher rental payments do offer some assurance but are disputed by the investor.

> Mr. Shafik Ladha, representing the lessee, requested that an amendment previously executed by the lessee and previously submitted to the Authority for execution and ratification be approved and ratified, which amendment would allow junior security interest to be placed upon the leased premises without investment or rental increase provisions ...

The request from the lessee here is twofold: allow the lessee to issue junior debt but lift the investment and/or rental increase and allow the issuer to be a non-Georgia entity.

It is unusual that the authority would approve such a request, but given that J.I. Investments Inc. is organized under Panama law, it does make sense that Panamanian financial institutions would be the first source of financing. There is also the pressure to decide quickly, without which the Corsair will sit idle and does not produce any revenue, while the debt and security deed, in the hands of the authority, need to be repaid in full and according to schedule.

---

[237] The Department of Natural Resources paid the authority $1,290,000 as part of the Supplemental Appropriations Act of 1979. The authority used the funds to purchase the security deeds of the Corsair and the Atlantic Carriage Inn. Both hotels were fully owned by the authority and secured by a $1MM loan, repayable to DNR over twenty years, starting in 1981.

The authority allows for two modifications to its original proposal, considering the urgency to open the hotel by the summer of 1980:

> The Authority considered a second proposal specialized amendment to the J.I. Investments, Inc. lease requested by the lessee and Tri-Continental Leasing, Inc., which amendment would permit the designated mortgagee to place a security interest upon the leased premises and upon the securing of possession of the leased premises by the designated mortgagee, by foreclosure or otherwise, would limit the financial liability of the designated mortgagee to an amount equal to the preceding twelve (12) months' rental ...

Not only does the new lessee receive permission to issue junior debt without any investment obligation thereafter, J.I. Investments Inc. also limits its financial liability to twelve months' rental income.

The authority clearly has no choice but to protect its investment by inserting the clause to have the option to buy the junior debt upon bankruptcy or default, lest it loses its investment in bankruptcy. It does increase the authority's risk, however, but for now the problem has been solved.

The Corsair opens again in June 1980 under a new name, Ladha Island Inn.[238]

But there is more good news. The once troubled Atlantic Carriage Inn, operated since 1978 by several management companies, is transformed into the Ramada Inn, and with that, all existing hotels and motels are once again fully operational. There is one more detail that needs attention, and that is a new request made by First Boston By-The-Sea Inc.

The company that now owns and operates By-the-Sea Hotel requests approval to assign the leasehold interest in Parcel No. 353 to Messrs. Emil V. Steele and Brenton S. Mongan. The authority approves the assignment, assumption, and agreement, subject to the following conditions:

---

[238] The Ladha Island Inn is Mr. Ladha's fourth hotel. He also owned the Ladha Downtown and the Ladha Continental, both in Atlanta, and the Ladha Beach Hotel on Tybee Island.

1) First National bank of Boston furnish the authority with a letter giving official notice that they will be the holder of the first mortgage in the amount of $3,900,000.

2) The proposed assignees furnish Mr. Case with the financial information they submitted to the bank.

3) The proposed assignees agree to remain a Sheraton franchise for at least six months.

It is unclear from archived documents why only Parcel 353 was subject to a change in lease assignment, given that the premises are constructed on two parcels, namely Parcel 353 and 354. It is also not clear why the authority would approve a change in leasehold estate while demanding the primary mortgage to continue to be held by First National Bank of Boston. One can assume that keeping the first mortgage intact gave the authority some sense of stability even though the assignees were individuals rather than a company or financial institution.

Since the authority is in the process of amending its commercial leases and securing the future of its hotel/motel structure, it also tackles a small and seemingly minor issue with the current ownership of the Holiday Inn Beach Resort[239] on South Beachview Drive.

Previously, Servico Inc. had sold a 50 percent stake of the hotel to Penmoco Inc. Now there is another merger of ownership, and the authority approves a lease amendment that makes Penmoco Inc. the full and sole owner of the Holiday Inn Beach Resort.

By the end of the summer, Mr. Case reports an increase of 19.5 percent in revenue versus the previous year, and it seems that all the hard work to keep the resort side of the island stable begins to pay off and bear its fruits. A renovated Sandwich Hut restaurant, courtesy of Domco Food Services, has been transformed into a hundred-seat full restaurant, and the newly dubbed Shoreline Restaurant[240] certainly adds to the increased success of Jekyll Island.

---

[239] The Holiday Inn Beach Resort was demolished in 2006. This location now features the Hampton Inn & Suites.

[240] The Shoreline Restaurant was previously known as Charcoal House Restaurant until it changed its name to Jekyll Sandwich Hut in the 1960s. In the mid-1980s, it was known as Shuckers Restaurant. The current location is now home to Tortuga Jack's.

By the end of summer, Hammer, Siler, George Associates are ready to present their findings to the authority. Their recommendations are not ready for public viewing or scrutiny yet and are presented in private at a regular board meeting.[241]

Mr. Jeff Wingfield of Hammer, Siler, George Associates prefaced his report by stating that it is necessary to protect the investment made as well as to promote visitation to the island. The areas of concern for this request for funds are: a) physical improvements, b) transportation improvements, and c) incentives to stimulate private investment.

a) Physical improvements:

- repairs to and utilization of Gould Casino (cost $350,000)
- repairs to Morgan Tennis Court (cost $35,000)
- restoration of Maurice Cottage[242] (cost $150,000)
- restore pilings and install new decking on Village Wharf (cost $300,000)
- dredge vicinity of Village Wharf (cost $250,000)
- additions and improvements in north picnic area (cost $170,000)
- at dredged basin, provide ramps for self-launching of trailered boats, parking lot, picnic area, wildlife observation dock (cost $190,000)
- restore Village Stables (cost $20,000)

Subtotal $1,465,000

b) Transportation improvements:

- construct approximately 8.1 miles of bicycle trails (cost $429,000)
- purchase components for an island tram system (cost $149,000)
- construct approximately 1.2 miles of boardwalks across marshes and dunes (cost $124,000)

Subtotal $702,000

---

[241] Board meeting, October 27, 1980.
[242] Also known as Hollybourne Cottage.

c) Stimulate private investment:

- clean up the Jekyll Club (cost $250,000)

Grand total $2,417,000

Prior to the report's release and recommendations, the authority launches the initiative "A Day on Jekyll Island"[243] to promote the island as a resort and to streamline advertising and marketing themes with the JI Tourist Bureau, Ltd.

The initiative brings hotel owners, managers, staff, and the authority together to brainstorm about how to jointly target their audience. A joint advertising campaign is launched in the Tourist Council Brochures, food and beverage guide to Jekyll Island, JI brochures, the Golden Isles Directory, and the *JI Gazette*.

Once again, the authority agrees to donate $20,000 to the JI Tourist Bureau, Ltd. to join the marketing efforts and to complement the contributions of the seven resort hotels. This a reversal of policy, since it was only one year ago when the same authority withdrew its support from Wayne Morrow and his JI Promotions Associations under the notion that the resort hotels must be self-sufficient in their marketing efforts.

One thing that does help the authority in its continued battle for funding is the support of Mrs. Iris Blitch, the original author of the 1950 Authority Act. She submits a request to the general assembly in September 1980 to approve an entry fee for Jekyll Island.[244]

The idea to somehow impose an entry fee to Jekyll Island stems from the Hammer, Siler, George Associates study. No specific recommendations are made as to what type of fee can be imposed, just that a daily entry fee can improve the financial situation of the authority and such fees will contribute to the overall improvement of the island.

---

[243] "A Day on Jekyll Island" was launched on September 28, 1980 (board meeting August 25, 1980).

[244] A resolution to that effect is issued by the authority on September 29, 1980: "The Authority is proud of the citizens of Jekyll Island, and believes they have contributed to the success of this State Park, to the Authority, and to the Tourist Industry of Georgia."

That does not prohibit the authority from appropriating other revenues, and despite opposition from the Jekyll Island Citizens Association, the authority raises its sewage and garbage fees by 40 percent but leaves the water rates untouched as a sign of compromise.

A new lessee, European Management Services Inc., also secures the much-needed extra revenue and proposes to lease the Shrady-James House[245] for ten years, with promised improvements of no less than $200K, paid for by the lessee. The intent is to open the house as a restaurant once renovations are completed.

With the search for funding and again the request to appropriate state funding, as per the Hammer, Siler, George Associates report earlier, the authority faces scrutiny again during its town hall meeting.

Mr. Issenburg, a member of the Jekyll Island Citizens Association, which is now a permanent fixture at regular open meetings, questions the authority members about the issuance of bonds and who exactly issues such bond series. The answer seems simple, and it is. "The State of Georgia issues the Bond Series, not the Authority" (board meeting minutes, October 10, 1980).

The answer is not entirely true, at least not for the early series that were explicitly issued, signed, stamped, and seal affixed by the Jekyll Island State Park Authority's chairman and treasurer/secretary, as per the board resolution dated February 10, 1964.

The state of Georgia issued the more recent series through a lease agreement and a security deed with a trust indenture placed with a designated trustee. The process is so complex that ultimately the authority is responsible for the payment of both principal and interest in the form of collateralized future revenue. It is not a surprise that to an outsider it seems that the authority issues the bonds rather than the state. In reality, the authority doesn't issue bonds itself after the 1965 Series but secures and collateralizes state bonds through their revenue stream, so the authority is responsible indirectly.

The entire financing component of Jekyll Island State Park can best be described as both innovative and risky, from a pure legal perspective. Without the innovative approach, the commercial development would probably not have been possible. That does not justify the lack of

---

[245] Now known and referred to as Cherokee.

transparency, nor does it substantiate the statements that state funds (i.e., taxpayers' funds) were never used in the development of the island.

The question is posed and answered in a simple fashion and without any further elaboration or explanation. The topic will never be addressed publicly either, except maybe in newspaper articles in later years.

Despite opposition from permanent island residents, and despite the friendly warning from state Representative John Greer, the authority decides to transfer the responsibility of the Jekyll Island Fire and Rescue Department to Glynn County. The total annual operating cost is estimated at $180,000, of which $99,000 is to be paid by the authority, with the remainder to be collected from residents through the imposition of a three per mill tax.

Now that Glynn County can prove it renders services to the island community, a requirement of the 1960 court ruling should the county execute its right to impose county taxes on Jekyll Island residents, the door is open to levy other property taxes like those applicable to Saint Simons Island residents.

The entry fee dispute is resolved early 1981 as well, and the general assembly approves the levy of a "parking fee" upon entering Jekyll Island. The authority unanimously approves a similar resolution during its regular board meeting of April 6, 1981, with the clear stipulation that such fee does not constitute an "entry fee" or a "toll fee."

Calling it a "parking fee" is a clever way around the legal prohibition of collecting either a toll fee, which was abolished in 1956, or the levy of an entry fee, which would have been contradictory to any other state park policy.

The daily rates are set at five dollars for buses and one dollar for motorized vehicles, with an annual pass to be available at thirty-five dollars.

The exact location of the tollbooth for collection of such parking fees is not a simple matter, as a dispute lingers between the Department of Transportation and the authority that even requires the intervention of Gov. Busbee.

Tom Moreland, director of the Georgia DOT, first disputes the legality of implementing a toll on roads that are constructed with federal funds, as such is prohibited. The authority counters that the fee is not considered a toll but merely represents a "parking fee" that will be used to beautify the island. Since the general assembly and Gov. Busbee are no longer willing to finance Jekyll Island and impose the mandate to become self-sufficient, this parking fee will help increase the annual revenue. That is the thought process of the authority, but most residents and the DOT disagree with the approach.

In return, the DOT threatens to remove GA-520 (Jekyll Island Causeway) and GA-50 (Jekyll Island perimeter road) from the highway system, in addition to the portion of SB-25 that runs between exit 29 at I-95 and the entry to the causeway. That means approximately forty-seven miles of state highway road that now becomes the sole responsibility of the authority for maintenance and repair.

The dispute lingers until the fall of 1981 when the arrival of a new executive director[246] leads to mutually acceptable terms.

Despite all the commotion and disagreements, it is interesting to note that DOT agrees to resurface roads on Jekyll Island one month prior to removing GA-50 from its highway system.[247]

The two decisions early in the year certainly improve the financial situation of the authority, at least for the immediate future, but there is more trouble looming. Unexpectedly, the authority decides to auction off the Jekyll Island Club furniture and solicits bids from appraisers to estimate the value of such. Any antiques are to be excluded from the auction, although no specific guidelines are provided as to what exactly qualifies as "antique." One can assume that any remaining furniture considered to pertain to the millionaires' era is excluded from the sale, although most of that furniture was already sold or removed twenty years ago.

The island, and the authority specifically, does not seem to get relief from the ongoing turmoil. Each time a problem is thought to be solved and fixed, another one rears its head. This time, it's the island's sole food service provider, Domco Food Services, that terminates its lease on April 30, 1981. The company, which took over the reins from Morrison Food

---

[246] Mr. George Chambliss joined the authority as executive director on October 20, 1981, replacing Mr. Robert Case.
[247] DOT resurfaced 2.351 miles of island roads in October 1981. The following streets were resurfaced: Hyde, Lanier, Hayes Avenue, Perkins Street, Baker Lane, Forest Road behind Seafarer, Pierson, Howland, Ogden, and Clark (authority board meeting, October 1988; addendum to the minutes of the board meeting).

Services barely two years ago, and that oversees the food services for the convention center, the Shoreline Restaurant, and provides catering services at Crane Cottage, leaves suddenly and receives a payout of $125,000 for improvements made to the Shoreline Restaurant. Without much delay, the authority enters into a lease agreement with Mr. Jim Rohr of Otter Management to manage all food services at all island facilities except the Shrady-James House,[248] which is in the capable hands of European Management Services Inc. It should be noted that Otter Management is not a newcomer on the island. When the Sand Dollar Motel was converted into a one-bedroom motel and renamed the Jekyll Island Hilton Inn in 1979, the Georgia Teachers Retirement System appointed Otter Management as its operator of the facilities after clearing the title and deed with the authority.

One major problem solved and a new and more urgent problem to address. Both the old wharf and the new Aquarama are showing signs of decay and warrant a new study and survey to address the issues at hand. Hussey, Gay & Bell, a Savannah-based engineering firm, is hired to conduct a survey of both buildings. The Aquarama opened its doors in the summer of 1961 and is barely twenty years old, but the roof shows cracks and deterioration. The recruited engineering firm is to determine whether the Aquarama roof can be repaired or whether it should be torn down. Pending the results of the study, both the old wharf and the Aquarama are closed to the public until further notice.

During all of this, an ex-employee of the authority files another lawsuit, the third one of its kind in less than one year. This time, Mrs. Diane Fouche files a sexual harassment case against the authority, which immediately requests that a new policy for employee practices be put in place.

Whether the three lawsuits, the study of the Office of Planning and Budget, or the multitude of recurring problems contributed to the resignations of Robert Case as executive director and Ray McCadden as director of services and development will never be known. When both resignations coincide with Mr. Weltch's request to be relieved from his duties as vice-chair of the authority, one can assume that the working

---

[248] Now called Cherokee Cottage.

conditions and the environment were not ideal and that the multitude of problems must have contributed to the simultaneous resignations.

Robert Henry, director of tourist and convention development, assumes the role of executive director ad interim, and Mr. Elfer replaces Ray McCadden as the new director of services and development. Mr. Weltch is requested to continue in his role as vice-chair by Governor Busbee until a replacement can be found.

Because of the three discrimination lawsuits, the authority orders that all procedures, leases, documents, and amendments are to be reviewed and approved by the attorney general prior to execution or implementation. The board further orders that a personnel manual be created and distributed to all employees and that a human resources department be created for such purpose. Each employee is to be evaluated each year, and a mandatory retirement age is introduced and enforced at the age of seventy. Exceptions for retirement can be reviewed, and requests for extension of employment can be granted by the board upon recommendation by the executive director. Neither one of these measures alters the course of the three discrimination lawsuits, which will be pending in court for several years until finally being settled out of court for undisclosed amounts.

It is not a coincidence that during this difficult period, the Jekyll Island Citizens Association offers its full cooperation to the authority in all matters and forthcoming projects. The sudden closure of the Aquarama and the old wharf without prior or timely notification must have triggered the desire to seek more direct involvement and cooperation between the residents and the authority. Although they are excluded from any Executive Committee meeting, and despite the assurance by the authority that such executive meetings are meant for discussion only and no decisions are made in closed meetings, residents want to play a more active role in the day-to-day business decisions or at least want to be recognized as a valuable partner, like the commercial businesses that are well represented.

The pending enforcement of an entry fee to the island and the past disagreement about the proposed tap-in fees to connect to the new water and sewage system are also contributing factors in their attempt to seek a closer relationship with the authority and above all with the new municipal management structure (i.e., the Executive Committee). After all, the residents have done their part. By the end of summer, all 136 residential homes are tapped into the water system as instructed by the authority, and now it is time to have some sort of voice and representation in the decision-making process.

It will take another twenty-four years before state legislation recognizes the island residents and allows them to participate as a Citizens Resource Council.[249] It does, however, result in Mr. Kaylor, as president of the Jekyll Island Citizens Association, partaking in the JI Master Plan Task Force together with a broad group of state agencies.

The newly formed task force is comprised of Robert Kerr, executive director of the Georgia Conservancy, Robert Reimold, DNR director, Greg Paxton, director of Georgia Trust for Historic Preservation, Willon Smith, Glynn County commissioner, Joe Kaylor, president of JICA, and Dan King, president of JI Tourist Bureau Ltd. Its task is to review the study and recommendation made by Hammer, Siler, George Associates.

The hotel-motel industry does not sit idle either and contracts, leases, and lease assignments change faster than the authority can anticipate.

Motel Properties Inc. requests a lease assignment for the Wanderer Motel and the Buccaneer Motor Lodge to Townhouse Inc. The company has been managing and operating both motels since 1970, and a reason for the sudden lease assignment is not immediately clear. The Ramada Inn follows suit, and its operator, Jekyll Island Group Inc., wishes to transfer its lease to Ocean View Associates. Again, no reason is given for the request to change the leasehold estate, but it does prompt the authority to review its policy pertaining to long-term leases for hotels and motels two years later and to insert such into its revised policy manual.

Both hotels continue to operate as usual and fare better than the Sheraton By-The-Sea, which proposes and introduces a time-sharing concept for the hotel. The concept is new for Jekyll Island and is the first of its kind, although Larry Morris proposed a similar concept for his Sand Dollar Motel when he requested permission to transfer his leasehold estate to 130 separate limited partnerships. His request was denied and subsequently led to the bankruptcy filing that resulted in the

---

[249] HB 120 Section 16.3. Passed July 1, 1995 (www.legis.ga.gov/legislation).

From Millionaires to Commoners

Georgia Teachers Retirement System taking control of the property and transforming it into the Jekyll Hilton Inn.[250]

A similar idea was also presented in 1961 when state Rep. Charlie Gowen proposed to construct a forty-eight-room cooperative; it was rejected initially but ultimately received approval to construct Ocean Terrace Apartments but without the requested individual ownership.

Sheraton By-The-Sea ultimately files for Chapter 11 bankruptcy protection on August 11, 1981, while the authority attempts to avoid foreclosure. Six weeks later, an agreement is reached between the authority and First National Bank of Boston, the primary mortgage holder, to assign a new management company and continue to operate without the Sheraton.

A new executive director and new members of the authority hopefully laud in quieter times or more comprehensive approaches to the many difficulties the island faces.

George Chambliss becomes the new executive director effective October 20, 1981, and Mary Walker becomes the new board member, appointed by Gov. Busbee, while John McTier replaces Mr. Weltch as the new vice-chair of the authority.

Mr. Chambliss, a native of Albany, Georgia, doesn't come to the island without prior experience. He previously earned his reputation as director of Parks and Recreation in Winder, Milledgeville, and Dalton, Georgia, prior to his move to Dallas, Texas, where he served as assistant director of recreation since 1978. Well accomplished in the recreation business, and being an avid golfer, fisherman, and pilot, it is no surprise that Mr. Chambliss takes the bull by its horns and focuses on what he does best: beautifying the island and making sure it is financially sound and self-sufficient.

It is now obvious that Mr. Chambliss also introduces the island to his favorite color, and before long, the entire equipment and vehicle pool undergoes another color change from white to hunter green.

No time is wasted before addressing the lingering maintenance issues, and funds from the 1972 Bond Series are allocated as per the task force's recommendation. The old wharf receives a capital injection of $110,000

---

[250] The Sand Dollar Motel operated as Jekyll Hilton Inn after bankruptcy filing in 1979.

to replace old pilings and reinforce the dock with additional new pilings. The JI Club receives an exterior facelift for $137,500, while both the Morgan Tennis Center and the Maurice House receive $30,000 each for renovation. An additional $300,000 is spent from the reserve fund to upgrade the golf cart paths.

The Aquarama roof seems to be beyond repair, according to the Hussey, Gay, and Bell study, and a decision is made to tear down the structure. The demolition alone costs $127,500, funds that are partially appropriated from reserve funds ($77,500) with the remainder to be reallocated from a previous Land & Water grant.

The good news at the end of the year is that there is finally hope for the old and deteriorating buildings in St. Andrews Beach division. The once prominent Dolphin Motor Lodge and Club may see a revival when the University of Georgia follows through with its plans to operate a youth camp year-round.[251] The preliminary deal between UGA and the authority provides for UGA to maintain and operate the existing facilities for at least ten years, while the authority commits funds to construct and improve the facilities with general assembly funds only.

The initial agreement between UGA and the authority is the beginning of a long-term cooperation that will eventually expand to include the JI Music Theatre, at least for a few years.

By March 1982, a formal lease agreement is in effect between UGA and the authority, whereby UGA commits to operate the old Dolphin Motor Lodge and Club, and the St. Andrews Auditorium as a 4-H Center for a period of ten years. The properties are leased at one dollar per year, and the authority commits a maximum capital contribution of $300K to renovate and repair the existing structures, while UGA is responsible for tapping into the water and sewer lines, the cost of which must be paid by the board of regents.

The old structures, despite being used as a youth camp for several years, are still using the old and original septic tanks and drainage fields. It seems odd that all commercial hotels-motels and the permanent residents

---

[251] The Dolphin Motor Lodge and Club closed its doors officially in 1960. Between 1960 and 1966, the authority leased the grounds and buildings for outdoor activities, primarily youth activities. All buildings were closed to the public in 1966 after several complaints of vandalism and unauthorized use.

are obligated to tap into the new system, while the property owned and operated by the authority continues to use its septic tank, a system that was prohibited as early as the mid-seventies.[252] Given the cost associated with the tap-in and the cleanup of the drainage fields, the conversion to island water and sewage will ultimately be completed a year later and after several warnings of noncompliance by the authority.

Funds are available to begin restoring the old wharf and construct bike paths on the island, thanks to an additional donation from the Jekyll Island Garden Club of $8,000, its second donation in one year. Mrs. Gates had previously offered a Garden Club contribution of $7,000 for the expansion of island bike paths if the authority would match the funding. Finally, the authority commits $10,000 to the project after it receives an additional $8,000 from the Department of Natural Resources for the same project.

But money is always tight and hard to come by, certainly when the general assembly continues to demand that Jekyll Island become self-sufficient as per the original Authority Act of 1950. The reality is that self-sufficiency is a loose term that has been interpreted in a variety of different ways for the past thirty years.

A more accurate and applicable term to use is "economically viable." It simply means that all operating costs must be covered with the revenue generation from hotels, motels, leases, and percentage payments of gross sales but that any capital outlay for construction projects, renovation, and maintenance that is intended to beautify and expand the island can be and are covered through general assembly funds. Such funds are and have been made available through the issuance of bond series, subordinate bonds, and outright capital outlays each fiscal year. The estimated budget for FY1982 is $7,117,662, yet reserve funds are depleted; hence a new capital injection of $955,000 to complete the improvement projects is made.

Despite $340,000 being earmarked to redesign and landscape all the picnic areas on the island, only $9,000 finds its way to the north picnic area, and $17,000 is used to upgrade the south picnic area and St. Andrews Beach. The same fate awaits the Gould Auditorium. Scheduled to receive a complete renovation as the first and oldest convention center on the

---

[252] Residents were notified in May 1976 that the use of private wells was prohibited, and all existing wells should be capped (authority board meeting, May 28, 1976).

island, estimated and budgeted at $350,000, it is never restored and is closed in 1983.

Some matters do get attention, and the old cafeteria in the shopping center does get a facelift, probably because the Georgia State Patrol needs a new temporary home, pending construction of the tollbooth for which $110,000 has been set aside as the maximum allowable construction cost. Changes and renovation in the first shopping center also coincide with Cecil Mason selling his 50 percent interest to Wright Parker, who now becomes the sole owner of the second shopping center next door. While it is pure coincidence, Mr. and Mrs. William Fitting lease commercial space in the same place for the first time, doing business as Jekyll Realty.

There are other ways to raise funds though. One way is to increase the water and sewage service fees for residents and hotels-motels by 37.4 percent and 100 percent respectively. Another way of reducing road maintenance cost is to provide a twenty-one-acre land easement southwest of the Sydney Lanier Bridge to the Department of Transportation in exchange for maintenance and upkeep of the island's perimeter road for the duration of the one-year lease and five-year easement agreement.[253] It is not possible to quantify the contract in annual monetary terms, but it certainly is a deal that works in favor of the authority since a decision about where to construct the "entry fee" tollbooth has not been made, and whoever owns or maintains the road alongside such booth is also responsible for the adherent road construction and rerouting.

During intense negotiations, an agreement is reached with DOT that leaves the highway system intact, except the removal of GA-50, Jekyll Island's perimeter road.[254] To that effect, the authority constructs the first Collection Station[255] on the Ben Fortson Memorial Parkway, east of the bridge and just west of the North Riverview Drive intersection. The new tollbooth opens in March 1982, and the daily parking fee of one dollar

---

[253] Authority board meeting of June 28, 1982.
[254] The twenty-one-acre land easement southwest of the Sydney Lanier Bridge was the incentive to keep GA-520 (Jekyll Island Causeway) and SB-25 within the state highway system.
[255] The Collection Station was built in the same style as the old schoolhouse in the Historic District.

goes into effect together with the sale of annual decals[256] at thirty-five dollars.

To avoid any congestion at the Collection Station, traffic bound for North Riverview Drive is prohibited from making a left turn immediately after paying the parking fee and is directed to proceed to the intersection with Beachview Drive where a legal but complicated U-turn must be made to proceed to North Riverview Drive.

On the beachside of the island, the odd lot, Parcel 352, that has been designated for development since the Sand Dollar Motel and By-the-Sea Hotel were constructed in the mid-seventies, suddenly receives interest from M&M Resorts. For reasons unknown but based on the recommendation of Executive Director George Chambliss, and without further explanation, the lease request is denied.[257] No plans or designs are presented, at least not according to archived material, other than the request is made to lease 175 feet of oceanfront property between the two existing motels.

At the same time, the question is raised whether the Jekyll Hilton Inn is being subsidized by the Georgia Teachers Retirement System and whether such subsidy creates an unfair practice on the island.

The entire hotel-motel lease and ownership comes under review to such an extent that the authority revises its "Long-Term Leases for Hotels and Motels" and adopts such as part of its policy manual. The most notable change or amendment pertains to the rental terms:

> D. Rental terms including, without limitation:
> Base rental of 8% of land value
> Percentage rental of 3% of total gross income
> Base rental adjustments every 10 years based on 8% of appraised land value
> Capital improvements of 1% of total gross income annually placed in escrow until withdrawn for such capital improvements

---

[256] Annual decals could be purchased at the offices of the authority in Crane Cottage.
[257] Parcel 352 still exists today and sits empty between Villas by the Sea and The Cottages.

> General description of receipts to be included within gross income of lessee, which receipts shall include without limitation, the gross receipts of any third-party concessionaire conducting business upon or from the leased property, <u>together with</u> the sum paid to lessee by such third-party concessionaire for the privilege of conducting such business ... (Jekyll Island-State Park Authority, Policy Manual, Section VII-A-7, Item III.D)

The policy manual also reiterates the process of how, when, and why certain commercial leases may or may not be reassigned and lists the requirements for the application and approval thereof.

The authority has certainly seen its share of lease assignments, specifically for hotels and motels. Given the continuing problems with some hotel properties, and the mere notion that one hotel, Jekyll Hilton Inn, is suspected of being unfairly subsidized,[258] it seems appropriate to clarify the applicable terms and conditions. After all, the Ladha Island Inn, whose lease was just reassigned to JI Investments Inc., is already seeking a reassignment to International Realty Properties Inc., and the 1976 ad valorem taxes on the same property remain unpaid and therefore become the responsibility of the authority.

The reason for revising the policy must be found a little deeper than just the simple ongoing problems with commercial leases.

Immediately following the policy revision, the authority also prepares a prospectus for the Jekyll Island Club, the Annex, and the Sans Souci. The notion is made that the base rent for the property should be based on a percentage of the appraised value, combined with a percentage of gross income, and that restoration of the buildings may result in a tax advantage for the prospective lessee, given that the property is recognized as and included in the National Registry of Historic Landmarks.

---

[258] The accusation of being "subsidized" needs to be taken with a grain of salt. It is indeed the only motel remaining on the island that is fully owned and operated by the Georgia Teachers Retirement System, hence it can set its own pricing. However, in the early days of 1957 and beyond, it was the same public pension plan that ignited the commercial construction on the island.

The property has been sitting idle and partially boarded up since late 1971, and most of its inventory has been auctioned off, so it is interesting that a prospectus for the historic hotel and its buildings is being prepared at the same time as the commercial lease policy is being amended and reinforced, yet it does not come as a surprise.

Simultaneously, the authority receives a proposal from a development group for the lease of certain properties in the Historic District and the lease acquisition and renovation of hotel properties on the island. The development group consists of McKennon-Holden Hotels, Collum & Associates, Design Continuum, Armour & Cape Inc., West Point Construction Co., Dean Witter Reynolds Inc., Laventhol & Horwath, and Townhouse Inc.[259] Financing of the project is to be provided primarily by a combination of private financing through the syndication of limited partnership interests and the sale of tax-exempt bonds.

Now the changes and the new prospectus make sense and shed a new and different light on the course the authority chooses to sail. The development group is not merely interested in renovating the historic hotel buildings. They are interested in acquiring the lease agreements of at least four existing hotels on the island in exchange for extensive renovation. The offer also marks the first time that a "syndication of limited partnership interests" and the "issuance of tax-exempt bonds" are offered as a finance mechanism and will be used later, albeit through different investors.

Only two of the four hotels mentioned in the offer are explicitly named in the archived minutes of the board meeting dated December 6, 1982, namely the Wanderer Motel and the Buccaneer Motor Lodge. The other two hotels are never specifically named, not even in the formal authority's response to the development group.

Given the current ownership and the frequent past troubles, the Ladha Inn (Corsair) and the Ramada Inn (Atlantic Carriage Inn) seem to be a good and educated guess.

The authority's official response is unanimously approved in executive session as follows.

---

[259] Townhouse Inc. also assumed the lease assignment from Motel Properties Inc. for the Buccaneer Motor Lodge and the Wanderer Motel on December 18, 1981.

1) The Authority does not object generally to the acquisition of the lease agreements for, and leasehold interests in, four certain hotel properties by an entity formed by or from the development group ...
2) In the event the project proceeds as contemplated, the Authority would grant a term of thirty-five (35) years for the lease of the hotel properties and the Millionaires' Village properties.
3) For each lease of the properties in the Millionaires' Village, no base rent would be required for an initial period of the term adjusted to offset defined deficiency (loss) for the project during such initial period ...
4) The Authority will exercise control of all use, development, and rehabilitation of the Millionaires' Village, directly and through the involved lease agreements ...
5) All lease agreements for the four hotel properties must be revised to provide for a reasonable economic return to the Authority and to require proper operation of the hotel properties as first-class hotels ...
6) All renovation and rehabilitation for the hotel properties and the properties in the Millionaires' Village will be in accordance with plan and specifications approved by the Authority.
7) The Authority will make available to the development group certain proposals and studied previously obtained by the Authority regarding the Millionaires' Village for use by the development group in securing a feasibility for the project ...

It must be noted foremost that the above motion is made in executive session and not in a regular board meeting, as prescribed by the authority's explicit policy of reserving executive meetings for advisory recommendations only, while all decisions are to be made by the board only.

Secondly, the authority's response indicates for the first time that default of any individual lease agreement by the lessee for nonadherence to the terms and conditions of said individual lease automatically constitutes a default of all other corresponding leases. In previous cases where one lessee held multiple individual leases on several properties (i.e., Motel Properties Inc. that operated and managed the Wanderer Motel and Jekyll Estates), a breach of lease on one of the properties did not affect the lease of any other properties when the lessee was identical. This is a new concept that is introduced for the first time in response to a development group but not to be found in any policy beforehand.

Lastly, the authority clearly indicates that it reserves the right to revise its existing lease agreements and adjust the base rent and percentage rent of gross sales prior to a lease reassignment. In previous cases, a lease assignment was a mere formality, and the terms and conditions of the previous lessee were automatically assigned to the new lessee without revision or appraisal adjustment.

The authority is clearly under pressure to maximize the annual revenue stream and is determined to use lease agreements and leasehold estate assignments as the opportunity to appraise the properties and adjust the base rents accordingly. The focus on becoming "self-sustainable" or "economically viable" is best confirmed in the outlined priorities of the board meeting of December 6, 1982:

> ... restoration of Millionaires' Village and the opening of the Jekyll Club; environmental education and recreational programs; and ensuring that Jekyll Island breaks even financially, noting this is a necessity because the General Assembly will no longer provide operating funds for the Island ... (Outlined priorities by Chairman Sam Williams)

Now that a possible agreement can be reached to renovate and reopen parts of the Historic District, George Chambliss recruits a director for museums and historic structures and hires Dr. Tom Rhodes at around the same time as Ed McCormick becomes the first superintendent for water and sewer facilities.

The hotel-motel industry is not the only one subject to major changes, as the authority begins to tackle its next project, namely the operation of the Cherokee Campground. Wayne Morrow has been operating the campground since its inception in 1958. Several lease amendments and extensions later, the authority wants to operate the campground itself. The decision doesn't come as a surprise, given that the golf course and miniature golf were once privately operated, only to be turned over back to the authority in the late 1960s.

Operating the campground in-house does make sense from that perspective, but the timing seems unusual unless such can be ascribed to the need for extra revenue and a desire to self-operate the state park side of the island, of which the campground is obviously a part. The problem is how to terminate the lease with good cause and how to avoid any payout to Wayne Morrow. A creative way will be found soon enough when the time comes.

The same fate befalls the Otter Corporation, who is relieved from its duties as the sole food services provider. The authority removes the beach stands from the lease agreement and begins to self-manage food services at the beach concession stands. This is a move that will soon be followed by an overhaul of the beachfront restaurant Shuckers[260] as well.

The development group's proposal falls through in early 1983, as the authority's request for full financial disclosure and a final list of island hotels under consideration is not forthcoming. The authority decides to go back to the drawing board and consider any other proposals that may come their way. Only one other seems to have been received that same year, namely a lease proposal for the Millionaires' Village buildings by Groupmark Canada, Ltd. that befalls the same fate as the previous one. The Canadian investment company withdraws its bid on April 25, 1983.

The withdrawal is obviously a disappointment and a missed opportunity to breathe new life into the Historic District, but it is also accompanied by the decision to demolish another island icon.

The Aquarama is demolished in the summer of 1983, leaving behind an open space that will remain unused for several years until new and improved plans are set in motion to overhaul the oceanfront convention center once again.

Trouble with some hotels persists, and it is again the Ladha Island Inn that requests a new lease assignment. Less than one year after International Realty Properties Inc. receives the lease assignment from Jekyll Island

---

[260] The Shoreline Restaurant, previously known as Jekyll Sandwich Hut, was renamed Shuckers Restaurant after the Otter Corporation took over management in 1981.

Investments Inc., the group turns around and reassigns its lease to Sea Ventures Inn Inc.

It is remarkable that each lease assignment is preceded two months earlier with a notice of default, which seems to be resolved by changing lessees for the same property. This is not only the case with the Ladha Island Inn. It also occurs with other troubled hotels, such as the Ramada Inn and even Sheraton By-The-Sea. It is then not a surprise that a fourth hotel joins the ranks of lease assignments when Jekyll Estates' lease is transferred from Motel Properties Inc. to William Minter. Mr. Minter also acquires the lease agreement for the Seafarer Inn & Suites the following year.

The struggling Ramada Inn finds itself in trouble again and is placed in receivership by court order. The hotel will soon be joined in pending litigation by Cherokee Campground, which has been found in default of its 1978 lease modification by the authority.

The Cherokee Campground default is not really a surprise given that the authority wants to self-manage the property, and it seems clear from archived minutes of the board meetings of the previous year that all lease agreements, extensions, and amendments were ordered fully researched and examined for full compliance of all terms and conditions. The default letter is based on non- or only partial adherence to the use of extra land and the construction of additional bathrooms and restrooms as per the lease amendment.

Despite multiple objections from Mr. Wayne Morrow, his lease agreement is terminated,[261] and the authority proceeds to renovate Cherokee Campground at a total cost of $717,000 as per the development proposal of Mr. Jack Ingram.

The necessary funds are obtained through a capital outlay, approved by the general assembly in 1984. The remainder of the funds are used to redesign the parking area between the convention center and Shuckers Restaurant, and to remove the beach concession stand and north picnic shelter. By the end of the year, one of the oldest structures on the island, namely the once-famous 1.5-mile boardwalk that connected the north

---

[261] Mt. Wayne Morrow and Cherokee Campground Inc. filed a lengthy lawsuit against the authority for wrongful lease termination. The case was finally resolved in July 1988. The terms of the settlement were never disclosed.

beach concession stand with the original south picnic area and was lined with palm trees between the Wanderer Motel and the Corsair, ceases to exist. The only reminder of what was once was is the still the visible retention wall and revetment at the north parking area.[262]

Despite objections from residents, the authority decides not to renew the JI Music Theater's lease agreement. Attendance has been dwindling and is very low, the Gould Auditorium is not renovated as planned and budgeted, and the $60,000 annual subsidy to keep the outdoor theater going is becoming too expensive. Given the growing relationship with UGA, the university is willing to take on a three-year term to perform at the amphitheater, and it seems outdoor performances are saved, at least for the time being.

As predicted the year before, Otter Food Services' lease agreement for the convention center is terminated, and the authority decides to add another layer of self-management to its ever-increasing management role on the island. The authority now manages all food services at the convention center, the wharf, and the Golf Club, but the 1984 food and beverage budget shows that the total gross profit for all three locations of $265,860 is largely offset by its operating cost of $221,170, barely leaving a net annual profit of $44,690. That does not include any capital improvements or depreciation, a cost largely carried before by the previous food service companies.

Maybe the arrival of Ski Rixen Inc. is the beginning of a new era and a new approach that will expand the recreational areas on the island, as was the chairman's priority the previous year.

Ski Rixen was the first water ski cable company, founded by inventor and water ski enthusiast Bruno Rixen. His water ski cableway became an international fixture and major tourist attraction in Europe during the late 1970s, including championships.[263]

---

[262] Small portions or steps of the original boardwalk can be seen at parking lot, south of the Holiday Inn resort. The retaining walls of the boardwalk and the rock revetment are still intact. Steps that led from the boardwalk and the original Charcoal House Restaurant (currently the location of Tortuga Jack's) to the beach can still be seen today.

[263] www.rixen-cableways.com.

Given that Jekyll Island has a perfect location for such an endeavor, and the fact that the sport or entertainment is new to the US market, it makes sense to add the attraction to the inventory of island tourist attractions.

The company signs a ten-year lease agreement to rent the freshwater pond left behind after the failed attempt to create a luxury yacht marina, and the terms and conditions seem favorable for the authority with a guaranteed $5,000 annual rent payment or 4 percent of gross income, whichever is greater. The water ski park is expected to open by June 1984, right before the heavy tourist season and just in time to accommodate the thousands of music lovers who attend the Beach Music Festival on July 7, 1984. The parking fees alone amount to $6,810 in revenue for the authority, although not all are happy with the new annual event.

Whether the opening of Rixen Pond,[264] as it came to be known, is the catalyst to pursue all water fun options is debatable, but soon after, the Economics Research Associates are ordered to make a feasibility study for a water park on Jekyll Island. The cost for the study is $15,000, and the site is still to be determined since the study is focused on visitors' analytics, usage, opening hours, and economic sustainability.

By year-end, the proposal for a water park is ready and is divided into two building phases. Phase I includes a wave pool, a water slide, and several other smaller attractions with an estimated construction cost of $4.9 million. Phase II will add a leisure pool and an innertube ride for $1.77 million. The proposed site is just south of the Rixen Pond at the new marina site, or at least part thereof. Funding, the perpetual problem, can be provided with the issuance of general obligation bonds that can be fully reimbursed and paid off in nine years or less with anticipated revenue from the park's operations, according to Mr. Chambliss's statement to the authority.[265]

Trying to revamp and reinvent itself, or to create as many diverse revenue-generating points of sale, the authority adopts the idea of creating a health spa in the old building adjacent to the demolished Aquarama. Construction and engineering for the new project is estimated at $112,400.

---

[264] Rixen Pond is now home to the Tidelands Nature Center and currently serves as a fishing pond with multiple piers and a boat ramp.
[265] Authority board meeting of November 26, 1984.

The proposed budget ends up being increased by an additional $16K to further improve existing walls and floors and to purchase equipment from the old Nautilus restaurant[266] that once was part of the Corsair and since converted to a simple breakfast area.

The Historic District doesn't get its expected investors, but that does not deter the authority from appointing Taylor-Ward Consultants to prepare drawings and engineering plans for the JI Club Hotel. Two years prior, Tom Collum was requested to prepare the same at a cost of $96,000, but none of the promised plans, drawings, or proposals were ever delivered to the authority.

Since the executive director is clearly focused and committed to bring the entire Historic District back to life somehow, he also pursues the opportunity to hire an architect to draw up renovation and restoration plans for the old stables so that they may become an island museum soon. After all, some of the lessees in the Historic District seem to be ready to vacate an already deserted and historic part of the island, so preparing for replacement attractions and activities seems like a good idea. Ms. Mary Miller's lease of Villa Ospo ends in October 1984, and Mr. Stauffer, who has been leasing the old power plant for his antique car collection, prefers to continue to lease month-to-month rather than renew long-term.

Changes are definitely coming to the Historic District, but how and when is a question of dollars and cents—and time of course. In anticipation of potential new lessees, adjusted monthly rents for the cottages on Pier Road, Claflin Road, and Maurice Road are published by the authority in April 1984.[267]

A new $75K grant from the DNR and an additional $100K from the 1984 budget are used to improve the island's recreational areas. The parking between Shuckers and the convention center is redesigned. The concession stand and picnic shelter are removed as well as the remaining asphalt and benches at the north picnic area.

---

[266] The Corsair featured a full restaurant, named the Nautilus, on the second floor with full ocean view.

[267] Historic cottages on Pier Road rented between $100/month and $175/month. The small houses on Claflin and Maurice Road rented at $115/month. The latter were mostly rented to JIA employees or supervisory staff.

How the authority is funding all these newly found initiatives is not very clear at the time, but a new and innovative way to pay both for the financing of new projects and accrue for the maintenance and repair of the Historic District is just around the corner.

The innovation starts with a resolution that unanimously passes during the August 23, 1983, board meeting. Although it seems rather innocent and irrelevant at first, further examination of archived documents and minutes of subsequent meetings shed a light as to what this resolution specifically sets in motion.

> ... NOW, THEREFORE, BE IT HEREBY RESOLVED BY THE JEKYLL ISLAND-STATE PARK AUTHORITY THAT the Authority agrees to the amendment of said lease agreements to provide for annual adjustments and changes in the amount of rental, which annually adjusted rental shall be equal to the annual amount of debt service and any trustee or administrative fees becoming due for each respective bond issue of the Authority, as such adjusted rental for each year of each such lease agreement shall be determined by the Office of Planning and Budget and the Georgia State Financing and Investment Commission, as confirmed by the Trustee designated in the involved Trust Indenture for each respective bond issue of the Authority ...
>
> ... Adopted and resolved pursuant to motion properly made and seconded and recorded in the minutes of the August 22, 1983 meeting of the Jekyll Island-State Park Authority.[268]

The resolution is of interest because of the agreed-upon change in annual payments that are now subject to changes in annual debt service, rather than the pre-agreed annual payments.

It means that the authority can adjust its annual payments to match the amount of debt to be matured rather than adhere to the original

---

[268] Authority board meeting, August 23, 1983.

amortization schedule of the bonds. It provides the authority with additional flexibility in paying down its outstanding debt.

Also, it recognizes the Department of Natural Resources as a party to the lease agreements. Previously, only the Department of State Parks was part of the lease agreements and trust indentures. The above amendment now clearly identifies the Department of Natural Resources as a "successor" to the Department of State Parks.

The fact that DNR is a recipient of annual rent payments will become important in the immediate future and will become a negotiating tool for the issuance of other general obligation bonds that follow.

CHAPTER 10

THE ROAD TO HISTORIC PRESERVATION

1985–1986

The authority faces tough financial choices with the beginning of the new year. The desire to preserve the JI Club Hotel and its surrounding Historic District will take more than obtaining the original design plans from Tom Collum and the completion of the engineering study by Taylor-Ward Consultants. It requires private developers to invest in the restoration and renovation of the Club Hotel, Sans Souci, and Annex building, but it also requires funding to restore and preserve the Historic District, specifically the millionaires' cottages.

Approximately twenty years earlier, the historic cottages received a major facelift and new roofs to preserve the structures for generations to come. However, no plan was in place to depreciate the capital, hence no funds were ever placed in reserve to maintain, renovate, and restore the historic homes. Now, two decades later, the cottages need extensive repair of damage caused by time, neglect, and the salty environment. The initial cost is estimated at $1,169,000 to repair seven of the major historic homes.[269]

Knowing that funding from the general assembly is limited and given that such funding obtained through either the Office of Planning and Budget or the Georgia State Finance and Investment Commission will be

---

[269] Indian Mound, Mistletoe, Goodyear, Moss, Crane, Cherokee, and Villa Marianna were identified as the seven cottages to be repaired.

needed for the construction of a water park, Mr. Chambliss has a better and more creative solution.

In late 1984, a board resolution stated that the DNR, as successor to the Department of State Parks, is the recipient of annual rent payments in accordance with the annual debt service. This annual payment, as described in chapter 9, now comes into play.

Excerpt from the regular authority board meeting:

> The Authority is required to pay $53,000 annually to DNR to retire a debt of $1,000,000 which was obtained from the General Assembly 6-7 years ago in order to reopen two hotels. Mr. Chambliss stated that he would like to request that the $53,000 paid annually be left with the Jekyll Island Authority and ear-marked for maintenance of the structures in the Village. Mr. Ledbetter stated that he supported the concept of the maintenance program but that he would have to oppose leaving the funds with the Authority without an arrangement to replace them from the State general revenue funds ...

The two hotels Mr. Chambliss is referring to are of course the troubled Atlantic Carriage Inn and the Corsair. One had to be saved from bankruptcy, and the other required title clearance by the authority.

It was not clear at the time where the funds originated from or how much was borrowed, and it was assumed that the required funds were obtained through the issuance of general obligation bonds. Now, six years later, we know that said funds, $1,290,000, were obtained through a DNR loan. "Acts and Resolutions of the General Assembly of the State of Georgia 1977 Session" confirms the capital layout of $1,000,000 by the Department of Natural Resources with a maturity date of 2001, or a duration of twenty years.[270]

The proposal to redirect the annual payment of principal and interest to DNR and divert such to the authority to maintain the historic cottages

---

[270] The Supplemental Appropriations Act of 1979 confirms that $1,000,000 of the capital layout of $1,290,000 must be paid back to the DNR starting in 1981 over a twenty-year period (p. 270, Section 33).

is not unusual. To compensate DNR with the same amount from general revenue funds (i.e., state funds) is more questionable. Nevertheless, the request for diversion of annual payment to the authority and the compensation from general revenue funds to DNR in the same amount is granted and approved by Governor Harris.

The redirection of state funds is very interesting when placed in the context of Jekyll Island being self-supporting, a mandate placed on the authority since 1950 and repeated frequently throughout the past thirty-nine years. Then again, the term has always been used liberally, and the interpretation thereof was changed or amended depending on prevailing financial conditions or simply depending on who represented the authority and who held office at the time.

With one funding problem solved, the authority proceeds to send the new Jekyll Island Club Hotel prospectus to six different development companies that have expressed interest. Four companies present their respective development plans during a regular board meeting in February 1985. The presentations are made by Ralph Cole and Sibley Jennings of Winn Development Company, Boston, Massachusetts; Larry Evans, Vance Hughes, and Burton Wiand of Circle Development Corporation, Brunswick, Georgia; Taylor-Ward Properties and Lincoln Financial Services, Atlanta, Georgia; and Latco Construction, Augusta, Georgia.

The water park development will have to wait and take a back seat, given that funding through general obligation bonds and approval of the Office of Planning and Budget is not possible in fiscal year 1985. The other option can be a request for commercial funding through the Georgia State Finance and Investment Commission, but there is hesitation at the board meeting given the high investment amount of $7,000,000. Mr. Chambliss comes to the project's defense:

> Mr. Chambliss discussed the possibility of using G.O Bonds to fund this operation and stated that the total pay-off of the bond could be accomplished in nine years. It was noted that even when ERA (Economic Research Associates)'s projection of number of attendees from surrounding areas was reduced by 11% and the projected

operating cost was increased, the park would still be financially successful ...

Ultimately, funding for the water park is rolled up in a $10.7 million grant request[271] for 1986 as a supplemental budget:

- $7,000,000 water park
- $2,000,000 Historic District renovation
- $1,000,000 new campground
- $700,000 tennis complex

Besides the two main projects, the authority has its hands full with other smaller but still pressing issues, as the day-to-day operations of the island do not stand still. A study to renovate the old stables in the Historic District results in conversion of the millionaires' building into a museum at a cost of $53,455, which also happens to coincide with the first annual payment withheld from DNR to restore the Historic District. By January 1985, a small theatre and gift shop are added. The opening of the island's first museum that serves as a catalyst to preserve the old Millionaires Village and this vignette of American history leads to the creation of the New Jekyll Island Club Inc.[272]

Ski Rixen International Inc. is constructing its main building by the new marina pond but requests a lease transfer from the parent company to its new affiliate, Ski Rixen Jekyll Island. The transfer of legal responsibility and liability from the initial investor to a subsidiary is common, but the precedents are well-known by now. In case of default, as experienced by several hotel and motel operations and other small business ventures, the lease assignment to a subsidiary typically has preceded the early closure or termination of the business involved. Ski Rixen JI will prove to follow the same path and fate the next year.

---

[271] Authority meeting on February 22, 1985.
[272] The New Jekyll Island Club Inc. changed its name to the Jekyll Island Museum Associates in 1990. The organization became later known as Friends of Historic Jekyll Island. (See Addendum 3.)

Clam Creek is in dire need of its picnic area renovation, but funds are not readily available. A grant from the Department of Natural Resources with matching funds from the authority make the renovation possible.

The Jekyll Island Fitness Center, located adjacent to the demolished Aquarama building, is fully operational, and operating hours and fee schedules are published. Frank Simpson manages and opens the center daily from 7 a.m. to 5 p.m. except on Monday, Wednesday, Friday, and Sunday when the center opens during afternoons only. Daily, weekly, and monthly rates are set, while annual memberships can be purchased for singles, married couples, and families at $150, $250, and $350 respectively.

The Causeway Welcome Center and Georgia State Patrol building is nearing completion by May 1985 and reason enough for the authority to announce a dedication ceremony in June 1985 for the grand opening of the welcome center, Georgia State Patrol, fitness center, and Ski Rixen.

Despite the successful additions or upgrades to recreational activities on the island, revenue for 1985 falls short of the projections and is below the 1984 revenue total. The overall hotel occupancy, parking fees, and golf passes all show a decline in comparison to the previous year, while most of the island's fee structure remains the same.

But what remains the same must always be offset with continuous changes, and it is no surprise that some existing hotels-motels go through their ritual of lease assignments or changes in ownership.

Villas by the Sea requests a lease transfer from Jekyll Villas Associates to Villas by the Sea Inc., owned and represented by George Heaton and Bernard Wolfson. The transaction involves more than just another simple transfer. This time, Villas by the Sea Inc. purchases the property outright from the previous owner and agrees to pay the authority 6 percent of the purchase price. No specific purchase prices are mentioned in the archived documents, but remembering that First National Bank of Boston held the primary mortgage on the property in the amount of $3,900,000 and that additional construction has taken place together with the issuance of junior notes, it is fair to assume that the purchase price exceeds the above amount. A 6 percent fee to the authority is therefore considerable, and it also marks the first time that the authority charges what amounts to a brokerage fee to accommodate a lease assignment. The precedents of the past must have compelled the authority to partake in the multiple changes of ownership and consider the lease assignments to be the equivalent of the purchase and sale agreement and therefore subject to the standard brokerage fees of 6 percent.

The Ramada Inn, which filed for Chapter 11 bankruptcy protection the year before, is finally purchased by Jekyll Island Group, who promises extensive renovations and upgrades to the property.

As the summer season ends with the second annual Beach Music Festival and its 23,000 attendees that cause the residents to file multiple complaints with the authority, more serious negotiations take place between the authority and Larry Evans of Circle Development Corp.

Of the original six development firms interested in the JI Club prospectus at the beginning of the year, and the four board presentations soon afterward, only two companies remain interested in the completion of the restoration project, namely Winn Development Co. of Boston and Circle Development Co. of Brunswick.

In the end, the local Brunswick company, despite being much smaller and certainly less prestigious than its Boston competitor, obtains a sixty-day lease option on the Jekyll Island Club Hotel and adjacent properties and begins to negotiate the financial arrangements.

The complete restoration is projected to cost $20 million, half of which is obtained through the issuance of industrial development bonds by Brunswick-Glynn County Development Authority and the assignment of such to a newly created company, Jekyll Circle Ltd. Project. The next step is to secure letters of credit to back the bonds and to find an additional $10 million to finance the entire project. Most funds, about $8 million in total, are pledged through a variety of partnerships, with the remaining $2 million coming from an Urban Development Action Grant with the help of the city of Brunswick and its director of downtown development, Roosevelt Harris.

With the required financing now in place, Jekyll Club Associates, the new lessee of the Jekyll Island Club Hotel and Sans Souci, through its partners/representatives Leon Weiner, Larry Evans, and Gene Murphy, begin the first round of negotiation of the terms and conditions for a long-term lease agreement.

Jekyll Club Associates stipulates four requests on August 25, 1985, during a regular board meeting:

1) The designation and use of 200 feet of beachfront between the existing Shuckers Restaurant and the North Beach House.
2) The permission to build one hundred additional guest rooms, attached or adjacent to the existing JI Club Hotel, with meeting space to be used by hotel guests only.
3) Meeting space shall be limited to 10 square feet per hotel room and based on double occupancy (two guests); that is, 144 rooms x 2 x 10 = 2,880 square feet (maximum allowance).
4) A five-year lease option to use four acres on the north side of Shell Road, aka the old driving range. All buildings shall be constructed as hotel rooms or suites only.

The authority sets forth the following terms for lease negotiations with Circle Development Corp:

1) Lease payments
   - Years 9–10: $100,000
   - Years 11–15: 3 percent of gross
   - Years 16–55: 3.5 percent of gross
2) Language regarding use by average income and price control by the authority softened
3) Default provision written in same language as the other hotels
4) Require approval of authority before lease assignment.
5) Fifty-five-year term
6) Designate area north of Shuckers as beach access for hotel and authorize construction of a boardwalk and bathhouse
7) Lease tennis center[273] for ten years with gross received included in hotel's lease payments (It was the consensus of the authority that these courts remain accessible to the public until the authority constructs additional courts.)
8) Security deposit
   - Years 1–8: $50,000
   - Years 9–10: $150,000

---

[273] The tennis center refers to the Morgan Tennis Center on Old Plantation Road in the Historic District.

- Years 11–55: $200,000
9) Performance bonds required to ensure completion of the project[274]

The lease agreement between Jekyll Club Associates and the authority is signed on September 12, 1985, and the restoration work starts immediately and coincides with the completion of the new Island Museum, the old millionaires' stables, and its new orientation center.

It seems that the authority has finally found a path to restoration and preservation after struggling to maintain and repair the old village structures. The millionaires' cottages will have to wait until grant money is received, but restoration of the historic Club Hotel is in full swing by early 1986. The required $20 million funding is now in place and secure, thanks to a letter of credit obtained from a French Bank, Banque Indosuez in Paris, and a franchise agreement with Radisson Hotels and Resorts. Full details about the financing, project development, and restoration of the Club Hotel, Annex building, and Sans Souci are described and narrated in detail in *The Jekyll Island Club Hotel*, written by June Hall McCash and Brenden Martin, published by the Donning Company Publishers, Virginia Beach, in 2012.

The letter of credit by a French bank is notable here. While it is standard practice to guarantee the issuance of bonds, in this case $10 million issued by the Brunswick-Glynn County Development Authority, with a letter of credit, it is unusual to find a foreign bank doing so rather than a federal bank or even a regional bank.

Despite Mr. Weiner's extensive business connections, no US bank was willing or could issue the required letter of credit, hence he resorted to contacting Banque Indosuez in Paris. In exchange for guaranteeing the $10 million loan, the bank requested that the hotel would be franchised to a reputable hotel company. In this case, the Radisson agreed to lend its name and management experience to the new JI Club Hotel.

With one major project underway and a heavy burden and concern lifted from the authority's shoulders, time and efforts can be spent on other island matters, and there are plenty. The idea is of course to ready the island's infrastructure, beauty, and recreational facilities by the time the Club Hotel and the Historic District reopen to the public for the first

---

[274] Board meeting on August 26, 1985.

time on December 29, 1986, as a soft opening, with the grand opening taking place three months later on March 31, 1987.

By early 1986, the roads, asphalt, and concrete at the north picnic area have been removed and piled up. Only a short stretch of the original access road remains intact today, but some of the road infrastructure, water drains, and remains of the concrete benches that once adorned the picnic area can still be found after heavy storms and beach erosion, only to be covered up again by Mother Nature as it did thirty years ago. Removal of road and picnic area debris must be taken with a grain of salt. Most of the debris was indeed piled up but never completely removed, leaving it to Mother Nature to take care of "natural" removal, covering it up with sand or simply displacing it somewhere else.

The authority follows up on its intention to self-manage and operate all food services on the island. The Otter Corporation's lease had already been amended in 1984 to exclude the old wharf, the convention center, JI Marina, the golf clubhouse, and Crane Cottage from the lease agreement. This time around, its lease for Shuckers Restaurant is also terminated, permanently ending the relationship. Jim Rohr, representative of Otter Food Services Corporation, demands payment in the amount of $200,000 for losses incurred and early termination of the lease agreement.

Shuckers Restaurant receives a complete makeover during the spring at a cost of $375,000 and reopens its doors on July 1, 1986, as Blackbeard's. The new restaurant, with seating for 164 patrons, is to provide an outstanding lunch and dinner experience on the island. But the authority does not stop there with its ambition of providing excellent dining facilities. While Shuckers Restaurant is being remodeled, the first plans to construct and open an additional restaurant at the old wharf surface. Ussery/Rule Architects of St. Simons Island write a proposal to the authority on April 28, 1986:

Latitude 31-Statement of Probable Cost

General Contract	$154,709.00
Site Work	$8,800.00
Furnishings	$55,597.00

Awnings & Covered Walk	$20,000.00
New Equipment	$50,000.00
Gazebo, Deck & Equipment	$31,000.00
Outdoor Furniture	$8,000.00
Signage	$2,500.00
TOTAL	$330,606.00

Local shrimpers are still using the docks at the wharf to conduct their business daily, and the authority decides to postpone all plans until the end of the 1988 shrimping season.

Ski Rixen Jekyll Island, which just assumed the lease agreement from its parent company a year earlier, proposes to sell all its equipment and the main building at Rixen Pond to the authority. It is unclear whether this questionable decision is based on less than anticipated revenue during its first two years of operation or whether Ski Rixen sees a business opportunity now that the authority is clearly focused on self-management of all island facilities. No action is taken by the authority at this time, and Ski Rixen will continue to own and operate the Rixen Pond until 1990 when the authority finally decides to purchase all buildings, equipment, and inventory.

The next action item on the authority's list is the airport and its current lessee, Shields Aviation, who has been in payment defaults several times. The authority abruptly decides to terminate the existing lease agreement and to upgrade the runway, expand the apron, and install MIRL (medium-intensity runway lights) at the recommendation of the Federal Aviation Administration. The estimated project cost is $458,000 but is fully funded by a grant obtained from the FAA. Davis Aviation will ultimately replace Shields Aviation and operate the newly renovated airport.

The golf courses are not immune to changes or upgrades either, as nothing seems to be on the island. The Oleander Golf Course receives a facelift when Benson Construction Co. rebuilds all greens for $259,000. Pine Lakes Golf Course, however, may see a different future altogether when the authority instructs Laventhol & Horwath to study the feasibility of constructing homes on and around the golf course. The study is presented to the authority that same summer, but no action is taken toward implementation. The same idea of creating a golf course community with luxury private homes will resurface again several times and at the time of writing is again a point of discussion and contention.

But what about the hotels? Certainly something must be brewing underneath the heavy and busy reorganization that takes place, given its long history of changes in ownership and operational management.

The first sign comes from one of the older motels on the island, the Seafarer Motel, which applies for a change from motel designation to become a condominium hotel, like previous requests from Villas by the Sea and others alike. Not surprisingly, the request is denied, and the motel is ordered to continue to operate "as is." The authority never liked the idea of condominiums on the island and has always preferred regular hotels or motels throughout its existence.

The second in line is the Jekyll Inn and Resort,[275] which requests another lease assignment from Jekyll Partners, Ltd. to Jekyll Inn & Resort, LP. But something bigger is brewing underneath the current, caused by the pending opening of the JI Club Hotel as a Radisson franchise.

A hotel owners' meeting is called with the authority to express their concerns about the multitude of changes and what is viewed by some as unfair competition.[276] The Jekyll Hilton Inn is viewed by its competitors as being heavily subsidized by the Georgia Teachers Retirement System, which still owns the hotel and is its sole mortgage holder since inception in 1971, and certainly since the original bankruptcy filing of the Sand Dollar Motel and its subsequent conversion to its status as a Hilton Inn.

The second concern of the hotel owners is the franchise agreement between the Jekyll Club Associates and the Radisson Hotels & Resorts. The agreement to allow one hundred additional hotel rooms to be built at or adjacent to the Club Hotel is viewed as unfair competition.

The fact that the authority is taking over all island food services, including restaurants, is another reason for concern. Most of the hotels operate their own restaurants on site but do not benefit from the large-scale food operations the authority is managing. It gives the authority an unfair competitive advantage in the tourist and visitor market against which no

---

[275] Previously the Ladha Inn and currently known as the Days Inn & Suites.
[276] The hotel owners-authority meeting took place on July 21, 1986.

hotel owner has any recourse. Add to this that the authority also owns and operates the convention center, and therefore directly and indirectly controls the visitors' budget, and it is no surprise that the owners want more direct participation and request that a general marketing plan be developed with the input and participation of all hotel and motel owners.

Lastly, the owners request the authority to examine and revise the operational cost of conducting business on the island. Specifically, the request points toward the prevalent cost of water, sewage, and fire services and the impact such monthly expenses have on their net income, while businesses operated by the authority are not subject to the same fee schedule, hence the creation of another disadvantage for the hotel and motel owners.

The sticking point is probably best described as the existing disparity between the island's hotels and motels as contributors to the Jekyll Island Convention and Visitors Bureau and its lack of control over or input in marketing strategy. The suggestion is made to open a sales office in Atlanta and jointly market the convention center and the available hotels/motels simultaneously. That still does not solve the authority's seeming food services monopoly, nor does it really solve the marketing control the authority has implemented during the last few years.

The positive outcome of the meeting is that both parties ultimately agree to expand their cooperation. At least that is what it looks like from the outside and high above, while the reality in between the lines is a continuation of what works best for the authority and the island in its entirety.

The water park is still a project under contention since the requested capital funds for 1986 are denied by the general assembly. What probably makes matters worse is that Jekyll Island's friendly competitor, Lake Lanier Islands, succeeds in appropriating $25 million in general obligation bonds from the general assembly to fund and implement its 1987 Revised Master Plan. That leaves the authority with the option of possibly using the issuance of tax-exempt bonds to fund the major capital improvement projects. The development of Lake Lanier Islands and the creation of the Lake Lanier Islands Development Authority (LLIDA) is well documented in a commemorative book published by LLIDA: *Building a Georgia Treasure, Celebrating 50 Years*, 2015.

Despite the denied capital funding, the authority orders a second study for the water park, this time to be completed by William Haralson & Associates. The first study was completed by Economic Research Associates (ERA) two years earlier in 1984, and both studies have substantial differences in cost and pricing.

ERA's estimate for Phase I was $4.9 million, while the second study estimates the start-up cost at $2.9 million. By the end of November, the board approves again to seek general assembly funding for the water park in the 1987 budget, after it receives support from the owners of Villas by the Sea and the Holiday Inn Beach Resort.

The supporting vote that is missing here is that of Motel Properties Inc., operator of the Comfort Inn Island Suites, previously known as the Wanderer Motel, and the Quality Inn-Buccaneer, previously known as the Buccaneer Motor Lodge. No reason is mentioned for the lack of support from one of the largest hotel management companies on Jekyll Island, but it is noteworthy here since a year later the same management company will acquire another hotel lease and increase its management share on Jekyll Island to 43 percent of the total hotel/motel rooms available.

The year ends well for the authority in the sense that the newly renovated Jekyll Island Club Hotel has its soft opening on December 29, 1986, and right on schedule, although a full opening will take place in the spring of 1987. It marks the first time the Millionaires' Hotel is open again for 144 eager guests in more than fifteen years.

With the hotel opening also comes the grand opening of Blackbeard's, the authority's own ocean-view restaurant, completely renovated and newly landscaped. The capital expense for landscaping alone is $90,000 because sewer lines must be installed and connected with the municipal sewage system.

The authority must have high expectations for its new restaurant, as its feasibility chart estimates a continuous 80 percent occupancy during 364 operating days. Reality falls well short of the estimate, but nothing can dampen the excitement the authority feels.

Forty years in the making and four decades of continuous struggles to overcome economic obstacles and financial setbacks, and yet here is Jekyll Island, bruised and hurt but not defeated and still standing. The future looks bright and promising, now more than ever before. Who knows what the next forty years have in store and what other changes are coming.

If the four-year Capital Improvement Plan, as presented at the end of 1986, is any indication, there are plenty of changes to be made and projects to finance and realize. And as always, some seem feasible, while others will require some serious adjustments to become successful.

One thing is certain: Jekyll Island is not done and finished growing up yet, and neither is its story.

EPILOGUE

The soft opening of the newly restored Jekyll Island Club Hotel rings in a new chapter and a brand-new beginning for the island. Set to open its doors again in March 1987, after having been closed for fifteen years, it is one of the most exciting moments in island history.

After several attempts to save the Historic Landmark Hotel, the collaboration between public and private capital proves to be the key to success, and most certainly when it pertains to preserve history. The newly found form of public private partnerships, or PPPs as they are commonly referred to, will be used again in the years to come. It even gives rise to specific legislation in 1993 that will allow for the involvement of private contractors in "the development, construction, operation, and management" of projects (Ga. L. 1993, p. 1781 [Act No. 600]).

The same PPP formula is used many times in the following thirty years of the island's tumultuous history that is yet to be written, sometimes successfully, and other times not so successfully. Suffice it to say that saving the Jekyll Island Club Hotel has become the blueprint for the authority to follow a path of development, management, and operation of Jekyll Island State Park that is both unique and innovative in its approach—most definitely so when placed within the timeframe in which it was first successfully executed: 1986.

The new approach is further solidified in the coming years with firm long-term agreements between both the public and the private participants/investors that provide either tax or lease advantages over a specific period when the private investors adhere to the duration of the initial agreements.

Despite the seemingly advantageous proposals, the next thirty years will see several development attempts collapse prior to the initial design and development phase, even after intense and long negotiations. The delay caused by the "business divorce with mutual consent" sets back commercial and recreational development on the island by several years.

In addition, the 1999–2000 market collapse and the subsequent international financial crisis of 2008 have major repercussions on the island's development and revenue stream. The impact is so damaging that even thirty years later, it can still be seen with the existence of empty hotel lots and fenced-in oceanfront lots that have been vacant since 2005 in some cases, while all of them were still occupied at the end of 1986.

If the first forty years in the island's history are any indication of what is to come next, then the following thirty years certainly do not disappoint. If the train of thought at the end of 1986 is, however, that the road to success has been paved with rose petals and that all will be well now that the Historic District has been saved from demolition or decay, then more hard-learned lessons need to be experienced.

Economic downturns and financial crises are hard to predict and even harder to protect oneself against, except of course when development plans fit within a well-thought-out vision. After forty years, there have been multiple plans, but there is still no vision.

Can a new chapter change the plan-making authority into a visionary board that can blend the financial desire for a "year-round resort" with the Gov. Thompson's vision of a "state park, accessible and affordable to the common people of the state of Georgia"?

Can the lessons of hardship and disappointment give rise to a new approach with a clear vision for the future, or will development plans be altered again in land-use plans as each decade passes?

Will the existing duality of Dr. Jekyll and Mr. Hyde, or the forced symbiosis of a resort-island and a state park, finally be resolved and come to terms with a shared coexistence without infringement or threat to affordability?

One thing is certain. Development and expansion do not end and are forever meant to evolve just as the natural ebb and flow of the island itself.

Maybe that is the answer to these rhetorical questions.

What erodes in the north must accrete in the south, as Mother Nature intends it to be, and as the story shall continue ...

Jekyll Creek drawbridge. Officially opened in December 1954, the bridge finally connected the JI Causeway, completed in 1949, with the island. The bridge remained operational until 1997 when it was replaced with the current elevated bridge. (Author's collection.)

Jekyll Island entrance. The two towers were constructed in 1959. One housed a public bathroom; the other was the first welcome center. The towers remain intact today, although the banner in the middle has since been removed. (Author's collection.)

Jekyll Island neon road sign. During the early sixties, the authority launched its first advertising campaign and placed several directional signs on US-17. This sign was placed at the entrance of the JI Causeway. (Author's collection.)

Jekyll Island sign. This sign could be seen next to the entrance of the old IGA Supermarket, temporarily located at the public beach parking area, south of the Holiday Inn Resort. (Author's collection.)

The old wharf. Also known as Jekyll Island Marina before the current marina was constructed in 1989. (Author's collection.)

The old wharf. Home to several shrimping boats until 1988. (Author's collection.)

Jekyll Island Parkway. Seen here in the late fifties or early sixties. The island entrance was renamed the Ben Fortson Jr. Memorial Parkway in 1979 in memory of Ben Fortson, secretary of state and chairman of the authority board. (Author's collection.)

Cherokee Campground. First opened in 1957 by Wayne Morrow. The authority terminated Mr. Morrow's lease in 1984 and took control of the campground. (Author's collection.)

Jekyll Sandwich Hut. Previously known as Charcoal House Restaurant, Jekyll Sandwich Hut changed its name to Shoreline Restaurant. It later became known as Shuckers Restaurant (early to mid-1980s) and changed names again in 1986 to Blackbeard's and later to Fin's on the Beach. It is currently known as Tortuga Jack's. (Author's collection.)

Blackbeard's Seafood Restaurant. Home of the original Charcoal House Restaurant. (Author's collection.)

Jekyll Island Clubhouse. The island's first golf clubhouse was constructed in 1958, using the original bricks from the demolished Albright-Pulitzer Cottage. It is now home to Red Bug Motor's Pizza. (Author's collection.)

Gould Auditorium. The old Gould Playhouse served as the island's first convention center until 1973. (Author's collection.)

Clam Creek Bridge. Constructed in the early sixties, the bridge connects Clam Creek with Driftwood Beach. (Author's collection.)

Clam Creek fishing pier. Constructed in 1969. A ticket booth was placed at the entrance to collect daily entrance fees. The fees were abolished in 1970 and replaced with fishing licenses. (Author's collection.)

Aquarama entrance. The indoor pool was constructed in 1961 and demolished in 1983. It was part of the new convention and welcome center. (Author's collection.)

The Aquarama and convention center. The convention center was demolished in 2010 to make room for a new convention center and beach village. (Author's collection.)

Welcome center. Located at the convention center and Aquarama. (Author's collection.)

Aquarama and convention center. South Beach House is visible on the left. The two shopping centers can be seen behind the convention center. (Author's collection.)

Old shopping center. The first of two shopping centers opened in 1959. (Author's collection.)

Old shopping center. The first of two shopping centers opened in 1959. (Author's collection.)

North Beach House. Three public bathhouses were located on the boardwalk in 1957—one to the north (south of current Holiday Inn Resort), one in the center at Shell Road, and one to the south, between the convention center and the current Days Inn & Suites. (Author's collection.)

South Beach House. Located between the convention center and the current Days Inn & Suites. All public bathhouses were demolished in 1984. (Author's collection.)

Jekyll Island Club Hotel (1965). Cars were still allowed, and Riverview Drive was open to two-way traffic in the Historic District until the mid-1990s. (Author's collection.)

Jekyll Estates Motel. The first motel on Jekyll Island, constructed in 1957. Currently known as the Beachview Club. (Author's collection.)

Wanderer Motel. Constructed in 1957 and the second motel on the island. Currently home to the Holiday Inn Resort. (Author's collection.)

Seafarer Apartments. Constructed in 1958 with salvaged bricks from the Oglethorpe Hotel in Brunswick. Currently home to the Quality Inn. (Author's collection.)

The Corsair. Built in 1960 as the third hotel on the island and the first one on the southside. Currently home to the Days Inn & Suites. (Author's collection.)

Dolphin Motor Lodge Inn. Completed in 1960, the motel only survived three years and closed by 1964, after which it became a youth camp until UGA transformed the properties into a 4-H Center. The buildings were demolished in 2015 to make room for Jekyll Camp. (Author's collection.)

Buccaneer Motor Lodge. Built in 1960, south of the Corsair. The hotel was demolished in 2007, and the land is currently vacant, awaiting development. (Author's collection.)

Stuckey's Carriage Inn (1963). The hotel was originally known as the Holiday Inn (1961). The hotel closed in 2003 as the Georgia Coast Inn and was demolished in 2005. The land is currently vacant. awaiting development. (Author's collection.)

```
              DEDICATION PROGRAM
         JEKYLL ISLAND STATE PARK BEACH HOUSE
              J. M. ATKINSON, PRESIDING
                    Jr. P. E.

NATIONAL ANTHEM                    RISLEY BAND
INVOCATION                         REV. JULIUS JAMES
MUSIC                              RISLEY SCHOOL
RECOGNATION OUT OF TOWN GUEST      J. P. ATKINSON &
                                   J. S. WILKINSON
MUSIC
PRESENTATION OF CITY, COUNTY AND STATE OFFICIALS
                                   J. L. CARRUECHE
MUSIC
INTRODUCTION OF SPEAKER            REV. R. W. MOORE
ADDRESS                            REV. J. Y. MAIN
MUSIC                              RISLEY BAND
PRESENTATION OF PARK               HON. B. B. BLALOCK
ACCEPTANCE                         PRES. LUCIOUS DACOTE,
                                   STATE TEACHERS ASS.
BENEDICTION

              W. P. HOLMES, MARSHALL, MOTORCADE
```

Dedication St. Andrews Beach House. September 5, 1955. (Author's collection.)

PART II

1987–2015

THE RISE AND FALL OF JEKYLL ISLAND STATE PARK

CHAPTER 11

THE PERIOD OF STAGNATION AND HESITATION

1987–1990

The Historic District is finally coming alive again, now that the Millionaires' Club Hotel has been restored to its original and natural beauty. A few changes are made of course as part of bringing the historic hotel up to par with modern accommodations and expectations of guests and visitors. Overall, the hotel retains its true character while offering modern conveniences.

After the soft opening in December 1986, the hotel launches its grand opening in March 1987 to the delight of many guests and residents who have been waiting patiently for fifteen years. The addition of two meeting or reception rooms[277] and the restoration of the original lobby staircase certainly do not go unnoticed. Neither is the removal of the elevator building and the carefully reconstructed porte cochere that is a reminder of the days when guests arrived by horse-drawn carriage and were greeted by their own private butler and housekeeping staff.

All 144 guests are treated in the same way, and the new Radisson-franchised hotel gets raving reviews for its service, accommodations, and dining experience. The new and upscale accommodations will soon be

---

[277] The Vanderbilt and Rockefeller rooms were not part of the original 1886 hotel design. Both rooms were added during the 1986 restoration/renovation.

used as a standard by which all other hotels and motels are measured with regards to lodging, service, and quality.

Apart from the Jekyll Island Club Hotel, the Historic District remains in the same condition as before. The millionaires' cottages on North Riverview Drive and the smaller cottages on Pier Road remain the same, but plans are being made to restore and rejuvenate the entire Historic District very soon. For that purpose, the authority, upon recommendation by Executive Director George Chambliss, creates the new position of superintendent of historic structures.

It needs to be mentioned that even in 1987, most of the roadbeds in the Historic District are asphalt and are open to vehicles and tour carriages, including North Riverview Drive, in front of the Jekyll Island Club Hotel, and Old Plantation Road, between the south and north end of the newly renamed Stable Road.[278]

Motor vehicles and tour carriages passing by the historic cottages on Riverview Drive, Old Plantation Road, and Pier Road in both directions are common sights and have been since the late 1950s. It is also common for tour operators to drop off their customers or to provide narrated tours while passing by. That too will change if George Chambliss gets his way and the much-needed funding to restore the entire Historic District.

Things are changing, and the restoration of the Jekyll Island Club Hotel serves as a catalyst to finally pay attention to the oldest structures on the island.

The opening of the JICH-Radisson also leads to the creation of private and designated parking areas, which is a new concept. The hotel, through its lease agreement with the authority, has full and private access to all parking areas between Stable Road and the back side of the hotel. Only hotel guests can park their vehicles there, which means the only remaining public parking in the Historic District is at the old wharf. For that purpose, the authority allows trailers to be parked there and allows overnight parking with special permit only.

The old wharf itself is in dire need of some upgrades, but Zachry's Seafood Market receives a one-year lease extension in March 1987. Concurrent with the extension and the plans for renovation and

---

[278] Old Village Boulevard was renamed Stable Road in May 1986 (authority board meeting, May 19, 1986).

repurposing, George Chambliss notifies the Jekyll Island shrimpers[279] that their wharf dockage agreement will not be renewed and that such terminates thirty days after the closing of the beaches to shrimping. The change rings in the end of an era and the end of a local piece of island history as it has been known for decades or longer.

The old wharf has served as a center for the local island shrimping business since the 1950s. That is not a surprise, since it was the only existing docking space on Jekyll Island. For several decades, ten shrimping families made a living by catching sweet white Georgia shrimp off the coast of Jekyll Island. They would dock their boats at the old wharf and sell their fresh shrimp right there. The shrimping business was so popular it led to one of the shrimp boat captains, David Zachry, opening a small seafood market on the old wharf in 1979 and expanding his business by starting a shrimp-packaging business right next door.[280]

The shrimp boats are still a daily sight on Jekyll Island but are no longer a staple in the Historic District. While one staple is on the verge of disappearing, another one gains in popularity. Santa's Christmas Shop, which opened in 1984 in the old power plant[281] and succeeded Mr. Stauffer's antique automobile museum, is becoming an attraction in the Historic District, so much so that the owners receive a three-year lease extension without any need to renegotiate the terms and conditions, a rare feat for business owners indeed. Despite the setback last year in obtaining funding for a water park on the island, a new request is made for the issuance of general obligation bonds in the amount of $4.6 million. The bonds are set to mature at five years, and $4 million is reserved for the water park, while $600K is earmarked for a new tennis center. In addition, the authority authorizes George Chambliss to request $2.1 million for stabilization of the Historic District and to build an additional nine holes

---

[279] Letter to John Roundtree, Kew McCall, Fred Dennis, David Zachry, Ed Roberts, Jeff Brannen, Bobby Waters, and Wesley Dickey, dated December 1, 1987 (authority board meeting minutes-addendum).
[280] The Wharf restaurant, previously known as Latitude 31, was the original location of Zachry's shrimp-packaging business. The Rah Bar, demolished in 2017, was the original location of Zachry's Seafood Market.
[281] The old power plant is now home to the Georgia Sea Turtle Center.

at the Oceanside golf course.²⁸² The additional funding will have to wait, as the general assembly does not see the need for golf course expansion beyond the existing sixty-three holes. It does approve funding for the water park,²⁸³ and by January 1988, construction of Phase I is right on schedule.

The year 1987 marks a change of direction not simply because of the grand opening of the new Radisson-JICH or the construction of what will become Summer Waves but also because of careful preparation and documentation of existing revenue-generating businesses, such as the hotels and small businesses in the shopping center. For starters, Mr. Chambliss orders a comparative study of the current rent per square footage for all businesses in the shopping center and the Historic District. The intent is obviously to streamline future revenue, and the results are surprising. Jekyll Realty, for example, pays five dollars per square footage, while William Bonamie, owner and operator of the Jekyll Island Beverage Center, pays $15.79 per square footage. All other shopping center business owners pay a monthly rent anywhere between those two numbers.

Businesses in the Historic District such as the Cottage on Pier Road, the Seafood Market at the wharf and Santa's Christmas Shop, pay twelve dollars per square footage. It is evident that monthly rents are set haphazardly at the time of lease commencement and that such guaranteed revenue needs to be streamlined.

Other commercial businesses undergo some dramatic changes as well. The Jekyll Inn,²⁸⁴ better known as the Jekyll Hilton Inn, changes ownership from Jekyll Associates to Greater Capital Corp. This change is merely a change of lessee, since the Georgia Teachers Retirement System is still considered the owner as holder of the primary mortgage. Since Jekyll Associates is deemed to be in default of its lease agreement, Greater Capital Corp. is approved by the authority as new lessee, effective June 22, 1987, and pledges to invest $3.1 million for renovation, construction of public

---

[282] The additional nine holes would restore the Great Dunes golf course to its original design of eighteen holes. The new nine holes would be located north of Shell Road (authority board meeting, November 10, 1987).

[283] The water park, Summer Waves, will open June 18, 1988.

[284] The Georgia Teachers Retirement System owns the Jekyll Hilton Inn and is considered a "subsidized" hotel. The hotel originally opened as the Sand Dollar Motel (1971) and was demolished in 2015 to make room for The Cottages at Jekyll Island (constructed in 2015–2018).

areas, tennis courts, and meeting rooms, while an additional $2.4 million is earmarked to renovate the guest rooms.

With the change of ownership also comes a change in management companies, and Motel Properties Inc., which already manages the Quality Inn Buccaneer[285] and the Comfort Inn Island Suites,[286] becomes the new property manager. This change makes Motel Properties Inc. the largest hotel management company on Jekyll Island, managing 43 percent of all available hotel rooms, excluding the Radisson-JICH.

Coincidentally, or maybe not, Villas by the Sea approaches the authority yet again with a proposal to convert the hotel to condominium ownership. The persistent push by owners and financers to convert large hotels to condominium ownership has been prevalent since the mid to late 1970s. Mr. Larry Morris, original owner of the Sand Dollar Motel, and Mr. Bernard Wolfson, owner of Villas by the Sea, have submitted requests for condominium conversion on several occasions but have always been met with resistance. Some of that resistance by the authority is warranted but not in its entirety.

Looking back at the origination of land lease agreement and leasehold agreement in the late 1950s and its evolution over the past thirty years, it is important to note that all effective lease agreements so far, whether residential or commercial, are always based on sole ownership of said lease and the buildings constructed upon it. In the case of residential leases, this is obvious, but in the case of commercial leases, the entity that constructs the hotel or motel has always been a single incorporated entity that collateralizes not only the building(s) but also the leasehold agreement upon which the hotel/motel is constructed, hence the first mortgagor can take possession of both the leasehold agreement and the hotel/motel in case of default.

When ownership of a single incorporated entity changes into a condominium ownership, then obviously a disconnect of ownership between the leasehold agreement and the individual condominium

---

[285] Previously known as the Buccaneer Motor Lodge and located just south of the current Days Inn & Suites. The hotel was demolished in 2007, and the lot has been vacant since.

[286] Originally known as the Wanderer Motel (1957) and currently known as the Holiday Inn Resort.

ownership is created, hence the reluctance of the authority to approve such requests. While this may not seem to be a complicated matter at first sight, it does have serious legal concerns for the authority and the way business is, or has been, conducted in the past thirty years.

This time, things may be different, as Mr. Wolfson finds a way to convince the authority to at least consider a transfer of leasehold estate for Villas by the Sea.

Summary of Villas Conversion to Condominium Ownership.

1. Establishes hotel as leasehold condominium under condominium law.
2. Lessee has right to sublease hotel units
3. Lessee is not relieved of obligation of lease after subleasing units.
4. Rights of sublessee (unit owner) subordinate to lessee.
5. Premises shall continue to be operated as a hotel during the entire term of this lease.
6. After 14 days use of a unit in the months of February through August, unit purchaser will pay substituted rent for any use during those months.
7. Substituted rent is 8% of average daily rate for double occupancy for the month of occupancy.
8. Unit purchasers that are employed on Jekyll are exempt from substituted rent. Only 6 units can be exempt.
9. Hotel unit mortgagees who acquire hotel units from a foreclosure are exempt from substituted rent.
10. Maintain membership in Jekyll Island Tourist Bureau.
11. Budget and books for marketing and sale of units are to be maintained separately from operational records.
12. Lessee will make good faith effort to complete the sale of the units by 1992.
13. Lessee will pay 2% of unit gross sales (up to $11,500,000) and 10% of unit gross sales over $11,500,000.
14. Gross sales payments are due December 31st in 2nd year after the initial sale. Each December after the initial sale the 2% is due on that calendar year's sales.

15. Lessee will provide a certified accounting statement of all sales on an annual basis.
16. Lessor will not allow the sublease of other hotel units on the island that are not equipped with separate dining room and kitchen during the first five years of Villas' unit sales.
17. Lessee must maintain books for period of not less than 24 calendar months.
18. Lessee must make books available to lessor.
19. Mortgagee that acquires unit by foreclosure shall have the right to pay lessor the proportionate share of the base rent.
20. Lessor agrees to release Jekyll Villa Associates (Wolfson, Heaton) from further obligation 12 months after last hotel unit sold.
21. Lessee will deliver a set of condominium instruments that sets out understandings with unit buyer prior to the initial sales offering.[287]

A few things are interesting in this proposal. Notice that although the units are offered up for sale individually, the authority demands payment of base rent even when the unit is owner-occupied.

Secondly, a clause in the agreement protects Villas by the Sea from any unwanted competition for the first five years of unit sales, thereby providing exclusivity on Jekyll Island and temporarily prohibiting any other hotel owners from competing in the same market. On the other hand, this clause may also be viewed as a careful attempt to curb any unbridled growth of the condominium market on the island and can be interpreted as a protective measure, given that condo conversions or cooperatives are an increasingly popular idea with existing owners of multifamily dwellings, including hotel/motel structures.

Of greater impact is probably the decision by the general assembly to raise the hotel/motel tax from 3 percent to 5 percent, effective July 1987.[288] While this increase may seem rather innocent, it must be noted that all government employees are exempt from this tax, which has serious financial consequences for the authority. Most of the larger conventions are organized by state agencies or government associations, and while

---

[287] Addendum to authority board meeting, November 6, 1987.
[288] HB 563 (Act 621), approved on April 2, 1987, during regular general assembly session.

this represents good business for the hotel and motel industry on the island, most, if not all, attendees are exempt from the hotel/motel tax as government employees. Moreover, they are also exempt from the daily parking fee. The loss of income due to the exemptions amounts to $123K by August 1987.[289]

Before the year ends, three new ideas are launched. The authority adopts a resolution on October 12, 1987, to request the governor "... to render all such assistance as his office may permit in advocating the placement of dredged, beach-quality sand from Brunswick harbor upon the eroded beach areas of Jekyll Island, Sea Island and St. Simons Island ..."[290]

This marks the first time that beach renourishment is mentioned rather than the placement of revetments or riprap. The idea itself stems from the beach renourishment program on Tybee Island that dates to 1970. Tybee City Council ordered a study of beach erosion in correlation with the dredging of the Savannah River shipping channel. The study determined that the Army Corps of Engineers caused excessive beach erosion by dredging of the shipping channel. Subsequently, Tybee Island has received grants from the Army Corps of Engineers, equally matched by city reserve funds to pay for the beach renourishment every seven years. Jekyll Island is obviously aware of this agreement and tries to lay the foundation to follow the same path. Unfortunately, the idea never materializes, as the future will show.

The second idea that takes shape is the replacement of the old drawbridge. To that extent, George Chambliss, executive director, takes it upon himself to contact his political allies in the general assembly and the Department of Transportation and plants the seed for a new and higher bridge to Jekyll Island. The seed that is planted in 1987 takes several more years to grow and materialize.

The third and last idea of the year is the implementation of regular hotel/motel inspections. Although no formal process is in place yet, the quality of service and cleanliness of the existing hotels is compared to the upscale service of the Radisson-JICH. In the next year, this process

---

[289] Authority board meeting, August 17, 1987.
[290] Addendum, authority board meeting, October 12, 1987. Signed by Mrs. Carolyn Stradley-Thompson, secretary.

will become a regular event and will be formalized in a set and required operating standard for all hotel owners.

The first monthly board meeting of the new year is always sparked with vigor, ideas, and immediate action, and the start of 1988 is certainly no exception to the rule. George Chambliss makes sure that all the commercial leases in the shopping center are renewed and extended for five years, and in the process, ensures that the rate per square footage is streamlined with other lease agreements. Jekyll Realty, a permanent island fixture since 1983, sees its monthly rent increased by 55 percent and is not the only one that is subject to large rate adjustments. It is the beginning of a new approach by the authority, under the leadership of Executive Director Chambliss, to start maximizing the potential revenue stream for the island.

For several decades, the authority has accepted the less-than-favorite terms and conditions of residential and commercial lease agreements, but a serious attempt is now made to change course. This is certainly not an easy task and will have to be accomplished piecemeal and with baby steps, but the idea is certainly made clear to the entire authority board. There are several obstacles that need to be addressed and resolved before such plans can be implemented.

Keep in mind that most of the hotel/motel lease agreements were signed in the late 1950s through the early 1970s and that all were based on a flat base rent plus the common 3 percent of gross sales. Nowhere in any of the agreements was it stipulated that base rent could be changed into a percentage rate based on the fair market value of the land in question. Secondly, although all the commercial lease agreements provided for renewal terms after the first ten or twenty years, the base rent would still be calculated as a flat rate and not percentage based.

The biggest problem, however, is that none of the lease agreements require the owners/operators to place funds in reserve for capital improvements, and nowhere do the agreements state that such improvements are mandatory, lest it represents a breach of contract and thereby default of said lease.

The authority, and certainly Mr. Chambliss, are very aware of the shortcomings of such old lease agreements and the financial impact they have on the island's operating budget, but they also recognize the legal challenge such a dramatic change represents. To make his point, Mr.

Chambliss presents a comparative study between the current hotel leases for Motel Properties Inc. and the base rental rate per acre of the Ramada Inn, Jekyll Inn, and Days Inn.

The Comfort Inn Island Suites, previously the Wanderer Motel, pays $8,000 per year plus 3 percent of gross sales until the first lease renewal in 2002. The Quality Inn Buccaneer on the south side pays $13,000 per year for both lots 251A and 251B/C with the latter lease effective until 2008. By comparison, that is less than half of what the other hotels are paying.

It must be noted that while a base rent adjustment for some properties, primarily Motel Properties Inc., seems justified, the authority stipulated the maximum allowable daily room rates in its original lease agreements[291] to allow affordability for the average Georgian.

This complicated matter leads to many debates and proposals to remedy this situation, deemed by some to be an impediment for growth and success. It also causes a period of stagnation and hesitation, as it takes several years to circumvent the legal obstacles and implement the long-term solution.

This means that Mr. Chambliss must focus on other potential revenue sources to somehow compensate for the loss.

One such revenue source is already under construction. Summer Waves should be referred to as George Chambliss's brainchild since he relentlessly pursued the idea of a water park both with the authority and his political allies in the general assembly. His persistence pays off, and by February 1988, 45 percent of the water park is completed, with the remaining construction to be finalized in the next six weeks.

In anticipation of its envisioned grand opening in June, the authority approves the first admission rates for the upcoming summer season. General admission is $7.95 for adults, $5.95 for children ages four to eight, and kids younger than three get admitted for free. Season tickets are also on sale and cost $47.95 for admission between June 4 and July 1; $39.95 allows entrance prior to June 4, and $31.95 gives daily access after July 1 and through August 5.

---

[291] The lease agreements referred to date to 1958 and 1959 (authority archives).

The first three weeks of operation draw a crowd of 29,366 day visitors and generate a gross income of $296,705.[292]

A second revenue generator is added to the authority's portfolio as the Cherokee Campground's legal issues are finally resolved on July 14.[293] It is not known from archived documents how the case between Mr. Morrow and the authority is settled, but the site and its title are now free and unencumbered.

There is more good news when a joint venture between Intercoastal Enterprises and Circle Development proposes to restore and lease the old wharf to operate a restaurant. The authority grants a ninety-day lease option as it seeks approval from the Georgia State Finance and Investment Committee to sublease the historic structure. Circle Development is not a newcomer to the restoration and revitalization of the island's Historic District. The company was instrumental in the restoration and renovation of the Jekyll Island Club Hotel in 1986.

The Jekyll Club Associates[294] also has big plans for the Gould Auditorium[295] in the Historic District. Once home to the first convention center on the island and since fallen into disrepair, the company proposes to restore the interior of the auditorium to create meeting space, while the authority will pay for the exterior stabilization and restoration. A preliminary proposal is presented to the authority on November 22, 1988, but no action is taken because of differences of opinion.

The Jekyll Island Club Hotel proposes the following terms and conditions:

1. The Jekyll Island Authority shall be responsible for the exterior renovation of the Gould Auditorium at a maximum cost of $625K.

---

[292] The average daily attendance is 1,398 visitors, with the July 4 weekend drawing 6,400 visitors (authority board meeting, financial reports, July 14, 1988).

[293] Mr. Wayne Morrow, owner and operator of the Cherokee Campground, challenged the authority's default notice in court in 1984. While the authority renovated the campground and operated the site since 1984, the legal battle was not settled until July 14, 1988.

[294] Jekyll Club Associates is the entity that manages and operates the Jekyll Island Club under the Radisson franchise.

[295] The Gould Auditorium was known as the Gould Casino during the millionaires' era.

2. The Jekyll Island Club Hotel shall lease the premises at $50K per year until 1998.
3. In January 1998, the premises will be added to the existing Master Hotel Lease dated 1986.

The authority has a slightly different plan and proposes the following:

1. The Authority shall renovate the exterior of the Gould Auditorium up to a maximum amount of $400K.
2. The JICH shall lease the remises at an annual rate of 9% and shall repay the principal over the next six years.
3. The premises will be included in the Master Hotel Lease starting January 1998.[296]

No agreement is reached at the meeting, but the topic will resurface early next year.

It seems that stabilization is becoming the trend, which also extends to the existing beachfront hotels. Regular inspections of the hotel properties are being conducted by Capt. Richard C. Caton, Jekyll Island Fire Department. The initial inspections are primarily focused on cosmetics, both exterior and room interiors, but later expand to include quality of service and even guest experiences. The average hotel ratings are above 85 percent satisfaction rating, including the newly renovated condo-hotel Villas by the Sea.

One hotel does seem to linger in defaults and controversy. Jekyll Hilton Inn, previously known as the Sand Dollar Motel,[297] is again in trouble when Jekyll Associates files for Chapter 11 bankruptcy protection.

The hotel is owned by the Georgia Teachers Retirement System, which requests a lease assignment to Royce Hotels Int'l Inc. to continue to operate the property while a sale of the property is being negotiated. Two months later, on August 29, 1988, a new buyer has been found in Mid-Atlanta Motel Associates Inc.

---

[296] Authority board meeting minutes, November 22, 1988.
[297] The hotel was ultimately demolished in 2015. The Cottages at Jekyll Island were constructed in the same location.

The sale is so complicated, and so many entities and shell companies are involved in the deal, that Mr. Chambliss calls the deal "fishy," as per his letter to Tom Stroud, chairman of the authority.[298] Because of the multitude of out-of-state registered shell companies and the limited liability of passive investors, the authority does not approve the sale, but the hotel continues to operate under new management.

The end of the 1988 fiscal year shows a net profit to the authority in the amount of $779K, derived from a gross revenue of $9.5 million, or 8.2 percent net return. This is certainly not a bad financial accomplishment when excluding the annual debt service and reserve, but one thing always seems to rise to the surface, namely the municipal services, their cost, and their revenue.

The island counts 686 permanent residents in the summer of 1988, all of whom are connected to the municipal water and sewage system and all of whom benefit from weekly trash and debris pickup. Because Jekyll Island uses the Glynn County landfill for its garbage, it is also subject to any rate change the county may make. There is also the cost of upgrades to the wastewater treatment facility that must be recovered, hence the new rate increase, effective January 1989, and a change to monthly billing cycles for the hotels only.[299] The new rates represent an average increase of 13 percent.

By the end of the year, Mr. Chambliss has created a tight reporting procedure among its directors, while he himself provides monthly reports to the authority board about the state of affairs on the island, the status of ongoing hotel/motel inspections, and the sources of income.

The island directors that report directly to Mr. Chambliss are:

- Pat Duncan: Convention and Visitors
- Betty Tomlinson: Marketing (Public Relations and Advertising)
- Al Elfer: Services and Development
- C.M. Green: Administrative Services
- Tom Rhodes: Museums & Historic Preservation

---

[298] Letter dated August 30, 1988 (addendum to the authority board meeting, September 19, 1988).

[299] The change in billing cycles was recommended by a study conducted by Tribble & Richardson in 1988 (authority board meeting minutes, August 26, 1988).

- James Bradley: Controller

The authority board at the time consists of the following appointees:

- Mr. Tom Shroud, Chairman
- Mr. J.W. Holloway, Vice-Chairman
- Mrs. Carolyn Stradley, Secretary
- Mrs. Judith Arrington, Mr. O. R. Cothran III, and Mr. Max Cleland, Secretary of State

When the parking fee issue raises its head again at the end of the year, most of the board members, and even the directors, cannot really remember what agreements were made with regard to road maintenance on the island, the causeway, or even the location of the first tollbooth. The Jekyll Island Citizens Association, however, is more than willing to enlighten the current members of the board since they were intricately involved in the issue, and they summarize the chain of events dating back to 1981 through the present.

The innocent parking fee generates $650K annually[300] for the authority and is obviously an integral part of the annual budget. While the archived documents do not clearly stipulate a specific reason for raising the parking fee issue after seven years, it can be assumed that the topic is directly related to the future plans of a new Jekyll Bridge and the possible rerouting of the Ben Fortson Memorial Parkway. If such is the case, the collection booth will have to be relocated as well, hence the refreshing of the collective memories.

In 1981, the Department of Transportation prohibited the authority from collecting any type of entrance fee—be it referred to as a toll or parking fee—on any road that was constructed and maintained with state funds (i.e., taxpayers' money). If an entrance fee were to be collected on such stretch of road, then the Department of Transportation would remove the road from their jurisdiction, thereby holding the authority responsible for all maintenance and repair issues. Ultimately, the decision was made

---

[300] Jekyll Island Authority Consolidated Budget Report, Final FY 1988 (authority board meeting addendum, November 22, 1988).

to place the collection booth on the east side of the Jekyll Bridge,[301] leaving the Jekyll Island Causeway[302] within the state highway system but transferring all maintenance issues of the island's perimeter road to the authority.

The Jekyll Bridge replacement is still a decade away, but both Mr. Chambliss and the authority actively pursue funding and design plans, hence their renewed interest in the exact placement and purpose of the collection station.

The continued revitalization of the Historic District takes front stage, now that Dr. Tom Rhodes is taking charge of historic preservation. The success of the old Club Hotel, now the Radisson-JICH, and the Historic Landmark designation certainly help redirecting the focus on what can become another revenue generator. For that purpose, Dr. Rhodes outlines the financial needs for full exterior and interior restoration of the cottages and the small shops on Pier Road.

In his estimate, $4,397,100 is needed for exterior renovation, and $3,128,000 for further interior restoration with an anticipated annual operating budget of $250K for regular maintenance. The funds are not immediately available but will be included in the midyear budget of 1989. His vision of what can become a new tourist attraction is presented in detail during a regular board meeting.

---

[301] The bridge was renamed the M. E. Thompson Memorial Bridge on July 17, 1989, by authority board resolution (authority board meeting minutes, July 17, 1989).

[302] The Jekyll Island Causeway was originally known as SR-50 and later added to the existing SR-520 as an extension. The island's perimeter road is still known as SR-50 but no longer falls under the jurisdiction of the state highway system (https://en.wikipedia.org/wiki/Georgia_State_Route_520).

Use of Structures by area and by structure.

1. South Museum Complex.

Macy, Goodyear, Mistletoe, Rockefeller, and DuBignon, tied together with the Pier Road Walk Structures and the Stables will provide a concise historic district experience.

A. Macy will be an area of exhibits highlighting recreational activities of Club Members, i.e. golf, tennis, skeet shooting, croquet, etc. The exterior is scheduled for restoration by June 30, 1990; the interior by June 30, 1990.[303]
B. Goodyear will continue to serve as an exhibit hall for local contemporary art and the sale of related objects and gift items. The exterior and interior are restored at the basic level.
C. Mistletoe will continue to exhibit historical exhibits and specialized collections storage.
D. Rockefeller will continue to serve as the exhibit area for decorative arts and period rooms. The exterior is restored; the interior complete by May 1991.
E. DuBignon Cottage will serve as a period room and historical exhibit area for the era, 1865 – 1914.
F. The Stables will be the center for providing information for the visitor to the district. The Theater will be used for special programs and orientation. There will be a Museum Sales shop. The Garage area will be converted to a display area for the Fiore Sculpture Collection in the next three years.

---

[303] The dates may be a typographical error by the author, Dr. Rhodes. The actual and correct dates could not be confirmed with certainty.

2. Peripheral Museum Area

This will include Faith Chapel, Crane Cottage, Cherokee Cottage, Maurice Cottage, and Villa Ospo. These structures will make up a support system which provides space for weddings, receptions, parties, lectures, and meetings.

A. Faith Chapel and Cherokee as both a reception/wedding service and an interpretive area for a short experience of the Jekyll Island National Historic Landmark District.
B. Baker Stables preservational display and support of horse and carriage operations.
C. Cherokee Cottage office space for the Museum Division and as rental space for receptions and social events.
D. Crane Cottage office space for the Authority and rentals for receptions and social events.
E. Maurice Cottage after basic interior restoration this would be used as a basic architectural and historic preservation test site and exhibit area for use by professional groups at a charge commensurate with Drayton hall and Biltmore Restoration Projects (as distinct from Biltmore Resort). To be operated by the Historic Preservation Department and the Museum Programs Department for specialized programs and related revenue generation.
F. Ospo Cottage will continue to be used for rentals to individuals for receptions and parties. Office space will be available for lease when DNR departs.

3. Commercial Leases Area

A. Sans Souci Power Plant will continue to be a sales area for material and services consistent with the nature of the Historic District. Rent will be $12.00 per square foot per year; if an in-house operation is started, it will have to satisfy a cost benefit ratio analysis. Restoration will be the point of negotiation in granting a business agreement.

B. Power Plant, the space available in the structure should be divided and part continue as a leased shop, part continue as working areas for restoration, and part serve as needed large object storage.

C. Commissary will continue as housing until such time as a business operation similar to the Sans Souci Power Plant is located and installed. Vendors are actively being sought. The details of the Business Agreement will also be similar to the Boiler House.

D. The Servants Sleeping Quarters, after extensive restoration, will be a commercial venture similar to the Sans Souci Boiler House. The exterior is scheduled for restoration by July 1991; the interior by July 1991.

E. The Assistant Boat Captains house, after extensive restoration, will be a commercial venture similar to the Sans Souci Boiler House. The exterior is scheduled for restoration by July 1992; the interior by July 1992.

F. The Boat Captain's House, now "The Cottage", will continue as a commercial operation for the next three years (FY92) under a long-term lease.

G. The Wharf will continue to function as a major adaptive reuse activity specializing in charter fishing and boat tours. The construction of the Restaurant Lounge Function is expected to begin in June 1987.

H. Gould Casino is to be leased to the Radisson partnership for meeting space. Construction to be completed in late 1989.

4 Special activity areas and residences.

   A. Old Motor Pool[304] will become:
      1. A major furniture and archives collections storage area if funds are available for interior temperature/humidity control.
      2. The site of the Historic Preservation Restoration workshop – heavy work such as stripping – and storage of structural elements.
      3. Storage area for Trams if no funds are available for reworking the structure.

   B. Mariana will continue to be used by the Executive Director.
   C. Goodyear Infirmary will serve as housing for the Director of Services and Development until he departs the Authority. At that time the structure will be included in the interpretive program of the South Museum Complex and provide exhibit space for the walking tour traffic.
   D. Small Dining Hall[305] will continue as housing for Maria Gilbert.
   E. Actor's Dorm[306]: When a long-term lease is negotiated with a music theater company, it is expected that the Actor's Dorm will be leased to that organization and serve as a permanent installation for that function. Summer staff may be housed in the structure as part of that agreement.

---

[304] The Old Motor Pool was located near the Georgia Sea Turtle Center and was demolished during the implementation of the Circulation Plan in the mid-90s.

[305] Maria Gilbert was the secretary to the executive director. She received free housing at the small dining hall, located behind the Island House on Pier Road (Historic District). The space was converted to a US post office in 2017.

[306] The Actor's Dorm located behind the Jekyll Island Club Resort currently houses the administrative staff of the Jekyll Island Authority.

F. Employees Dorm. This is a structure which will require extensive work. For the immediate future it will continue to be a site for temporary employee housing.

The detailed study entails a lot of changes and reassignments of current historic structures, most of which materialize over time. Others do not fare so well, such as the restoration of the Gould Auditorium, despite a new proposal made by the Radisson-JICH partnership in early 1989.

The Jekyll Island Club Hotel agrees to a maximum exterior restoration of $400K, to be completed by June. It also agrees to pay 9 percent interest on the authority's investment for five years with a first repayment of principal in the fifth year in the amount of $200K. For the next four years, 9 percent interest will be paid again on the remaining balance of $200K, which will be repaid in full at the end of the ninth year.

Despite some concessions and the assurance that capital repayments are secured by $1.2 million in operating reserve, no agreement can be reached, and the restoration project never materializes.

The proposal to lease the old wharf by the same partnership does find solid footing. By May, the lease is being finalized, and work to accommodate a wharf restaurant[307] is underway.

Other historic structures that rely on the continued long-term presence of a Jekyll Island Music Theatre do not fare as well and follow in the footsteps of the Gould Auditorium when UGA informs the authority it will not renew its lease for the upcoming season—a major loss for the authority and more so for the many loyal fans and residents. The amphitheater and its JI Music Theatre have been a staple on the island since the early seventies, and although most shows lacked the attendance needed to sustain the financial burden, it has been a unique and personal experience that is unrivaled by any of the coastal barrier islands.

This means that the authority not only has to search for a possible replacement, but it also affects the Actor's Dorm, its use, and its future. Most of the proposals for the Historic District, including the Gould Auditorium, the Actor's Dorm, and the Baker-Crane Carriage House,

---

[307] The new wharf restaurant would become Latitude 31, currently known as the Wharf Restaurant.

take a back seat as bigger problems need to be resolved first and existing revenue centers need to be stabilized as best as possible.

To that extent, the authority is able to execute an agreement for the construction of a wharf restaurant that will ultimately become Latitude 31. It also finalizes a new lease agreement with MAPAR, owner of the second shopping center on Beachview Drive. It reviews a proposal by Mr. Robert Moye to construct a new marina, just south of the newly renamed M. E. Thompson Memorial Bridge.

The marina plan calls for the construction of a dock with forty boat slips with a hoist, restrooms, laundry facilities, and bathrooms. Within five years, a dry storage facility is to be constructed adjacent to the marina, and an access road is to be surfaced to connect Harbor Road with the new JI Marina.

The project cost for the authority is estimated at $115K, including road stabilization and the installation of utilities. In exchange, JI Marina agrees to pay 8 percent of the land value, to be revalued every ten years, and 3 percent of gross sales.

The first-year success of Summer Waves and its financial contribution to the authority's bottom line is enough reason to explore an expansion during the off-season. The $438K project cost can easily be funded through the net revenue derived from the water park. Unfortunately, the same cannot be said about all the other projects the authority wishes to tackle.

First on the list is the upgrade to the water and wastewater facility that is expected to cost $751K and will be completed in four phases between 1989 and 1994. The first thought is to pass on the cost to its users (i.e., the residents and hotels) by increasing the water and sewage fees by 17 percent together with an 8 percent increase for garbage fees. The proposal leads again to a dispute between the authority and the JICA representatives.[308]

It is pointed out that if users are to absorb the cost for a water treatment plant upgrade, the authority should consider itself a user of the system as well and bill itself accordingly.[309]

The authority also envisions an expansion of the old Cherokee Campground now that the court case has been settled. The popularity of

---

[308] Jekyll Island Citizens Association.
[309] The authority used approximately 14.5 percent of the municipal water supply but didn't bill itself for water usage (authority board meeting minutes, July 1989).

the campground surpasses revenue expectations,[310] and since adjacent land on the east side is available for development, a survey proposal is launched. Among the RFP bidders are Quille E. Kinard & Associates from Jesup, Georgia; George P. Underwood & Associates from Brunswick, Georgia; and Atlantic Survey Professionals from Brunswick, Georgia. The request is to survey the available land to create an additional two hundred campsites.

Fiscal year 1989 marks the first year the authority generates more than $10 million per year, but with expenses running at $9.9 million, the net revenue is declining and will continue to do so unless new investments can be made with the help of state funds. Most of the revenue, 23 percent, is still generated by golf fees, while the food and beverage industry now generate approximately 16 percent of total revenue. Probably the one disappointing contributor is the convention center, which only generates $300K annually.

The period of hesitation finally results in an action plan that authorizes the authority to request state funding in the amount of $13.5 million through the issuance of general obligation bonds. The proposed term is thirty years at 8 percent annual interest, with debt service to commence four years after completion of the projects.

The detailed proposal is submitted to the authority during the December 1, 1989, regular board meeting:

<u>Construct new 200 space campground to include store, group shelter, swimming pool and attendant's housing.</u>

Estimated cost: $1,500,000
Debt service source: fees and charges from facility.
Background: campground generated $70,000 net for FY89 (did not include July and August).
Campground estimated to net $147,000 in FY90.

<u>Construct 9 new holes and renovate existing 9 holes on Oceanside Golf Course. Pro Shop will also be renovated.</u>

---

[310] During the filming of *Glory*, the Freddie Fields Production Co. rented half of the campground for its filming crew at a cost of $61K.

Estimated cost: $1,500,000
Debt service source: fees and charges from facility.
Background: Currently 30,000+ rounds played on nine-hole course. Carts used by 30% of golfers. 30,000 rounds at 18-hole green fee will generate $195,000 in additional green fee revenues and $102,500 in additional cart revenues. Additional maintenance estimated $150,000. Net gain $147,500 new revenues.

Water/Wastewater Plant Renovation

Estimated cost: $351,410
Debt service source: increase user fees to cover cost spread over 20 years.
Annual projection is $37,500 by increasing fees 6%.

Construct new 40,000 sq. ft. shopping center behind existing center (which would be torn down).

Estimated cost: $1,650,000
Debt service source: rental fees
Background: Existing 21,012 sq. ft. facility generated $195,000 in FY89. New facility estimated to generate $400,000 annually in rental fees ($10/sq. ft. x 40,000).

Renovate Convention Center Complex and Restore Historic District.

Estimated cost (Convention Center): $3,000,000
Estimated cost (Historic District): $5,000,000
Debt service source: increase parking fee to $1.50 in July 1991 and to $2.00 in 1994.
Background: Parking fees generated $750,000 in FY89. 50% increase is estimated to generate $350,000 and an additional 50% increase in 1994 is estimated to generate $700,000.

SOURCE OF FUNDS

State Bond Issue	$13,500,000
Debt Service Annually	$1,189,000
- 30-year term	
- 8% Interest	
- 4-year delay after project complete	

SOURCE OF ANNUAL DEBT SERVICE

Camping Fees	$147,500
Golf Course Fees	$147,500
Water/wastewater Fees	$37,500
Shopping Center Leases	$195,000
Parking Fee Increases	
FY91 (50%)	$350,000
FY94 (50%)	$350,000
Total	$1,227,000

That now leaves the authority with one remaining problem that has plagued the island since 1986, namely the overall condition and appearance of its aging hotels, the quality of service by hotel staff, and the overall satisfaction level of customers. The authority calls a formal meeting with the hotel owners on October 9, 1989, to address the issues based on surveys done in 1986, and again in the spring and summer of 1989. The dissatisfaction is across the board and includes all hotels,[311] except the Radisson-JICH, which receives an "excellent" rating of 70 percent. The newest survey ratings show a steady decline in service since 1986.

The owners commit to improving their hotels and training staff but refrain from providing any details on how such will be achieved, nor is any deadline imposed by the authority by which improvements must be made. Although regular hotel inspections continue, the authority takes no action against the hotels that underperform.

---

[311] The hotels surveyed include the Jekyll Inn (formerly the Hilton Inn), Jekyll Estates, Villas by the Sea, the Seafarer, the Ramada Inn, the Holiday Inn, the Quality Inn, the Comfort Inn, and the Days Inn.

It needs to be noted that the authority has no legal ground to enforce physical upgrades or renovations. The original lease agreements or leasehold estates date back to the 1960s, and although most have been renewed since, the terms and conditions do not stipulate that hotel owners are obligated to reinvest in upgrades, nor can they be forced to make capital improvements. The inspections and the semiannual customer surveys can only encourage hotel owners to improve their service, but lack of upgrades does not legally constitute a breach of contract or a default of the lease.

The authority will diligently work on amending the terms and conditions when commercial leases are eligible for renewal to remedy this "unforeseen" oversight.

CHAPTER 12

THE FINANCIAL CONUNDRUM

1990–1994

Leaving a complicated period behind that is marked by hesitation and intertwined with stabilization efforts, and a clear action plan that outlines in detail the new construction projects that are envisioned and the funding needed to further enhance Jekyll Island, the authority has high expectations for the new decade and the years to come.

Things don't always work out the way they are planned, and the first disappointment comes when the general assembly refuses to approve the issuance of general obligation bonds in the amount of $13.5 million. Without the requested funding, the authority is forced to find an interim solution until a new request can be submitted in 1991.

The setback does not stop the expansion of Summer Waves, but even there, problems and conflicts between Foster & Cooper, as installer of the selected ProSlide Technology product,[312] and Heery Engineering, as installation supervisor, surface when the final product does not operate according to standards. The conflict does not halt the opening of the water park for the summer season, but it does result in a two-year-long lawsuit

---

[312] The firm was selected to provide four new waterslides as part of the approved expansion in 1989.

that will not be settled until 1991. Ultimately, the authority agrees to pay for the remediation of the installation errors.[313]

The lack of state funds does present a problem for the upgrade of the wastewater treatment plant. The authority attempts to obtain the necessary funding from other sources and contacts Mr. Leonard Ledbetter, DNR commissioner, and Mr. Leamon Scott, executive director of GEFA (Georgia Environmental Facilities Authority). Both respond in April that the planned wastewater project does not meet the qualifications of either DNR or GEFA, and the authority needs to go back to the drawing board to come up with alternative funding sources.

The one logical funding source is a rate increase for the user and recover the project costs over a period of time rather than immediate project funding. The idea itself again sparks a debate during a regular authority board meeting about the large shortfall in providing municipal services and how the proceeds of revenue producers on the island are being used to fund the shortfall.

Mr. Chambliss presents a very thorough "background agenda" detailing the responsibilities of the authority, pertaining to providing municipal services on Jekyll Island.

Subject: JIA'S SERVICE RESPONSIBILITIES

<u>Business & Residential Municipal Type Services.</u>

The legislation that created Jekyll Island Authority addresses the provision of services on the island through permissive language. The following are excerpts from legislation that references the provision of services:

12-3-235, 20 To grant franchises to and make contracts with utility companies both public and private, providing electric light or power, gas, steam heat, telephone, telegraph, cable television, water, or sewerage services …

---

[313] The authority had retained $28K in final payment from Foster & Cooper after installation but was forced to pay for the remediation of the problems (authority board meeting minutes, November 1990).

to permit the rendering of such utility services upon such conditions and for such time as the Authority may deem appropriate or convenient.

12-3-235, 22 To provide and operate at the discretion of the Authority, a fire department of a county, municipality, or other political subdivision.

12-3-235, 23 To charge fees to all persons, natural and artificial using or relying upon the fire department.

12-3-236 Exercise of police power of Authority: delegation of power to State or County.

As you have read, the legislation that created JIA does not require the providing of any municipal type services.

Presently the Authority is providing the following municipal type services at the stated cost:

	Revenues	Expenditures		Net	% Short
Water/Wastewater	766,700	913,890	(147,190)	0.19
Fire/EMT	138,000	420,570	(282,570)	2.05
Garbage	158,000	176,000	(18,000)	0.11
Roads		60,000	(60,000)	N/A
Street Lights		41,200	(41,200)	N/A
Convention Ctr.	222,600	516,210	(294,610)	1.33
Museums	241,600	598,475	(256,875)	0.75
Recreation	128,300	328,905	(200,605)	1.56
Landscaping	2,500	448,200	(445,700)	N/A
Total		1,756,700	3,503,450	(1,746,750)[314]

---

[314] Background Agenda Item 3 provided by Mr. Chambliss at authority board meeting on April 28, 1990. All figures and percentages provided as per the original document.

Mr. Chambliss correctly lists the relevant legislation as it pertains to the provision of services but includes in his list of current services items that are not necessarily considered municipal in nature. Maintenance of the island's natural beauty (i.e., landscaping) and recreation are considered mandatory services according to the Authority Act of 1950. One can argue that the maintenance cost of the convention center and the museum, including all buildings in the Historic District, are to be considered the responsibility of the authority and thereby excluded from what can be viewed as municipal services.

One point of contention is the current fire/EMT fee and the annual shortfall it creates. Mr. Chambliss takes the position that the authority should introduce an ordinance to charge a rate that will cover all associated costs with providing such services. The Jekyll Island Citizens Association, however, takes the position that the authority may be in violation of the Georgia Code by charging a higher millage rate than Glynn County.[315] Upon further examination, and as per Charles Stewart, county administrator, the rate differential is explained in the referenced letter, dated February 14, 1990:

1. Assessed millage rate   1.4
   (This millage rate is used for Fire services only)
2. Millage per property for EMS Services   0.6
   (This comes from the General Fund)
3. Millage derived from Insurance Premiums   0.5
   (Every insurance policy sold in Glynn County has a refund of which an amount equal to 0.5 mill is allocated)
   Total Millage 2.5

Mr. Chambliss further makes the case that Jekyll Island residents receive far more fire and safety protection for their fire fee than do their counterparts in Glynn County. His assessment is based on the number of fire apparatus and ambulance per resident that are available on Jekyll Island. He furthers his case with the authority by calculating the portion for which the authority

---

[315] The authority charges 2.5 mills versus Glynn County's millage rate of 1.4 (letter from George Chambliss to Tom Stroud, authority chairman, February 14, 1990).

is responsible if the millage rate is applied to the total assessed value of buildings under the authority's jurisdiction and responsibility.[316]

The debate about municipal services and the applicable fees to recover most, if not all, service costs leads to the request for a new comparable study of costs, fees, and taxes for businesses in Saint Simons Island and Jekyll Island versus Brunswick. The study is completed by UGA through the Carl Vinson Institute of Government. Ironically, a similar study was conducted in 1977 with the conclusion that the unincorporated areas, including Jekyll Island, paid more for fewer services than the incorporated areas and the city of Brunswick. The recommendation in 1977 was to create a Service District, encompassing police and fire/EMS services, which would reduce the applicable millage rate but would have an adverse effect on the General Fund of Brunswick.[317] Findings of the new study are to be presented to the authority by August 1990.

The authority has other and more immediate problems to deal. The lack of funds and the resulting delay in historic preservation lead to the sudden resignation of Tom Rhodes, director of historic preservation, and Pam Meister, chief curator. Both positions will again be filled the following year with the hiring of Bob Rathburn as director of museums and historic preservation, and the hiring of Martha Teal as curator. Funding for completion of the necessary capital improvements of the Historic District are not forthcoming any time soon, and the entire capital improvement plan, as envisioned last year, is modified to a new four-year capital construction plan, pending a new request for general obligation bonds.

If the above delay is not enough for the authority to handle, there is always something brooding on the commercial side of the island. Servico, owner of the Holiday Inn, files for bankruptcy protection in November 1990, while the owners of the Days Inn request a new but complex lease assignment to a new group of joint ventures. Diversified Innkeepers becomes the new general owner and manager of the Days Inn, releasing JI Investments

---

[316] Jekyll Island Authority assessed value: $45,076,752, which results in a share of $165,057 at 3.35 mills (addendum to letter of February 14, 1990, from George Chambliss to Tom Stroud).

[317] Executive Summary, Carl Vinson Institute of Government, Brunswick-Glynn County Tax Benefits Study, 1977.

(Ladha). The deal is valued at $3.3 million, while the assessed value of the hotel is listed at $4.7 million with an estimated debt of $700,000.

An interesting note here is that Senshu Bank financed the entire deal.[318]

The Jekyll Inn also faces some cashflow problems and requests authorization to defer its quarterly rent payment (November 1990–January 1991) to June 1991.

Can this be the first sign of hotel erosion and the beginning of hard times to come? The Comfort Inn seems to be doing brisk business in both its hotel occupancy and its restaurant business, so much so that hotel management requests extra parking spaces on the west side of Beachview Drive to accommodate both its patrons and its employees. The authority grants a temporary permit on a partially empty residential lot. The Ramada Inn, on the other hand, requests a consolidation of its lease agreement. Lee Forehand, part owner of the hotel, relinquishes his 50 percent stake to co-owner William Forehand, who now becomes the sole owner. Not long after the consolidation does Mr. Forehand decide to make his three children, William Forehand Jr., Debi Fry, and Hollie Forehand, his three co-owners.[319] The change in ownership will play an important role in the future of the hotel.

By April 1991, the authority is ready to implement a new and improved strategic plan for 1991–2000 that includes both proposals for cost savings and finding new sources of income, be it increasing current fees or implementing new ones.

The first cost saving is the implementation of a new Part-Time Employee Retirement Plan, effective July 1, 1991. While this may seem contradictory in nature, the plan results in savings of $72,700 annually. Instead of the obligation to pay full Social Security (i.e., 15.3 percent) by the authority, it now only must pay 3.9 percent into the retirement plan, hence the savings. In addition, and by order of Gov. Zell Miller, a mandatory furlough of

---

[318] Senshu Bank's primary shareholder is the Bank of Tokyo-Mitsubishi. The two main partners in the acquisition are Ken Otokawa and Kyonichi Fukei. This marks the first time that Japanese investors acquire commercial property on Jekyll Island, financed by a non-US bank.

[319] The transfer to co-ownership was approved on January 7, 1992, six months after becoming sole owner of the Ramada Inn (minutes of the authority board meeting January 7, 1992).

one day per month is imposed on all state employees, and a hiring freeze is issued until further notice.

The second proposal is to increase the daily parking fee from one to two dollars, effective July 1, 1991, while the price of annual decals remains the same. The expected increase in revenue of $536,000 is never materialized, as the sale of daily parking passes drops 21 percent, while the sale of annual decals increases by 79 percent. This is reason enough for the authority, upon recommendation of George Chambliss, to examine the possibility of raising the price of decals from $35 to $42.50[320] for residents and island employees, and to $60 for visitors and nonresidents. The proposal is not approved but rather postponed to July 1, 1992. Instead, the authority changes the duration of the decals from the current calendar year to coincide with the authority's fiscal year that runs from July 1 through June 30. This encompasses of course a partial reimbursement to existing decal holders by selling new ones at half price to bring all in line. The matter is so complicated that it takes more man-hours to adjust all the decals than it results in actual savings—more so given the fact that in the end, annual decals are again adjusted to coincide with the actual calendar year after all. But for one fiscal year, the authority gets the benefit of matching one revenue source to its fiscal year spending.

The one steady revenue source that never seems to be scrutinized is the well-producing Summer Waves, which is largely considered one of the best investments made by the authority. Despite regular maintenance costs and upgrades, the popular venue easily services its own debt and interest and is indeed one recreational area that can be called self-sustainable and economically viable.[321] Given its continued success, it entices George Chambliss to consider yet again whether to outright purchase Ski Rixen, given its proximity to Summer Waves, with the ultimate goal to incorporate the water ski adventure into the park. A first proposal was made the previous year but was postponed. Since the authority is looking for extra revenue sources, now may be a good time to revive the old proposal. James Bradley, JIA controller, supports the purchase of Ski Rixen in his August 29, 1990, memorandum to George Chambliss, although he suggests reducing waterskiing and instead expanding

---

[320] The suggested price of $42.50 is based on the St. Simons toll fee of the same amount that includes a $7.50 debt service surcharge.

[321] Attendance in 1990 was 127,599 versus 97,382 in 1989. Total revenue was $1,217,484 versus $875,460 in 1989.

the operations to include boat and canoe rentals: "Bringing the operations under Authority control would add a new revenue source and complement our operation of Summer Waves. Promotion of the complex can be easily combined with Summer Waves promotional efforts."[322]

The authority is clearly preparing for another round of funding through the issuance of general obligation bonds, while it continues to tinker with projected budget shortfalls. What is missing in the overall assessment of expenditures and revenues is the Historic District. In September 1991, the authority requests a $9 million loan from the general assembly, $4.5 million less than the 1990 funding request. A detailed proposal shows that funding for the Historic District is omitted from the request, which explains the reduced loan amount. It does show, however, the inclusion of a brand-new project: a new shopping center.

CAPITAL CONSTRUCTION SCHEDULE AND PAYBACK PROPOSAL

$9 million loan with drawdown scheduled over a four-year period. Interest payments to be made as money is drawn and payback to begin upon completion of the project. Interest rate 4.5%

Drawdown Date	Convention Center	Golf Course	Shopping Center
Mar. '92	$2,425,533	$200,000	
Jan. '93	$866,000	$1,529,500	
Jul. '93	$750,000		
Jan. '94	$1,432,426	$324,000	$750,000
Jan. '95	$488,000		

---

[322] A pro forma proposal projects a negative return in fiscal years 1991 through 1993 with a positive cashflow of $54,876 in 1994. The negative return includes three annual principal payments to Ski Rixen of $53,333 for a total purchase amount of $160,000 (addendum to James Bradley's memorandum dated August 29, 1990).

Interest and Debt Service Funding

The Authority implemented a Debt Service Surcharge on green fees and the parking fee beginning July 1, 1991. This surcharge will generate over $300,000 annually. Based on the payment schedule above, over $1,6 million will have accumulated in the Surcharge Fund prior to the first principal payment.

George Chambliss makes a convincing argument to demolish the existing two strip malls on the northwest corner of Beachview Drive and replace them with a "Victorian-style" shopping complex that can contain 32,000 square feet of retail space and parking for five hundred cars.[323] The interesting part of his argument is his reference to a historic era as the desired architectural style for the new shopping center. He derives his inspiration from a master plan prepared by the Phoenix Group, Architects, Brunswick, Georgia, that states: "This shopping complex, replicating a Victorian-era street, is not a new concept. Many New England towns have prospered with this concept for over a hundred years."

It may seem that the existing Historic District is placed on the back burner for now, yet George Chambliss proposes to use the same architectural style for his new commercial spaces. He clearly has a lot of respect for the history of Jekyll Island, and he understands the attraction of historic architectural styles that enhance the visitor experience.

One of the main reasons funding for the Historic District is excluded is that George Chambliss knows that the Jekyll Island Club Hotel will begin to pay $100,000 annually,[324] and the extra funds, combined with an annual capital layout of $300,000, are enough to maintain the integrity of the Historic District without the extra burden of debt and interest servicing.

---

[323] Shopping Pavilion Construction project detail as addendum to the Capital Construction Schedule and Payback Proposal. Dated September 1991. The strip malls contained 19,000 square feet in 1991.

[324] According the original lease agreement, the JICH was exempt from annual lease payment for the first ten years. Annual payments of $100K were scheduled to begin in 1996 (minutes of authority board meeting, September 1991).

The issuance of the above loan and the implementation of a new strategic four-year plan seem to be the solution Jekyll Island needs to survive its projected budget shortfalls, but another proposed legislation, this time by Glynn County commissioners, may cause another major problem with long-lasting financial impacts.

HB1212, or the proposed legislation that would allow Glynn County to collect bed tax on Jekyll Island, can drastically reduce Jekyll's promotional efforts, with far-reaching negative impact on the local and state economy.

The 3 percent bed tax has been collected on Jekyll Island since 1976, with 100 percent of the proceeds dedicated to Jekyll Island's promotional efforts since 1981. In 1987, the bed tax was raised to 5 percent upon the request and recommendation of the ten independent hotel owners and two rental companies that rely heavily on the island-wide advertising program. A strong case is made to oppose HB1212 given Glynn County's record of accomplishment and the fact that Jekyll Island contributes 5 percent of Glynn County's General Fund but only receives 1.4 percent in services.[325]

Ultimately, HB 1212 is not approved, but it opens the door again for a lengthy discussion about fire fees and the cost of doing business or living on Jekyll Island.

For that purpose, a Fire & Emergency Services Committee is formed to discuss and propose an amiable solution for all parties involved and to resolve the long-standing dispute between the authority, Jekyll Island residents, and Glynn County. The current fire millage rate is 3.35 mills, which results in annual fee collections of $302,000.[326] An additional $15,000 in expected ambulance fees brings the total fee collection to approximately $315,000, while the actual service cost is listed as $459,000, thereby creating an annual shortfall of $144,000 that is at the center of the dispute.

As a result, the committee writes the following proposal for the consideration of the Glynn County Commission:

---

[325] Detailed explanation of the negative effects of HB 1212 on Jekyll Island, George Chambliss's letter to the authority, December 1991.
[326] Amount calculated based on total assessed and/or insured value of non-JIA property and JIA structures of $90 million (addendum to authority board meeting minutes, March 1992).

To cover this $144,219 deficit, the fire fee committee respectfully requests that the Glynn County Commissioners consider the following proposal:

Fire Services

Currently, Glynn County reduces Jekyll leaseholders' taxes by the Jekyll portion of the insurance premium tax rebate.

That Glynn County, instead of reducing the leaseholders' taxes, use Jekyll's portion of the insurance premium tax rebate to help fund Jekyll's fire service. The amount of the rebate would be determined annually and issued to the Jekyll Island Authority. Currently this amounts to an estimated $61,000.

Emergency Medical Services

Currently, Jekyll leaseholders' taxes go into the County's general fund from which the County funds emergency medical services.

That Glynn County, instead of using the taxes collected on Jekyll Island to fund County emergency medical services, use these taxes to help fund Jekyll's emergency medical services. The amount of taxes would be determined annually and issued to the Jekyll Island Authority. Currently this amounts to an estimated $46,000.

Remaining Funding

Fire Services	$61,000
Emergency Medical Services	$46,000
	$107,000

> That Glynn County concur in this methodology for reimbursement of Fire Services and Emergency Medical Services, and in addition, consider funding the remaining short-fall deficit of $37,000.
>
> Committee members:
> Karen Moore, Glynn County Commissioner
> Charles Stewart, Glynn County Administrator
> Ray Rerhig, Jekyll Island Citizens Association
> John Kjellstrom, Jekyll Island Resident
> Ed Brophy, Jekyll Island Hotels
> Jimmy Veal, Jekyll Island Hotels
> Lamar Fender, Jekyll Island Businesses
> Douglas C. Adamson, Jr., Jekyll Island Businesses
> Bill Fitting, Jekyll Island Businesses
> George Chambliss, Jekyll Island Authority

Simultaneously, the general assembly decides to amend Section 235 of Chapter 3 of Title 12 of the Official Code of Georgia Annotated (OCGA 12-3-235), establishing the general powers of the Jekyll Island State Park Authority to change the manner of determining the annual amount of fire fee to be charged to persons using or relying upon fire protection.

> The total amount charged under this paragraph each fiscal year shall not exceed the actual cost to the Authority and the Uniform Division of the Department of Public Safety for providing fire protection and suppression services and public safety services during the next preceding fiscal year. The Authority is required to charge itself, in the same manner that it charges persons, the fees authorized by this subsection.[327]

Both actions ultimately have the same result. The authority has the right to charge all residents for the actual cost of providing fire and

---

[327] Excerpt from OCGA 12-3-235, Section 1.

emergency services, independent of whether Glynn County contributes to the budget shortfall.

The time and effort that goes into the fire fee dispute diminishes when placed within the total budget shortfall of fiscal year 1992, which amounts to $700,000. Half of this shortfall is attributed to golf alone ($300K) and parking fees ($130K), but other areas such as the campground, the convention center, public relations, and catering business are not immune to a drop in annual revenue.

New parking fees that take effect on July 1, 1992, and the pursuit of the earlier Ski Rixen proposal may ease the financial burden some but are certainly not the solution to the problem. The only good news may be that at least the hotel occupancy rates have been stabilized, although they are still well below the highs of 1989, and the convention center continues to lose money.

An interesting memo, written by George Chambliss to Pat Duncan, adds more credibility to the dire situation Jekyll Island and the authority finds itself in.

George Chambliss makes a comparison of the food and beverage spending cap between Jekyll Island and Stone Mountain Park, Hampton Point, St. Simons Island, and Birmingham Country Club, Michigan. Jekyll's per cap[328] is $1.67 versus $3.38, $9.05, and $22.97 respectively. He makes a case to expand the food services at the island's golf courses into a full-service restaurant but refrains from further extensive expansion. According to his letter, dated August 10, 1992, he estimates that gross revenue could increase from $193,000 to $440,000, if implemented.

Stabilization of the current situation is the order of the day for the authority, and expansions, wherever they may be, will have to be postponed until next year. Previous plans to expand the exhibition hall at the convention center are postponed, and the request for a new shopping center is denied.

George Chambliss does not sit idle, despite the apparent financial setbacks. In an elaborate letter to John McTier, chairman, Jekyll Island Authority, Mr. Chambliss addresses the issue of leasing parameters on Jekyll Island. He does not only delve into the legislative aspect of the issue;

---

[328] The per cap is considered the food and beverage spending per rounds of golf played.

he also addresses the past management philosophy to determine that Jekyll Island must set its own course due to the lack of a model that applies to the island and its uniqueness due to its structure. His recommendation at the end reads: "A suggested approach to developing leasing parameters could be considering any activity or business that enhances tourism and beautifies the Island. Staff recommendation of a lessee would include a statement that outlined how the proposal would be of benefit to tourism, and that it would not be in conflict with the Island Land Use Plan."[329]

It becomes evident that the authority is in dire need of revamping its management approach, and George Chambliss feels the pressure to keep costs below budget and maximize the existing revenue stream. For two consecutive years, requests have been made to the general assembly for additional funds to finance capital improvements or expansion projects, but both requests were denied or postponed until the next fiscal year.

It is therefore no surprise that George Chambliss pursues the only available options to him, namely taking control of private enterprises and placing such under the direct management of the authority to increase the revenue stream.

Mr. Shortridge, owner and operator of Ski Rixen, finally comes to an agreement with the authority to sell the entire operation, including three annual payments of $53,333 for the equipment. Ski Rixen retains the lease agreement for the next three years, but instead of paying its annual rent of $5,000 to the authority, Mr. Shortridge receives $3,000 for the exclusive use of its leased property.[330]

The authority also makes immediate changes to the island's food service industry. It takes possession of the Wharf restaurant until a buyer can be found, and it revamps Shuckers Restaurant that will now operate as Blackbeard's Restaurant. But changes do not stop there. The authority

---

[329] Authority board memo from George Chambliss to John McTier, dated December 23, 1992 (authority board meeting minutes).

[330] Ski Rixen's lease agreement provided for an annual lease payment of $5,000 plus monthly payments based on gross receipts. The sale of the property and equipment to the authority kept the original lease agreement intact for three years with the agreement that all gross sales proceeds would be retained by the authority, the annual lease payment would be forgiven, and the authority would pay $3,000 annually as the cost of subleasing the operation.

also opens a new full-scale restaurant at the golf complex, just as George Chambliss envisioned and as per his previous comparison study.

Morgan's Grill opens at the golf course on March 8, 1993, and the Wharf Restaurant opens for business one week later, on March 15, 1993.

The extra revenue from the expanded food services cannot offset the continuing decline in revenue. Hotel occupancy is down again from the previous year, and while golf activity still seems to go strong and hold steady, there is no visible growth. Add to the problem that the parking fees continue to decline, as they have done since 1989, one can only wonder how and why the change in food and beverage can solve the annual budget deficit.

The year 1993 is of slow economic growth throughout the US, and the signs of declining consumer spending on food and beverages, combined with fewer visitors, should be a warning sign for the authority.

Nevertheless, when funds from general obligation bonds are finally made available, largely in part through the intervention and negotiation of the GSFIC (Georgia State Finance and Investment Commission), the authority adheres to its original investment plan that includes the design and construction of a new nine-hole ocean course and the renovation of its aging convention center.[331]

A proposed plan by the Army Corps of Engineers to alleviate continued beach erosion on the north end of the island must take a back seat, as funds are not available in the budget for such an expensive endeavor. The plan proposes to pump sand from the Brunswick Bar Channel to an offshore location northeast of the island, allowing the sand to slowly and naturally accumulate onto the northern beaches.[332]

One can question why the authority is keen on absorbing privately held business endeavors on the island, while simultaneously the general assembly passes HB 941. The bill specifically requires the recreational authorities to involve the private sector in the development, construction, operation,

---

[331] The general assembly, through GSFIC, approved the issuance of $7.5 million general obligation bonds, made available in November 1993 (authority board meeting minutes, March 22, 1993).

[332] The estimated cost for the project was between $400K and $600K, and $50K per 1,000 feet of pipe (authority board meeting, March 22, 1993).

and management of each authority's projects prior to undertaking any new projects.

The content and purpose of HB 941 seems contradictory to the policy the Jekyll Island Authority is implementing under the guidance and upon advice from George Chambliss. It is understandable that as executive director, Mr. Chambliss works within the limitations and parameters set forth by the original Authority Act (i.e., adheres to the requirement of being self-sustainable and/or economically viable). The new House bill, however, seems to steer the authorities in general toward the use of private investments and marks the beginning of public private partnerships. The law now requires that a copy of the feasibility evaluation be filed with the Office of Planning and Budget.[333]

This results in the authority being forced to hire a private and independent consultant to complete a feasibility study for the renovation and expansion of the convention center. As such, the Mescon Group, Atlanta, is hired to complete a primary study at a cost of $8,000.

Despite every effort possible to survive a difficult year, the budget falls well short of its projections, and for the first time the authority records a 2 percent negative return on revenue, or a net loss of $187K. The upcoming year does not provide any comfort either, given the negative trend in visitation and consumer spending, hence the projected decline in revenue of $361K for 1994, twice the amount of the current year.

But there may be some light at the end of the tunnel if Jekyll Island can benefit from participating in another round of county SPLOST funding.

Without hesitation, George Chambliss drafts a project list of public works that can be considered for such funding. The total amount of his wish list, which includes culvert replacements, road repair or resurfacing, parking area resurfacing, bike trails, and placing the south-end residents finally on a sewer line system, is $574,000. But he goes beyond his "must-have" wish list and also includes $1 million for the restoration of the museum and Cherokee Cottage. Since the general assembly did not approve the requested $5 million for historic preservation in 1991 and 1992, Mr. Chambliss finds another creative way to fund these important projects.

---

[333] HB 941, Phase I and Phase II (addendum to the minutes of the authority board meeting, July 18, 1993).

Or at least he attempts to, since his request is subject to the approval of the Glynn County commissioners.

In the background of these tumultuous years, where both the executive director and the authority members are scrambling to delicately balance a limited budget, also looms the large construction plan of a new bridge across Jekyll River. Archived documents show that discussions about joint responsibilities between the Department of Transportation and the authority are ongoing, and permits and approvals are discussed at length. One point of contention early on is the design and placement of the collection booth. Current DOT commissioner, Wayne Shackelford, is instructed to seek the help and advice from former DOT member, Mr. Downing Musgrove, to clarify the requirements. Mr. Musgrove proves to be instrumental in the ongoing negotiations and can be credited with ultimately reaching a mutually beneficial agreement on May 5, 1994, that would set in motion the replacement of the 1954 drawbridge.[334]

> Article 1, Scope and Procedures. 1.... The DEPARTMENT shall also provide funds for the construction of the related roadway and to construct paving and parking facilities for the new information booth and shall provide a maximum amount of $20,000.00 for the construction of the new information booth. The DEPARTMENT shall let the PROJECT for the construction.

In early discussions, the Department of Transportation demanded that the authority take financial responsibility for its new or temporary information (collection) booth. The DOT's original refusal to agree to the collection of parking fees in 1981 certainly contributes to their renewed stance of refusal. Intervention by Mr. Musgrove leads to the DOT's concession to absorb the construction cost of the information booth, although a limit of $20,000 is placed on such. The original agreement further states that any cost above the agreed-upon amount is the responsibility of the authority.

---

[334] Project: STP-BRF-007-4(44) Glynn County, P.I. NO. 521330, May 5, 1994 (addendum to authority board meeting, May 1994).

> 7. Upon completion of the PROJECT, the AUTHORITY will own and be responsible for maintaining the remaining west side of the existing bridge and its approach for use as a fishing pier ...

While the authority does not contest the assigned responsibility for the remaining west side of the old bridge, the topic will become a point of contention between the county and the authority later. It is also noted that the agreement does not specify how the remaining east side of the old bridge should be maintained.[335] The project is scheduled to be completed by August 31, 1997.[336]

The struggle for a sound and solid financial equilibrium somehow takes its toll on its long-serving executive director, George Chambliss. His sudden resignation at the end of 1994 is as much wrapped in obscurity as personal stories surround it. Neither the archived minutes of the authority board meetings nor the summaries of the executive sessions give any indication of the reasons or background behind Mr. Chambliss's sudden resignation and disappearance from the Jekyll Island scene; however, theories abound, yet unsubstantiated.

Lauded in and welcomed in 1981 as the new executive director, George Chambliss certainly made an immediate impact on how Jekyll Island was to be managed. He consolidated the early municipal structure even further and solidified his position as executive director versus the authority board by absorbing all day-to-day management decisions and allowing the board to function as a policy-making body.

His focus on financial stability and his passion for recreation, including golf, earned him a favorable spot amidst island residents. Yet his unabashed personality and independent decision-making is also what sometimes got him in troubled waters.

---

[335] It can be safely assumed that since the east side of the old bridge is under the jurisdiction of the authority, as per the Authority Act of 1950, that therefore the authority assumes full responsibility, hence the omission in the agreement. (Author's note.)

[336] Original agreement as addendum to the authority board meeting minutes, May 1994.

A multitude of personal stories and recollections point to an irreconcilable argument between Mr. Chambliss, the authority, and the DNR as the primary cause of his resignation.

When in 1993 the general assembly finally approved funding for a new nine-hole oceanfront golf course, George Chambliss saw his dream come true—the reconstruction of one of the oldest golf courses on the island, namely Great Dunes. Reduced from a links-style eighteen-hole golf course in the aftermath of Hurricane Dora in 1964, the once prominent golf jewel of the island had been reduced to a mere nine-hole course ever since. The extra funding would allow George Chambliss to recreate the 1927 design of Walter Travis.

Upon approval of the DNR, George Chambliss orders to stake out the median of the nine new fairways so that the architects can start the design. Instead of adhering to the specific DNR authorization and man-cut the linear median, Mr. Chambliss decides to speed up the work and orders the medians to be cut by a bulldozer, thereby effectively damaging the natural woods and marshes in and around the prospective area.

Several residents are astonished by the methodology and document the damage with a multitude of photographs. They also file a complaint with the DNR and substantiate their claim with the pictures taken.

What happens from here on out is based on personal stories, none of which are substantiated by official archived documents, but Mr. Chambliss is found in violation of the DNR regulation and hence in violation of the Jekyll Island Authority policy, both of which would support a termination or mandatory resignation.

It is believed that George Chambliss resigned upon the advice of and pressure from the authority board members. His resignation brings an end to an era that began fourteen years ago and is the beginning of a new relationship structure between the executive director and his staff, and the authority board members.

CHAPTER 13

THE COSMETIC CHANGE HIDES THE UGLY

1995–1996

The sudden departure of Mr. Chambliss as long-serving executive director cannot come at a more complicated time in the forty-five-year existence of Jekyll Island State Park. The visible downturn in island visitation, combined with the multitude of large and expensive capital improvements, calls for a steady hand at the helm of the day-to-day island operations. The authority, or maybe the governor himself, does not seem ready for a permanent replacement and instead appoints James Bradley, director of administrative services, to become the acting executive director.

The authority board also requests that a representative of the Department of Natural Resources attend the regular board meetings as well as the executive sessions. Bill Donohue,[337] as DNR representative, makes his first appearance on the scene of Jekyll Island.

Whether the requested attendance of a DNR representative is the result of the incident the previous year remains unconfirmed. It is safe to assume that the DNR wishes to play a more direct role in the decision-making process, or at least have some oversight over the pending capital improvements. Such would coincide with its original proposal to restrict outdoor beach lighting and its request in 1991 to amend the Official Code

---

[337] Bill Donohue will serve as executive director from 1997 through 2006.

of Georgia (OCGA).[338] The proposal never materialized into an ordinance issuance on Jekyll Island until 2008[339].

A more tangible explanation for the sudden interest of the DNR in the daily activities on Jekyll Island can be traced back to a letter submitted by Mr. Thomas Swift, attorney at law, representing the interest of several island residents and the Coastal Georgia Audubon Society, to Mrs. Carolyn Stradley on August 15, 1990. While the letter itself, or any official response by the authority, is largely missing from the archived documents, the topic of the letter is worth mentioning in this context.

In the summer of 1990, the authority had approved plans to construct a new marina, just south of the M. E. Thompson Memorial Bridge. This new development was viewed by many residents as a possible violation of OCGA Section 12-3-243, which restricts the authority's ability to develop more than 35 percent of the island. The new marina development would exceed the maximum-allowable land above the high tide marker that could be developed. The development proceeded as planned with only minor alterations to the shoreline access to alleviate any possible violation.

The story does show how the wording of a specific law can easily be interpreted differently, depending on which interested party does the interpretation and for which purpose. The specific OCGA Section 12-3-243 does limit the development of Jekyll Island to 35 percent, reduced from 50 percent as originally described in the Authority Act 1953 Amendment. When the authority requested the attorney general for his interpretation of said restriction, his ruling stated: "The limitation applies only to the amount of ground which may be leased or sold and that there is no limitation whatever on the Authority's power to develop and improve the island."[340]

Nevertheless, the culmination of "possible violations" over the past five years may very well have culminated into a more direct oversight of daily

---

[338] DNR proposal to change chapter 15 of the OCGA, Statute 15-114 (outdoor beach lighting) (board meeting minutes, January 1991).

[339] The authority adopted the new ordinance at its regular board meeting in August 2008 (http://www.savejekyllisland.org/EnvJITurtOrd.html).

[340] Letter from Michael Egan, House of Representatives, to the Jekyll Island State Park Authority, August 7, 1972 (addendum to letter from Michael Swift to Carolyn Stradley, August 15, 1990).

operations by the DNR, be it only as a presence during board meetings or executive sessions.

During the course of the year, two large-scale development plans are launched in addition to the renovation and expansion of the convention center.

A three-year Historic District master plan is proposed to address the continuing decline of some of the historic buildings. This can be achieved with the use of extra public funding and the attraction of private capital. The plan also calls for the full restoration of Cherokee Cottage, with the intent to ultimately include the structure in the Jekyll Island Hotel Club portfolio, creating extra guest rooms and ballroom space.[341]

It also mentions for the first time the weakness of the Historic District, namely the confusing traffic pattern within its boundaries and the seven different roads that provide access to the area. The pilot study[342] recommends a single point of access by opening Riverview Drive to allow restricted guided tours. The entire traffic plan is to be implemented in different phases over a period of three years to reduce traffic and enhance the overall experience of visiting one of the most unique and largest Historic Districts in the state of Georgia.

The next big undertaking is another request for Master Planning Services. The scope of services, as listed in the request, is vague and nonspecific with maybe one exception. The study requests: "D. Recommendations for the protection of unimproved areas. Advice with respect to access, nature experience, interpretation and educational opportunities that are not disruptive and are consistent with remaining unimproved. A balance is sought in preserving the natural setting, while serving as a classroom of the barrier, coastal island environment easily accessible by the general public."

Could it be that a DNR presence on the authority board has its benefits and influence on the scope and focus of development and master plans after all? It certainly marks the first time that so much emphasis is placed on protecting and preserving the natural integrity of unimproved areas.

---

[341] Restoration cost is estimated at $300,000 and $10 million in private funding for hotel expansion (addendum to authority board meeting minutes, July 1995).

[342] EDC Pickering conducted the pilot study with input from authority staff and Historic District constituencies.

With two development plans in motion, the first large construction project on the island, namely the renovation and expansion of the convention center, is awarded to Beer's Construction. The total cost is estimated at $5.95 million, and work is set to start early October 1995. A smaller but similar expansion also takes place at the newly renamed Blackbeard's Restaurant with new and elaborate landscaping to enhance the customer's experience.

The focus on visitor experience may come a little late when the authority launches its first "Guest Services Initiative." The Tourist Accommodations Quality Inspection Process provides a good insight about the quality of hotels, rooms, and overall condition of the island hotels. Most hotels receive a score around 85, except the Seafarer (74) and Jekyll Estates (75). The only hotel that scores higher (91) is the JICH-Radisson.[343]

Common complaints in the inspection report mention old and worn-out furnishings, mildew, the presence of bugs in the rooms, worn-out carpets, lack of exterior maintenance, structural interior damage (holes in the interior walls and doors), and inadequate, leaking air conditioners.

A letter by Gail Jordan, president of Rising Sun Talent Productions, whose company held its annual dance competition at the convention center during the summer, sums up the poor conditions of the hotel accommodations on the island even more descriptively than the official inspection report. Mrs. Jordan calls the hotel situations "… the hotel situation was deplorable, to say the least. Not only were the room conditions appalling, but the hotel staffs were rude to the guests. Hotel services were intolerable."[344]

This is just a small excerpt of a long list of complaints that not only points to a continuing decline in hotel accommodations but also accuses the hotels of "fudging" its occupancy rates to avoid mandatory contributions to the convention center:[345]

---

[343] Scores are based on exterior and interior appearance, maintenance, service, and overall quality of the accommodations and are awarded on a scale of 100.

[344] Letter from Mrs. Gail Jordan to Ms. Misty Olinde, CVB, September 4, 1995 (addendum to the authority board meeting minutes, September 1995).

[345] The hotels and the Convention Visitors Bureau had the agreement that each hotel would contribute five dollars toward the CVB for each guest room occupied by a convention visitor.

> On top of everything else the hotels were taking advantage of their own convention center. By giving false information on the number of room nights they had kept them from paying the $5.00 rebate to the convention center who was responsible for the number of guests they had in the first place.
>
> We received an approximate room count two weeks before we came down and our room nights were over 2,000 but after the convention was complete we were told the room count was less than 1,000 ...
>
> ... The hotels are taking an unfair advantage of the convention bureau by making a quick buck of the hard work of the convention center and its staff.

Quite an accusation and a sad depiction of the state of affairs in the island hotels and the guest accommodations and experience in general. Sadder may be that this situation will not remedy itself any time soon, as harder times are yet to come that will impact overall visitation even more negatively, despite the large amount of capital spending on the convention center.

Maybe the island residents can make an impact or direct the authority to change course. For numerous years, and since the early 1980s, residents have asked the authority to allow them to partake in the decision-making process by granting them a seat on the Jekyll Island Authority Board. The request has always fallen on deaf ears, until now.

The general assembly passes HB 120 on July 1, 1995, which allows for the creation of the Jekyll Island Citizens Resource Council.

OCGA 12-3-233.1 stipulates:

> (a) The Governor shall appoint a body to be known as the Jekyll Island Citizens Resource Council. The purpose of the Citizens Resource Council shall be to improve, foster, and encourage communication and the exchange of thoughts and ideas between the authority and the community of persons interested in Jekyll Island

including, but not limited to, residents of Jekyll Island; owners, operators, and employees of businesses located on or providing services to Jekyll Island; and environmental organizations.

(b) The Citizens Resource Council shall consist of seven members. Three members shall be representative of the Jekyll Island residential and business community with two of these members being residents of Jekyll Island and one being an owner, manager, or employee of a business or commercial facility located on Jekyll Island …

The first seven members appointed are Tim Goddard, Kevin Runner, Jean Poleszak, Jimmy Veal, Ed Brophy, James Bradley, and Cecil Passmore. Three months later, the composition changes[346] already for unknown reasons, but the new council uses its newfound voice to communicate its ideas directly to Gov. Miller, as per their mandate.

A letter dated November 3, 1995, to the governor clearly indicates their support for the authority's Historic District Master Plan and requests annual funding of $810,000 for the next three years to be used solely for the Historic District renovation, as per the authority's budget request.[347]

In conjunction with the attention on the Historic District and its future, Valdosta State University takes the opportunity to address the future of its musical program. VSU has operated the Jekyll Island Musical Theatre Festival for the past six years, and while the Historic District Master Plan does not mention the amphitheater specifically, it does raise questions about future lodging for the summer production company and its actors. Rumors about potentially renovating the Gould Auditorium and reassigning the use of dorm space may affect the future of the Musical Theatre.

---

[346] Cecil Passmore and Tim Goddard left the Citizens Resource Council for unknown reasons and were replaced by Joe Iannicelli and Ralph Steffan. James Bradley, executive director ad interim, left because of a potential conflict of interest.
[347] Citizens Resource Council letter, signed by Ed Brophy, Kevin Runner, Joe Iannicelli, Ralph Steffan, Jean Poleszak, and Jimmy Veal (authority board meeting minutes, November 1995).

Jan Lane Harper, president of the Jekyll Island Musical Theatre, addresses the concerns in a letter to Charles Jenkins, chairman of the authority, on September 15, 1995. Two months later, VSU proposes to lease the Gould Auditorium for five years to secure its future on the island and to convert the auditorium into the Gould Casino Arts Center. Securing the future of the musical program is so important that Valdosta University is willing to pay $10,000 annually in addition to $600 per performance. Despite the generous offer, no long-term contract can be agreed upon, but VSU retains its annual subsidy through 1996.[348]

Whether the ongoing expansion of the convention center, the envisioned renovation of the Historic District, or the construction of the new bridge triggers the need to reexamine the actual land use on Jekyll Island is not immediately clear. Nevertheless, a new Land Use Acreage Analysis is presented to the authority by year-end.

The report documents in detail, per area and usage, the total acreage and percentage of undeveloped, developed, disturbed, and ponds/wetlands land:

Undeveloped:	2,256.91 acres	59.5%
Developed:	1,233.55 acres	32.5%
Disturbed:	192.76 acres	5.10%
Ponds/Wetlands:	108.36 acres	2.90%

> Besides these land totals there is approximately 2,200 acres of natural areas east of Jekyll Creek. They comprise of beaches, shell banks, salt marsh, and beach hammocks that are not included in the totals above.[349]

By January 1996, the bid for a new island-wide master plan is awarded to Robert Charles Lesser & Co. and Tunnell-Spangler & Associates. A

---

[348] The annual subsidy, as provided by the authority, was between $40K and $50K (authority board meeting minutes, March 1996).

[349] The report reflects current development levels on Jekyll Island as of February 1995. Development that has occurred after March 31, 1980, was calculated by aerial photography, surveyed plats, and field surveys (authority board meeting minutes of November 1995).

proposal or recommendation is not forthcoming until April, by which time renovation of the convention center is already completed,[350] and construction of the new bridge is well underway. The $6 million facelift of the old convention center and the $10 million new bridge that is under construction cannot hide the ugly problems the island faces and the constant battle the authority must fight each day to stabilize a deteriorating situation.

The authority, under the leadership of James Bradley, tries to reinvent itself to meet the ever-changing demand for high-quality services by restructuring itself organizationally. The new and improved structure in 1996 shows a change of responsibilities with consolidation of some services under the management of directors:

- James Bradley, Executive Director
- Al Elfer, Director Maintenance & Services
- Vernon Yawn, Director Human Resources & Customer Service
- James Rivers, Director Administrative Services
- Jim Weidhaas, Director Public Relations & Special Events
- Ken Opel, Director Food & Beverage
- Bob Rathburn, Director Museum & Historic Preservation[351]
- Johnny Paulk, Director Golf & Tennis
- Ed Schroeder, Director Convention & Visitors Bureau

The authority also counts 360 full-time employees and 946 temporary employees.[352] The new structure may be impressive and justified to tackle the problems the island faces, but the visitation numbers reflect another image.

Hotel occupancy rates are stagnant and disappointing, given that large crowds are expected now that the Olympic Games are held in Atlanta. The tourism boom does not materialize, as documented in an editorial of the *Brunswick News*:

---

[350] The convention center was dedicated on May 10, 1996, by Gov. Zell Miller.
[351] Dr. Bob Rathburn resigned in March 1996 and was replaced by Warren Murphey (authority board meeting minutes, March 4, 1996).
[352] Jekyll Island Authority payroll, July 1996 (authority board meeting minutes, August 1996).

> The boom to tourism that was to accompany the Olympics has not materialized. Tourism is down throughout the state and even in the Atlanta area shopping malls, restaurants, and other attractions are experiencing a decline in business. In the Golden Isles, tourism officials say the loss could amount to about $6 million or more. What happened? ...
>
> ... Local visitor statistics are down, especially on Jekyll which saw 10,000 less cars go through its parking fee gate the first three weeks of July compared to the same time last year. Summer Waves has had 8,000 less visitors in July, and hotels and restaurants on St. Simons and Jekyll are seeing sluggish sales ...[353]

The hotels are not the only ones suffering from the decline in visitation, as the number of golf rounds declines by 30 percent, and Historic District tours declines 20 percent to an all-time low of 41,000 annually.

The newly enhanced convention center may be able to accommodate more and larger convention groups, but if the hotel standards are not following suit, the complaints from visitors remain the same. In response, the authority forms a Hotel Standards Committee, chaired by Tom Lewis, that in turn hires Ritchie International[354] as hotel consultants. The intention is to develop a hotel standard for Jekyll Island to measure customer satisfaction and to gather and analyze guest reviews to recommend improvements.

In addition, the authority also forms an Audit Committee to inspect all commercial island properties and suggest improvements, using the new convention center as a benchmark for customer satisfaction. Given that the convention center is brand-new and has been completely renovated, it seems hardly possible to hold the island hotels, some of which are forty years old, to this new standard. It is obvious that most of the hotels do not pass the litmus test. When the Hotel Standards Committee issues its first report in September 1996, the average guest satisfaction rate is 78.1 percent

---

[353] *Brunswick News* editorial, July 30, 1996.

[354] Ritchie International is a brand consulting firm based in Massachusetts (http://www.ritchieinternational.com/main.htm).

and well below the national average of 85 percent. The only positive note and result of the island-wide exercise is that at least both the authority and Ritchie International now have a base to work with. The first results are used as a standard for future inspections and satisfaction ratings to detect any decline or increase.

Only one island hotel scores well above the island and the national average with 94 percent. The Jekyll Island Club Hotel-Radisson has carried the torch of excellence in service, guest experience, and hotel amenities since its grand opening in March 1987. It has also continued to invest its entire net revenue[355] in hotel maintenance and upgrades; hence the high guest satisfaction and rating.

Its continued success leads to a proposal to further expand its facilities and services. More specifically, David Curtis requests the authority to favorably consider the application to add sixty-six hotel rooms and approximately 8,000 square feet of meeting space, but such comes with a caveat.

> In order to make the expansion viable from a financial viewpoint, we must request a new lease with the Authority.
>
> We propose a lease rate of 2% of gross revenue for the expanded 200 room property commencing one year after the date of completion and with an expiration of 2049 which we understand is the furthest date for which the Authority may lease properties.
>
> Our current lease calls for an increase in our annual payment from $100,000 to 3% of gross income commencing January 1, 1998 with a further increase to 3½% commencing January 1, 2003. We request a revision to the current lease that provides the payment remain constant at $100,000. The reason for this request is that our current lender, Banque Indosuez of France, has decided to cease its North American operations and has informed us that it intends to call the loan (notwithstanding the

---

[355] The JICH invested more than $8 million over eleven years of ownership (letter from David Curtis to James Bradley, October 9, 1996).

fact that we are current on all obligations) as of December 4, 1996.

The impact of such a call would be to force the partnership to file for bankruptcy protection if we have no substitute lender available. As yet, no lender is willing to replace Banque Indosuez, in large part, due to our escalating obligations under the current lease.

We believe if the lease payments were fixed at $100,000, we would be in a much stronger position to find a new lender and thereby avoid a drawn-out bankruptcy action which would not only hamper our ability to operate the Hotel as a top-flight resort, but also cripple our prospects for expansion ...[356]

The letter is accompanied by financial exhibits, containing projections of lease and tax payments to the authority after hotel expansion and with the implementation of the new lease terms and conditions as proposed in the letter. The total annual revenue stream to the authority is to increase by $115,568 by 2002.

Two architectural site plans, attached to the above proposal, show that the new hotel, featuring sixty-six guest rooms on three floors, is to be constructed at the northwest corner of the JICH, with the building set diagonally between the hotel's swimming pool and Crane Cottage. The new meeting rooms, totaling 8,000 square feet, are to be constructed behind the Rockefeller and Vanderbilt meeting rooms, facing east.

The architectural style proposed for both new additions, based on submitted site plans and architectural renderings, is similar in style and complementary to the existing 1887 style of the original Club Hotel.

Before the authority can consider the new additions, Bill Donohue reaches out to the Georgia Department of Natural Resources for an

---

[356] Letter from David Curtis, executive vice president of Leon N. Weiner & Associates, to Jekyll Island Authority Board, c.o. Mr. James Bradley, executive director (authority board meeting minutes, October 20, 1996).

opinion on the matter, specifically Mark Edwards, division director and state historic preservation officer.[357]

Given that the JICH is classified as a National Historic Landmark (NHL), and the fact that the natural landscape is cited as a significant feature of the district, according to the Jekyll Island Historic District Pilot Master Plan, the proposed new structure is deemed to have a detrimental effect and protrudes into the historic front landscaped lawn of the hotel.

Mr. Edwards further points out in his letter that according to the Jekyll Island Historic Pilot Master Plan, expansion might occur through the adaptive reuse of the Cherokee and Crane Cottages. He also recommends contacting either his staff preservation architect, Michael Miller, or any of the enclosed list of architects with previous experience in the treatment of historic resources. Interesting to note is that Larry Evans,[358] the original architect involved in the renovation and restoration of the JICH, is listed as one of the recommended preservation architects.

The fact that DNR recommends the adaptation of Cherokee and Crane Cottages to accommodate further expansion is noteworthy.

Both cottages are in dire need of restoration, but lack of funding in recent years for the Historic District has taken its toll on most prominent historic structures, certainly those that are north of the Jekyll Island Club Hotel.

The authority's administrative offices are still located at Crane Cottage, and Warren Murphey, director of museum and historic preservation, and his museum curators work out of Cherokee Cottage. The historic archives, once housed in Cherokee, are being moved to Villa Marianna in anticipation of funding. The latter may be in better shape than Crane and Cherokee but has its own moisture and water problems as well.

The authority is never short on problems or fires that need to be put out immediately. Maybe the highlight of their good intentions or ideas can be the expected grand opening of the new bridge across Jekyll Creek next year.

A new bridge, a new tollbooth, or even a new and improved Ben Fortson Jr. Memorial Parkway cannot hide or solve the island problems.

---

[357] Letter from Mark Edwards to Bill Donohue, December 16, 1996 (authority board meeting minutes, January 1997).

[358] Larry Evans worked closely with Vance Hughes as Circle Development Corp. in Brunswick, Georgia, and was instrumental in the renovation design and historic preservation of the JICH in 1986.

CHAPTER 14

THE NEW BRIDGE TO AN OLD ISLAND RESORT

1997

The story of the new Jekyll Island Bridge begins in 1986, ten years before the opening and dedication ceremony. One can attribute the length to the complexity of the project, the difficulty in obtaining federal and state funding, or even the multitude of agencies involved and their specific permitting process. Yet all would fall short and omit the relentless efforts behind the scene to secure better island access amidst the turmoil of hotel neglect, disappointing guest reviews, and managerial problems.[359]

Back in 1986, it was George Chambliss's vision to modernize Jekyll Island State Park and to promote the island as a resort, rather than a family destination. His vision also included the appearance of the island, starting with the Ben Fortson Jr. Memorial Parkway, the convention center, the strip mall, and of course the Jekyll Creek Bridge.

Most of the island's planned upgrades are completed, including renovation in the Historic District that now has a clearly marked boundary, west of Stable Road, with a newly installed wire fence, much to the dislike of some adjacent neighbors. The fence is just the beginning of the transformation the Historic District awaits if the promised funding of $1.725 million comes to fruition.

---

[359] See addendum A for more details about the bridge project.

For the time being, the entrance to the island looks impressive, but what lies in front of eager visitors is not always what one expects, as so many renovations are needed to old, outdated hotels that need more than some tender, loving care.

Hotel guest reviews, as compiled and analyzed by Ritchie International, show a continuing downtrend, even in comparison to the previously recorded average satisfaction rate of 78.1 percent.[360] The island hotels average a rate between 54 percent and 75 percent,[361] well below the benchmark and far below the national average of 85 percent.

Because of the latest guest reviews, three island hotels respond to the authority's request for improvement plans to address guest complaints and remedy the situation: Days Inn, Villas by the Sea, and Jekyll Inn. None of the plans entail major renovation work or upgrades and are largely limited to increased upkeep of the property and small maintenance solutions—barely a band-aid for a dying patient.

The reviews also bring to light that one hotel, the Ramada Inn, adds 3.5 percent to all customer bills, including lodging and food and beverages. The added-on cost is in addition to the regular bed tax and is the equivalent of the hotel's lease payment to the authority.[362] The hotel implies to its guests that the additional 3.5 percent is a tax imposed by the authority and therefore passed on to all guests. Needless to say, this situation is rectified immediately.

Jekyll Estates, the oldest island hotel,[363] seems to take its low ratings seriously and makes arrangement for a lease transfer from Diversified 84-1, Ltd. to Maranatha Corp., owned by Robert Phillips. The new lease has a term of twenty years with an option to renew for an additional ten years. The agreement also requires the new owner to build three more kitchenette apartments in the north wing of the property, a new conference

---

[360] The average standard was implemented as a benchmark for all island hotels in September 1996 (Ritchie International, first guest review study).
[361] The ratings are largely based on bad reviews from conference attendees.
[362] The lease agreement between the Ramada Inn and the authority provides a lease payment of 3.5 percent of gross sales.
[363] Jekyll Estates was built in 1957 and was the first motel to be constructed on Jekyll Island and most recently called the Beachview Club. The motel is currently owned and operated by the adjacent Holiday Inn Resort.

room on the south end, and a tiki hut by the pool. All construction and improvements must be completed within the first year.

The Jekyll Island Club Hotel, consistently scoring high ratings in guest satisfaction, continues its pursuit of expansion. In response to the letter from DNR and its concern about the possible detrimental effect on the Historic District, and the protrusion the new building will have on the historic front lawn, Jekyll Development Associates proposes a new architectural plan in March 1997. Instead of the initial diagonal structure, Smith Dalia Architects[364] submits a new linear proposal between the garden of Crane Cottage and the north wing of the JICH. The structure is to allow for sixty-six additional guest rooms, as per the original proposal, on two floors.

That proposal does not gain any more favorable opinions with the authority or the DNR, as it is still found to be obtrusive, independent of the complementary historic style.

Robert Charles Lesser & Co. also has an opinion about the proposal—not just about the request for a lease amendment but also about the entire expansion plan. It is not surprising the developer of the new Island Master Plan pursues the DNR recommendation to include the adaptive use of Crane and Cherokee Cottages to accommodate the desired expansion.

A letter dated January 10, 1997, from Robert Charles Lesser & Co. to Clay Long, Jekyll Island Authority, makes the following recommendations:

> Our conclusions and recommendations are based on the following findings:
>
> - The welfare of the Jekyll Island Club is critical to the Jekyll Island Authority as the Club represents the only upscale accommodations on the island, and the only unique lodging experience on the island.
> - The current lease for the subject property does not reflect current market standards for commercial land leases. Market land lease deal structure for hotels generally range from 3% to 8% of gross

---

[364] Smith Dalia Architects, Atlanta. (http://www.smithdalia.com/about/)

income with some base minimum lease rate. Lease terms are typically longer-term (30 years or more) with some provision for adjustment every five years.

- According to their own unaudited financial statements, the Jekyll Island Club has not been a highly profitable property since reopening and has lost money (after repayment of debt) seven out of the ten years the hotel has been in operation, including an estimated loss in 1996.
- In reviewing the cash flow projections provided by Jekyll Development Associates, L.P., the expansion of the hotel appears to be necessary to enable the hotel to be profitable, allowing the hotel to further tap into the conference/meeting market.
- The re-negotiation of the lease as proposed by the Club would result in reduced lease payments to the Authority relative to the 1985 agreement while revenues for the Club are projected to increase (i.e. the Jekyll Island Authority would not directly benefit financially from the re-negotiation of the lease and the expansion of the hotel).

Upon our examination of the current situation, we offer the following recommendations relative to the lease on the Jekyll Club Hotel:

- The current lease, which calls for lease payments of $100,000 in 1997, 3% of gross income in 1998 through 2002 and 3.5% of gross income from 2003 through the life of the loan appears to be reasonable from a market standpoint, though at the low end of the range. There should be a provision that over the same period of time, the lease payments increase closer to market, say between the proposed 3.5% and 8%. This could be tied to an increase in the debt service coverage ratio exceeding the lenders required minimum, so as not to impact financially.

- The extension of the lease through 2049 is reasonable as improvements made to the property will require significant time to be amortized.
- Some concessions in the lease rate appear to be required for the Jekyll Island Club to undergo expansion and become a potentially profitable property, should either be considered an equity investment or a loan. Thus, the two options are as follows:

-The amount of the concession provided to the Club could be considered a loan, like a second mortgage on the property, and could be repaid to the Authority with interest over time after some grace period, or

-The Jekyll Island Authority could become a partner in the property with the amount of the concessions representing a percentage of the ownership, resulting in a share of profits being paid to the Jekyll Island Authority.

- While re-negotiating the lease to accommodate the aforementioned concessions, the opportunity exists to enforce minimum maintenance and appearance clauses. In leased property, these clauses are typically needed as assurance that lessees maintain the property in a manner appropriate to the Authority and to ensure the Authority that needed maintenance in the latter years of a lease are not deferred.

- The Jekyll Island Authority should reserve the right to have the Club's financial records audited by an independent entity to assure accuracy in gross income, net cash flow reporting.[365]

Robert Charles Lesser & Co.'s opinion letter sets forth two new ideas pertaining to the future management of commercial properties on the island.

The indication that the current and future JICH lease payments (3 percent) are not in line with prevailing market rates (3 percent to 8 percent) marks the first time a land-use plan developer compares the existing lease payments to overall market conditions. This simple comment will have far-reaching consequences for all the island hotels very soon.

The second important idea is the mentioning of a possible partnership in the hotel between the existing lessee, Jekyll Development Associates, LP, and the authority. While not explicitly mentioned in the letter, such partnership refers to public private partnerships, or PPPs, that exist elsewhere.

Of more importance, however, is the proposal to include two historic cottages in the hotel expansion. While this may seem innocent enough and will certainly accommodate the hotel expansion through the adaptive use of the cottages, it will also mark the first time a private firm has exclusive access to structures that carry a National Historic Landmark designation and are meant to be open and accessible to the public.

A *Brunswick News* editorial on March 18, 1997, comments on the proposal with similar concerns:

> There are some questions that need to be answered and explored by the board before it agrees to the hotel's request. The main ones are whether the JIA wants to turn over two of its historic properties to the management and use of the resort, and whether this will be a one-time deal or set a precedent of private leasing of other state-owned historic properties …

---

[365] Addendum to the minutes of January 1997 authority board meeting.

> ... Many tourists come to the island just to visit the historic village, and we would not want to see a majority of the properties given up to private enterprise ...[366]

A subtle but fair warning, with the intention to protect the integrity of the Historic District and to ensure continued public access.

In response to both the recommendations of the DNR and the opinion letter of Robert Charles Lesser & Co., the Jekyll Island Club Hotel submits a second proposal to the authority that includes the use of Crane and Cherokee Cottages. Instead of forming a public private partnership, the hotel proposes to invest $1.1 million as matching funds if the authority commits to invest the anticipated $1.725 million through general obligation bonds.[367]

The purpose of the funding request through appropriation includes far more than the restoration of Crane and Cherokee Cottages. The Jekyll Island Historic District Masterplan Implementation Summary 1997, as submitted to Gov. Miller and members of the general assembly, includes upgrades of the site facilities at the Club Stable, stabilization of Hollybourne Cottage, Chicota site exhibit, restrooms at the Historic Wharf, upgrades to the interior of Indian Mound and Villa Marianna, and restoration of Moss Cottage.[368]

It seems that most of the above proposed renovations will take a back seat in favor of capital improvements to Crane Cottage and Cherokee Cottage, both of which will be leased and managed by the Jekyll Island Club Hotel.

As one partnership comes to fruition, another similar proposal for the restoration of the Gould Auditorium does not receive the same welcome or attention from the authority.

It is no secret that Valdosta State University has pursued the idea of a permanent arts center on the island for some time now, given the less than

---

[366] *Brunswick News* editorial, March 18, 1997, "Jekyll Tourism growth."
[367] Gov. Miller committed $1.725 million in general obligation bonds for FY 1998 and for the exclusive use of Historic District renovation.
[368] "Jekyll Island Historic District Masterplan Implementation Summary—1997" (authority board meeting, addendum to the minutes of January 1997).

accommodating environment at the amphitheater, let alone the condition of the Actor's Dorm.

A proposal is submitted by James Bradley, executive director, to Charles Jenkins, chair of the board, on April 2, 1997:

> Following are initial design plans for Valdosta State University to facilitate a Capital Fund-Raising Campaign for the renovation of Gould Auditorium. An estimated $1.5 million would allow the structure to become a year-round Arts Center operated by the University.
>
> This proposal presents multiple advantages to the Authority. Primary among them are the restoration of another building and the addition of an entertainment option for our guests.
>
> I recommend that the Authority endorse this proposal and participate fully in the efforts to raise the funds needed ...

The attached design plans, developed by Richard Hill Associates, Valdosta, Georgia, include a 442-seat theater, dressing rooms, meeting rooms, office space, and concession stands for patrons.

The proposal is lost amidst the multitude of other renovation projects in the Historic District that seem far more attractive from a future revenue perspective. Ultimately, the opportunity to restore and repurpose the first island auditorium is lost forever.

By the end of 1997, the Historic District has been somewhat stabilized, despite ongoing projects of the historic cottages on Riverview Drive. Pier Road cottages and the small businesses that occupy them attract a steady flow of curious visitors. The Santa's Christmas Shop, located in the old power plant, seems somewhat isolated from the regular foot traffic, but that doesn't seem to be an impediment. It is therefore not a surprise that the other "isolated" building in the Historic District, the old infirmary,[369] gets a permanent lessee when Jekyll Books & Antiques Inc. signs a three-year lease agreement.

---

[369] The old infirmary, also known as the Furness Cottage, was used as housing for the island's superintendent and later for its director of services until mid to late 1996.

Pier Road itself now prominently features several small stores and offers ample shopping opportunities for visitors and locals, in addition to the two strip malls on Beachview Drive. The historic character of the Pier Road Cottages allows for a stroll down memory lane, and the merchandise of the Commissary, the Cottage, Nature's Cottage, the Old Bath House, Jekyll Trading Post, and the Sweet Shoppe[370] enhance the visitor's experience with a multitude of old-style and local smells, mementos, and replicas. The inventories match their historic surroundings perfectly, although once outside, asphalt and constant drive-through traffic bring visitors back to the stark reality of modern times, despite the historic setting.

It will take several more years before a new and improved circulation plan is completed and finally matches the true character of the Historic District and its century-old cottages.

In the two years of his tenure as executive director, James Bradley succeeds to stabilize the day-to-day management of Jekyll Island, while still pursuing and completing important capital improvements. While Mr. Bradley is certainly the shortest-serving executive director in island history, he has achieved what was needed the most after the turbulence created by his predecessor, George Chambliss. He created an operational environment that mended and bridged the distance created between the island's management team and the authority. Bradley restored that mutual respect and cooperation at a time when stabilization, trust, and, above all, adherence to the rules of oversight, regulations, and mandatory approval processes by the relevant authorities and agencies is critical to the continued success and credibility of Jekyll Island, its authority board, and its future demands for continued funding.

Mr. Bradley effectively paved the way for the future of Jekyll Island by uniting and unifying all parties involved, thereby restoring and solidifying a much-needed solid foundation upon which a new course for the island could be charted.

---

[370] Lois Acheson operated the Commissary. Milton and Cheryl Smith owned the Jekyll Trading Post. C. N. and Billie Croft operated the Sweet Shoppe, while Susan Hamer owned both the Cottage and Nature's Cottage. Both leases were transferred to Cheryl and Van Hart and Beverly and Larry Wade respectively in 2000. Leigh and Steve Baumann owned the Old Bath House, behind the Commissary.

All these unwritten requirements and requests are now fulfilled successfully, and it is time to appoint a new executive director who can guide and steer Jekyll Island toward the future.

Bill Donohue takes over the reins as executive director in September 1997.

He is certainly no stranger to the island. On the contrary, Bill Donohue has attended regular board meetings and executive sessions for quite some time in his capacity as the DNR representative.

Besides being credited, at least behind closed doors or maybe during informal conversations, for halting the unauthorized clearing of land north of Shell Road in 1995[371] to pave the way for a new nine-hole golf course addition, thereby saving natural habitats and marshlands from being permanently damaged, Bill Donohue also earned the respect and admiration of his superiors and the political powers in Atlanta during the 1996 Olympic Games. He was instrumental in the design and construction of the Olympic Village and its security. More importantly, his vision led to the repurposing of the village for low-income housing.

His arrival marks a new beginning and chapter in island history, one that is both challenging and paved with more than a fair share of setbacks, changes, improvements, and victories. But when a predecessor smoothens and stabilizes ground level and relationships, upcoming challenges can be tackled more easily and without the usual or expected resistance.

It is exactly this well-understood and stable relationship between the island's management team, under the direction of Bill Donohue, and the authority that puts the mark on his tenure and allows him to take control from the start.

---

[371] George Chambliss ordered the clearance of land north of Shell Road by heavy machinery to draw the median for nine new fairways. The clearance was not approved by the DNR and was considered a violation. It ultimately led to his immediate involuntary resignation.

CHAPTER 15

SETTING A NEW COURSE

1998–2002

Launching a new phase and a new beginning for Jekyll Island requires a strong and stable management team. Besides the appointment of Bill Donohue as the new executive director, positions that will play a key role in the island's future are also secured. John Hunter is well placed as chief curator and assistant museum director to ensure the stability of the Historic District, while Laura Bonds keeps a close eye on the island's checks and balances as the chief financial officer.

The island's golf courses are undergoing continued change under the supervision of John Neidhardt, senior golf superintendent, with the implementation of new irrigation sources. The project that will provide golf course irrigation using new Miocene wells, rather than continuing to use valuable potable water from the Floridian Aquifer, began in 1997 and was recommended by the Environmental Protection Department.

The conversion from six Floridian Aquifer wells to four Miocene wells costs over $1 million but will reduce potable water usage by 33 percent. Jekyll Island is the first municipality to convert to the shallow Miocene wells among the twenty-four coastal counties between Charleston, South Carolina, and St. Augustine, Florida. The project is completed in 2001, well before the EPD enforces the conversion by law.

The Historic District undergoes major changes with the ongoing renovation and rehabilitation of Crane Cottage and Cherokee Cottage.

The total project cost for both is estimated at $4.25 million, of which the authority contributes $1.9 million. The remainder is private investment made by Jekyll Development Associates, the current owners of the Jekyll Island Club Hotel. The project is expected to be completed by December 2000, but both cottages will not open to guests until March 2001.

The main reason for the duration of the project and the delay is the implementation of a new circulation plan for the entire Historic District that is both time-consuming and expensive.

In 1997, the Historic District is easily accessible by car, and the fact that there are seven entry points[372] through which tour cars can guide visitors past all historic buildings and cottages for a quick and easy narrated tour makes for a congested scene, let alone the potential damage to the buildings.

The Circulation Plan Phase I removes all the asphalt from the main roads in the Historic District and narrows the surviving roads to twelve feet while repaving with faux tabby.[373] The changes definitely alter the character of the Historic District and give it more definition as a tourist destination. The sudden absence of multiple motorized vehicles and the expansion of pedestrian, bicycle, and horse-drawn carriages add to its own historic value. Several entry points are eliminated in the process, and extra parking lots are added to facilitate pedestrian access to the shops in the district.

The later Phase I-b will close the northern entrance of Old Plantation Road and Riverview Drive altogether. The removed asphalt is used to create roadbeds at the Cherokee camping ground and as rock revetment on Clam Creek.

---

[372] The Historic District could be accessed by car through Riverview Drive, north and south; Old Plantation Road, at the north and south intersection with Stable Road; Pier Road; James Road; and Old Schoolhouse Road.

[373] Faux tabby refers to the modern and more cost-effective road surface that resembles old tabby made from crushed oyster shell, limes, sand, and water.

The entire project is paid for with the same general obligation bonds used to renovate Crane and Cherokee Cottages, while some of the additional parking lots[374] are resurfaced by the Department of Transportation.

As part of another major infrastructure project, the authority embarks on its last phase of water/sewage expansion and mandatory tap-in. Since most of the island residents and commercial properties have been using the municipal water/sewage system since the late seventies, one small development has continued to use individual septic tanks until now.

St. Andrews Beach subdivision, including the 4-H Center, never converted from septic tanks to municipal sewage. The authority now addresses the issue and demands a ten-foot easement from all fourteen residents through the issuance of a quit claim deed and demands a $1,600 tap-in fee per property. The proposal meets so much resistance that it takes more than a year for twelve residents to finally agree to the one-time tap-in fee and sign the required quit claim deed. Two residents are holding out until mid-2000 when the authority resorts to extreme measures and authorizes the executive director to enforce the ordinance and use condemnation proceedings if needed. The extreme measure is never used, and all residents ultimately sign the deed agreement so the entire subdivision can be connected.

It is remarkable that the 4-H Center, once home to the Dolphin Motor Lodge and later acquired by the authority to serve as a youth camp, could operate its own septic tank system for more than twenty-five years, even when UGA signed a lease agreement in the early seventies. Part of the explanation is that at the time, such an expensive conversion would have been the financial responsibility of the authority. Now that the adjacent residents are forced to tap in the municipal sewage system, the authority, or UGA as lessee, has no choice but to do the same and has the advantage of cost-sharing with the residential property owners.

---

[374] The JICH parking lot was private guest parking only until the Circulation Plan Phase I was completed. Part of the renegotiated lease agreement with Jekyll Development Associates was to remove the exclusive parking lot and to allow public parking for visitors other than hotel guests. In exchange, the authority constructed extra private parking around Crane and Cherokee Cottages and public parking around Faith Chapel.

As planned projects seem to progress smoothly, and required funding is secured to finance all or part of the improvements, two interesting things occur around the same time: a major discussion about taxes, as proposed by an obscure and surprising House bill (HB 1427), and new language that accompanies the issuance of General Obligation Bonds-2000B in June of the same year.

The General Appropriations Act for fiscal year 1999–2000, Act No. 499, 2000 Regular Session, signed by Governor Roy Barnes on April 17, 2000, makes the following appropriation to the General Obligation Bond Sinking Fund:

> ... WHEREAS FURTHER, the Jekyll Island-State Park Authority is aware of the provisions and requirements of the Internal revenue Code of 1986, as amended (the "Tax Code") and the regulations issued thereunder respecting arbitrage bonds, and private activity bonds, and is aware that the Projects must proceed with due diligence and be timely complete following receipt of the proceeds derived from the sale of general obligation bonds, ...[375]

It is the first time that an official document, pertaining to the appropriation of general obligation bonds, mentions the applicable Tax Code about the restrictions placed for use as arbitrage bonds and/or private activity. The restriction strictly prohibits the use of sale proceeds of said bonds to leverage against any other previous bond issue and further prohibits its use for any project other than the one(s) listed in the addendum of the appropriations request.

Given that the referenced Tax Code dates to 1986, and several other appropriations have been issued since, it raises the question of whether the Georgia Finance and Investment Committee found any unusual or inappropriate use of proceeds in the past, hence the inclusion of the specific paragraph.

The second interesting event of the year is the obscure HB 1427. It is not the bill itself that is questionable but the method used to attain its goal.

---

[375] Resolution of the Jekyll Island State Park Authority, June 12, 2000 (authority board meeting, addendum to the minutes, July 2000).

HB 1427 is a measure that requires Glynn County to help with the costs of providing services to residents and businesses on Jekyll Island. The dispute between island residents and Glynn County commissioners dates back several decades and always centers around the ad valorem taxes levied against the residents in relation to county services rendered in exchange. Although Jekyll residents receive a tax rebate through a reduced millage rate, Glynn County does not provide police or emergency services as it does for its other residents, hence the ongoing dispute about the disparity between levied taxes and services rendered.

Jekyll residents want a portion of SPLOST taxes to be earmarked for capital improvement projects on the island, given that they pay their fair share. Glynn County, however, already struggling to raise sufficient funds for all the projects that need completion, refuses to share the financial pie.

Initially, a compromise is reached that would give Jekyll Island $50,000 to construct bike paths, but even that deal seems to fall apart due to projected budget shortfalls in Glynn County.

The Preservation Alliance, formed by Tise Eyler and the Jekyll Island Citizens Association, rallies the political troops wherever possible. By February 2000, the group has amassed so much support that sponsors of HB 1427 in the House looks like a Who's Who of the general assembly.[376]

According to the bill, it places an ultimatum on Glynn County. Failure to help defer the cost of services to residents and businesses on Jekyll Island would result in forfeiture of the local option sales tax and the special local option sales tax altogether.

The request to help defer service costs on the island is reasonable, but HB 1427 smells more like a financial ultimatum than a proposal to negotiate. Given the multitude of newspaper articles about the topic and the numerous letters to the editors, the general sentiment is that the request for sharing the financial pie is more than fair but that the road taken to achieve this goal is less than commendable.

The unorthodox way does achieve its ultimate goal: plenty of publicity and the ear of Glynn County commissioners who fear they may lose the legal grounds to levy and collect LOST and SPLOST funds altogether should they fail to provide services to Jekyll Island.

---

[376] The *Brunswick News*, February 15, 2000. Article by Hank Rowland.

The controversy in this long-standing and lingering dispute is of course the special status Jekyll Island enjoys as being managed by a state agency, and funding for capital improvements primarily comes from fund appropriations through the general assembly—a complicated and complex matter indeed and one that still prevails to this day.

Also consider that, at the same time, the authority just raised its parking fee from two to three dollars, a 50 percent increase that is supposed to fund general projects, including bike paths.

As the battle continues for extra revenue sources, be it SPLOST funds allocation or general assembly appropriations, the commercial island properties are never exempt either.

For several years, Ritchie International has closely monitored the service quality of the island hotels by carefully reviewing and documenting guest reviews and comments regarding their accommodations, service, hotel personnel, and overall satisfaction ratings.

A new study by Bare Associates International[377] reveals a continued downtrend in guest satisfaction, and six out of the ten hotels reviewed score below the national average of 85 percent.

The continued decline leads the authority to establish a new standard lease agreement, which requires 6 percent of the annual revenues to be reserved for capital improvements and implements an evaluation process to assist in monitoring and enforcing quality standards and raising insurance requirements.

This is a major change from the original lease agreements that were signed in the previous four decades. It forces the hotel owners to upgrade their properties to meet the required industry standards and satisfaction rating, but it also places a sudden and unexpected financial burden on them.

---

[377] The six hotels with a score below 85 percent are Villa by the Sea, Ramada Inn, Comfort Inn, Holiday Inn, Jekyll Inn, and Clarion Hotel. The four hotels that score above the average are JICH, Beachview Club, Days Inn, and Seafarer Inn. The JICH receives the highest score of 91.3. (Bare Associates International, Executive Director's Report, 1st period 2001. Addendum to the authority board meeting minutes, May 2001.)

The authority goes one step further in its quest to increase and revise the current rent structure, since it is in the process of revising all its commercial lease agreements.

Upon the advice from Atlantic Hospitality Advisors, an independent industry consulting firm hired by the authority in February 2000, the current rent structures are not in line with industry standards. That doesn't come as a surprise, given that some of the leases or even the lease renewals never adjusted the base rent, based on land value, or the gross percentage based on sales.

Initially, all commercial leases consisted of a fixed base rent payment plus 3 percent of gross revenue. In later years, the authority used two segments to determine rent: the first as a percentage of gross revenues; the second as 8 percent of the fair market value of the land.[378]

Because the lease agreements are typically renewed every ten years, it results in a new land appraisal that affects the new base rent. When such was done for the Jekyll Inn in 1999, the old formula of 8 percent base rent plus 3 percent of gross revenue put the hotel well over the industry standard of 4 percent to 7 percent of gross revenue, hence a new approach must be found.

The recommended solution is to change the rent structure for all hotels to be the higher of either 4.5 percent of gross revenue or 8 percent of the fair market value (FMV) of the land.

The FMV base used in existing lease agreements was $40K to $45K, but a new appraisal for the Jekyll Inn and the Ramada Inn result in a land value of $218K to $350K. The dramatic change in FMV alone represents a challenge for the authority.

On one hand, the authority wants to be compensated according to industry standards, but it also wants the hotel owners to be able to improve their properties and generate enough revenue to continue to exist.

A compromise is reached by gradually adjusting each hotel's lease agreements, rather than enforce the new standard at once and across the board. This flexible approach avoids the underdeveloped assets from facing potential bankruptcy should the new rule be strictly enforced.

---

[378] In 2000, the average total rent paid to the authority is 3.72 percent of the hotel's gross income (authority board meeting, March 2001).

The Holiday Inn, Jekyll Inn, and Villas by the Sea are all spread out over large properties yet do not generate enough income to sustain the proposed rent increase.[379]

The Clarion, Comfort Inn, Days Inn, Jekyll Inn, and Ramada Inn are all adjusted immediately upon the authority board's decision. The Holiday Inn will become effective in October 2002, and Seafarer Apartments in February 2003. Villas by the Sea will be effective December 2003; however, it is limited to a 50 percent increase in base rent as per the current lease agreement. Beachview Club will not be adjusted until 2007. The only exception is the Jekyll Island Club Hotel, which doesn't have a base rent.

The result of this extensive exercise is that three hotels[380] are envisioned to pay the base rent (8 percent of the land value, set and agreed upon at $200K per acre), until they can increase the gross revenue to support the property; all other hotels pay 4.5 percent of gross revenue.

By implementing the new plan, the authority increases its revenue stream by $500K annually and sees its return on commercial properties increase from 3.72 percent to 4.93 percent.

But not all is well in the island's hotel industry. Besides struggling to meet industry standards and client satisfaction rating, one owner struggles to meet its financial obligations and contacts the authority with the proposal to reassign one of its leases.

Motel Properties Inc. (owner of the Clarion Resort Buccaneer and Comfort Inn) is in such financial hardship that it proposes to assign the Clarion lease to a single entity, thereby protecting the Comfort Inn and the Beachview Club[381] from any potential financial fallout.

By assigning the Clarion lease to a single asset entity, Atlantic Ventures Inc., Sterling Partners Capital is willing to issue a $5 million loan to pay off the existing loans, property taxes, and payroll taxes. The remainder of

---

[379] The Holiday Inn occupies 12.4 acres, Jekyll Inn is built on 14.53 acres, and Villas by the Sea is spread over twenty acres. In comparison, all other hotels use between five and ten acres and feature more guest rooms. (Hotel Rent Summary, letter dated March 2001 from Bill Donohue to Members, Jekyll Island Authority.)
[380] Holiday Inn, Jekyll Inn, and Ramada Inn.
[381] The owner of the Beachview Club is also a cosigner on the Motel Properties loans (letter from Laura Bonds to Bill Donohue, dated October 9, 2000).

the funding, $1.25 million is earmarked for renovations, while less than $500K is left as working capital.

It is clear from Ms. Bonds's letter that the renovation amount is deemed inadequate to bring the property to such a service standard that revenue will be enough to meet the new base rent or gross revenue percentage, thereby satisfying the new lease terms. There certainly are not enough funds to even consider complying with the new 6 percent capital reserve.

Should the loan not be closed, because of failure to reassign the lease to a single asset entity, then Motel Properties will most likely seek bankruptcy protection, which would involve both the Comfort Inn and the Beachview Club. It is not an attractive prospect for the authority, who does not wish to see three of its hotel properties closed or entangled in a complicated and complex Chapter 11 court proceeding.

The Ramada Inn also submits a request at the same time to sublease its hotel restaurant to a subsidiary of Zachry's Seafood Restaurant Inc. The Surf Steakhouse Inc., owned and operated by David Zachry and Patrick Cawley, will pay the percentage rent directly to the authority rather than the Ramada Inn. The hotel has also caught the attention of Remington Hotels, who is willing to acquire the property and make a major investment in complete renovation.

The small business leases are next in line and subject to either standard renewal to secure the immediate future or a base rent adjustment to streamline the lease agreements.

All the shops in the Historic District pay an average of seven dollars per square foot plus 3 percent of gross revenue. The stores in the shopping centers all receive a five-year renewal notice.[382] The only noticeable change is the new requirement of a security deposit.

The first two years of the new management team, under the leadership of Executive Director Bill Donohue, seem like a repeat of the late 1980s with one exception. This restructuring effort is well thought out and with a clear focus on the future stability of the island as a whole. The complex island puzzle doesn't necessarily change, but the individual pieces are reshaped in such a way that each fits better in the whole picture, so that the total is more valuable than the sum of its individual components.

---

[382] IGA, Maxwell's, the pharmacy, and the US post office.

It is therefore not a surprise that the Convention & Visitors Bureau (CVB) goes through a thorough review process to eliminate any possible redundancy and to ensure efficiency.

The proposal recommends that the JIA contract with the Brunswick Golden Isles CVB to provide direct sales, advertising, and public relations services for Jekyll Island. In return, the JIA will pay 60 percent of the collected hotel tax to the BGI-CVB, estimated at approximately $750K, and will eliminate two full-time employee positions. The JIA will retain a marketing staff and certain CVB functions, including the welcome center, convention services, and printing. The contract proposal, if approved, will be for one year and take effect on July 1, 2000.[383]

There is room for one more piece in the puzzle that apparently has been missing since the early days of the Jekyll Island Committee Fund.[384] Its new replacement, the Jekyll Island Foundation (JIF), is formed with the purpose of raising, managing, and disbursing funds for Jekyll Island improvements. Like its predecessor, the JIF will raise funds as a nonprofit organization to subsidize capital improvement projects for which no adequate state funding can be obtained.

It seems that by early 2001, all the pieces are in place, and the hope is that the overall plan will slowly bear its fruits, or at least avoid any further decline in revenue and deterioration of valuable assets.

Looking at the first hotel evaluations in April 2001, the results are less than stellar, and the scores continue to decline. with only two hotels scoring in the low nineties and two barely reaching the national average of 85 percent.[385]

---

[383] Bill Tipton is the executive director of BGI-CVB. Kevin Runner would become BGI-CVB Board chairman for two years. (Letter from Bill Donohue to Members, Jekyll Island Authority, June 5, 2000.)

[384] The Jekyll Island Committee Fund was established in 1951 to accept state funding and finance 80 percent of the operating and improvement expenses on Jekyll Island (authority board meeting, July 1951).

[385] The Jekyll Island Club Hotel received the highest score of 91.3, with the Beachview Club as a close second with a score of 90. The Seafarer and the Days Inn both scored 85.3. (Hotel Evaluation Responses, May 2001.)

From Millionaires to Commoners

To make matters worse, the Jekyll Inn suffers major damage from a fire in one of its buildings,[386] and the Clarion and Comfort Inn are not able to meet the required capital reserve budgets, resulting in Motel Properties filing for bankruptcy protection altogether.

Not a good beginning and one that unfortunately will continue to plague Jekyll Island, despite the welcoming news from Remington Hotels to acquire and renovate the Ramada Inn.

The only positive news at this time is that the Historic District is stable, and Phase II of the Circulation Plan is set in motion now that Crane and Cherokee Cottages are finally open to hotel guests after several delays.[387]

It is remarkable that the Historic District, once the stepchild on Jekyll Island that barely received any attention, let alone funding, is finally being recognized as the stabilization factor on the island. While the much-praised oceanside hotels and resorts long overshadowed, the priceless and timeless treasure of what makes Jekyll Island unique finally gets its well-deserved day in the sun. Much of the praise is due to the continued efforts of the Jekyll Island Club Hotel and its owners, who persisted on expanding their hotel and thereby revitalizing an entire underappreciated district.

No better tribute of this revival and accomplishment can be found than the visit of Mr. Christopher Elliman in February 2001. Mr. Elliman is interested in visiting the Historic District and the cottages but has a special interest in Indian Mound. After all, he is the great-great-grandson of Mr. Rockefeller himself.[388]

The shops on Pier Road are doing well and are appreciated by visitors and hotel guests, so much so that Ms. Juliana Germano, who already operates Yesteryear at the JICH and the Island House on Pier Road, now also takes over the operations of the Commissary from Lois Acheson.

Ongoing renovation also means one popular shop must make room for bigger and better things. Santa's Christmas Shoppe,[389] which has been

---

[386] The Jekyll Inn Inverness Building caught fire in May 2001 and caused serious fire and water damage.

[387] Both Crane Cottage and Cherokee Cottages opened March 31, 2001, after a three-month delay due to the implementation of the Circulation Plan.

[388] Mr. Elliman's visit to Jekyll Island was covered in detail by both the *Columbus Ledger Enquirer* and the *Atlanta Journal-Constitution* on February 19, 2001.

[389] Marie Stubbs, Martha Harvey, Mary Bishop, and Pat Taylor operated Santa's Christmas Shoppe.

operating out of the old power plant since 1984,[390] must relocate to Pier Road, a much smaller space, so that extensive renovation and restoration can take place.

The celebration of the renovated Historic District ultimately culminates in an official visit from Gov. Roy Barnes himself on July 21, 2001, where he can see firsthand the result of appropriated state funding, and the success of a public private partnership, when he tours Crane and Cherokee Cottages, while also paying a visit to the new welcome center and Georgia State Patrol offices on the causeway.

But as summer ends, America is shocked by the events of 9/11, and although Jekyll Island is miles away from New York City, the effect can be felt immediately in the number of visitors or regular vacationers. A nation mourns, and rightfully so, and vacations or weekend getaways are as far from the average American's mind as anything. Although the economic impact is not as dramatic as in other resort areas across the country, the reduced number of visitors is enough for the authority to carefully reduce its budget projections for 2002 by 2.5 percent and to reduce or postpone its spending plan.

Barely seven days later, the much-anticipated SPLOST IV issue is approved by a majority of the Glynn County voters. Part of SPLOST IV projects and listings, as listed on the ballot, includes funding for Jekyll Island projects. Before the votes are tallied and the list of projects finalized and approved, the controversy surrounding the fair allocation of SPLOST funds roars its ugly head again with a lawsuit that is filed in Glynn County Superior Court on October 1, 2001.

---

[390] The old power plant featured an antique car showroom, operated by Mr. Stauffer until his retirement in 1984.

The Civil Action File # 01-01439 states:

> Ken Plyman and others similarly situated
> Plaintiff
> V.
> Glynn County
> Defendant
> PETITION TO SET ASIDE SPECIAL ELECTION
> Comes now Plaintiff and petitions this Court as follows:
>
> 1. The special election for the SPLOST vote contained matters that are unacceptable and without basis under law. Said election being held on September 18, 2001.
> 2. The SPLOST listings contained funds for Jekyll Island, GA which is a State Park and not a municipal or county governmental body.
> 3. Any funds allocated, collected, and paid would be illegal and unenforceable and therefore should be set aside and vacated.
> 4. Plaintiff requests that this Court set a time and date for hearing to determine the validity or invalidity of such special election and to set aside same for the reasons set forth above.[391]

Summons by the Glynn County Clerk, Superior Court are sent to Glynn County with the request to file a response within thirty days. Failure to do so may result in a default judgment.

Pending resolution of the lawsuit, the authority halts and postpones all projects identified as being funded with anticipated SPLOST revenue

---

[391] Executive Director's Report, Attachment 3A (authority board meeting, October 2001).

allocation, including the bike path extensions for which $50K was earmarked earlier and the incomplete ADA improvements.[392]

As expected, 2002 has a difficult beginning with less than expected revenue due to a decline in hotel room occupancy, rounds of golf, and overall visitation.

To make matters worse, the Holiday Inn files for bankruptcy protection, joining Motel Properties, who filed for Chapter 11 six months earlier. While the affected hotels remain open for business as usual, it is the first sign of a major game changer for the island's hospitality industry. Four out of the ten hotels are now under bankruptcy protection, and it is unclear how or when each will reemerge. Will the court-approved restructuring plans allow for enough capital to be invested in complete renovations that will ultimately improve the revenue? The second question on the authority's mind is whether enough operating funds will be made available to secure the mandatory 6 percent capital reserve.

Only time will tell how the four hotels will fare, but the remaining six hotels do not score high marks either, and client satisfaction is at an all-time low. Without a clear solution to the problem, despite the new lease agreements that provide the authority with the power to declare any hotel to be in default due to consistent underperformance, no forceful measures are taken. Instead, Bill Donohue uses his diplomacy and continues to work with hotel management to come to a consensus, in the hope that time and patience will heal the dire situation.

Clients do not have the same patience as Mr. Donohue or the authority and take measures into their own hands. One of Jekyll Island's biggest convention clients, the annual All-Star Challenge Cheerleading and Dance Competition, based in Durham, North Carolina, informs the authority in April 2002 that it is moving its annual event to Florida.[393]

The cited reason is a lack of accommodations and convention facilities that are too small. This is a major loss for Jekyll Island, as the organization has brought over five thousand competitors to the island over the past two

---

[392] Most of the American Disability Act (ADA) improvements were completed between 1996 and 2001. Some remained incomplete pending SPLOST allocation funds.
[393] The *Brunswick News*, April 18, 2002.

years and has spent more than $1.5 million on lodging during its three or four days on the island.

The problem is clearly not just the convention center or its size. No hotel is large enough or accommodating enough for such large gatherings, hence the idea starts floating of building a new three-hundred-room oceanside hotel that can serve as a dedicated convention hotel.[394]

On May 15, 2002, the authority issues an "Invitation to prequalify to bid on the development and management of a first-class resort hotel on Jekyll Island, Georgia."[395]

The invitation is launched upon the recommendation of a private consulting firm, PKF Consulting Inc., that was retained earlier in the year to study the feasibility of first-class destination resort accommodations in the area.

One paragraph in the invitation is of particular interest, as it reads: "The Authority is interested in forming a venture with a developer or development group to build, finance, and operate a first-class resort hotel on the subject site."

Not everyone is happy with the new and bold approach of building another three hundred hotel rooms on the island, given that the average occupancy rate is 55 percent, and the guest satisfaction rate remains consistently below the national average. That is the argument Ted Smith makes, a real estate marketer from Cornelia.

Mr. Smith has been working diligently with the owners of the Ramada Inn, recently renamed the Georgia Coast Inn, to convert the property from motel to "condotel," a time-share arrangement. Despite an expensive study, his presentation receives a lukewarm reception from the authority board in May, and his request for conversion is ultimately denied four months later.

The reason for denial has some rationality to it, since the authority already struggles with the arrangement of 140 condominium owners at Villas by the Sea. Mr. Smith's proposal will create another possible complication with 135 condominium units and a foreseeable total of 2,025

---

[394] The idea of an oceanside convention hotel was first launched in May 2001. It materialized with the opening of the Westin Hotel in 2015.
[395] Authority board meeting, April 2002. Addendum to the meeting minutes.

time-share owners. The collection process and the revenue-sharing process is problematic at best, hence the refusal for conversion.

The authority has enough headaches already with several distressed hotels and four properties under bankruptcy protection. The sense is that the situation needs to be stabilized before any new venues are to be considered, but the perception is also that both the authority and Bill Donohue know that the island is at important crossroads, and a decision needs to be made that can and will change the future of the island. It is just uncertain at this time which fork in the road to take.

The good news is that by July, Motel Properties emerges from bankruptcy with a new $8.54 million loan, of which $820K is placed in escrow for capital improvements. That amounts to the required 6 percent as per the lease agreement.

The Seafarer, which has recently completed extensive renovations and improvements, successfully negotiates an affiliation with the Quality Inn. The affiliation with a major hotel franchise is viewed as a good indicator for the hotel industry overall.

The sentiment cannot undo, however, the fact that by the end of the year, yet again the Jekyll Inn is found to be in default for underperformance, and the Holiday Inn is still working on financing to exit bankruptcy.

That same sentiment of uncertainty also finds its way to the general assembly, where both House Resolution HR 1105 and Senate Resolution SR 826 are passed to create a Joint Study Committee on Jekyll Island.

The committee consists of six members, three members of the House of Representatives to be appointed by the Speaker, and three members of the Senate, to be appointed by the president of the Senate.

SR 826 stipulates: "... BE IT FURTHER RESOLVED that the committee shall undertake a study of the conditions, needs, issues, and problems mentioned above or related thereto and recommend any actions or legislation which the committee deems necessary or appropriate ..."[396]

The issues and problems referred to are further explained as pertaining to the ninety-nine-year lease of the authority; the fact that some residential leases will come due in the near future, which will make transfer, refinance,

---

[396] Excerpt SR 826. Full text 02 LC 8 5145. March 8, 2002 (addendum to the minutes of the authority board meeting, May 2002).

or sale of the property difficult; and the need for state funding to renovate historic property and golf courses.

The latter is certainly becoming a problem lately since the Senate denied the authority's request to issue a $1.2 million loan for improvements of Summer Waves attractions earlier in the year. An alternative way of financing must be found by the authority, but such route requires an amendment of the Official Code of Georgia Annotated (OCGA). In September 2002, such amendment is forthcoming, and Code Section 12-3-232(a) and Code Section 12-3-241(a) are amended as follows:

> Part 1 of Article 7 of Chapter 3 of Title 12 of the Official Code of Georgia Annotated, relating to Jekyll Island-State Park Authority, is amended by striking the existing last sentence of Code Section 12-3-232(a), which reads "The Authority shall exist for 99 years," so that, as amended, Code Section 12-3-232(a) shall read as follows:
>
> (a) There is created a body corporate and politic to be known as the Jekyll Island-State Park Authority, which shall be deemed to be an instrumentality of the state and a public corporation, and by that name, style, and title such body may contract and be contracted with, sue and be sued, implead and be impleaded, and complain and defend in all courts. The Authority may delegate to one or more of its members, or to its officers, agents, and employees, such powers and duties as it may deem proper ...

The implication of this seemingly minor change is dual.

First, the authority no longer has a limited time of existence, as per the original Authority Act of 1950. Another section amendment will further explain this change.

Secondly, the fact that the authority is known as an instrumentality of the state and a public corporation allows it to seek private financing in addition to the general assembly appropriation proceedings. This paves the way to private borrowing, with the approval of GSFIC and/or the

Office of Budget and Planning and opens the door to form public private partnerships for future capital improvements.

Section 2 of the same bill further reads:

> ... Part 1 of Article 7 of Chapter 3 of Title 12 of the Official Code of Georgia Annotated, relating to Jekyll Island-State Park Authority, is amended by striking from the first sentence of Code Section 12-3-241(a), the words "for a term of 99 years," and inserting in that same sentence, after the date "February 13, 1950," the words "and ending at midnight on February 12, 2100," so that, as amended, Code Section 12-3-241(a) shall read as follows:
>
> (a) To the Authority is granted, for and on part of the State of Georgia, a lease beginning on February 13, 1950, and ending at midnight on February 12, 2100, to all of that island of the State of Georgia ...

This new amendment explains the extension of the ninety-nine-year lease agreement to 150 years, expiring in February 2100. This change is important if and when the authority executes its rights and powers to borrow funds from private banking institutions, or if it enters into long-term public private partnerships.

These changes may seem subtle to the average Georgian, but they are very well crafted, and the authority does not waste time approving a resolution for the issuance of a master promissory note that only needs GSFIC approval to execute. The resolution, the first of its kind, specifically refers to the authority's new status as a public corporation and an instrumentality of the state of Georgia:

> WHEREAS, the Jekyll island Authority (the Authority) is now existing as a public corporation and an instrumentality of the State of Georgia, created pursuant to an act of the General Assembly, as amended, codified at O.C.G.A 12-3-232, et seq; and
>
> WHEREAS, the General Assembly empowers the Authority pursuant to O.C.G.A 12-3-235 (8) to borrow

money for its corporate purposes and to execute evidences of indebtedness therefore, to provide security for such indebtedness in such manner as the Authority may provide by its Resolution authorizing the indebtedness to be incurred, provided that the Authority shall not pledge to the payment of the indebtedness revenue pledged to the payment of any other indebtedness then outstanding or encumber in violation of the terms of any existing contract, agreement, or trust indenture securing existing indebtedness; and ...[397]

The proposed resolution requests funding of $2.5 million to be issued as a master promissory note, pending approval by GSFIC; $1.5 million is designated for the water park expansion and improvement projects, funds that were previously denied by the general assembly; and $1 million is earmarked for the purchase of a garbage truck and other capital equipment.

---

[397] Resolution, addendum to the minutes of the authority board meeting, October 2002.

CHAPTER 16

THE HARD ROAD TO REINVENTING JEKYLL

2003–2006

As 2002 ends, the future of Jekyll Island is more uncertain than in any of its previous years of existence, and the reason is not solely due to economic or revenue problems, although there are plenty to be found.

This time, a dramatic change in political climate at the state capitol adds more fuel to the smoldering fire. For the first time since 1871,[398] the voters of the state of Georgia elect a Republican governor when Sonny Purdue defeats incumbent Roy Barnes in the 2002 gubernatorial race.

The political shake-up in the capitol has serious consequences for Jekyll Island as they manifest themselves on several different fronts.

Bill Donohue is asked to tender his resignation as executive director and is one of eighty heads of state agencies to be mandated to do so by then Gov.-Elect Sonny Purdue. The politically motivated decision cannot come at a worse time for the island and the authority.

Just weeks away from sending out a request for proposal to construct a large three-hundred-room new convention hotel, and a request for bids for major improvements to the convention center, a possible change in executive leadership seems the last thing Jekyll Island needs right now.

---

[398] The last Republican governor was Benjamin F. Conley, who served from 1871 to 1872 (https://en.wikipedia.org/wiki/Sonny_Perdue).

Although Bill Donohue, as all other heads of state agencies, can reapply for the job via the internet, the process itself creates uncertainty, as any waiting game does.

To make matters worse, the Jekyll Island Study Committee,[399] a joint committee with members of both the Senate and the House of Representatives, formed at the beginning of 2002 with a mandate to produce their findings prior to year-end, fails to produce any recommendations or results. All six members have been so wrapped up in their reelection campaigns, to the point that the committee never met with any of the island residents to discuss the issues at hand. Since all members are Democrats, and the committee's mandate ends December 31, 2002, it is too late to act, and the entire study committee is dismantled.

Not all is bad news though, and the change of guard may present an opportunity for island residents to tackle a long-standing issue and renew interest.

Since the mid-1990s, island residents have petitioned both the authority and the general assembly to allow representation on the authority board through the creation of one extra board seat. The effort never materialized and was even considered a conflict of interest by the attorney general. The residents had to settle for a compromise with the formation of the Citizens Resource Advisory Council, formed and appointed by Gov. Zell Miller in 1995.

Sen. Tommie Williams, a reelected Republican from Lyons, Georgia, and previously representing Jekyll Island in the state Senate, becomes the warrior for Jekyll Island in the battle for representation on the authority board.[400] He promises to propose to the newly elected governor to reserve two seats on the board, one for a permanent Jekyll Island resident and one for an island business owner who resides in Glynn County. Currently,

---

[399] Lt.-Gov. Mark Taylor and House Speaker Tom Murphy appointed the committee in early 2002. Sen. Rene Kemp and Rep. Richard Royal cochaired the committee but never met with island residents, businesses, or the authority to draft recommendations and proposed solutions (*Brunswick News*, December 13, 2002).

[400] Sen. Tommie Williams was first elected in 1998 and represented Jekyll Island until district reapportionment in 2002 (https://en.wikipedia.org/wiki/Tommie_Williams; *Brunswick News*, December 14, 2002).

none of the nine board members reside in Glynn County, let alone on Jekyll Island.[401]

The *Brunswick News* is so interested in the public opinion that it launches its own online poll, in addition to asking readers to express their opinion in "The News Forum: Giving Jekyll residents a voice" and through letters to the editor.

The opinions are spread over a wide range, but about one-third prefers to eliminate the need for the Jekyll Island Authority altogether, while 22 percent prefers either one or two board seats included for either a Jekyll resident or Glynn County resident.

The debacle about additional board seats is never seriously discussed or even considered and quietly dies amidst the politics in Atlanta. What does prevail is the reappointment of Bill Donohue as executive director in June 2003.[402] At least the daily management is again stabilized, and Jekyll Island can continue its vision for the future, no matter how unstable and tricky this will prove to be.

The hotel industry continues to underperform, with low satisfaction ratings at the Comfort Inn, the Georgia Coast Inn, and the Holiday Inn. This doesn't come as a surprise, given that all three hotels struggle to make the necessary improvements and thereby suffer from a lower than expected revenue stream and low occupancy.

But it also reflects negatively on the other island hotels. Rebuilding and rebranding Jekyll Island with a fifty-year-old hospitality industry is like playing Catch-22. Demanding enough capital improvement reserves from all the hotels places some of them in financial hardship, yet the reserve requirement is the only way to force owners to maintain their buildings and improve service.

Motel Properties Inc. just exited Chapter 11, and the Holiday Inn is preparing to do the same with a new loan from Merrill Lynch. The debt restructuring allows the hotel to hold a 4 percent capital reserve, payable

---

[401] Authority board members, December 2002: Dan Williams, Kingsland; Lonice Barrett (DNR); Randall Booker, Savannah; Jack Collins, Smyrna; Daniel Halpern, Atlanta; Charles Jenkins, Blairsville; Thomas Lewis, Cartersville; and Linda Underwood, Atlanta (*Brunswick News*, December 13, 2002).

[402] *Brunswick News*, June 20, 2003, and June 30, 2003.

to the authority and be able to pay the new base rent of $20,976.66 per month.[403]

The Georgia Coast Inn doesn't fare so well and continues to struggle now that its request to convert the motel into time shares is denied. There is also a dispute between the owners, the Forehand family, and the management company, Philbeck Inc. The owners want to liquidate the property under bankruptcy law,[404] while the management company believes a restructuring and reorganization during Chapter 11 proceedings are the solution.

In any event, another island hotel seeks bankruptcy protection, this time without a clear exit plan, given the dispute between owners and operators.

The state park aspect of the island is tranquil as usual, a nice balancing act that can somewhat counter the oceanside turbulence.

Thanks to a $50K grant from the DNR, two fishing piers can be installed at the old Ski Rixen. The new attraction leads to the island's first Family Fishing Derby in the fall, cosponsored by the DNR and Tidelands Nature Center.

Summer Waves also gets a facelift during the spring, in anticipation of the upcoming summer crowds, thanks to a $2.5 million master promissory note.

Both the central and north bathhouses[405] are being remodeled and connected to the municipal water-sewage system, and the authority agrees to a new lease with Georgia RSA 12 that will allow the use of its water towers to place additional antennas.[406] The agreement allows for the cellular partnership to upgrade its analog service on the island to digital signals.

The lease renewals in the Historic District are going smoothly except maybe for a small hiccup at the Old Bathhouse, operated by Steve and

---

[403] The new base rent is based on a land valuation of $253K per acre at 8 percent. The Holiday Inn occupied 12.4 acres of land and was the fourth largest land property on Jekyll Island behind the JICH at twenty acres, Villas by the Sea at 16.13 acres, and the Jekyll Inn at 14.53 acres.

[404] The Georgia Coast Inn was listed for sale in July 2003 for $5.2 million.

[405] The central bathhouse is located near Shell Road. The north bathhouse is located just south of the Holiday Inn Resort.

[406] Water tower #4 is located on the south end, across Camp Jekyll. Water tower #5 is located at the north end, across Villas by the Sea.

Leigh Baumann, who are not in compliance for placing unapproved outdoor signage and for selling food items without the proper permit. Both also recently acquired a 49 percent stake in Jekyll Books and Antiques from Mr. David Hamer but without the proper approval process. Now that the lease renewal is upcoming, the authority is hesitant to grant an extension until the other "small issues" are resolved satisfactory. Ultimately, the lease renewal is granted but only in the name of Mr. Hamer instead of the corporation.[407]

The spring of 2003 has more good news in store for Jekyll Island. The sticky SPLOST IV issue, and the lawsuit filed against Glynn County by ex-Commissioner Ken Plyman, is finally settled by the Georgia Supreme Court. A unanimous decision upholds the Glynn County Superior Court ruling that the lawsuit was filed forty-two days too late before seeking an injunction to stop the collection of the special purpose sales tax.

That is not only good news for Glynn County and Brunswick, who can now continue with their planned water and sewer projects, but is also good news for Jekyll Island, which will benefit from SPLOST allocations to fund its own infrastructure projects.

Add to this the grand opening and dedication ceremony of the new Sidney Lanier Bridge on April 7,[408] and it seems that the mild spring breezes are all blowing in favor of Georgia's Jewel.

But not all winds blow in the same direction, and some come as a complete surprise and when one least expects it. When island resident Thornwell Parker decides to tear down his old house on Dexter Lane and build a new home, he never imagines that his flood insurance will go sky-high, certainly not when his new home is built several feet above the flood zone.

The "adder in the grass" is a little-known federal law called the Coastal Barrier Improvement Act of 1990,[409] signed into law in 1991.

---

[407] The corporation was known as Jekyll Books and Antiques Inc. and was owned 51 percent by Mr. Hamer and 49 percent by Mr. and Mrs. Baumann (authority board meeting minutes, and letter from Laura Bonds to Bill Donohue, dated July 8, 2003).
[408] Lyneath Musgrove, widow of Department of Transportation board member Downing Musgrove, who worked hard for a replacement bridge before his death, was the first to cross the new bridge (the *Georgia Times-Union*, April 8, 2003).
[409] https://en.wikipedia.org/wiki/Coastal_Barrier_Resources_Act. https://www.fema.gov/media-library/assets/documents/20375.

The intention of the act was to protect certain areas known as "otherwise protected areas," or OPAs, from further development by no longer offering FEMA-backed flood insurance on all new construction. Since OPAs consist of land owned by public agencies, and Jekyll Island is owned by the state of Georgia, the island falls under the new regulation, although most homeowners and the authority are not aware of the possible impact, nor can they be, as there is no precedent.

All homes constructed prior to March 16, 1991, are grandfathered in[410] and retain their FEMA backing if the properties are not improved by more than half of their value.

While the law has been in effect for over a decade, its potential impact on Jekyll Island, both residential and commercial, is unknown. Imagine the effect of a hurricane and residents needing to rebuild their homes, or hotel owners choosing to dramatically improve or rebuild their properties, thereby exceeding the 50 percent property value. And what about new construction such as the planned three-hundred-room convention hotel, or even a new convention center?

Those are all unanswered questions that suddenly become known because of one island resident who chooses to build a brand-new home rather than face costly improvements to his old house.

Both the authority and the Jekyll Island Citizens Association take up the cause to seek clarification about how and why Jekyll Island was included in the 1990 Act as an OPA, and more importantly, how the island can be excluded.[411] Both recognize that it will probably take an act of Congress to exclude the island from the original Coastal Barrier Act and the subsequent Coastal Barrier Improvement Act. In the meantime, the law may very well deter growth on the island until the issue is resolved.

Adding fuel to the fire is the renewed fear that lenders are becoming more reluctant to issue loans, let alone agree to reversed mortgages, as some residents wish to pursue. While the authority's lease with the state is

---

[410] The *Brunswick News*, February 7, 2003.

[411] This marks the first time that the authority and JICA join forces to address and try to resolve an issue. In the past, both have always been on the other side of the argument, but this time is different, as the resolution to the OPA restriction is mutually beneficial. JICA will benefit through the reinstatement of FEMA-sponsored flood insurance, while the authority's benefit lies within its future growth.

secure until 2100, the residential and commercial leases are set to expire in 2049. This doesn't seem to be a major problem, since more than forty years are left on all current leases, were it not for the ten-year renewal clause that went into effect in 1999 for the first time and is again up for review in 2009.

Nobody fears that existing leases will not automatically renew in 2009 at the same guaranteed annual lease payments as set forth in 1950,[412] but the automatic renewals and the diminishing duration are cause for concern, and residents would like to see an earlier renewal and a longer lease extension beyond 2049.

No action is expected from the authority before Robert Charles Lesser and Co.[413] completes its study of Jekyll Island with a mandate to look toward the future and the need to become self-sustainable very quickly.

To make matters worse, Jekyll Island stands to lose eighteen acres of undeveloped high ground if the Army Corps of Engineers and the Georgia Port Authority get their way. The Brunswick port project, which creates a new turning basin for deep-draft ships, destroys about eighteen acres of wetland that need to be replaced somewhere else.

That preferred "somewhere else" place is the high marsh just south of Summer Waves, according to the Army Corps. This means that 20 percent of undeveloped land will be taken away from the remaining hundred acres available for growth. Some residents see that as a good sign, but ecologists may have a different opinion.

The history of the eighteen acres that are designated for scraping down and thereby creating low marshland begins in the early sixties, when the area was altered from low marsh into high marsh because of debris deposited there. In essence, the scraping of the designated area will bring it back to its original state prior to 1960, but it has an adverse effect on the available acreage for future development.

Despite some opposition, the project plans are approved. The only victory for the island residents is that the Corps agrees to remove the

---

[412] The annual lease payment was set in 1950 at a ninety-nine-year fixed rate (Authority Act 1950).
[413] Robert Charles Lesser & Co. completed the 1995 Jekyll Island Master Plan, approved in June 1996. The new study would begin mid-November 2003 (*Brunswick News*, November 10, 2003).

350,000 cubic feet of dirt by barge rather than trucks that would cause an unsightly appearance for several months.

The turmoil and debates circling around Jekyll Island overshadow the new initiatives the authority brings to the island that are designed to bring more visitors, and specifically day-trippers, to the island.

The year 2003 marks the twentieth anniversary of the popular Beach Music Festival[414] and the first Birding & Nature Festival[415] on the island that attracts four hundred bird watchers from near and far.

The Beach Music Festival always attracts thousands of music lovers, rain or shine, and has amassed a loyal following throughout its years of existence. When the Beach Boys are announced as the main attraction that year, only the weather has a dampening effect on the anniversary celebration.

Not only new events deserve attention and are noteworthy on the island. Johnny Paulk,[416] the Jekyll Island Golf Club head pro for thirty-five years, is honored as the recipient of the first-ever President's Award by the Georgia PGA in recognition of his lifetime commitment and contributions to golf. Harry Kicklighter is also recognized and wins the Assistant Professional of the Year Award at the same ceremony held in Macon, Georgia.

But celebrations and new initiatives last only that long. When the new year announces itself, it is with a bang of bad and unexpected news.

The Clarion Resort Buccaneer and the Comfort Inn both file for bankruptcy in separate filings. Although the authority ensures the public and the media that the filings will have no immediate effect on guests, as both hotels will continue to operate as usual, the filings come at a very bad time.

---

[414] The Beach Music Festival was held annually in June at the Beach Deck, located just north of the Days Inn. It was later moved to Great Dunes Park.

[415] The festival was the brainchild of local bird enthusiasts, including Ms. Lydia Thompson. The first festival was held from October 10 through October 12, 2003 (*Brunswick News*, October 8, 2003).

[416] Johnny Paulk is credited with organizing the annual Georgia Florida Golf Classic since its debut in 1979. The annual tournament has grown from the initial forty participants to six hundred golf enthusiasts.

The authority and Jekyll Island are busy preparing for the upcoming G-8 Summit on Sea Island,[417] and all available rooms are expected to be reserved by the Secret Service to accommodate the summit attendees and security personnel.

Both hotels are placed in receivership with Corcoran Jennison Hospitality Co. Inc. while operating to secure the cashflow and the payments due the authority.

While both continue to operate during restructuring, the Georgia Coast Inn abruptly announces it is closing its door immediately. That means 110 fewer rooms are available, and guests with reservations need to find other accommodations on or nearby the island.

Despite the closing, the hotel and all its properties are ultimately placed in receivership as well.[418]

The hotel shake-up does not stop here. The Jekyll Inn, now owned by Capstar Jekyll Co. LLC, submits a proposal to convert the hotel to condominiums, at least part of the property.

The hotel owner is able to place $4 million in escrow for capital improvements and agrees to pay 8 percent of the appraised land value or 4.5 percent of gross revenue, whichever is greater, with a minimum monthly payment of $20K per acre.[419] The new lease agreement is signed on January 5, 2004, with the right to renew every five years, and the hotel changes its name to Jekyll Oceanfront Resort.

The initial conversion plan calls for seventy-eight existing suites to be converted to condominium units, with the remaining rooms and suites[420] to follow and based on the successful sale of the new condominiums.

The confusion and changes continue when Mr. Holloway Strickland, CFO of Lighthouse Point, current lessee of the now defunct and closed Georgia Coast Inn, requests permission to demolish the motel and

---

[417] The 2004 G-8 Summit took place from June 8 through June 10, 2004. The Secret Service planned to take all available rooms on Jekyll Island before and during the summit (*Brunswick News*, January 15, 2004).

[418] A court order also assigns Corcoran Jennison Hospitality Co. Inc. to act as temporary receiver for the Georgia Coast Inn.

[419] The total acreage of the Jekyll Inn is 14.53 acres, which results in a guaranteed monthly payment of $290,600.

[420] The Jekyll Inn has a total room capacity of 263 rooms/suites on the property.

construct condominiums on the property, and submits an offer to purchase the Holiday Inn from Servico Inc.

All requests and proposals are postponed until there is more clarification about the pending master plan update. The authority staff does not support a lease transfer from Servico to Mr. Strickland, probably because of the dire situation of the Georgia Coast Inn and its track record.

By February, Robert Charles Lesser & Co. presents its first progress report on the Jekyll Island update. The first major conclusion of the report best summarizes the report and is a clear indication of where both consultants and the authority see the future of Jekyll Island.

> The JIA needs to better decide whether Jekyll is to function more as a park or a resort. While there is certainly a mandate for Jekyll to remain a park, a mindset shift needs to occur to recognize that Jekyll is competing against resorts and resort locations for visitors. In doing so, the JIA needs to better determine who it's "target market" should be (which RCLCo[421] will help identify), and the facilities, amenities, and attributes the island should take on to attract those markets. This does not mean abandoning Jekyll's charge to be a location for the "average Georgian", yet provides a greater focus again as to who Jekyll's target market should be.[422]

Since the creation of Jekyll Island State Park in 1947, this duality or fear of duality between being a state park and a resort has always resulted in a hybrid future. Now that the commercial side, or maybe a more suitable name is "the resort side," of the island is suffering from a major shock, with several aftershocks to follow, it is indeed time to reexamine what Jekyll Island should be.

A follow-up paragraph of the same report also touches briefly on the residential aspect of the island: "… There is no central community identity

---

[421] RCLCo stands for Robert Charles Lesser & Co (author's note).
[422] Robert Charles Lesser & Co. letter to Mr. Warren Murphey, Jekyll Island Authority, dated January 12, 2004 (addendum to authority board meeting, February 2004).

and community gathering place, a 'downtown' if you will. People are either doing an activity or [are] in a small hotel room. There are few, if any places for people to linger."

Jekyll Island is at crossroads, both commercial and residential, and needs to decide what its future will look like, but reinventing oneself is not an easy task achieved overnight.

A long and hard road awaits until a new future is materialized, and residents are making sure their voices and opinions are heard.

The media are predicting more retail spaces, replacing some hotels with condominium-like rentals, and allowing more houses on Jekyll as the general consensus but fails to elaborate on the details.

A public planning session on February 9, 2004, sheds more light on the opinion of island residents. While the entire questionnaire is subjective and maybe even suggestive by nature, some interesting conclusions can be drawn.

When asked to identify potential sites on the island for redevelopment, a clear majority identifies the Comfort Inn, the Georgia Coast Inn, the Clarion, and the Holiday Inn as the most desirable.[423] That doesn't come as a surprise, given that all the hotels identified also consistently score the lowest customer satisfaction rating in guest surveys. In addition, two of the hotels are currently in bankruptcy, while one is closed altogether.

The questionnaire does point out that the natural setting of the island and the campground are considered valuable assets.

The remainder of the survey is not so clear cut, with some residents preferring the status quo in redevelopment but wanting to see an increase in tourism. Others want hotels to be converted into condominiums to create more diverse lodging options.

The opinions certainly do not point to a consensus, even within the island residential community, and are often at odds with each other.

However, it seems that a main and important conclusion is drawn pertaining to the convention center and the need for a designated convention hotel, which is exactly what the authority already had in mind.

---

[423] Comfort Inn: 100 percent; Georgia Coast Inn and Holiday Inn: 92 percent; Clarion: 90 percent. Results from the Jekyll Island Public Planning Session, February 9, 2004 (authority board meeting, addendum to the minutes of February 2004).

Further recommendations and amendments to the master plan will take a back seat, as all hands are on deck to prepare for the upcoming G-8 Summit on Sea Island in June.

The first signs of preparations are immediately visible as two new signs greet visitors as they enter the causeway from Highway 17. The new signs, "Jekyll Island—Georgia's Jewel," measure 8 feet high by 24 feet long and are surrounded by timber walls that hold reflecting pools with decorative fountains.[424] New palm trees are planted east of the two welcome towers, and underbrush is cleared to give drivers a better view of the marsh and the bridge. Funding for the project comes from the three-dollar parking fee.

The summit itself is a negative experience for Jekyll Island overall, despite the extra publicity and the marketing strategy set in motion to promote the island to the world. Security is so tight that the entire Cherokee Campground and the Jekyll Island Club Hotel are closed for the duration of the summit. The lost revenue is not just contained to the campground either. Blackbeard Restaurant and Morgan's Grill both suffer from empty seats and lost patrons, not to mention the loss in parking fees since government vehicles are exempt and its occupants are also exempt from any state taxes on lodging.

In the end, the free publicity is a welcome gift nicely wrapped in shiny paper that sets high expectations but ultimately disappoints because the box inside is empty.

The remainder of the summer and the fall do not compensate for the losses when Jekyll Island must deal with not one hurricane but three in less than one month. When Hurricane Frances hits on Labor Day 2004, and Hurricanes Ivan and Jeanne[425] follow three weeks later, revenue for what is normally a busy fall is down dramatically compared to the previous years.

Several beach crossovers are damaged due to the storms, and there is severe beach erosion on the north side of the island, specifically on Driftwood Beach and the nearby Villas by the Sea.

---

[424] The signs were made from tabby with brass lettering and are still flanking the causeway entrance to this day.

[425] Hurricane Ivan passed through on September 17, 2004. Hurricane Jeanne brushed the island on September 25, 2004.

The Huddle House suffers some severe tree damage as well, complicating things even more since the owner/operator is still in litigation with its corporate headquarters.[426]

The Jekyll Island Foundation (JIF) does bring some good news to the island, in contrast to a seemingly difficult and complicated year.

JIF has been raising funds since the summer of 2000 to finance capital improvements on the island that may or may not be eligible for ordinary financing through general obligation bonds by tapping into the private market of foundations, charitable organizations, or endowments.

In addition, the JIF also launched a private fundraiser in 2002, with the assistance of the island hotels, by asking hotel guests to donate two dollars to support the JIF initiatives. The donation is added to the guest bill upon checkout and collected and disbursed by the hotel owners.

Instead of using the raised funds to rehabilitate and restore the old Actor's Dorm,[427] a Turtle Rehab Center becomes a priority project in March 2004.[428]

How does one come up with the idea to construct such a center and find it to be of higher priority than other projects in the Historic District? After all, the entire district has accumulated a deferred capital improvement of $40 million.

Sea turtles are no strangers to island residents, and their annual nesting visits were first discovered by Harvey Smith, owner/operator of the Peppermint Amusement Park, back in 1963 when some loggerheads got entangled in the rides' wiring and tracks.

But since May 2004, several sea turtles wash up on Georgia beaches, either injured or dead. No one can find a specific reason for this sudden occurrence, but it is suspected that some may be the result of commercial

---

[426] Jeannine Kettles was the franchise owner of the Huddle House. Ms. Kettles wanted to replace the old Huddle House with a new structure and expand operations but did not receive permission from Corporate HQ; hence the litigation (authority board meeting minutes, October 2004).

[427] The Actor's Dorm, originally one of the two servants' quarters during the millionaires' era, was initially used by the Jekyll Island Music Theatre, hence the popular name for the building. Today the building serves as offices for the authority's administrative staff.

[428] Authority board meeting minutes of March 2004.

shrimpers whose nets are not equipped with the mandated TED devices (Turtle Excluder Device).[429]

The nearest turtle rehab centers are either in Florida or South Carolina, and the long journey there can prove too much for the injured turtles. The two-week spike[430] in turtle deaths and injuries gives rise to the idea of opening a turtle rehab center right here on Jekyll Island, as the very first of its kind in the state of Georgia.

The Georgia Sea Turtle Center,[431] as it became known, is scheduled to open by 2006 once all the restorations and rehabilitations are completed at the old power plant. The 5,200-square-foot center will house an exhibition area with video presentations and hands-on activities for visitors, while a window will provide a view of the veterinary clinic, staffed by Terry Norton and Mark Dodd.[432] Both are the founders of GSTC and widely recognized as experts on sea turtles, not only on Jekyll Island but all of Georgia's barrier islands and far beyond.

The total cost is estimated between $1.75 and $2 million, most of which is already funded by year-end.

Sadly enough, and happening on so many prior occasions, when one new initiative is launched to attract a new market segment to the island, another loyal or sentimental visitor sees its cherished attraction abolished and left behind.

For the past fifteen years, Valdosta State University has kept the Jekyll Island Music Theatre alive and well on Jekyll Island, despite some difficult years and consistent low attendance. Somehow, they always seemed to survive and even had hopes of refurbishing the old Gould Auditorium with the help of the authority as an additional indoor venue for their dedicated actors and supporters.

---

[429] *Brunswick News*, May 29, 2004. The *Times-Union*, May 22, 2004.
[430] Seventy-three sea turtles washed ashore between May 7 and May 22. Seven had been reported dead the week after (*Brunswick News*, May 29, 2004).
[431] The Georgia Turtle Center was the brainchild of Elizabeth Hines, then executive director of the JIF (*Brunswick News*, July 15, 2004).
[432] https://gstc.jekyllisland.com/about-us/our-staff/staff/.

VSU terminates its contract with the authority in the spring of 2004,[433] hence the amphitheater will sit empty and abandoned for the first time since its construction in 1972, and the Jekyll Island Music Theatre disappears with it.

When the dust finally settles over the G-8 Summit, island residents recover from the long months of preparation and aftermath of intense security and closures, and business owners have recovered from their financial hangover while trying to recuperate lost revenue, the new and improved master plan rears its ugly head again, this time with amendments and recommendations that are subject to public scrutiny and review.

The recommendations[434] are listed and highlighted as follows:

- Retain the 35 percent developable / 65 percent undevelopable restriction.
- Create a development/revitalization plan.
- Develop a conservation plan.
- Restructure the residential leases.
- Technical amendment to the 3.9-acre parcel of land that lies between the 4-H Center and the existing residential development from undeveloped to developable.

For the authority to amend or alter the 1996–1997 Master Plan, specific procedures are established in the Georgia Code 12-3-294.1(d).

- September 13, 2004: JIA schedules a board meeting, submits the records to the appropriate organs of public record in Glynn and Fulton Counties, runs announcements in *Brunswick News* and *Atlanta Journal Constitution*, and submits three copies to the office of Legislative Counsel.
- October 4, 2004: Conducts a public hearing to review amendments and receive public comments.

---

[433] Valdosta State University decided to move their music theater back to their own campus. Their decision was based on the authority's refusal to renovate the Gould Auditorium and the Actor's Dorm.

[434] Robert Charles Lesser & Co. Updated Jekyll Island Master Plan Recommendations, September 13, 2004.

- October 21, 2004: Submits to Office of Legislative Counsel copies of public comments and appropriate JIA responses.
- November 15 or December 16, 2004: JIA Board publicly and officially either adopts or rejects the proposed amendments at its regularly scheduled meeting.

The race to the future has begun in earnest for Jekyll Island, and residents are weary about unbridled growth, given that several developers are eyeing Georgia's Jewel and its pristine oceanfront that may be up for grabs, be it redevelopment or brand-new development.

The technical amendment on the south side alone is reason for concern. The 3.9 acres were originally designated in August 1955 for residential development when St. Andrews subdivision was created and became the Negro subdivision that would see the rise and fall of the Dolphin Motor Lodge, the Dolphin Music Hall, and the St. Andrews Auditorium.

With the 4-H Center so close, residents fear that the reclassification may open the doors for high-rise condominiums. Only commercial hotel and motel properties have a height restriction of thirty-five feet, but condominiums would be exempt from such unless a new height ordinance is approved.

A lot is at stake, certainly when Jekyll Island, and the authority specifically, is in dire need of increased revenue that can only be generated through major renovations or new construction.

The approval or rejection of the proposed amendments can mean the difference between stagnation and further deterioration, or a capital injection of close to $300 million.

The newly amended master plan for Jekyll Island seems to reverberate all over the state of Georgia, and particularly in Atlanta, when Gov. Purdue announces his plan and new legislation to boost Georgia tourism.

The New Georgia Tourism Foundation, created by Gov. Purdue, will be chaired by Craig Lesser, commissioner of Georgia Department of Economic Development, and will include the DNR commissioner, executive directors of Jekyll Island Authority, Stone Mountain Memorial Association, Lake Lanier Islands Development Authority, North Georgia Mountains Authority, and the Southwest Georgia Railway Excursion

From Millionaires to Commoners

Authority, in addition to five members at-large, appointed by the governor, and one member of each of the five Halls of Fame.[435]

Almost simultaneously, the governor also wants state agencies with a stake in the development of coastal Georgia to create a master plan for the entire region. The effort is to be coordinated by the Georgia Department of Community Affairs.[436]

While the efforts are applauded in the media and Atlanta, and a coordinated effort across multiple coastal areas is certainly more efficient than a single-location approach that may impact surrounding areas willingly or unwillingly, it raises the question of how much influence other counties or communities will have on the much-needed development of a small coastal island such as Jekyll.

There is also the small and often overlooked or forgotten conveyance of Georgia State Parks to the Jekyll Island Authority in the early 1960s. Such conveyance was done to facilitate financing through the issuance of trust indentures and needs to be undone by placing all state parks back under the jurisdiction of the state of Georgia, except for those that are managed under the auspices of a designated authority.

For Jekyll Island, this means that the authority no longer has access to or jurisdiction over any state park other than Jekyll Island.

The fear of getting lost or being overlooked in the grand scheme of consolidated master plan development is eased by the announcement of Gov. Purdue that a third Glynn County resident is joining the Jekyll Island Authority. It is the first time that a Georgia governor looks for leadership within Glynn County rather than beyond the waters of the Golden Isles. Even Gov. Zell Miller did not search for board members within Glynn County.

Michael Hodges of St. Simons Island is appointed to the authority and joins Ed Boshears, former state senator, and Richard Wood, retired FBI agent, both also St. Simons residents.[437]

---

[435] Press release, Office of Communications, February 2, 2005.
[436] *Brunswick News*, February 19, 2005. The *Times-Union*, February 19, 2005.
[437] Ed Boshears was appointed on March 14, 2005. Richard Wood was appointed on February 14, 2004 (*Brunswick News*, April 6, 2005).

The new authority seems to be in good hands or at least is believed to be more balanced in its approach now that island residents have local representation, an issue that has always been a sore point of contention.

A multitude of decisions will have to be made to guide Jekyll Island toward a more modern and accommodating future and to secure much-needed stability in tourism.[438]

Despite the windfall the island hotels enjoy because of the nearby Super Bowl XXXIX in Jacksonville, Florida, guest ratings keep falling in most of the hotels, as has been the trend for the past fifteen years. The only exceptions are those hotels that have managed to completely renovate their properties and guest rooms, such as the Days Inn and the Beachview Club.[439] Both rank #1 and #2 respectively in the 2004 island hotel rankings, with Villas by the Sea and the Jekyll Island Club Hotel taking third and fourth place.

The remaining five hotels are those that need extensive renovation or are candidates to be torn down completely and replaced with newer and maybe other structures.[440]

But the authority is also planning major changes to the existing shopping centers. All current business leases are renewed for two years, expiration date 2007, and the added clause to relocate afterward.[441] The expiration date coincides with Gov. Purdue's mandate for the Department of Community Affairs to draft a Coastal Georgia Master Plan by the end of 2006 and the time it takes for public input and possible amendments.

Two separate committees are also formed in June: a Parking Committee, whose task it is to investigate whether the three-dollar parking fee can be abolished, and a 4-H Center Committee to examine the future

---

[438] In 2005, tourism was the fastest growing industry in the state of Georgia and an ever-growing mainstay of Glynn County's economy (*Brunswick News* editorial, April 14, 2005).

[439] The Beachview Club was completely renovated in 1998 when Jimmy Veal purchased the property.

[440] Holiday Inn, Jekyll Oceanfront Resort, Quality Inn, Buccaneer, and Oceanside Inn. The Georgia Coast Inn, which is closed and completely fenced in, was approved for demolition in June 2005.

[441] Jekyll Pharmacy, Jekyll Realty, Sand Pail, Jekyll beverage center, IGA, Maxwell Variety Store, US post office, and Barnett Bank all signed the two-year lease extension in March 2005 (authority board meeting minutes, March 2005).

of the site with the addition of 3.9 acres of land that is in the process of being reclassified as per the Robert Charles Lesser & Co. amendment recommendation.

Both are sensitive issues since the first one means a loss of $1.4 million that needs to be supplemented somewhere else, and the second because of the reclassification and the close proximity of the St. Andrews subdivision that is entirely residential.

Ultimately, the parking fee remains unchanged. Instead, sanitation fees and yard debris pick-up fees are increased to offset the rising fuel cost.[442]

The Jekyll Island Foundation also contributes to the intense preparation of upcoming change, or maybe takes advantage of the situation. That depends on who interprets the JIF's latest fundraising effort when it decides to use the vacated amphitheater as a new drive-in movie theater but without the cars. Now that Valdosta State University is not returning for its annual musical performances, the JIF decides to use the venue to present family-friendly "made in Georgia" movies. The initial program runs from June 9 through July 3, but if attendance is steady, a second late-summer series is envisioned. A five-dollar donation is requested to benefit the new Georgia Sea Turtle Center.[443]

The annual Beach Music Festival also returns to the island after a two-year hiatus, much to the delight of its many loyal followers who are more than happy to shuffle and dance to the tunes of their favorite bands, The Tams, The Swingin' Medallions, the original Swingin' Medallions and Hack Bartley and Shuffle.

The authority has organized the festival since 1982 but decided in 2003 to allow a public private partnership to take control of the annual festival. Unfortunately, the festival was cancelled due to major sponsors

---

[442] Sanitation fees are increased by $1.00 to $9.50 (first increase since 2002), and yard debris pick-up fees increase to $14.30 from $12.30 (first increase since 1998) (authority board meeting minutes, August 2005).

[443] "Made in Georgia" refers to films for which at least "some production" was done in the state of Georgia. The movie series included *Smokey & the Bandit*, *Fried Green Tomatoes*, *Bobby Jones*, *The Legend of Bagger Vance*, *Forces of Nature*, *Beauty Shop*, *Wild America*, *Independence Day*, and *The Bear* (*Brunswick News*, June 4, 2005).

pulling their support just days before the event and did not return until 2005.

A new, exciting hotel deal gets the attention of local newspapers when plans are announced of a possible purchase of the Holiday Inn by the Jekyll Club Associates, owners of the Jekyll Island Club Hotel.

The visionary group's appetite for island expansion certainly doesn't stop with the inclusion of the Crane and Cherokee Cottages in their portfolio. Both historic cottages were added to the amended lease agreement in March 2001 and now operate as a combination of private events and guest accommodations.

The Jekyll Club Associates propose to assume the lease from Lodgian Inc. and to extend the current lease from 2014 to 2049. The hotel will remain under the Holiday Inn flag until the end of the franchise agreement in about five years, but first the property will have to be renovated to meet the required franchise standards. To that effect, the buyers agree to an initial capital investment of $2.5 million.[444]

While the authority grants the requested lease transfer and extension, adhering to the Holiday Inn franchise standards proves difficult, if not impossible, from a financial perspective. The envisioned $2.5 million capital injection barely scratches the surface of what the total renovation cost amounts to, according to the franchise-imposed requirements.

The Holiday Inn's corporate standards require a total renovation cost of $8.2 million, or $40K per room, which is triple the amount pledged.

Add to the equation the new FEMA rules that are in effect since 1991 and applicable to any coastal development, and one can see why renovating the 1972 structure is no longer feasible. Instead, demolishing the old hotel to make room for a new development starts to make more sense.

The new FEMA rules impose a specific height variance to comply with flood zone requirements. In the case of the old Holiday Inn, built well before the new FEMA rules went into effect, this would mean that the entire ground floor cannot be used for guest accommodations, meeting rooms, or any guest activity. It would significantly reduce the number of guest rooms and negatively impact the future revenue stream of the property, even after extensive upgrades.

---

[444] The Holiday Inn features 204 guest rooms. The total capital investment equates to $12,200 per room.

The revised proposal for the Holiday Inn, as prepared by Jekyll Ocean Oaks, LLC[445] reads:

> The Managing General Partners of the Jekyll Island Club Hotel are negotiating the purchase of the lease and existing Holiday Inn structures on Jekyll Island. In our due diligence in the last week, we obtained the PIP from Holiday Inn which recommends substantial improvement that would cost a minimum of $40,000 per room to bring the existing structure to **minimum** Holiday Inn Standards. Also, as we began our boundary and survey work, we found the top of the lower level floors to be 12 feet-4 inches above mean sea level. The FEMA requirement for the site is 13 and 14 feet above mean sea level.
>
> Since substantial improvement must be done to the buildings, all new and existing structures must meet current FEMA requirements according to the International Building Codes. This would require reconstruction of the structures or eliminating the use of the lower floor level. The economics of this kind of improvement to existing structures is not feasible.[446]

A new redevelopment proposal, designed by Cooper Carry of Atlanta, is submitted to the authority for review. Oceanside Dunes, as the new development is to be called, is a mixed-use development consisting of a limited-service 120–150-room suites hotel with a small amount of meeting space, a casual restaurant, and sixty to one hundred residential units of varying sizes and building types, including flats, terrace units, townhouses, row houses, and detached houses. All units, including the

---

[445] Jekyll Ocean Oaks, LLC, became the new lessee of the Holiday Inn. The company has the same four partners as the Jekyll Club Associates, owners of the JICH (authority board meeting minutes, September 2005).

[446] Jekyll Ocean Oaks, LLC, revised proposal for Holiday Inn. Addendum to the authority board meeting, October 12, 2005.

hotel, the restaurant, and the residential units, are to be managed by the Jekyll Island Club Hotel.[447]

According to the proposal, the hotel and adjacent restaurant will be constructed on the north side of the property, with the residential units to be built around landscaped parks with alleys between the back side of the units.

The natural environment of dunes and trees are to be preserved, and the entire development is focused on being a beach-access property rather than a beach-view property. The architectural style for both the hotel and the residential units is inspired by historic Jekyll details and shapes and resembles the unique historic architecture of the Jekyll Island Club Hotel.

Ultimately, the design and proposal are not approved, although specific reasons are not documented in any of the archived materials. One can assume that a combination of factors such as financing, scope, or design contributed to a change of plans and approach for the property in question.[448]

When summer season ends, there are more than just a few things to worry about. Last year's record three hurricanes disrupted the Golden Isles' tourist season and left hospitality industry with a sour taste. This year, it seems that Hurricane Katrina may very well have the same effect on tourist traffic, but if not, then Tropical Storm Ophelia[449] will keep its grip on Jekyll for more than a week. Strong, gusty winds keep day-trippers and visitors away, putting another dent in tourism revenue, also exacerbating the existing beach erosion problem at Villas by the Sea and nearby Driftwood Beach.

Besides the prevailing weather, visitors are also struggling with rising gas prices and the fear of actual shortages. Gas prices already top three dollars per gallon in Glynn County, but Atlanta reports show spikes of as much as seven dollars per gallon, while other metropolitan areas face

---

[447] Excerpt from the revised proposal for Holiday Inn, page 8 of 11 (Jekyll Ocean Oaks, LLC-2005).

[448] In 2006, a new proposal is submitted that ultimately leads to the construction of the Hampton Inn & Suites.

[449] Hurricane Katrina struck New Orleans on August 29. TS Ophelia battered the Golden Isles one week later, causing major beach erosion (*Brunswick News*, September 7, 2005).

outright shortages. The return of state tax on fuel, fifteen cents per gallon, also looms right around the corner, adding even more concern to the immediate future of leisure and business travel.[450]

The immediate effect of Hurricane Katrina on the Gulf states also has a ripple effect on Jekyll Island, which is still trying to come to terms with the Coastal Barrier Act of 1982 and its subsequent amendment in 1990. While US Rep. Jack Kingston takes the lead in Congress to reverse the OPA status[451] of Jekyll Island, legislators are particularly weary to add even more government liability to an already massive amount of FEMA funds needed after the devastation of Hurricanes Katrina and Rita.

The proposed HR-138, which will exclude about 68 percent of Jekyll from the CBRA[452] map by lifting the erroneous OPA status, will take more time and patience than envisioned. It will also slow down or even cancel plans for other commercial development, such as condominiums. With a ban on available flood insurance, or at least affordable insurance, conversion or construction of condominium complexes is out of the question, hence the authority places a moratorium on condominium conversions altogether, much to the chagrin of existing hotel owners.

It looks as 2006 will be another challenging year, both financially and fiscally, and difficult decisions to cut costs are needed. Summer Waves urgently needs a capital injection of at least $1 million to repair the waves pool; the Buccaneer and the Oceanside Inn are still up for sale, and buyers are nowhere in sight; the Georgia Coast Inn is still in disarray and should be torn down; and there is the persistent request from the Jekyll Oceanfront Resort to pursue the sale of individual condominiums, despite the moratorium.

The need and the desire to pave the road to success is present, but somehow, somewhere, obstacles keep popping up that prevent the reinvention of Jekyll Island as a whole.

---

[450] The fifteen cents per gallon in state tax was added on October 1, 2005 (*Brunswick News*, September 30, 2005).
[451] Otherwise protected area.
[452] Coastal Barrier Resources Act.

Jekyll Oceanfront Resort, formerly the Jekyll Inn,[453] continues its large-scale renovation project. Since Mr. Lurken purchased the 260-room property from Meristar in 2003, he has spent more than $4.5 million to renovate thirty-six suites and 144 sleeping rooms. The near completion of another twenty-four sleeping rooms by February 2006 leaves only forty-two suites to be renovated by year-end.

The sleeping rooms are combined to make one three-bedroom suite that can also be split up into separate rooms should the guests only require a simple hotel room. The suites can also be rented as a whole, and this is where Mr. Lurken envisions his original plan for condominium conversion to come to fruition.[454]

The property itself has also undergone a complete makeover with a new lobby, meeting rooms, restaurant, bar, and the addition of a fitness center and a stand-alone spa facility.

But there are still some problems to be resolved before conversion can be considered, let alone approved by the authority.

While the authority placed a temporary moratorium on all condominium construction in the previous year, the resolution does not affect Mr. Lurken's request directly. After all, his renovation of existing property does not fall under the moratorium, or so it seems. Secondly, and more importantly, the CBRA and its 1990 amendment does cause a problem since the total renovation cost, more than $6 million, may exceed the imposed renovation limit of 50 percent.[455]

In contrast, negotiations to purchase the Holiday Inn are moving along. Lodgian, current owner of the hotel, has accepted the offer of the Jekyll Island Club Hotel owners, paving the way for approval by

---

[453] The Jekyll Hilton Inn location now features the Cottages at Jekyll Island.

[454] The price levels for the condominiums were tentatively set at $150,000–$195,000 for one-bedroom units; $225,000–$260,000 for two-bedroom units; and $375,000 for three-bedroom units (all oceanfront). The pricing was below the equivalent units offered by Villas by the Sea and one-third of the equivalent prices in Florida (Jekyll Oceanfront Resort, history to date and long-term strategy, December 21, 2005. Addendum to authority board meeting, January 2006).

[455] The renovation completion requires another $1.5 million in addition to the initial $4.5 million already spent. The limit of 50 percent of the total fair market value of the property was imposed by FEMA. If renovation exceeds such limit, then the property no longer qualifies for FEMA flood insurance.

the authority.[456] The Holiday Inn is undergoing extensive renovations in preparation of the 2006 tourist season, but all come to an abrupt halt once the deal is sealed.[457]

The purchase increases the number of hotel rooms, owned and managed by Jekyll Club Associates, from 157 to 355, making it the largest hotel complex in Glynn County and certainly on Jekyll Island.

The plan for Phase I is to tear down the hotel and construct a new hotel under the different hotel-franchise name. Phase II remains a question mark. The intent is to construct townhouses and flats in natural surroundings of parks and alleys, but such plans are not approved yet.

By May 2006, the Holiday Inn is found to be in default of the lease agreement, and the hotel closes for business. The repercussion of the default notice is that the owners of the Holiday Inn are now responsible for demolishing the property, instead of the new buyers. One may call it a nice and welcoming financial windfall for the Jekyll Club Associates, or its affiliate and new owner, the Jekyll Ocean Oaks, LLC.

The Georgia Coast Inn, on the other hand, does not fare so well. Not that such comes as a surprise anymore, given that the hotel has been sitting idle since its abrupt closure in 2004. The abandoned property is prone to vandalism, and the authority has no choice but to completely fence in the property to keep it from further deteriorating and being a continued eyesore on the island.

Besides delinquent lease payments, the property owners are also found to be in default of county taxes, hence the property is placed in a forty-five-day compliance notice and is found to be in default by the authority. While default notices are being prepared, the owners of the Georgia Coast Inn file for bankruptcy protection in the state of Florida, which prohibits a default filing by the authority.

It is becoming a cat and mouse game, unfortunately. The denial by the authority to allow for condominium conversion and the inability to reach an agreement about the future of the Georgia Coast Inn ultimately lead

---

[456] A formal resolution for approval was made during a regular authority board meeting on February 13, 2006.

[457] Heidi Cook, general manager of the Holiday Inn, confirms halting all renovations on January 13, 2006 (*Brunswick News*, January 13, 2006).

to its demise but not until a legal battle can be settled between all parties involved. The Chapter 11 filing in a state different from the physical location of the property and outside the legal jurisdiction of the authority only complicates matters even further, causing unforeseen delays.

The authority does manage to move the bankruptcy case to a Chapter 7 liquidation case, forcing the owners to sell the buildings or demolish the structures. It prohibits the owners from initiating a long process of financial restructuring, thereby only delaying the inevitable.

Ultimately, the property is offered for sale through federal court but not without some controversy. Two interested buyers are bidding on the property during public auction, the Southeast Landco, LLC (Reynolds Plantation), and 150 Beachview Holdings, LLC (Patton Group). While the Reynolds Plantation makes the final and winning bid for $3.9 million, the Patton Group demands immediate payment. As representatives from Reynolds Plantation try to obtain a certified check for the purchase price, the property is re-auctioned, and the Patton Group winds the bid at $3 million. Needless to say, a lawsuit is soon filed in federal court to dispute the auction process and the subsequent second auction during the absence of the primary buyer.[458]

The pending lawsuit does not prohibit the new owners from demolishing the Georgia Coast Inn, but it will encumber any new construction on the site until the case is settled to everybody's satisfaction.

That leaves the Buccaneer Beach Resort[459] and the Oceanside Inn & Suites.[460] Both hotels, previously owned and operated by Motel Properties, and subsequently assigned to Western United Life Assurance Co. (WULA) in 2002 following the bankruptcy of Motel Properties, now face a new dilemma.

If both hotels wish to pursue renovations, as desired and encouraged by the authority, lease assignments will have to be made. Georgia Coast Holdings, LLC, (GCH) currently has both hotels under contract through a purchase and sale agreement with WULA. However, in order to start

---

[458] Authority board meeting, August 14, 2006.
[459] Originally known as Sam Snead's Buccaneer Motor Lodge (1961) and located just south of the present Days Inn & Suites.
[460] Formerly known as the Wanderer (1957) and currently known as the Holiday Inn Resort.

renovation, GCH needs a lease assignment and a lease extension for both hotels.[461]

The company envisions demolition of the old Buccaneer Beach Resort and construction of two new hotels, one a Marriott hotel and the second a Hilton franchise, while GCH plans to invest $500K in capital expenditures to improve the Oceanside Inn & Suites.

While the authority approves the requested lease assignments, extensions are not granted, as such must coincide with new base rent and/or percentage of gross revenue payments, neither one being of interest to GCH.

It is unknown why the lease assignments are approved, knowing in advance that building not one but two new hotels in its place and barely investing $500K in another property is almost impossible and certainly unrealistic given the difficult times other hotel owners are facing.

Prior to and during these changing times in the island's hotel scene, the authority does manage to come up with a new marketing idea: the Jekyll Island B2B FAM trip, or business-to-business familiarity trip. One can question whether this is really the most opportune time for the island to highlight its amenities, given the turmoil on the ocean resort side, but when placed within the island's desire to seek new investors and partners to complete its new master plan, it does seem logical to show its potential. The accent here is *potential* and not necessarily the existing environment, which is earmarked for demolition and drastic change, rather than a simple renovation or upgrade.[462]

Although the effort is touted as part of the larger concept to revitalize the island and the strategy to push for change, not everybody is as excited about the proposals that include a condominium village complex near the soccer complex and 4-H camp, a golf village, and beach-side villas.

But the island's marketing team takes the effort one step further. To keep the authority's revenue stream steady and to compensate for lost

---

[461] The original lease agreements with Motel Properties, assumed in 1999, expired in 2009.

[462] The idea is Eric Garvey's brainchild, senior marketing director. According to Mr. Garvey, "The hardest part is getting them to commit the time to come down. Once that happens, the hard part is over" (*Brunswick News*, January 24, 2006).

revenue due to hotel closings and demolitions, the authority adds more festival components to its existing list of annual festivals.

Besides the annual Fourth of July and Christmas Island, new events such as a Classic Car Festival in August and a Wild Georgia Shrimp Festival[463] in September are born, more out of necessity to increase parking fee revenue and to offset the declining hotel revenue than anything else. By the end of the year, Jekyll Island only has one thousand hotel rooms available, a drastic change from 1,500 rooms only two years ago.

What is interesting is the authority's clear shift from convention and hotel business toward promotions of special events. On one hand, this shift can be viewed as the result of three island hotels going offline for the entire 2007 season. On the other hand, and probably in hindsight, it can be seen as a preparation for the storm that will hit in 2008.

It certainly is not the first time the authority changes strategies from "resort development" to "state park promotion" and vice versa. Such changes have happened since the creation of Jekyll Island State Park and have always been subject to the prevailing economic conditions and roller coasters.

This time is no exception, and the preparations to attract day visitors through weekend festivals and entertainment to offset the lost hotel revenue may well be a very good and intelligent decision after all—certainly considering what is lurking on the horizon, the impact of which nobody could have predicted so early in the game.

It is therefore not surprising that the authority enters into a formal agreement with the Jekyll Island Foundation to "continue its pursuit of fundraising for projects, solely directed to the preservation or conservation of an historic or natural resource of Jekyll Island, or to the education of the public about some aspect of Jekyll Island history, its environment or natural resources."[464]

---

[463] The first annual Shrimp & Grits Festival was held in September 2006. It attracted 13,100 attendees (authority board meeting minutes, October 2006).

[464] Jekyll Island State Park Authority-Jekyll Island Foundation Operating Agreement, February 13, 2006 (authority board meeting, addendum to the minutes, February 13, 2006).

Immediately following the agreement, the authority formally approves the Georgia Sea Turtle Center Project and funding in the amount of $2,613,000 for restoration of the 1903 power plant.[465]

In addition, it seems the authority is serious about sprucing up the recreational parks on the island. The pavilion at Clam Creek is completed, the new restrooms at St. Andrews are nearly finished, and the faux-tabby ruins are installed on both entries of the Horton House-Historic District. Even the cupola that adorns the old wharf is newly gilded and restored to its original beauty.[466]

The pursuit of hotel improvements is not lost during this change of attention, and the authority acknowledges that in order to implement its new master plan that entails new construction and most likely the conversion of some existing hotel structures, a solution must be found for the Coastal Barrier Resource Act.

The initial agreement to remove the 35 percent developed area on Jekyll from the OPA[467] map seems the most suitable proposal to convince US Congress to act quickly.

The Unites States Fish & Wildlife Service (USFWS), using the same Jekyll Island Master Plan Map of 1996, agrees only to remove 33 percent by excluding some roadways on the island.

The goal is to find other state lands on the coast that are currently not in the OPA that can be added without any hardship on the state. Such marshlands can be best found under the control of the Georgia Ports Authority, who received eighteen acres of marshland to construct a turning basin at the harbor at the expense of high marshland on Jekyll Island.[468] This compromise further strengthens Jekyll's case for a swift and

---

[465] The JIF had already raised $2,035,000 at the time of the approval and further committed to raise the full $2,613,000 (resolution of the Jekyll Island State Park Authority, February 13, 2006).

[466] The restoration of the cupola was an initiative of Friends of Historic Jekyll Island (FOHJI). Funding was obtained through a donation from FOHJI.

[467] OPA, *other protected areas*, not suitable for development and flood insurance coverage through FEMA.

[468] The turning basin was constructed in 2003 by eliminating eighteen acres of marshland at the Brunswick River and designating eighteen acres of high marshland on Jekyll Island in return.

acceptable solution in Congress where Rep. Jack Kingston spearheads the political effort.

The authority is not immune to change either. In September and by executive order of Gov. Purdue, Robert Krueger is appointed to the authority board as a member at-large to replace Steven Scheer, and Benjamin Porter replaces Jack Collins by the same order.[469]

Whether the two appointments are directly or indirectly related to questions that arose in June 2006 about the protocols followed vis-à-vis the Georgia Open Meetings Act[470] is unknown and remains unconfirmed. It is known that all state agencies, including the authority, received a letter from the attorney general on April 17, 2006, about strict adherence to the prevailing act.

The letter is the result of several lawsuits that are filed regarding the bidding process for Super Bowl XLIII, in which Atlanta was a contender but ultimately lost the bid to Tampa, Florida.

Irregularities and apparent closed meetings led to the multiple lawsuits, hence the AG's reminder to strictly adhere to the Open Meetings Act.[471]

---

[469] Robert Krueger's term ends in 2010, while Benjamin Porter's terms ends in 2009 (authority board meeting, September 2006).
[470] Georgia Open Meetings Act: OCGA 50-14-4 (b).
[471] The authority's response to the attorney general's letter was to sign affidavits to justify the need for closed executive meetings (authority board meeting minutes, June 2006).

CHAPTER 17

JEKYLL BECOMES EVERY DEVELOPER'S FAVORED CHILD

2007–2008

Sixty years ago, at the conception of Jekyll Island State Park, the state of Georgia, as proud parents, could never have imagined that their little child would become every developers dreamchild, nor could the authority, as its conscientious godparents, ever have envisioned so many suitors.

But here we are after sixty years of decision-making about who and what the little duckling should become when she finally grows up, and the line of suitors, better known as private developers, is endless, as all of them want a piece of the newly crowned "prom queen" or "Georgia's Jewel," as the Atlanta politicians like to refer to her.

There is no shortage of ideas, concepts, plans, or suggestions, as all of them seem to know what is in Jekyll Island's best interest, including the newly appointed board member Ben Porter. He makes his vision for the future of Jekyll Island clear in a letter addressed to all Jekyll Island Authority members and Bill Donohue, executive director.

I hope our discussions will produce a bold, creative plan that will:

- Protect and preserve forever the natural beauty and feel of Jekyll Island's vast natural areas and grand historic heritage, and that will
- Entice a strong, experienced, capable Master Developer to enter into a viable public-private partnership with the Authority to plan, build and operate a continuity of public and private facilities, which will provide lodging, food, retail, recreational, entertainment, residential and convention accommodations designed to revitalize Jekyll Island. The goal of the Master Redevelopment plan will be to enhance the value, beauty, and appeal of Jekyll, and to attract large numbers of Georgia citizens to visit and enjoy "their island."[472]

The excerpt of the letter does not necessarily bring any new ideas to the discussion table, but it does provide insight in Mr. Porter's way of thinking and handling his new position. After all, Mr. Porter's term is only for two years, expiring in 2009, so it seems he will use his tenure as effectively as possible to make an impact. And an impact he will definitely make, once development plans are submitted for review and approval.

Rumors and opinions run rampant, in both the media and on the island, about the future of Jekyll Island and the multitude of large-scale development projects. While most plans seem to agree on replacing the old shopping center, the convention center, and the revitalization of existing hotels on the island, some developers take their plans a little bit further, much to the dismay of the residents.

Two developers specifically, E. Wade Shealy, developer of the Hampton Plantation near Savannah, and Mercer Reynolds, builder of the Reynolds Plantation in Greensboro, plan to build luxury homes on the sites of the

---

[472] Letter from Mr. Porter to the authority board, November 8, 2006 (addendum to the authority board meeting, December 2006).

4-H Center and the Jekyll Island Soccer Complex. In addition, they envision building hundreds of condominiums and homes along the island's beachfront and public golf courses, creating lodging for 10,000 to 20,000 visitors on an island that barely has a thousand permanent residents. The idea alone of such a drastic change is viewed as an intrusion of the quiet and peaceful life on Georgia's Jewel, and it is not surprising that residents take their plight to the newspapers to get their opinion heard.

The *Brunswick News* clarifies in its December 29, 2006, editorial what is at stake and what the developers really have in mind:

> Plans for the future: E. Wade Shealy and Mercer Reynolds have each submitted development proposals to the Jekyll Island Authority for consideration.
>
> Both plans recommend tearing down the existing Jekyll strip mall and convention center and rebuilding both closer to the island's entrance. New hotels, condominiums and shops would take up their existing space.
>
> In addition, Mercer Reynolds is proposing the conversion of one of Jekyll Island's three golf courses into a private membership club.
>
> In addition, Shealy is proposing:
>
> - 1,500 condos with $1 million price tags.
> - 192 houses selling upwards of $1 million.
> - 200 golf course houses beginning at $500,000.
> - Transforming the Jekyll Island Airport into a residential area.
> - Building a South End Village where the 4-H Center and soccer complex are now located. The project would include $4 million beachfront homes, condos, a small hotel, shops, and restaurants.
>
> The Jekyll Island Authority also has a redevelopment plan on the table. Its proposals include:
>
> - A new Convention Center.

- New and improved shopping.
- New hotels.
- Rebuilding the 4-H Center on the north end of the island.
- Doing away with the Soccer Complex.
- ...[473]

Tensions are building so high that fifty Jekyll Island residents depart by bus for a trip to Atlanta to protest the proposed development plans that could potentially transform the entire island into an upscale resort. Despite the protests, the authority votes unanimously to move forward with the plans.[474]

The vote is actually a decision by the board to hire a real estate consultant to help find a master developer, willing to enter into a public private partnership and to build hotels and homes to ensure an acceptable and realistic rate of return for the authority. This is exactly what Ben Porter had in mind just one month ago.

The board also votes on the four options that were presented to Gov. Purdue last year:

1) Status quo until 2049.
2) Extend the lease and life of the authority; the authority and the staff operate and redevelop the island.
3) Extend the lease and the life of the authority and contract with a private sector partner to redevelop and manage the commercial aspects of the island.
4) Sell or convert to fee simple.

Since Gov. Purdue is opposed to options 1 and 4, the authority unanimously approves option 3 and directs Mr. Porter[475] to inform Mr. Richardson, Speaker of the House, of the decision made.

The unanimous decisions can be viewed as perfunctory since neither one has a direct impact on the future development plans per se, yet they

---

[473] The *Brunswick News*, editorial, December 29, 2006.

[474] The authority board meeting, January 8, 2007, was held in Atlanta.

[475] Mr. Porter was chair of the Legislative Committee and a member of the Hotel Committee (authority board meeting, January 8, 2007).

form the start of what will become the new foundation and the possible future of the island.

The general assembly does not waste any time proposing a renewal of property lease and provisions when HB 214 is introduced to the floor on February 2, 2007.

HB 214 extends the authority's current lease, set to expire in 2049, for another forty years.[476] Gov. Purdue approves the new bill on May 30, 2007, thereby giving the authority the green light to go ahead with its request for proposal to find a revitalization partner and start the search for a real estate consultant.

While the door for new development and changes may have been opened slightly, the authority, and Bill Donohue in particular as executive director, still need to bridge the gap and make ends meet until a partner is found and approved.

The first order of the day is to secure the commercial leases for small businesses in the old shopping center. All current occupants receive a two-year lease extension, set to expire in 2007. That secures the stability of the strip mall until 2009 and leaves plenty of time for new development to be proposed, reviewed, approved, and materialized.

The time line and extension of two years seems adequate at the time, but it is a fairly aggressive approach to assume that all can be altered and improved in such a short time.

Stabilizing the hotel leases is slightly more complex and complicated. The Hotel Committee decides to extend the current leases for the Beachview Club and the Jekyll Harbor Marina for five years at the present terms and conditions.[477] To enforce the new base rent, based on actual FMV, or the new 4.5 percent of gross revenue on all remaining hotels seems hardly possible given the low occupancy rates.

The only exceptions to the above are the Buccaneer Beach Resort and the Jekyll Oceanfront Resort. Both receive a lease extension to 2049, which allows the Buccaneer Beach Resort to be demolished and to be

---

[476] HB 214 amended Code Section 12-3-241, relating to the lease to the authority.
[477] Both the Beachview Club and the Jekyll Harbor Marina paid 8 percent of fair market value, set at $40,000 per acre (letter from Bill Donohue to the authority board, January 3, 2007). The real FMV in 2001 was $250,000 per acre, as per JIA Policy VII-A-6.

replaced with a new three-hundred-room hotel, and allows the Jekyll Oceanfront Resort to sell the north-end buildings, recently converted to condominiums, and to demolish the south-end buildings to make room for a new hotel, potentially an Embassy Suites hotel or similar hotel concept.

Trammell Crow Co., a Dallas-based developer of commercial real estate, makes its first appearance on the island as the company not only expresses interest in acquiring the lease of the Buccaneer Beach Resort to construct the new hotel but is also interested in purchasing the Days Inn. The interest doesn't come as a surprise. Both are large properties, adjacent to each other, and have the best unobstructed beach view.

But other parties also have a keen interest in both properties, and the Days Inn is quietly being purchased by none other than the Southeast Landco. Acquisitions Fund, LLC, a branch of the Reynolds Plantation, is still fighting a legal battle with the Patton Group about the Georgia Coast Inn.

Trammel Crow does succeed in acquiring the Buccaneer Beach Resort property through its affiliate Jekyll Crow Replacement Hotel I, LLC, a joint venture between Trammell Crow Co. and Noble Investment Group, LLC. The new lessees submit a budget proposal totaling $113.6 million for the construction of the new three-hundred-room hotel.[478]

The Georgia Coast Inn lease is left untouched until development plans can be submitted. Such are depending on the ultimate outcome of the federal lawsuit between the two bidders, Reynolds Plantation and the Patton Group. The authority does impose a deadline for resolution by June 11, 2007, after which the lease agreement will be terminated.

As new investors position themselves to grab a piece or multiple pieces of the Jekyll Island pie prior to the selection of a private partner, existing hotel owners quietly work on their own new development plans.

The JICH owners have not been sitting idle with their acquisition and demolition of the Holiday Inn. Initially, the new owners envisioned building a smaller 139-room SpringHill Suites, a Marriott Corp. franchise, with

---

[478] Budget proposed at the authority board meeting in October 2007: $61.6 million is designated to the hotel construction, $43 million is reserved for new condominiums, $9 million for a new parking lot, totaling $113,6 million in new investment. The hotel would ultimately close in October 2007.

an adjacent freestanding restaurant, a conference facility, and additional cottages to make up the balance of the two-hundred-room Holiday Inn.

But not all on the island centers around the commercial resort side, as other state park events take place and deserve attention.

The Georgia Sea Turtle Center finally opens its door to the public on June 17, 2007, after extensive renovation and rehabilitation. The first of its kind in the state of Georgia, completely funded by private donations raised through the Jekyll Island Foundation, it attracts more than its fair share of visitors, who for the first time can learn about the wonderful creatures that make the island their preferred place of nesting and birth.[479]

Besides the visit to the tourist shop, visitors also can tour the sea turtle hospital where they can watch the daily feeding and learn all about the care for the animals from expert staff members.

And since environmental issues and concerns are being addressed and incorporated in the overall Jekyll Island experience, it is not surprising that the beaches receive renewed attention.

The first time that beach erosion was officially mentioned on the island dates to the aftermath of Hurricane Dora in 1964. Since then, rock revetments on the north end and around Clam Creek may have slowed the erosion process, but the issue is brought up again. This time, the authority is committed to finding a more permanent solution and looks at various options that may be available.

One option is to submit a request for beach renourishment to the Army Corps of Engineers, similar to the Tybee Island approach.[480] Bill Donohue thinks the same situation may exist on Jekyll Island, following the deepening of the Brunswick channel from 30 feet to 36 feet.

The problem this approach faces is that it may take ten to fifteen years before the Army Corps of Engineers will approve such a project, and such still depends on the favorable outcome of a federal lawsuit that will have to be filed, claiming that deepening of the channel did indeed cause the beach erosion.

---

[479] The annual pilgrimage of the loggerheads was accidentally discovered in 1963 as they got stranded in the wires and rails of the Peppermint Amusement Park.

[480] The Army Corps of Engineers conducted a study of sand loss on Tybee Island in 2007. City officials contended that the deepening of the Savannah River accelerated the erosion of an already renourished beach (*Brunswick News*, January 6, 2007).

The advantage of taking this route is of course the financial impact, half of which would be funded by the Army Corps of Engineers, but any future need for renourishment due to a major storm or hurricane would be eligible for disaster relief, another major financial benefit.[481]

The advantage of the authority completing the beach renourishment itself is timing, as the project can be finished in three to four years, but the funding problem is hard to overlook, as no extra revenue is available, certainly not in these complex times.

Besides the dire need for sand and lots of it, the beaches also need another solution to a lesser-known problem.

In the summer of 2004, elevated levels of viral pathogens were found in the coastal waters of Jekyll Island and St. Simons Island. At first no logical explanation could be found for the high concentration of pathogens, but further research concluded that a rise in pathogen concentration coincided with heavy rainfall and thunderstorms.

In early 2007, when the oyster restoration project at Clam Creek and Beach Creek is initiated, after DNR approval, it is noted that the presence of oysters reduces the level of pathogens naturally. Oysters are perfect and natural water cleansers that break down the pathogens and release cleansed water back into their surrounding habitat.

It is not surprising that the state park and the natural environment all receive so much attention. After all, who knows what is coming and what is ahead when so many developers are eyeing the island to materialize their next big commercial projects.

Residents do not stand alone in their plight for conservation and limited development. Actually, it seems as if the entire state and the nation is watching about future developments and the future of Jekyll Island.

The *Athens Banner-Herald* carries an article, "Jekyll planning will be watched by entire state," but the *Los Angeles Times* takes it a step further when the West Coast newspaper publishes its article on February 19, 2007. The title, "Splitting a Georgia retreat's personality," cannot be more fitting, as Jekyll Island is really viewed as the last bastion on the eastern seaboard. Neighboring Florida and South Carolina are already heavily developed, including high-rising condominiums and hotels. Only Jekyll Island has

---

[481] Estimates indicate that beach renourishment would cost between $10 million and $12 million (*Brunswick News*, January 6, 2007).

always been protected by strict environmental laws and height restrictions, and it has also benefited from the 65/35 development rule.

But some residents believe stricter control and oversight is needed, hence local resident David Egan leads a grassroots movement, Initiative to Protect Jekyll Island, and starts his own survey to gauge public feedback on the proposed developments.

The survey receives more than 1,400 responses in its first month alone and finds an unexpected ally in the general assembly with Rep. Debbie Buckner.

She immediately goes to work and introduces HB 548 that places a cap of 1,500 housing units on the island, almost double the existing number of seven hundred housing units, calls for a growth limit of the south end of the island, the recycling of wastewater and its reuse for irrigation, and the enacting of height restriction of thirty-five feet.

The bill is clearly geared toward maximum protection and conservation of the island and is submitted to the floor of the general assembly without support, input, or involvement of the authority.

All this attention on natural conservation does get a boost from the DNR when its board votes to add a fifty-foot buffer to the Marshlands Protection Act of 1970. It's welcome news for state environmentalists but not such great news for developers, who see their plans curtailed and wing-clipped with this new buffer zone.

Now that the state agency has adopted the new rule, it is only a question of time before the rule becomes state law.[482]

By the end of summer, the battle for a public private partner comes to an end as the authority selects Linger Longer Communities as its new private partner. The announcement is not met with a lot of enthusiasm. Instead, the choice sets off a fire of newspaper articles, led by state Sen. Jeff Chapman.

The media scrutiny is not solely directed at Linger Longer Communities but also focuses on Trammell Crow Co., whose proposal to demolish the old Buccaneer Beach Resort and replace it with a the new three-hundred-room luxury hotel and 120 two-bedroom condominiums is met with the same concerns.

---

[482] HR-51 is introduced by Rep. Harry Geisinger (www.legis.ga.gov/legis/2007_08/fulltext/hr51.htm).

The combination of such two large-scale developments that seem to be geared toward the high end of the hospitality industry and the condominium market is enough reason for concern and raises serious questions. The news that the authority grants a $10 million rent rebate to Trammell Crow Co. in exchange for its $90 million hotel investment only adds fuel to the fire.

The questions Sen. Chapman asks publicly in several *Brunswick News* articles are very specific and require a serious rebuttal from the authority and more specifically from Ben Porter, chairman of the authority.

The *Brunswick News* article dated August 17, 2007, formulates the questions as follows:

> What is the board's general policy with regards to tax subsidies and other incentives to developers.
>
> What evidence exists that a significant subsidy or other financial incentive is warranted in the contract with Trammell Crow and partnering companies.
>
> Would knowledge of the possibility of such a subsidy have affected the bidding of other developers in ways that might have offered greater benefits to the authority.
>
> What criteria did the board use to determine that a subsidy was appropriate, and what is the mathematical or economic calculation for determining the appropriate level of such a subsidy.
>
> What recourse is available to mediate or alter any of the contract provisions if examination of the process proves such change is warranted.

Ben Porter's response on August 23, 2007, immediately refers to the authority's practice to use an escalating rent formula as an incentive for large-scale projects. The formula was first used in 1986 when Jekyll Associates restored the Jekyll Island Club Hotel and the rent structure provided for a no-rent period for the first ten years. The following two years, rent was structured as fixed annual payment, while the following years, 3.5 percent of gross revenue was charged.

Mr. Porter further states that this specific arrangement made it possible for the investors to service its $19 million debt, necessary to renovate the original clubhouse.[483]

The issue is also openly being addressed by the Jekyll Island Oversight Committee,[484] together with the questionable process of selecting a private developer that will ultimately build the forty-five-acre town square center. It also raises the question of affordability, as mandated by the original Authority Act of 1950.

As the discussion continues, the battle between Chair Ben Porter and Sen. Chapman gets a new tail and starts raising some valid concerns about the board's transparency, or lack thereof, during the selection processes.

The selection of Trammell Crow and the decision on the rent rebate were not made public until one day before the panel voted on both agenda items. That left the public with little or no time to comment or ask questions.

The same lack of transparency is now also becoming visible during the selection process of a public private partner.

A final winner for the town square center development is to be selected from the three finalists on September 24. Prior to this selection date, the public does not have access to any of the proposals, as such are being held confidential and are discussed only in closed meetings. The form of meetings to use the selection process also comes under fire.

Georgia's Open Records Act requires that all state agency meetings be held in public. However, the rule applies only if the agency meets in full quorum (i.e., if the majority of the board is present). In the authority's case, being a nine-member board, meetings must be open to the public if five or more of its members meet for a specific purpose or vote.

In the case of the public private partner selection process, which is conducted by the authority's Hotel Committee, the rule does not apply. The committee only has four members and therefore does not constitute

---

[483] The owners of the JICH did receive a ten-year rent-free period. However, the total rent rebate amounted to $1 million, or 5 percent of the total amount invested. The Trammell Crow rebate amounts to $10 million, or 11 percent of total investment.

[484] Jekyll Island Oversight Committee meeting on August 30, 2007 (the *Times-Union*, September 7, 2007).

a quorum—an innovative and politically correct way to abide by the law while circumventing it at the same time.

The same process was used for approval of Trammell Crow and the exuberant rent rebate, when the Hotel Committee members, including Ben Porter, approved the rebate while leaving little choice to the other board members to even question the decision.

The selection of Linger Longer Communities as the prevailing winner is already shrouded in controversy when a letter to the editor of the *Brunswick News*[485] raises even more eyebrows.

A typical procurement consists of either an invitation to bid (IFB) or a request for proposal (RFP). In the case of Linger Longer Communities, the authority opted for an RFP process. All bidders must abide by the specific instructions as set forth by the RFP, and their proposals must adhere to the limitations placed on the project size by the authority.

Linger Longer Communities submitted a bid that exceeded the proposed development acreage of forty-five acres by eighteen acres.[486] This would mean that the proposal is considered invalid, and the authority has two options available.

First, the authority can declare Linger Longer Communities to be "nonresponsive" since they exceeded the specified acreage. This would result in an automatic elimination from the bidding process. The second option is to revise the original specifications and to request all bidders, including Linger Longer Communities, to resubmit their bids accordingly.

Neither of the two options available are executed, and Linger Longer Communities is awarded the bid, behind closed doors and by a minority of the authority board members.

The question now is whether this deal can be delayed, altered, or declared void.

What makes this process and proposal even more interesting is that in the end when all calculations are made and final, the authority ends up with a public debt of $84 million, while the revenue only accounts for $67 million. Hardly a lucrative deal for Jekyll Island State Park or the

---

[485] *Brunswick News*, October 10, 2007 (letter to the editor, submitted by Brian Blue).
[486] Linger Longer Communities' proposal was submitted for sixty-three acres, rather than the requested forty-five acres.

Georgia taxpayers since in the end someone will have to cover the $17 million shortfall.

In the meantime, Linger Longer Communities acquires the exclusive rights to sixty-seven acres of pristine ocean view property at the expense of the average Georgian, who is required to give up its public beachfront parking to make room for exclusive condominiums, homes, and hotels.[487]

The controversy that surrounds the bid-awarding process does result in a legal challenge by one of the competitive bidders. The Jekyll Island Revitalization Group, whose bid ranked third, files an injunction in Fulton County Superior Court and challenges the selection process.[488]

Judge Jerry Baxter tosses out the injunction on January 14, 2008, clearing the path for the authority and Linger Longer Communities to proceed with the final design and permitting process.[489]

Following Judge Baxter's court ruling, the Glynn County Commission expresses its support for the revitalization project when Commission Chair Don Hogan publicly endorses the authority's selection and plan.[490]

The total project cost is estimated to be $450 million, with $25 million earmarked by Gov. Purdue in the 2009 budget for road and infrastructure improvements on Jekyll Island.

But the battle is far from over, as multiple articles and letters to the editor in the *Brunswick News* reveal the opposing stances and, more importantly, the various underpinning reasons to proceed with this large-scale development.

Linger Longer Communities' project Executive Director Jim Langford takes his fight straight to the people of Georgia when he offers a resolution to all Georgians:

> … Be it resolved, in view of the aging infrastructure and of declining visitation to Jekyll Island, that just 1 percent of

---

[487] The Linger Longer Communities' proposal would develop all beachfront property between the Days Inn and the current Tortugas Jack's location, removing the public parking lot, now known as Great Dunes Park.

[488] The three finalists in the bid for the private partnership were Linger Longer Communities, Trammell Crow Co., and Jekyll Island Revitalization Group.

[489] The *Brunswick News*, January 15, 2008.

[490] The *Brunswick News*, January 16, 2008.

the island's acreage, including land adjacent to less than 8 percent of the island's total beachfront, shall be revitalized to the quality standards that Georgians deserve, without reducing public parking or beach access points, and with adherence to extensive and rigorous environmental guidelines to create one of the most accessible and eco-friendly communities on the east coast ...[491]

The resolution is promptly placed on Linger Longer Communities' website, www.rediscoverjekyll.com, and all Georgians are encouraged to vote "yes" on the proposed resolution.

Unfortunately, the website only allows *yes* votes and does not seem to be able to accommodate any opposition, as a simple *no* vote is not allowed.[492]

But Mr. Langford takes his fight a little bit further. His letter also states that Jekyll Island is in dire need of revitalization because of declining visitation since 1990. According to his estimate, visitation has declined by 47 percent since 1997 due to aging infrastructure and facilities.

While it is true that the traffic count dropped by 44 percent compared to 1996, the steep decline is caused by excluding decal traffic from the total count and not because of a total decline in visitation.

The hotel occupancy only declined by 6 percent in 1997, compared to the previous year, and the average hotel room nights actually increased between 1997 and 2001 in comparison to 1996.[493]

This comparison alone strongly suggests that decal traffic was excluded from the total count in 1997, hence Mr. Langford's argument is debatable.

According to Mr. David Egan's Visitation Statistics: "Overall, we can project that visitation to the island has declined by 12% since 1996, a far cry from the 47% being reported by the JIA and LL. Furthermore, the significance of this 12% decline has to be weighed against a 30% drop in the island's total number of hotel rooms available since 1996."

---

[491] Jim Langford's letter to the editor, the *Brunswick News*, January 15, 2008.
[492] Letter to the editor by Chuck Diefenderfer, the *Brunswick News*, January 16, 2008.
[493] Visitation Statistics by David Egan, Initiative to Protect Jekyll Island (addendum to the authority board meeting, January 2008).

There is also the fight for affordability on the island and many residents fear that such large-scale development, whether it infringes on beach access or not, will increase hotel prices, thereby making Jekyll Island less affordable for the average Georgian.

Sen. Jeff Chapman spearheads the fight for affordability, together with the opposition groups to the project,[494] and requests a ruling by the attorney general's office on issues such as affordability.

But Mr. Langford disputes the claim and assures all that 72 percent of the new development, including condominiums and hotel rooms, will be priced below $139 per night.

While his claim can obviously not be verified, it is hard to imagine that a $450 million development is financially sustainable when three-quarters of the properties fall within such a low-price range.

What gets lost in the big political debate and controversy is the removal of Bill Donohue as the island's executive director. The removal comes by order of Gov. Purdue, who reassigns Mr. Donohue to a similar position at the Lake Lanier Islands Authority.

While there is no reason to question whether the turmoil that will soon reach its peak in the following years caused the sudden shift, it does seem odd that a trusted leader is removed at such a crucial time in island history.

One would think that steady, proven, and experienced leadership is the key factor for stabilization and the perfect buffer to bridge the gaps between opposing parties. After all, which head coach pulls his trusted quarterback out of the game in favor of a newcomer[495] and then expects the team to bring home the Super Bowl?

Bill Donohue has been leading Jekyll Island for more than a decade, taking over the helm during controversial times[496] and steadily guiding the island toward peace, quiet, and, above all, consensus building among the many interested parties involved.

---

[494] Initiative to Protect Jekyll Island and Center for a Sustainable Coast were amongst the opposing groups.

[495] Jones Hooks will replace Bill Donohue as the new executive director in June 2008.

[496] Bill Donohue succeeded George Chambliss in 1997 after the DNR controversy on the island.

Maybe it is therefore only appropriate that he gets reassigned during another raging political controversy.

The Linger Longer Communities development plans are at the forefront of many newspaper articles in 2008 and somehow overshadow the plans of existing hotels on the island.

The Jekyll Island Club Hotel launches a major renovation project in January 2008 to overhaul 134 guest rooms at the Club Hotel, Annex, and Sans Souci. The total estimated cost is $4.2 million.

Keeping true to its original Victorian design, all bathrooms receive an upgrade with new floors, walls, tiles, granite-topped vanities, and new light fixtures, while the guest room floors are refinished and adorned with new furniture that preserves the historical integrity of the original design.[497]

All the commotion about redevelopment and how it can add a spark to the Golden Isles' economy largely ignores what is brewing nationally where the economic news is less than encouraging.

The new housing slump that has a firm grip on the nation also has its effect on the state of Georgia. Last year alone, Georgia saw its construction permits drop 40 percent, and while those largely pertain to residential construction, it is a clear sign on the wall of what may be in store.

In comparison, Glynn County permits only drop by 20 percent, and local economists feel that somehow the Golden Isles will be spared. Don Matthews, economics professor at Coastal Georgia Community College, admits that "the Golden Isles may not escape all the shuddering going around the nation, though it may fare better than other regions of the state and the nation."[498]

His optimism stems from the proposed revitalization and the $25 million that is set aside in the 2009 budget, and the 19 percent increase in tourism in the Golden Isles the previous year.

What is missing from this assumption is that nationwide and regionally, the retail industry is taking an unexpected hit due to the housing slump and a sharp drop in consumer spending, both of which are early signs of a possible recession, or at least a serious economic slowdown.

While so early in the year the jury is still out on whether the economy is heading toward a true recession, the economic outlook is less than rosy.

---

[497] The *Brunswick News*, January 17, 2008.
[498] The *Brunswick News*, January 19–20, 2008.

Rather than hoping that the large-scale development that will pump close to half a billion new dollars in the local economy can offset the looming recession, local economists should have heeded the advice of national economists to play a defensive game, protecting current assets, rather than gambling aggressively and offensively in the hope that one will offset the other so that the end result is a zero-sum game.

Whether the drastic change in plans by Linger Longer Communities to scale down its original $450 million revitalization plan is the result of a more realistic economic approach, the continued opposition by residents, or a combination of both is hard to tell.

Suffice it to say that preservation groups such as IPJI and the Center for a Sustainable Coast, with the support of the island residents, played a large roll in scaling down the project to protect the beachfront property, the beach parking lots, and the public beach crossovers, most of which would probably have disappeared despite the multiple and continued assurances of Linger Longer Communities.

The fact remains that in less than one year, a $450 million project is reduced to a mere $170 million plan, while the total acreage is scaled back from its original sixty-three acres.

The proposed 141,000-square-foot new convention center is changed to renovation of the existing convention center, which is half the size. Instead of building three new hotels with a total capacity of 750 rooms, Linger Longer Communities agrees to build two hotels instead with a capacity of 350 rooms total. The proposed new shopping center, to be 59,000 square feet, is now reduced to 30,000 square feet.

That still leaves the controversy over the multimillion rent rebate for the two new hotels over the first ten years of the lease agreement, and the low 1 percent cut of time-sharing sales the authority accepted in the original deal. Never in the history of commercial leases or agreements has the authority granted so many discounts and rebates, so it is obvious that when more details of the deal become known, both the public and some politicians like Sen. Chapman question the integrity of the authority.

The residents are not the only ones expressing their opinions about integrity, due process, and public input.

Former board member Ed Boshears joins the plight for transparency and integrity in a letter to the *Brunswick News* on September 24, 2008.

He implies that Gov. Purdue, Authority Chair Bob Krueger, former chair Ben Porter, and Mercer Reynolds, founder of Linger Longer Communities, have acted unethically and held secret meetings.

Mr. Boshears implies that:

> Gov. Purdue directed the Board to choose Linger Longer Communities to develop the island because the governor and the governor's business partners would reap the benefits from profitable developments.
>
> Porter and Krueger are both developers, and their being on the board is a complete conflict of interest. Revitalization has been delayed over a year because board members are more concerned with Linger Longer making money on condos. Porter and others care more about lining their pockets.[499]

It is a well-known fact that Mercer Reynolds is a large campaign contributor for Gov. Purdue and Georgia Republicans in general, and it is not the first time Ben Porter is associated with tax rebates and rent reduction or forgiveness while he chaired the authority.

But the fight is not won yet. Linger Longer Communities still plans to move ahead with its smaller development, and it still holds the exclusive management and development contract on the island. The twenty-five-year exclusivity deal was part of the original negotiations but rarely mentioned in the newspapers. The no-compete clause in the contract is far more threatening to the future of Jekyll Island than the acreage, type of development, or even affordability.

The fact that the *Brunswick News* calls any and all disagreement with the development plans, be it the original or its revised and smaller-scale plans, to be "resident obstructionism"[500] is duly noted, hence the multitude of letters to editor.

The turmoil does result in other developers, such as Trammell Crow Co., slowing down their own development plans, although one can

---

[499] Letter to the editor, *Brunswick News*, September 24, 2008.
[500] The *Brunswick News*, editorial, September 22, 2008.

conclude that such is actually more the result of an uncertain economic climate than any other factors.

Nevertheless, all development, revitalization, and redevelopment on Jekyll Island faces some serious headwinds and unpredictable delays.

So much for the "cautiously optimistic" local economic outlook at the beginning of 2008.

CHAPTER 18

ISLAND DEVELOPMENT: SLOWER, SMALLER

2009–2011

By the beginning of 2009, it is clear that the nation has been in an economic recession since 2007 and that the economic forecast, both nationally and regionally, as "cautiously optimistic" was a clear understatement.

The bank bailouts and the large quantitative easing by the Federal Reserve, combined with high unemployment, 0 percent interest rates, and a total collapse of the real estate market certainly have a serious impact on the Golden Isles and Jekyll Island in particular.

What impacts the controversial Linger Longer Communities' deal and its partnership with the authority the most are the tight credit markets. Despite downscaling the original project from $352 million to a mere $170 million, financing is hard to come by in these difficult economic times.

For the past two years, the authority has now struggled to materialize this newfound public private partnership that is supposed to laud in a new and brighter future for Jekyll Island.

Everybody agrees that revitalization of the old and crumbling hotel infrastructure is crucial to the island's future. So is the building of a new and bigger convention center, but that is where the agreements end between developers, the authority, and the island residents.

The sticky point is not just the sheer size of the new development, sixty-three acres of beachfront property. It is also a question of density and capacity, or better yet, the fear of oversaturation.

At the height of Jekyll's tourism years, the island featured 1,800 guest rooms. That number has been reduced by a third since the closing and demolition of three hotels. The new development calls for doubling this number to almost 4,100 available accommodations, including hotel guest rooms, condominiums, time-shares, and townhouses, which will clearly impact the current infrastructure and possibly the island's saturation point.

For that purpose, the authority issues a development impact study, conducted by the Bleakly Advisory Group, who reports its findings to the board in late 2008.

The interesting side note of the study is that although Jekyll Island reported a positive cash flow for fiscal year 2007,[501] the island is living on borrowed time. When assets depreciate faster than the incoming revenue to replenish them, the existing infrastructure will soon need to be replaced. The extra funds needed will have to come from additional development, estimated to generate $100 million over the next fifteen years, which equates to around 6 percent of island redevelopment to make all the figures work in favor of the authority.

Nowhere in the report is it mentioned, however, that the practice to depreciate faster than income generation also applies to new development—meaning the income generated for new development must not only be adequate to compensate for the loss in depreciation of existing infrastructure. It must also be able to serve its own depreciation, therefore effectively doing financial overtime, which is hardly feasible.

In essence, the large-scale development contract must be constructed in such a way that the public private partnership almost needs to tilt toward the authority to make this work efficiently.

In reality, based on prevailing and agreed-upon terms and conditions, the public private partnership with Linger Longer Communities favors the private side and is therefore contradictory to what Jekyll Island really needs to brighten its future, at least long-term.

The only reasonable parity that can be found in the deal is maybe the capital injection. The authority has access to $50 million in state bonds, all of which have been sold, to invest in the construction of the new

---

[501] The authority's annual report states a loss of $210,575 in 2006, while the state auditor's report states a profit of almost $2 million (the *Times-Union*, February 2008).

Beach Village, including the new convention center, while Linger Longer Communities provides a similar investment amount.

Where the parity disappears quickly is the distribution of income generation and sharing, the rent abatements for the first ten years, and the exclusive development contract anywhere on the island for the next twenty-five years. That can hardly be called a well-balanced public private partnership.

It is interesting to note that during the many discussions, in public or private meetings, in the press, or during regular board meetings, the voice of the executive director is absent, as if the new development does not affect him or his staff. This is prevalent not only for outgoing Executive Director Bill Donohue but also for newcomer Jones Hooks.

All conversations and press releases or commentaries are handled by the authority board members, primarily Chairman Bob Krueger; Eric Garvey, senior director of marketing; and Bert Brantley, spokesperson for Gov. Purdue.

The only other voice that is often heard is that of Sen. Jeff Chapman, who relentlessly pursues the abolishment of the Revitalization Partnering Agreement, or RPA as it is commonly referred to.

Despite the initial plan to break ground on this massive undertaking in 2009, the end of the year approaches without any discernable progress.

Sen. Chapman attempts one more time to urge the authority members to "... Take advantage of contractual opportunities that would allow for the termination of the Revitalization Partnering Agreement (RPA) between the JIA and Linger Longer Communities on the grounds that it includes a number of provisions that are inconsistent with sound financial stewardship for Jekyll Island State Park, the crown jewel of Georgia's Coast ..."[502]

The reference to the RPA in question specifically refers to three questionable terms that are currently under consideration:

> - A series of upfront payments and financial incentives for Linger Longer totaling millions of dollars-financial incentives to build on prime oceanfront land make little, if any, fiscal sense.

---

[502] *Atlanta Journal-Constitution*, November 24, 2009.

- A 99 to 1 split in revenue sharing from the Jekyll time-share project - the oceanfront public land on which the time-shares will be built accounts for more than half of their market value, yet the JIA is settling for a penny on the dollar.
- Some $50 million in state bonds to pay for the infrastructure for Linger Longer's town center project – the bulk of those costs should have been covered by Linger Longer in return for the privilege of developing prime beachfront public land for which it does not have to pay anything ...

... The financial terms of the RPA are even more questionable when considering that they are the same, or in some cases worse, than the ones in the Linger Longer proposal that was rejected by the JIA in August 2007 during the private partner bid contest ...[503]

There is no doubt that the overall consensus points toward the preferred treatment given to Linger Longer Communities by the authority, certainly in comparison to previous agreements with other developers such as Jekyll Ocean Oaks,[504] as outlined in detail in a frontpage article of the *Atlanta Journal-Constitution*.[505]

On December 7, 2009, Gov. Purdue and the authority members symbolically break ground for what is to become Great Dunes Park. The project is part of the Beach Village project, which includes a new 78,000-square-foot convention center and is financed by the $50 million bond issuance previously approved by the governor.

---

[503] *Atlanta Journal-Constitution*, November 24, 2009.
[504] Jekyll Ocean Oaks constructed the Hampton Inn & Suites in 2009. The 138-room hotel opened in the spring of 2010.
[505] Investigative reporter Carrie Teegardin examined the authority's long-term agreement with Linger Longer Communities in detail and published her findings on March 1, 2009 (http://www.savejekyllisland.org/AJCMr109.html).

Additional private funding is expected to complete the retail portion of the Beach Village and to construct a convention hotel on the opposite beachfront side.

What is not clear yet at the time of groundbreaking is what role Linger Longer Communities will now play in the grand redevelopment plan, given that the authority is eager and ready to start.

Residents do not need to wait very long, as the newspapers break the news the next day that contract negotiations with Linger Longer Communities have been suspended "by mutual consent." The main reason provided by both parties is the uncertain economy, preventing Linger Longer Communities from providing an exact construction schedule. According to a statement released by the authority on December 8, 2009, and reported by Atlanta Unfiltered, "... With today's announcement, Linger Longer collects nothing, Garvey said. No money has exchanged hands between Linger Longer and the Jekyll Island Authority, he said. They have participated in some planning work ... but because there was no final contract, there was no money exchanged."[506]

It seems hard to believe that after two years of intense planning and negotiating, a major developer walks away from a multimillion-dollar deal by simple mutual consent without any minimal compensation for planning services rendered.[507]

While it is true that the economic climate is not favorable for any commercial development, tight credit markets are a more realistic explanation, given the size and scope of the project and the financing needed to begin construction, let alone completion by 2012, as agreed upon by both partners.

The contract provided that construction timelines would be submitted, and construction would start no later than January 2010. A draft amendment, presented to the authority in October, would have delayed construction by two to four years if no financing could be obtained. It

---

[506] Atlanta Unfiltered, December 8, 2009. Jekyll Island News Release, December 8, 2009.
[507] Archived documents do not show any payment agreement between the authority and Linger Longer Communities at the time of dissolvement.

also shifted half of the responsibility for the new shopping center to the authority.[508]

By slicing the large-scale development into smaller components, the authority can now open bids to multiple developers; finding financing for smaller bite-sized projects as part of a whole vision will be easier.

It also puts the authority back in charge of its own destiny and timeline. But breaking up such a large-scale project also has its downside. Breaking ground on a twenty-acre beachfront park and constructing a new state-of-the-art convention center without the contractual commitment to construct a designated convention hotel simultaneously is risky business. The authority should remember its struggles after the renovation of the existing convention center when visitors complained about the lack of centralized lodging and the aging hotel infrastructure.

If a partner-developer for a new convention hotel is not found soon, the same scenario may play out again, only this time the price tag is much larger, and so is the debt-servicing burden.

The breakup between the authority and Linger Longer Communities does not affect the groundbreaking and the initial phase of Great Dunes Park, or what is to become the Beach Village that initially still entails retail stores and residential condominiums on the second floor.

Southern Wilderness of Edison, Georgia, is tasked with Phase I of Great Dunes Park, while Thomas & Hutton is overseeing all engineering work in close cooperation with architectural firm HHCP of Maitland, Florida, and landscape architect Glatting, Jackson, Kercher, Anglin of West Palm Beach, Florida.

Since retail stores are an important component, not simply because of the new Beach Village but because they are an integral part of island living and important to visitors, plans are being made to move the stores to temporary facilities just south of the Oceanside Inn & Suites.

Accommodations are made to complete the move by spring 2010 but no later than the third quarter, after which the old shopping center will be demolished to make room for new access roads and the construction of the Beach Village.

The authority still envisions completing the entire project by 2012, including a new convention hotel. The aggressive deadline may be feasible

---

[508] The draft amendment was never signed or approved by the authority.

for the completion of the new convention center and Great Dunes Park, but the other two components may present more of a hurdle than anticipated.

As the prevailing economic conditions were underestimated in 2007 and 2008, the same "cautiously optimistic" forecast for 2010 is used again, this time by Eric Garvey, senior marketing director for Jekyll Island.

While probably influenced by the political announcement that the US recession had "officially" ended in September 2009, credit and liquidity conditions in the financial markets do not improve immediately, thereby still holding a firm grip on new construction and inherent large-scale commercial financing.

The persistent slow growth of the US economy, 0 percent interest rates, and high unemployment make a speedy recovery almost impossible and affect the envisioned completion time of the entire project, estimated at a total cost of $120 million.[509]

It also convinces the authority that an additional revenue source will be needed to support this now self-financed mega project and therefore increases the parking fee from two dollars to five dollars to offset some of the infrastructure cost, at least partially.

As sixty developers descend on Jekyll Island in January 2010 to jumpstart the island's stalled development and revitalization plans, hopes run high that a new developer can be found to quickly deliver one building, a three-hundred-room convention hotel, by early 2012 to coincide with the planned completion of the convention center. But hopes can be as aggressive as they wish to be. The lingering recession, now renamed a "slow recovery," can again dampen the high expectations and delay future development.

Tight credit markets and slow recoveries always tend to burst bubbles, just as it caused the demise of the partnership only a few months before.

It is true that the incentives to partake in oceanfront development and thereby shape the future of Jekyll Island are all present, but if economic circumstances are not favorable, quick and fast development automatically take a back seat.

The authority is encouraged though by the sheer interest of developers and hopes it can at least attract one to build an economy-class hotel on the island, a project that is very high on the authority's wish list.

---

[509] The *Brunswick News*, December 8, 2009.

While construction of Great Dunes Park is moving along, expected to be completed by June 2010, plans are being made to ensure continuation of convention business elsewhere on the island. For that purpose, the Morgan Tennis Center[510] is in the process of being remodeled to become part of the temporary convention center in the Historic District. Next to the Morgan Center, two large tents are to be constructed, one 17,000 square feet, and one 10,000 square feet, together with restroom trailers for men and women, ten chalets of 565 square feet for breakout space, a storage building, and an office trailer.[511]

A new concession stand, Doc's Snack Shop, is added prior to the official opening. The shop is not new construction in the Historic District but rather an expansion of the existing public bathrooms.[512]

The temporary convention center becomes available by the end of September and holds its first large convention in the Historic District on October 9, 2010.

That leaves the relocation of the small businesses in the shopping center. Nine merchants submit their request to be included in the temporary retail space. The one merchant missing is Jekyll Pharmacy. Owner John Waters opts not to relocate and instead closes the only pharmacy on the island prior to the start of summer. A second merchant, Larry Crews's bait-and-tackle business, requests to be relocated to Clam Creek instead. Larry Crews proposes to temporarily place his business under the existing Clam Creek pavilion until he can construct his own new store, adjacent to the pavilion.

His requests are approved in January 2010, upon which the authority also decides to close its own concession stand on the pier. That function will be taken over by Larry Crews once his new store opens for business prior to the summer season.

---

[510] The Morgan Tennis Center was officially renamed the Morgan Center in March 2010 (authority board meeting, March 2010).
[511] Authority board meeting, May 2010. The large tents and temporary facilities were built by Proteus On-Demand Solutions.
[512] Doc's Snack Shop opened in September 2010 on Pier Road as a building extension to the existing public bathrooms. The shop was named after its original and current owner, "Doc" Dougherty (authority board meeting, September 2010).

Although repaving of the parking lot just south of the Oceanside Inn & Suites[513] is underway, cabling and water/sewage connections delay the relocation until after the summer.

Despite some delays, the island seems to be the center of activity during the first nine months of the year, as demolition and new construction seems to be happening in multiple places.

The island also gets a new gasoline station, combined with a convenience store and Dairy Queen restaurant, when a new lease is signed with Flash Foods. The new construction will replace the old gas station and Huddle House and is anticipated to open midyear, depending on environmental mitigation by removing the contaminated soil and installation of the new gasoline tanks.

The only other requirements are that all existing trees on the site are to be retained, the site only gets one entry/exit lane, and that there will be no drive-through window at the new Dairy Queen.

Since remodeling is the name of the game and a large-scale overhaul is underway, the Historic District is not left behind either. Museum Director John Hunter presents his special projects to the authority board:

- Shift the daily presentations to the public to handheld devices, replacing some of the tram-guided tours.
- Remodel the Historic District Museum, including climate control. Cost estimate: $2 million.
- Restoration of Hollybourne Cottage to highlight the process of historic restoration and preservation. Cost estimate: $2.5 million over a five- to ten-year period.

Funding for projects two and three is to be provided by the Jekyll Island Foundation through fundraising.

Amid construction and changes, the island residents are also faced with a major change of their own, namely the proposed residential lease extension.

---

[513] Oceanside Inn & Suites is the current site of the Holiday Inn Resort.

All current residential leases, the earliest one signed in January 1955, expire in 2049.[514] Since the general assembly approved a forty-year extension to the authority to expire in 2089, the authority, together with the attorney general, has been working diligently behind the scenes to prepare a similar extension for island residents.

A simple extension does not seem too complicated to prepare, except that the terms and conditions are being revised at the same time. Moreover, some of the residential leases pertain to multifamily dwellings, hence an acceptable solution must be found in case one of the families decides not to renew the land lease, while the other lessees wish to renew.

Two separate version of a new residential lease agreement are offered:

- The "special" version, to be signed during 2010 and prior to December, takes effect January 1, 2011. The version requires a new lease payment of 0.4 percent of the land value, with discounts for signing during 2010 and for having homestead-exemption status.
- The "standard" version, to be signed after December 2010, takes effect immediately upon signing and requires a lease payment of 5 percent of the land value.

The new terms and conditions represent a big change from current land lease payments, which are based on an annual fixed amount. The new leases use the fair market value (FMV), as determined by Glynn County appraisers, to calculate the annual amount due.

In one aspect, the authority's proposal is in line with the previous change in commercial leases, as applicable to all hotel/motel property, but questionable in the sense that the existing leases do not expire for at least another thirty-nine years.

On the other hand, island residents have benefited from the old model of fixed annual payments without being subject to any inflationary index adjustments; nor have their leases ever been subject to regular extensions with the subsequent price adjustments, as has been the case with commercial leases since 1957.

---

[514] The residential lease expiration had to coincide with the authority's charter that was granted by the state of Georgia for a duration of ninety-nine years. This was stipulated in the Authority Act of 1950.

The residents do not really have much choice but to agree to the new terms and conditions, in exchange for keeping their land leases current. After all, banks and mortgage lenders may not be willing to underwrite or guarantee loans for a potential buyer if the land lease expires in less than forty years.

Complaints about the process and the short time frame given to either agree and sign or decline are heard several times during regular and special informative meetings, but it seems that the actual lease payment calculation, replacing the fixed lease amount, takes a back seat.

In the end, all but six residents[515] agree to sign the new lease agreement prior to year-end, thereby at least benefiting from the reduced annual lease payment of 0.4 percent instead of the inflated 5 percent, as proposed after December 2010.

Redbug Pizza is not immune to a lease revision. The restaurant, operating quietly next to the miniature golf and Great Dunes golf course, seems to have been the only commercial lessee to have escaped the drastic change in 1996. Its current lease is still based on base rent and a percentage of gross revenue. The new lease proposes an increase in rent to fifteen dollars per square foot with no percentage of income. That aligns its lease with all other small business and commercial lessees on the island.

By May 2010, two developers are selected to construct a full-service hotel and a limited-service hotel adjacent to the Beach Village. Jekyll Landmark Associates, owners of the Jekyll Island Club Hotel, is selected for the full-service hotel,[516] while Phelps Development will construct the limited-service hotel in the same vicinity. Winding Road Development of Arizona gets the contract for the Beach Village retail development.

Brasfield & Gorrie (B&G) of Kennesaw, Georgia, is selected as general contractor for the convention center and site-development-related work.

---

[515] The number of residents who declined the new lease is a guestimate at the time of writing. The actual number may well be anywhere between six and fifteen. The specifics and exact location of each land lease are not known (author's note).

[516] The contract provides a payment of $2,000 per acre per month from commencement date to operations date, and $240,000 per year thereafter; 3 percent of gross room revenue up to $8 million; and 4 percent thereafter; 2 percent of gross food and beverage, and 3 percent of other gross revenue (authority board meeting, September 2010).

It seems that the authority's development partners are all aligned and ready to go but not before the official ribbon-cutting of Great Dunes Park on September 20, which also coincides with the opening of the temporary Convention Center-Pavilion space in the Historic District.

To coincide with the grand opening, Blackbeard's Restaurant changes its name to Major Horton's Seafood & Ale House.[517]

The pending demolition of the convention center does present a unique problem. Back in 1974, local artist Esther Lippincott, an early organizer of the Jekyll Island Arts Association, painted several murals in the convention center. Conservation and Preservation Committee Chair Richard Royal asks John Hunter what plans are being made to preserve the murals.

Removing the murals requires special skills, not present among the museum staffers, and will cost $270,000. Instead, Mr. Hunter proposes to document the murals with a large-format camera so that images can be printed in a future convention center display.[518]

Mrs. Lippincott's son, Stanley Stewart Jr., pleads at the same board meeting to preserve the artwork and attempt to remove one mural to see whether preservation is possible.

The question whether the Jekyll Island Foundation would be interested in funding the preservation effort is answered with a stern "probably not," leaving no other option than to seek private capital.

A possible bid to preserve the unique artwork never materializes as the demolition date gets near. The groundbreaking ceremony for the new convention center takes place on December 7, 2010, on top of the rubble of the old center. Despite some delays, the authority still hopes to complete the project by the summer of 2012, at least the completion of the convention center.

The two envisioned hotels and the retail side of the Beach Village may have to wait a little bit longer.

---

[517] The name change was submitted by the authority to the Park's Naming Committee with the request for approval in September 2010. The restaurant was still owned by the authority but was managed by MMI (authority board meeting, September 2010). It is unsure whether the name change was made official since the restaurant was renamed in 2011 and became known as Fins on the Beach (authority board meeting, January 2011).

[518] The proposal never materialized, and to this day no images of the original murals have been on display, nor can they be found in the archives (author's note).

From Millionaires to Commoners

Almost hidden in between the ongoing projects and the collapse of the Linger Longer Communities partnership is the presence of Trammell Crow Co. that still owns the leasehold of two combined sites, namely the Georgia Coast Inn and the Buccaneer Beach Resort.

The company has made no effort to propose design or construction plans for new hospitality development on the two sites, as required by the lease agreement. To remedy the situation, the authority proposes amendments for the ground lease that include an increase in the base rent.[519]

In addition, during the six-month lease extension, several milestones are added as an extra condition, including feasibility reporting, study of financing alternatives, and so on. If these conditions are met, Trammell Crow Co. will be allowed to seek another six-month extension.

If no agreement can be reached after the two extensions, the authority can terminate the leases with a ninety-day notice.

But Trammell Crow Co. is in no hurry to submit design and construction plans. The company is perfectly happy with keeping its options open while it patiently waits to see what type of lodging will be built around the Beach Village and the new convention center. In the meantime, it is happy to pay the required $330,000 base rent.

The reaction is not surprising, given the continuing financial climate and the uncertainty about whether Jekyll Island State Park is ready for new hotel development.

This same uncertainty also plagues the now-closed Jekyll Oceanfront Resort. Leslie Lurken, owner of the resort, decides to close the resort despite his agreement with First Guarantee Bank of Jacksonville to keep the hotel open. As a result, the bank petitions the court to place the property in receivership so that it may be sold once the foreclosure process is complete.

---

[519] The base rent for the Georgia Coast Inn increases from $200K to $214K, while the rent for the Buccaneer Beach Resort site increases from $139K to $149K (authority board meeting, December 2010).

The sudden closure has a negative impact on conventioneers, who now need to find alternative accommodations, but it may also affect owners of the condominiums that have been sold.[520]

The good news is that base rent payments continue to be paid to the authority, despite the foreclosure proceedings and the pending sale, so there is no loss of revenue other than the percentage of gross sales.

That leaves the authority in a difficult situation, as least temporarily, as the new hotels will not open until 2012 or maybe later, depending on financing and development.

The opening of the new Hampton Inn & Suites[521] the previous year is good news but certainly does not make up for the loss of guest accommodations while convention business is supposed to continue as usual.

Design plans for both the full-service hotel and the midprice hotel move along according to schedule, but no financing or hotel brands have been completed yet. The expected completion around midsummer 2012 seems hardly possible unless construction can start in the summer.

The same financing problem plagues Winding Road, the retail center developer. The combination of 46,000 square feet of retail space and sixty-three loft condominiums on the second floor proves to be an impediment for banks to commit financing. It is not the size of the project that makes banks hesitate. It is the presence of condominiums and the illiquid secondary market to sell the units that makes them hesitate.

To resolve the problem, Winding Road agrees to bring a non-US investor on board, which makes matters even more complicated. A non-US investor requires the issuance of EB-5[522] visas through the Economic Development Office, and the application process may delay the project initiation date unless bridge loans can be secured.

---

[520] During the extensive renovation of the original Jekyll Inn, renamed the Jekyll Oceanfront Resort, several guest rooms were converted into condominiums and sold individually.

[521] The Hampton Inn & Suites opened in 2010 in the same location as the original Holiday Inn Beach Resort that was demolished in 2006.

[522] The non-US investor can obtain EB-5 visa status if and when a minimum investment amount is met and a minimum of fifty jobs are created as a result of the investment. After completion, the investor can be granted permanent residency (green card) based on the EB-5 visa issuance.

By September 2011, it is clear that timelines for construction and hotel opening need to be revised. The amendments pertain to not only the Beach Village but also to Landmark Associates, developer for the full-service hotel, and Phelps Development, the midpriced hotel that is pursuing a Hyatt franchise with 135 guest rooms.

The new date for completion of construction is now agreed upon to be June 2013, moving the current schedule by almost a full year.

The consequence of moving the completion time is that Trammell Crow Co. receives the same leniency in its lease extension. The previous six-month extension with strict progress requirements is no longer applicable. In fact, Trammell Crow Co. receives a much more lenient schedule than other developers.

The new deadlines, applicable to the former Buccaneer and Georgia Coast Inn sites, will be:

- November 30, 2013 for schematic design documents for the lots.
- March 30, 2014 for a written development proposal.
- September 30, 2015 for hotel-design documents.
- Failure to produce the required documents by these dates can result in termination of the lot leases on December 31, 2015 …[523]

The authority also prepares to redesign the island's entryway and decides to move the greeting station[524] back to the welcome center on the causeway. Plans for the complete redesign and the construction of three entry lanes will be completed by March 2012.

The roundabout on the east end of the newly redesigned parkway is also in its planning stage, so overall, a lot has been accomplished given the difficult circumstances.

In more or less than one year, Executive Director Jones Hooks and the authority can take credit for the grand opening of the new Hampton Inn & Suites, the revitalization of Great Dunes Park, the construction and opening of a new gas station with convenience store Flash Foods and

---

[523] Excerpt from the authority board meeting, September 2011.
[524] The greeting station was commonly referred to as the tollbooth, which was moved on-island after the new bridge opened in 1997.

Dairy Queen, the construction of a new island corridor, and several small business lease extensions.

Add to this equation a newly found marketing partnership with Young International Beverages, which plans to open a restaurant at the Atlanta Hartsfield/Jackson International Airport to promote Jekyll Island as a "brand name," and one must admit that 2011 is a successful year.

With the new convention center nearing completion, except for interior design and final additions, the authority's Naming Committee submits its first choice of new street names in the Beach Village. The entry will be named Main Street, while a proposal to name the cross street "Convention Way" does not please the developers of the new Westin Hotel. David Curtis, representing Jekyll Oceanfront Hotel, LLC, responsible for the full-service hotel, objects to the name and instead suggests Ocean Way.

The convention center itself also receives specific name assignments. The main ballroom will be "Atlantic Hall," as was the case in the former convention center, while the principal meeting room is renamed the "Ben G. Porter Oceanside Salon."

With this small disagreement out of the way, the authority moves ahead and selects a winning bidder to manage the new convention center.

Previously, the authority had unanimously approved the proposal that the new convention center be operated by a qualified facilities-management group. At the time, Chairman Krueger noted that: "It is the Board's plan to move all Park enterprise functions to private management groups."[525]

SMG of Pennsylvania is the winning bidder.[526] A five-year agreement with the company will cost roughly $475,000, and it is envisioned that the convention center will probably run a deficit in its first two or three of operations, after which the savings in marketing and strategic costs will offset the contract cost.[527]

---

[525] Authority board meeting, January 2011.
[526] The other two bidders were Global Spectrum of Pennsylvania and Venue Works of Iowa (authority board meeting, July 2011).
[527] Alysson Jackson is introduced by SMG Senior VP Greg Caren as the new General Manager for the Convention Center. Freda Brady, regional sales manager based in Savannah, will provide operational, sales, and marketing support (authority board meeting, January 2012.)

CHAPTER 19

THE FINAL CUT

2012–2015

With the successful completion of Great Dunes Park and the near completion of the new convention center, all signs point toward another active and rewarding development and revitalization period for Jekyll Island.

The years of planning, both strategically and developmentally, seem to come to fruition in the final cut and push to reinvent the island after all. But some plans are meant to be changed, altered, or cancelled altogether, as financing for such large-scale projects is still trepid and complex in the depleted liquidity world of commercial finance.

Once the new convention center opens its doors in April 2012 through a soft opening, island hotel accommodations become a problem, given that no new hotels have been constructed, the planned convention hotel has been delayed by at least one year, and the three hotels[528] remain offline.

This forces Eric Garvey, senior marketing director, to look elsewhere for conventioneer lodging. He successfully secures eight hotels off-island[529]

---

[528] The Jekyll Island Clarion Resort closed in 2011, the Georgia Coast Inn was demolished in 2005, and the Buccaneer Beach Resort was demolished in 2007. The three hotels total over six hundred rooms.

[529] Exit 38 on I-95 features several hotels: Courtyard by Marriott, Hampton Inn & Suites, and Holiday Inn. All became partners in the Housing Bureau in 2012. To this day, conventioneers still use the hotels, as room rates are more attractive compared to on-island rates.

to partner in the park's Housing Bureau to compensate for the possible shortfall once the convention center is fully operational.

The planned Westin Hotel, a full-service hotel designated to become the convention hotel, is still in the financing stage. Davis Curtis of Landmark Associates, one of the partners to construct the Westin Hotel, confirms that completion date is still on target for February 2014 but that the bankers[530] are still negotiating a loan guarantee with the US Department of Agriculture that is crucial to complete the financing.

The USDA underwriting is tied into the application for State of Georgia Tourism Tax Credits[531] and delays the entire finance project for several months until the authority comes to the rescue with the establishment of the Jekyll Island State Park Tourism Fund.

The new fund is the brainchild of Executive Director Jones Hooks, who proposes to use 30 percent of the "bed tax"[532] and divert the collected monies directly into the new fund.

According to Georgia state law, 60 percent of the collected bed tax may be used to cover associated costs (i.e., tourism development and related projects). To this date, Jekyll Island has never used the bed tax in such fashion, but Jones Hooks sees an opportunity to allocate the proposed 30 percent to advance the delayed development, since it is tourism and revenue related.

His proposal to the authority on September 24, 2012, indicates the reason, purpose, and the qualification criteria for use of the funds:

> It is now proposed that in FY2014, for the purpose of stimulating development projects in the Park that would substantially increase tourism income, up to 30% of the bed-tax monies would be used. Fundable projects must meet the qualifying criteria:
>
> - They must result in income from future bed taxes.

---

[530] PNC Bank is financing the construction of the Westin Hotel. The bank also financed the Hampton Inn & Suites in 2010.
[531] http://www.georgia.org/competitive-advantages/tax-credits/investment/.
[532] Jekyll Island charged a 5 percent bed tax.

- They must represent new investment in the tourism business in the Park.
- They must promote convention business in the Park.

The funds could cover multi-year projects. Application would be made by fundable business planners in July, and the Authority would make funding decisions by October. The proposed program has been reviewed by the State's Attorney General's office.[533]

The authority board approves the proposal unanimously, with the comment that the tourism fund will help making Jekyll Island State Park financially self-sufficient, as required by law, and while it is unclear how the funds will be used at this time, it is possible the tourism fund may be used to help fund the Westin project.[534]

The proposed retail center at the Beach Village does encounter its own set of problems. Winding Roads Development, responsible for construction of the Beach Village, cannot obtain financing despite several months of negotiations. The underlying problem is the presence of several residential condominium units in the development plan, and banks are reluctant to finance the project given the less-than-favorable market conditions in the residential real estate market.

The authority decides to terminate the contract with Winding Roads Development, raising serious concerns about the future of the Beach Village. It also impacts the construction of the Westin Hotel that is relying on near completion of the retail center when it plans to open for business in mid-2014.

PNC Bank had previously indicated three specific conditions for funding the Westin Hotel:[535]

1. A loan guarantee from USDA

---

[533] Authority board meeting, September 24, 2012.
[534] Chairman Kruger's remarks and comments after acceptance of the proposal (authority board meeting, September 24, 2012, transcripts).
[535] Authority board meeting, May 21, 2012.

2. Approval of the project under the Georgia Tourism Development Act
3. Assurance of completion of the Retail Center in the Beach Village prior to completion of the Westin Hotel

The only other component of this mega-project is the midpriced hotel, envisioned to be a Hyatt limited-service hotel and to be developed by Phelps Development, which still seems on track despite some changes.

The Chhatrala Group,[536] contracted by Phelps Development to construct the midsize Hyatt Hotel, cannot complete its financing and is terminated as a project partner, another setback in the grand scheme of things. Ultimately, the Phelps Development Group selects two new partners for the project in November 2012. Spherical Energy and Environmental Systems LLC (SEES) and Provartis AG, a Swiss financing company, take over the responsibility for financing and developing the Hyatt.[537] The goal is to open the hotel by the end of 2013 or early 2014, with a financial closing date set at December 31, 2012. Both parties reserve the right to terminate the contract should closing fail to occur before the deadline.

The hotel will also receive $1.5 million from the new tourism development fund.

It seems that the entire mega-project is built on so many contingencies and interdependencies that somehow one development is waiting for the completion or commitment from another piece of the construction puzzle; one must wonder which of the developers will actually break ground first.

Things become even more complex and complicated when Landmark Associates, through David Curtis, proposes to build three additional vacation accommodations buildings with a total of thirty-nine rental units as an extension of the Jekyll Island Club Hotel.[538] The new hotel accommodations will be constructed on the south side of the Westin Hotel and will have a separate check-in desk and guest parking.

---

[536] The Chhatrala Group is based in San Diego and operates hotels across the US.
[537] SEES will become the primary leaseholder as SEES Jekyll Island Hotel LLC (authority board meeting, November 19, 2012).
[538] The buildings would originally be called the Club Hotel at the Beach (authority board meeting, April 23, 2012).

Despite the complexity of managing yet another hotel project, the authority is not averse to the request but wants assurances that one does not interfere with or delay the completion of the other. The completion of the Westin Hotel is paramount to the future success of the convention center and the Beach Village. Any possible delay caused by a parallel project would be detrimental.

The authority is adamant that the proposed deadlines should be adhered to. Given that the financing of the Westin Hotel is dependent on the completion of the Beach Village, as per the previous PNC Bank mandate, the authority decides to take on the retail center's construction themselves. The plan is to build the center in multiple phases, starting with the sectors closest to and furthest from the beach.[539]

Financing is obtained from the One Georgia Authority[540] in the amount of $4 million, which covers two-thirds of the estimated $6 million project cost. The loan is approved by the Georgia State Financial and Investment Commission, after discussions with the Governor's Office and the State Office of Planning and Budget.

The proposed twenty-year loan does not require repayment until the retail center reaches a "stable point of revenue" or ten years after closing date. The first condition for repayment seems ambiguous and open for interpretation, while the second one constitutes a free loan for at least ten years.

Given the financial commitments the authority is making to push the large-scale project further, it does not come as a surprise that an increase in parking fee is proposed at the June 2012 authority board meeting. The Authority Finance Committee approves an increase in the daily parking fee to six dollars, and a change in the ten-dollar daily bus fee to include all oversized vehicles. The weekly passes will increase to twenty-eight dollars, while the price of annual decals will remain unchanged at forty-five dollars.

The change also coincides with the completion of the new parking fee station by the welcome center. The new multiple-lane entry booths will

---

[539] The two sectors were identified as R1, closest to the beach, and R3, farthest away from the beach (authority board meeting, May 21, 2012).
[540] http://onegeorgia.org/.

not open until the end of the summer and until the collection devices have been thoroughly tested.

With all the turmoil and attention being given to the new island construction, one can easily forget what happens to the empty commercial lots Trammell Crow still holds and the defunct Jekyll Oceanfront Resort, which is still in foreclosure and under the control of First Guaranty Bank of Jacksonville.

Earlier in the year, FDIC sold First Guaranty Bank of Jacksonville to CenterState Bank, who, as the new owner, pursued the sale of the property.

The property is first listed at $7.2 million but does not attract any interested buyers. The price is lowered in May to $6.9 million, and despite the forty-plus prospects and the continued interest of three investors, the property continues to sit idle, while the maintenance cost is surpassing $1 million.

CenterState Bank claims that the delay has been due to the completion and opening of the convention center, but since this issue has now been resolved, a property sale will be imminent, and the property will be under contract within the next sixty days. The current price will be reduced further, and the bank is willing to offer financing to any potential buyer.[541]

In August, the FDIC authorizes CenterState Bank to lower the asking price for the Jekyll Oceanfront Resort from $6.2 million to $5 million.[542]

Trammell Crow Co., who still owns the land leases on the lots of the Buccaneer Beach Resort and the Georgia Coast Inn, did not stand idly by when completion deadlines were renegotiated for the Westin Hotel, the Hyatt Hotel, or even the Beach Village.

By the end of the year, Trammell Crow Co. requests a lease modification for both lots that will allow them to submit schematic documents by November 2015 and design development documents by September 2018. The proposal will immediately delay any design or construction by three years, which the authority views as unjustified.

The original plans included a $120 million project, called Canopy Bluff, that would feature 301 rooms, 127 condominium units, a conference center,

---

[541] In 2012, three GSP officers lived on the property to avoid further damage, looting, and thefts (authority board meeting, May 21, 2012).

[542] The original asking price was $7.2 million, reduced to $6.9 million in May 2012, and further reduced to $6.2 million in July (authority board meeting, August 20, 2012).

five swimming pools, a full-service restaurant, and a spa.[543] A second hotel, the Inn and Suites at Georgia Coast, would combine a small inn with thirty beachfront cottages. The plans were subsequently revised in 2009 because of the financial crisis, and the two projects were combined into one.

Pending development, Trammell Crow Co. continues to pay $330K for the annual land lease. The authority takes no action but tables the proposal until early 2013.

By the end of the year, the Jekyll Beverage Center becomes the first approved commercial lessee of the proposed Beach Village. Other business categories, such as restaurants, spa and beauty shops, snack shops, clothing stores, and general merchandise are under consideration. The concerns about the island's only grocery store, IGA, are easily addressed when the announcement is made that Marty Fender sold his interest to Steve and Leigh Baumann in September 2012. A new license agreement, approved that same month, facilitates the new owners' application for designated space in the retail center.[544]

Construction of the two phases, R1 and R3, are expected to begin in March 2013, with a completion date of early 2014.[545]

As the new year moves in quickly, only good news seems to come ashore. Jekyll Landmark Associates receives permission from the authority to lease an additional 1.95 acres adjacent to the Westin Hotel construction site, bringing the total beachfront acreage to 6.42 acres. That doesn't mean that the design and construction plans are not subject to board approval, but the approval guarantees at least the land lease.[546]

A second announcement that Oceanside Inn & Suites will be gutted to its structural bones and replaced with a Holiday Inn Resort certainly brings hope and positive news. The $16 million makeover coincides with

---

[543] The *Brunswick News*, January 9, 2013.

[544] A *Brunswick News* article started the rumor that Marty Fender would cease to operate the IGA store and was looking for a potential buyer, hence the concern.

[545] By April 2012, ten local retailers had expressed interest in commercial space at the Beach Village. Forty to fifty other retailers from Savannah to Amelia Island and the Atlanta area also considered joining the Beach Village (authority board meeting, April 23, 2012).

[546] The original idea for construction included three three-story buildings with guest rooms, similar to the JICH suites, a swimming pool, and a small lawn for events (the *Brunswick News*, January 23, 2013).

the official announcement of a groundbreaking date for the long-awaited Westin Hotel, set for April 15.

The deteriorated Oceanside Inn & Suites, originally known as the Wanderer, has not seen such a major renovation since it was first constructed in 1957 as one the island's first hotels.[547] The exterior architectural design will remain intact, as will the original footprint. Other than that, the Holiday Inn Resort will be a brand-new hotel, featuring 155 rooms, a fitness center, swimming pool, and meeting rooms.

But the good news doesn't quite stop there, as the southern end of the island receives its own upgrade.

Following a visit by Gov. Nathan Deal, the newly elected authority chair, Richard Royal, announces a $12 million upgrade of the 4-H Center. The new center gets a new name and new owner, as the authority assumes responsibility from UGA Cooperative Extension Services, although the university will continue to run programs there.

The new facility is temporarily named the Jekyll Island Children and Youth Center and includes a new education building, dormitories, a new auditorium, and other new buildings, set within extensive ground improvements.[548]

But the highlight of the year must be the controversy surrounding the new Jekyll Island Master Plan and the revisions that both the authority and its multiple task forces have been working on since early 2012. The authority expected to finalize and approve the revisions by the end of last year, but differences of opinion between the authority board and members of the "65/35 Task Force" result in submitting the proposal to the Attorney General's Office for a final ruling.

The dispute centers around the question of whether the authority is adhering to the Coastal Marshlands Protection Act, established in 1970, and the 1971 amendment of the Authority Act, which limits development

---

[547] The first motel constructed on Jekyll Island was Jekyll Estates, later known as the Beachview Club Resort, just north of the Wanderer.

[548] The original 4-H Center buildings were the remnants of the Dolphin Motor Lodge and the St. Andrews Auditorium, all dating to the mid-1950s. All original buildings were demolished, including the Beach Pavilion, St. Andrews Auditorium, and Dolphin Motor Lodge.

on Jekyll Island to 35 percent of the total landmass above mean high tide (MHT).[549]

The 65/35 Task Force determines that the authority has overdeveloped the island by 3 percent (i.e., only 62 percent remains undeveloped instead of the mandated 65 percent). The authority, on the other hand, insists that according to the latest 2006 Jekyll Island Development Plan, it can still develop 106 acres or 3 percent.

The calculations are based on the question of whether marshland is actually considered land. As simple as this question may seem, the answer has far-reaching consequences for the future development on the island, not because the authority is considering building new hotels on marshland but because the attorney general's ruling will ultimately determine the total landmass of Jekyll Island, possibly including marshes, and therefore impact the 65/35 rule.

A ruling in favor of the authority means that an additional six hundred acres can be developed, even within the mandated restrictions of 35 percent developable land, and that is where the shoe doesn't quite fit the foot anymore.

The authority insists that the new development, planned, under construction, or soon to be undertaken, does not affect the imposed limit since none of the new construction is taking place on previously undeveloped land. That includes Great Dunes Park, the convention center, and the soon-to-be-constructed Westin Hotel, Hyatt Place, and the Beach Village.

Bob Krueger, former chairman and authority board member, offers a solution for the potential problem by suggesting using the exact amount of acreage available for development, rather than using percentages of total acreage.[550]

If only this methodology had been used since the 1971 Authority Act amendment, this dispute would never have materialized, nor would it have been covered so extensively in the local media.

In June 2013, Attorney General Sam Olens rejects the findings and conclusion of the task force, a clear victory for the authority.

"Excluding 'marsh' from Jekyll's measurement would constitute an inappropriate alteration of the statutory language," Mr. Olens writes in his opinion.[551] He effectively bars the authority from adopting a smaller

---

[549] Ga. L. 1971, p. 452 (Act No. 427).
[550] The *Brunswick News*, May 21, 2013.
[551] The Associated Press, June 27, 2013.

acreage but suggests that additional public input is appropriate, leaving the door open for further discussion or alternative suggestions. "The practical effect of our opinion is the status quo. Normally we would just answer the legal question. But we feel Jekyll Island is so important, additional public input is appropriate before any major change gets made."

The authority does agree to classify the island's golf course ponds, dirt roads, and bike trails as developed land, while all were previously considered undeveloped.

While important, Mr. Olens's opinion does not equate to law, and the final decision can be made only by the general assembly, which is exactly where supporters to protect Jekyll Island from unbridled development will take the fight next.

The acreage of developable land and the 65/35 rule are not the only points of contention on Jekyll Island.

As soon as ground is broken for the Westin Hotel, questions arise about the USDA guarantee for two loans, totaling $15 million.[552] Dan Chapman's article questions whether the USDA can underwrite commercial loans for upscale hotels that are built in a state park, and whether this falls within the legal mandate of the US Department of Agriculture altogether.

Quinton Robinson, head of USDA's Rural Development Office in Georgia, believes the Westin Hotel fits the agency's rural eligibility requirements. But even USDA is not sure what the term "rural" really means. Depending on the type of loan program, a rural community can be defined as 2,500 residents or less, or 20,000 or fewer, or even 50,000 or fewer. There is plenty of room for interpretation and apparently plenty of applicable loan programs to match the varied degree of "rural."

In the strict sense of the law, Jekyll Island qualifies for USDA loan programs based on the number of residents, but the fact that the island is a state park and the development in question is an upscale luxury hotel raises some serious questions.

David Kyler, executive director of the Center for a Sustainable Coast, explains in the same article, "It is a perversion of the federal program to use those funds for an oceanfront hotel at a state park. Between the government subsidies and the lease breaks, the hotel developer is playing the state and federal agencies for a sucker to make extra profit."

---

[552] The *Atlanta Journal-Constitution*, August 4, 2013.

Besides the disputed USDA loan, Jekyll Landmark Associates, through its banker PNC bank, previously tried to obtain a special tourism tax break as well, but Gov. Deal halted the plan, calling it unfair to competing hotels.

The authority, however, comes up with roughly $7 million in bed tax revenue it earmarked for its new tourism fund and other financial incentives that are spread over a decade—not to mention the $4 million received from the One Georgia Authority to finance the construction of the Beach Village and the $40 million in state funds to construct the new convention center.

The incentives are justifiable according to the authority. Without the extra financing and the incentives, Jekyll Island cannot grow and develop enough to remain financially self-sustainable, and the foreseeable revenue growth for the next ten years is predicted to be greater than the initial investments. Hence, the investments and subsidies create a good return on investment and are warranted. It also serves as a catalyst for more private investments and further commercial development.

It is not unusual for the Westin Hotel to become such a target of scrutiny. It just happens to be the first major luxury hotel being constructed on the island in the past thirteen years, or even the past forty years if size is taken into account.

And the size is what triggers the next dispute in the newspapers, both locally and in the Atlanta area.

Without dispute, the Westin Hotel is labeled as the tallest structure on Jekyll Island, reaching sixty-seven feet in height. It is also the tallest building on the barrier islands, nearly double the allowable height on Tybee Island and 50 percent taller than any beachfront property allowed on St. Simons and Sea Island.[553]

The height is within the authority's height restrictions as per its 2008 height and design ordinance, set at seventy-two feet. The proposed and adopted height at the time was motivated by the exact height of the Jekyll Island Club Hotels' turret that sits atop the presidential suite.

Concerns are also voiced about the lighting restrictions for beachfront properties, since both the Westin Hotel and the Beach Village are not only constructed in close proximity to the beach but also dominate in height.

---

[553] The *Atlanta Journal-Constitution*, September 19, 2013. Excerpt from Atlanta Forward blog, moderated by Tom Sabulis and submitted by David Kyler.

And then there is always the question about affordability on Jekyll Island. Gov. Melvin E. Thompson's promise to keep the island open and affordable to all Georgians still resonates with the island residents. That promise now seems to come under threat with new and luxurious guest rooms, a sharp contrast with the old hotels.

Then again, what was once affordable was also deemed dilapidated, hence the multitude of complaints and the authority's promise to force the hotel owners to renovate. The result was foreclosures and demolitions of the old, and construction of the new, which comes with different pricing levels in comparison.

As construction of the Westin Hotel is underway and debates about subsidizing hotels or recalculating the island's total acreage continue, the envisioned construction of the Hyatt Place, the midsized, limited-service hotel, comes to an abrupt halt.

Spherical Energy and Environmental Systems (SEES), together with Provartis AG, had assumed Chhatrala Group's responsibility for managing the new hotel, once open.

Now this deal falls through, as SEES cannot obtain financing for the project, and another little piece of the revitalization plans dies. Phelps Development Group must find yet another new partner/operator to replace SEES, the second time since signing its development intention with the authority in 2010.

But Phelps Development is not alone in its struggles. CenterState Bank, owner of the closed Jekyll Oceanfront Resort, is unable to find a buyer for the property despite a drastic reduction in asking price. The authority weighs its options and considers enforcing the foreclosure provision in the hotel's lease agreement. The agreement provides that the owner, CenterState Bank, must operate a hotel on the site during the terms of the lease. Since this is not the case, the authority can find the owner in default of the lease and commence foreclosure proceedings.

The debate over development limits on Jekyll Island and the disagreement about the island's total acreage continues well into the new year. With the proposed new master plan, as implemented in 1996 and amended in 2006, also comes the necessity to include exact measurements upon which the original 65/35 rule, as legally adopted in the 1971 law, can be calculated.

From Millionaires to Commoners

With multiple commercial developments in progress and several more envisioned in the near and even distant future, the calculations become increasingly important, hence the furious debate between the authority, environmental groups, residents, and lawmakers.

Rep. Mark Hamilton finally proposes House Bill 715 in the House Natural Resources Committee for discussion. His proposal is based on the authority's acceptance that only 1,675 acres of Jekyll Island can be developed,[554] leaving 66 acres available for future development, of which only twenty acres can be used for commercial development.

This is a big change from any previous and historic development calculations and certainly a big step forward to accurately measure and limit development, be it commercial or residential, in the future.

Previously, the 65/35 percent rule was applied, meaning that prior to any exact number of remaining acreages, one first must agree on the total island acreage. That has always been the dispute between developers and environmentalists since the results vary based on the methods used to survey the total landmass. Add to the equation the dispute about whether marshland is to be defined as actual land, and one understands the conundrum.

In the early years, the original standard was set at 50/50 and later changed to 65/35. Now it seems that exact acreage will replace the vague percentages, if HB 715 passes the House.

If the proposal passes both the House and the Senate, only seventy-eight acres can be developed, of which twelve acres are already earmarked for expansion of the campground. The question is not only whether common ground and agreement can be found but also whether this proposal will be final and not subject to future amendments.

It is hard to predict what politicians do and even harder to predict what they may or may not do in the future, but the authority chair, Richard Royal, assures, "As long as I am chair and as long as I am on the Jekyll Island Authority, we'll never ask for any more."[555]

---

[554] The Jekyll Island Master Plan of 1996 determined the island's total acreage to be 4,226 acres. When the new master plan was proposed in 2012, the authority measured the total acreage of the island to be 5,530 acres by adding marshland. The new acreage would have allowed the authority to develop an extra six hundred acres.
[555] *Savannah Morning News*, January 22, 2014.

His statement is in response to Rep. Debbie Buckner's question during a subcommittee meeting: "Does that mean we can take it to the bank that 1,675 acres is going to be developed land on the island and you won't be coming back for any more?"[556]

On April 14, Gov. Nathan Deal signs both House Bill 715[557] and Senate Bill 296[558] at the Great Dunes Park beach pavilion in the presence of a very appreciative crowd.

So many times, Jekyll Island has been at serious crossroads when it comes to development. This swift bill approval and signing may indicate whether a specific road has been chosen and whether the road will continue to be traveled by future authority members.

And while the signing is indeed a milestone, other issues still remain to be addressed and solved, such as density, affordability, and height restrictions.

The authority addresses the height restriction issue in June 2014 when it lowers the maximum height limit for buildings from seventy-two feet to forty-five feet. The new limit matches the Glynn County height limit but is still ten feet higher than the allowable height on Tybee Island.

Nevertheless, the amended height restriction is welcomed and appreciated, even though it comes after the development of three more hotels is approved.

Trammell Crow Co., which has been holding on to its land leases of the demolished Georgia Coast Inn and Buccaneer Beach Resort, receives approval to build three oceanfront hotels on both combined lots.[559]

The company intends to build a Courtyard Marriott with 210 rooms and a Springhill Suites, featuring 150 rooms. In addition, a third 175-room, full-service hotel, yet to be named, is planned at a later stage.

Both lots have now been vacant since 2007 and 2011 respectively, and while multiple proposals had been made to construct cottages or condominiums, neither project materialized due to financing complications.

---

[556] Savannah Morning News, January 22, 2014. Rep. Buckner was one of the most ardent development opponents.
[557] http://www.legis.ga.gov/Legislation/en-US/display/20132014/HB/715.
[558] http://www.legis.ga.gov/Legislation/en-US/display/20132014/SB/296.
[559] The total acreage for both lots is 15.5 acres.

The investments total is $88 million, of which $32 million is reserved for the Marriott hotel, $24 million for the Springhill Suites, and the remainder for the last luxury hotel.

Each hotel will be four stories high and will meet the fifty-four-foot maximum allowable height,[560] lower than the Westin Hotel but still nine feet higher than the new height limit.

In exchange for the new development and to help construction get started as soon as possible, Trammell Crow Co. requests and receives a 50 percent reduction in annual land lease payments.[561]

The news also coincides with ongoing renovation work on the north side of the island. The Oceanside Inn & Suites, under a $20 million complete makeover, is progressing as planned and is expected to be completed by early 2015.

The adjacent restaurant, to be named The Jekyll Island Beach House, will open at a later date. It was originally envisioned to simply renovate the existing restaurant, but unanticipated problems led to the total demolition of the old structure.[562] A brand-new restaurant and meeting rooms will be constructed once the new Holiday Inn Resort is open for business.

During renovation, a small pond was found underneath the kitchen floors and foundation, hence the need for total demolition. It is believed that this was the original location of the Beach Pond, which was covered with sand from the dunes in 1953 to construct the roadbed for Beachview Drive.[563]

That would explain the complete demolition of the original structure in order to stabilize the grounds and rebuild the foundation.

---

[560] The height restriction of fifty-four feet applied to any oceanfront construction outside of the Beach Village and the central business district around the convention center.

[561] Trammell Crow Co. paid $330,000 annually as land lease payments. The authority granted a 50 percent reduction to $150,000 for the duration of the construction (*Georgia Times-Union*, April 22, 1014).

[562] The old restaurant building once housed Denny's Restaurant and Pizza Inn.

[563] Archived materials point to the existence of the Beach Pond, about half the size of the Horton Pond, in this specific location. The same documents mention that "a beachfront pond was filled in with sand to construct Beachview Drive and to dry out the land for commercial development in 1957 (Jekyll Estates) and 1959 (The Wanderer)" (minutes of the authority board meetings, 1950–1957).

A little further north, the Jekyll Oceanfront Clarion Resort that has been bank owned for several years finally receives two proposals to develop the property. The authority selects Carolina Holdings Inc., Greenville, South Carolina, preapproved by CenterState Bank, to take over the land lease and submit design proposals.

Instead of trying to renovate the abandoned hotel structures, the new owner proposes to demolish the resort and construct ninety-eight cottage-style town homes and seventy garden apartments. The new development is called The Cottages at Jekyll Island and Oceanfront Apartments at Jekyll Island.

The first eight cottages are expected to be finished by December 2015, with phased-in completion in December 2016 and 2017. The apartments will be finished by May 2016.

Ultimately, the initial plans for mixed-use change, and the apartments are eliminated altogether to make room for more cottages.[564] The change is due to the high demand, given that this is the first new residential development on the island in forty years. By early 2015, Parker-Kaufmann Realtors, acting as property and rental management company, receives one hundred paid reservations. Despite the fact that none of the reservations are binding, the overwhelming interest leads to a change of plans.

Although the initial development plans for mixed use of the lot and the design plans were approved by the authority and the main reason for selecting Carolina Holdings Inc. as the new land lease holder, the authority allows the change to take effect despite the specific language in the land lease agreement. The omission of seventy garden apartments also eliminates the potential for low-income and affordable housing on the island, a concept that was highly desirable, specifically for the local workforce in the hospitality industry.

---

[564] The original plans for ninety-eight cottages and seventy apartments changed early 2015. The new plan eliminated the apartments altogether and called for 120 cottages to be constructed.

The projected revenue stream from 120 cottages instead of ninety-eight, including sales commissions and bed taxes,[565] is the main argument that convinces the authority to approve the change in design.

But rapid growth also comes with renewed fears of the impact on quality of life for the residents, not to mention traffic, parking problems, cost of living, and change of lifestyle.

Overall, the growth and development of the island is viewed as positive, as tourism is needed to cover the cost of providing municipal infrastructure and to pay for the continued maintenance and beautification of the island, all under the umbrella and mandate of being self-sufficient (i.e., economically viable).

Controlled growth is a necessary evil according to some residents, even if it spoils some of the quietness and the natural beauty.

The reaction is not surprising. Since the late nineties, residents have witnessed declining numbers of visitors, dilapidating or closed-down hotels, and complaints about the status of affairs on the island. Hoping that the turn of the century would hold promise of rehabilitation and renovation that would bring in a breath of fresh air, residents were disappointed again with the consequences of an economic recession and investors fleeing Georgia's Jewel, waiting for better times to come.

Now that the economic tide has turned, the change and multitude of new construction, including large-scale development, a new convention center, a seemingly out-of-scale Westin Hotel, and a Beach Village, all within three years, is a lot to absorb and get adjusted to, even if it is ultimately for the better.

Add to this the change in structure and visual appearance in comparison to the late 1950's and 1960's look, and one can understand that Jekyll Island is going through more than just a simple rejuvenation.

This is a total extreme makeover and resembles Pink Floyd's finale of "The Final Cut," as it summarizes the aftermath of the transition.

---

[565] The authority received an agreed-upon percentage of every sale in addition to the regular bed tax based on rental income. The archival documents do not specify the exact percentage, but using the same formula as the Villas by the Sea condominium conversion, the percentage is probably 1 percent or more.

> **"Two Suns in the Sunset"**
> … finally I understand
> the feelings of the few
> ashes and diamonds
> foe and friend
> we were all equal in the end …[566]

But the change is not finished yet, and more plans surface as the economic tide continues to favor investments.

In January 2015, Shan Pollachi purchases the Beachview Club with the intent to completely refurbish the thirty-eight-room hotel. The original structure dates to 1957,[567] and the last remodeling was already five years ago.

The $2.8 million renovation entails a complete makeover of the guest rooms, the addition of a business center in the lobby, a new breakfast bar, cooking area, and extra guest seating. Outside, a new tiki bar will be added, and the new owner plans to add cocktail hours as well.

The original exterior structures will remain intact, and while they will receive a much-needed facelift, no additions or alterations are planned.

The plans go hand in hand with the major renovation of the Holiday Inn Resort and the planned construction of the Jekyll Island Beach House next door.

The resort is still on target to open by March, at least with ninety-five guest rooms, with a new coffee/cocktail bar, Northshore Coffee & Cocktails, on the third floor and a cabana bar and grill, the Rusty Anchor,[568] alongside the pool.

As guest rooms are completely renovated with a nautical theme, one original room feature is discovered and incorporated in the new theme. The beamed ceilings, dating back to the original design of the Wanderer,[569] are left exposed in the refurbished rooms.

---

[566] "The Final Cut," Pink Floyd, 1983, was the final chapter of their well-known album *The Wall*.

[567] The original motel, Jekyll Estates, built in 1957, was the very first motel on Jekyll Island.

[568] The name changed to "The Anchor" in 2017.

[569] The design dates to 1959 when the Wanderer was constructed. The beamed ceilings were covered up with dropped ceilings that were installed during previous renovations.

The brick wall that surrounded the swimming pool of the Oceanside Inn & Suites is replaced with a glass wall to allow for ocean view from the pool and the guest rooms.

It is not just the island's commercial side that undergoes major changes. The state park, and specifically the Historic District, comes up with big plans to contribute to the new island look when the authority approves the complete renovation of the Jekyll Island Museum. The museum, both its interior and its permanent historic exhibit, has not changed since 1982, and a complete makeover seems appropriate.

The new name for the museum is the Jekyll Island Mosaic. The decision paves the way for the Jekyll Island Foundation to start one of its largest fundraising campaigns since its existence, as it seeks to raise more than $3 million for the ambitious project.[570]

Executive Director Dion Davis starts off the campaign with $400,000 in pledges, and the authority commits $500,000 to the renovation of the museum. The remainder will be raised through a request for funding from the Robert W. Woodruff Foundation and private donations.

The renovation plans include:

- Renovating and redesigning the interior while maintaining its historic structure and character.
- Creating a modern lobby with a convenient welcome desk and iconic visual mosaic stations.
- Combining the island's natural and cultural history in the main exhibit area with a mini-nature walk and boardwalk inside, along with exhibits of historic events, people, and cultures.
- Installing hands on learning stations throughout the facility, as well as virtual Red Bug driving and quail hunting exhibits, photo ops, Voices from the Past stations, and video recording booths.
- Expanding the retail area.
- Adding an indoor multi-purpose room and an outdoor stage; walking and audio guides; family activity kits; child collection cards and stickers.

---

[570] The first large fundraiser was for the Georgia Sea Turtle Center in 2006, when the Jekyll island Foundation raised $2.6 million.

- Installing smart phone apps to use throughout the historic district ...⁵⁷¹

It is a very ambitious plan that will not be set in motion until 2017 when the museum closes its doors temporarily to the public and the historic guided tours are moved to the old infirmary cottage.⁵⁷²

As one memory of the seventies disappears, a new hotel finally opens its doors. The Jekyll Island Clarion Resort is ready for demolition once the new owners conclude their massive yard sale. Anything and everything from beds, guest room furniture, TV sets, and even pizza ovens are offered for sale to anyone interested. Once the yard sale concludes after thirty days, the buildings are demolished, and the grounds are prepared for the construction of The Cottages at Jekyll Island.

The new and imposing Westin Hotel opens its doors to the public with an official ribbon-cutting ceremony on April 20, 2015. Only the second new hotel to open on the island in the last four decades,⁵⁷³ its 187 rooms and thirteen suites are a welcome addition to the depleted guest room availability on the island.⁵⁷⁴

At the same time as the Westin opens for business, the Beach Village welcomes its Phase I shop owners. With 99 percent complete and eight tenants working on the interior build-out, Kennedy Outfitters and Fuse are the first owners to move in, followed by Tanya's, Parker-Kaufmann Realty, the Collection, Jekyll Realty, Club Café, and Whittle's.

Public spaces open on April 13, once the fencing comes down around the construction zones of Phase I.

Phase II is finished by the end of April, and tenants are expected to move in within ninety days, depending on the build-outs.

Once the shop owners complete their move to their new permanent homes in the Beach Village, the temporary trailers at the northern beach parking lot will be removed, the parking surface is to be restored to its original state, and beach access and parking will again take its natural course.

---

⁵⁷¹ *Brunswick News*, January 21, 2015 (excerpt from the article by Donna Stillinger).
⁵⁷² The old infirmary is also known as the Furness Cottage.
⁵⁷³ The first hotel since 1972 to be built was the Hampton Inn & Suites in 2010.
⁵⁷⁴ At the peak of Jekyll Island visitation in the late nineties, there were 1,500 hotel rooms on the island. In April 2015, there were 750 left, excluding the Westin Hotel.

Once officially opened, the business center on the island can finally be viewed in its entirety. The once imposing Westin with its seventy-two-foot height suddenly looks less out of place when surrounded by natural landscapes and the Beach Village. The other side of the retail center is flanked by the new convention center that opens into the newly designed Great Dunes Park that in turn connects to the beach parking adjacent to what once was Fin's on the Beach but has been renamed Tortuga Jack's.[575]

That leaves the space available for a limited-service hotel west of the Westin. Those plans are temporarily put on hold as the authority determines it is time to take a break and digest all the new developments for a while before committing to another commercial project.

This is a wise and careful decision given that The Cottages at Jekyll Island will soon start construction.

But there is also another project that is being proposed and approved by the authority. This time, adjacent to the Hampton Inn & Suites, Jekyll Ocean Oaks proposes to construct thirty-four new luxury homes and a ten-unit condominium building around a pool and clubhouse.

The new proposal replaces the previous one that included a small eighty-eight-room hotel and sixty condominiums just north of the Hampton Inn & Suites.[576]

The project is not considered ocean view but merely oceanfront since the homes will be nestled in between the natural oaks and the existing tree canopy, while providing beach access through boardwalks and viewing platforms that blend into the natural habitat.

Construction is envisioned to begin early 2016 but will eventually be delayed until 2017.

In March, the same company purchased three vacant parcels from Trammell Crow Co. between the Days Inn and the newly approved Ocean Oaks development.[577]

---

[575] Michelle and George Stewart, managers of Slider's Restaurant on Amelia Island and the Village Inn and Pub on St. Simons Island, were selected out of four candidates to manage the former Fin's on the Beach. The new restaurant would become a Baja Mexican restaurant and open early 2015.

[576] The proposal was approved June 15, 2015 (*Brunswick News*, June 16, 2015).

[577] The parcels previously housed the Georgia Coast Inn and the Buccaneer Beach Resort.

Both parcels will remain vacant for the next three years as Jekyll Ocean Oaks, LLC, restructures its current assets and until the planned oceanfront boutique hotel[578] can begin construction next to the Westin Hotel.

From a bird's-eye view, Jekyll Island has seen some drastic changes when compared to the late 1990s. Old hotels have gone and been replaced with new modern accommodations that fit the style and demand of island guests, while others have undergone an extreme makeover.

These dramatic changes take a while to get used to for both visitors and residents. Prior to 2015, Jekyll Island never featured a town center, and certainly not a Beach Village, embraced by a convention center on one side and a designated high-rise convention hotel on the other. The concept takes a little time to find its place on the island.

When the Jekyll Market opens its doors in June 2015, the Beach Village seems complete. A big departure from the customary IGA the island residents have been accustomed to for so many decades, the new island grocery store brings upscale and gourmet food shopping to Jekyll Island for the first time.

Although all the empty spaces are now carefully lit with orange and dim lights, one large corner remains dark. The promised Jekyll Island Seafood Company,[579] to be located on the northeast corner opposite the Westin Hotel, remains absent.

On November 15, 2015, during the Jekyll Island Rededication Weekend, the authority and charter tenants celebrate the official opening of the Beach Village, the convention center, and the Westin Hotel. A dedication plaque is unveiled by board members of the Jekyll Island Authority,[580] and representatives of each of the original shops sign the sidewalk to commemorate the new beginning.

---

[578] The new luxury hotel will be known as the Jekyll Ocean Club and will feature forty ocean-view suites. Construction of the boutique hotel was completed late 2017.

[579] The Jekyll Island Seafood Company will open its doors in 2017 after its original space is reduced by almost half. The remainder of the space will be occupied by other tenants.

[580] https://www.goldenislesmagazine.com/columns/coastal_seen/jekyll-beach-village-opening/article_3ead44da-a4f5-11e5-8cbe-07e065bc85f8.html.

EPILOGUE

The history of Jekyll Island State Park is paved with controversy as much as it is built with ingenuity, persistence, and, above all, love for Georgia's Jewel. I sincerely hope that such sentiments prevail throughout this book.

The noticeable duality of the island and the continuous battle between the state park recreational side and the resort side, as clearly tangible throughout its seventy-year history, is still present to this day.

Time, combined with trial and error, has ultimately led to a peaceful coexistence, although every so often, shots are fired across each other's bow when new development ideas see the light of day. This coexistence for such a long time can best be described as a mutually agreed-upon symbiosis where time has revealed that both sides need each other to be successful and one can no longer exist without the support of the other.

Or maybe it can be viewed as an arranged marriage. Neither party voluntarily chose each other, but after seventy years, a divorce is far more expensive and complicated than trying to work out the differences. Who knows?

It is my opinion that such will always be the case, but that does not necessarily need to be a detriment to the continued development and simultaneous preservation of the island's natural beauty.

At the time of writing, several more construction projects are in progress or have been completed already.

Jekyll Ocean Club, a boutique hotel adjacent to the Westin Hotel, opened in the fall of 2017. The forty-suite hotel is home to the Corsair, an upscale dining facility that is open to the public. The vacant property between the new Jekyll Ocean Club and the Days Inn, previously the home to the South Beach House and later the location of the annual Beach

Music festival, has been repurposed as a public parking area with beach access.

Ocean Oaks, another private development by the previous owners of the Jekyll Island Club Hotel, is currently in progress. Most of the forty luxury private homes have been sold, with the majority of the homes in the final construction phase. The property was previously home to the original Holiday Inn (1972) and has been vacant since the opening of the Hampton Inn & Suites in 2010.

The two vacant lots between the Days Inn and the new Ocean Oaks, once occupied by the Buccaneer Beach Resort and the Georgia Coast Inn, are now owned by Ocean Oaks, LLC, and designated for future hotel development. No time frame for construction has been announced yet, but development should commence in early 2019.

A second convention hotel is to be constructed west of the Westin Hotel, just south of the Beach Village. Preliminary construction of Home2 Suites, a Hilton franchise, started mid-2018.

It is also envisioned that the empty parking lot, south of the Holiday Inn Resort, will receive a complete makeover, including new bathroom facilities. The proposed design will be similar to Great Dunes Park, adjacent to the convention center.

The history of Jekyll Island State Park is never-ending, and changes are meant to continue to occur. Such is the destiny of Georgia's Jewel—forever flexible and adaptable to changing demands, always seeking to meet the demands of the visitor, tourist, or future residents.

Let's hope that Mother Nature continues to guide and inspire those who seek to please the island experience. After all, the greatest public private partnership any entity or authority can ever find is the one between nature and humankind. Let's hope that we can be a reliable partner with Mother Nature as we seek such partnership.

ADDENDUM 1

JEKYLL ISLAND STATE PARK AUTHORITY LEGISLATION[581]

1765. Islands annexed to the province and subject to its law. Jekyl (old spelling) designated a part of St. James Parish. *Digest of the Laws of the State of Georgia,* compiled by Robert & George Watkins, p. 114.

1796. An Act to relieve the heirs of Francis Maria Loys Dumousay de la Vave, the heirs of Hyacinth de Chapadelane and Christopher Poulain Dubignon. Provides for the recording of certain deeds lost at sea. This act helps establish the title to land on the island and explains why the early deeds are missing. *Digest of the Laws of the State of Georgia,* compiled by Robert & George Watkins, p. 592.

1929. Corrects the spelling of Jekyll and reiterates island was named for Sir Joseph Jekyll, a friend of General Oglethorpe. Ga. L. 1929, p. 1505 (Resolution No. 4).

1950. Jekyll Island State Park Authority Act. Defines the powers and responsibilities of the Authority. Ga. L. 1950, p. 152 (Act 630).

---

[581] Legislation, as compiled by the Jekyll Island State Park Authority. Courtesy of Mr. Bruce Piatek, director of historic resources.

1951. Jekyll Island State Park Authority Act. Provides for the Authority to sell and dispose of junk, salvage, obsolete, unused, or surplus materials, machinery, and equipment now or in the future located upon its leasehold and to apply the proceeds thereof to permanent improvements; to provide for and increase the term of said authority's lease, powers, rights, and existence to a term of ninety-nine (99) years. Ga. L. 1951, p. 782 (Act No. 490).

1951. Jekyll Island Bridge. Authorizes the Authority to enter into a contract for the building of a bridge across Jekyll Creek to be operated as a toll bridge. Ga. L. 1951, p. 694 (Act No. 448).

1952. Jekyll Island State Park Authority Act-Amendments. Authority may improve not more than one-half of the highland portion of Jekyll Island and other restrictions. Ga. L. 1952, p. 276 (Act No. 860).

1953. Jekyll Island State Park Authority Act-amended. Authority granted 99-year lease. Authority may improve and lease not more than one-half of the land area of Jekyll island which lies above water at mean high tide. Ga. L. 1953, p. 261 (Act No. 261).

1956. Temporary Jekyll Island Legislative Study Committee created to determine whether it is advisable to make change to the present method of operation and report to General Assembly on or before January 15, 1957. Ga. L. 1956, p. 819 (Resolution No. 152).

1957. Jekyll Island State Park Authority Act-Amendment. Provides for new and different members of the Authority and provides for the Authority to sell and lease certain lots. Ga. L. 1957, p. 608 (Act No. 464).

1959. Authority to Convey Easement to Property in Glynn County. Authorizes the Governor to execute a spoil disposal easement to the U.S. Government. Ga. L. 1959, p. 101 (Resolution No. 4).

1960. Jekyll Island State Park Authority Act-Amendment. Revises the Revenue Anticipation Certificate and Bond Provisions. Ga. L. 1960, p. 89 (Act No. 447).

1963. Recognizes Governor Thompson for purchase of Jekyll Island and states that "Jekyll Island has become the best and soundest investment which the State has ever made ..." Ga. L. 1963, p. 324 (Resolution No. 40).

1963. Jekyll Island State Park Authority Act-Amendment. States in part that income arising out of the operation of the Park "shall be used by the Authority for the sole purpose of beautifying, improving, developing, enlarging, maintaining, administering, managing, and promoting Jekyll Island State Park at the lowest rates reasonable and possible for the benefit of the ordinary people of the State of Georgia." Ga. L. 1963, p. 391 (Act No. 330).

1971. Jekyll Island State Park Authority Act-Amendment. Reduces the maximum amount of land area of Jekyll Island that the Authority is empowered to survey. Ga. L. 1971, p. 452 (Act No. 427).

1972. Executive Reorganization Act of 1972. Assigns the Authority to the Department of Natural Resources for administrative purposes only. Ga. L. 1972, p. 1015 (Act No. 1489).

1976. Jekyll Island State Park Authority Act-Amendment. Franchises Provided. Provides for granting of franchises to utility companies and liberal construction. Ga. L. 1976, p. 1560 (Act No. 1403).

1981. Jekyll Island State Park Authority Act-Amendment. Provides for adopting and enforcing ordinances and resolutions of the Authority. Ga. L. 1981, p. 1436 (Act No. 769).

1983. Authorizes any fire department operated by the Authority to have the powers of a fire department of a county, municipality, or other political subdivision. Ga. L. 1983, p. 643 (Act No. 268).

1983. Brunswick and Glynn County Development Authority-Jekyll Island State Park Authority. Provides the power to Contract One with the Other, etc. Ga. L. 1983, p. 4057 (Act No. 169).

1984. Conservation and Natural Resources-membership of Jekyll Island State Park Authority changed. The most recent of many acts that specify membership in the Authority and the terms. Ga. L. 1984, p. 430 (Act No. 823).

1985. Commissioner of Natural Resources-Powers, Coastal Marshlands Protection Committee. Allows the Commissioner of Natural Resources to delegate his authority and power. Ga. L. 1985, p. 1465 (Act No. 739).

1987. Jekyll Island State Park Authority-Ordinance Violations, Prosecutions: Glynn County, magistrate, State, and Superior Courts, and Jurisdiction. Provides the Authority with legislative power to adopt ordinances and resolutions relating to the property, affairs, and government of Jekyll Island. Ga. L. 1987, p. 1117 (Act No. 736)

1990. Authorities-membership of Secretary of State. Removes Secretary of State from Authority. Ga. L. 1990, p. 872 (Act No. 1220)

1993. Directs the Authority to evaluate the feasibility of involving private contractors in "the development, construction, operation, and management" of projects. Ga. L. 1993, p. 1781 (Act No. 600)

1993. Transfers certain functions to the "Office of Treasury and Fiscal Services" as it relates to the lease of Jekyll Island. Ga. L. 1993, p. 1402 (Act No. 546)

1995. Provides for a Citizens Resource Council for the Authority on matters concerning Jekyll Island and to provide for a master plan of Jekyll Island. Ga. L. 1995, p. 105 (Act No. 10)

ADDENDUM 2

JEKYLL ISLAND ARTS ASSOCIATION[582]

Patricia Bowman. *Origin: The Founding Stories. Celebrating 50 Years.* January 10, 2017.

> The Storyteller's Beginnings. As Tricia Tells It.
>
> It all started in the 1990's when the public library I was working for in Chicago sent me to the international Storytelling Festival in Jonesboro, Tennessee. I was hooked and have been going to that storytelling festival almost every year since. Doing storytelling at the library with young children and families gave me an opportunity to gain experience. Next came a job in a middle school where I was media center director and taught storytelling and literacy to 6th graders. Chicago had a vibrant storytelling Community, so I was able to feed my storytelling habit. I consider myself more of a storytelling listener than a teller but I do love telling a good story.

---

[582] Jekyll Island Arts Association. *Origin: The Founding Story*, January 10, 2017, by Patricia Bowman. Reprinted in its entirety with express written consent and permission.

Preface

In February 1975, the President of the Jekyll Island Arts Association, Mrs. Shaw Benderly asked Mrs. Walter B. Yeager and Mrs. Joseph D. Baird to act as historians. We immediately began collecting data and learned that it is much easier to write, collect and assemble history as it is being made.

The purpose of this history is to give the origin and development of the association. As we look backward over the past 10 years certain events stand out as landmarks on our highway of growth. As history, we measure the progress by the Art Associations worthwhile accomplishments.

The Presidential plaque, a replica of the Charter membership plaque, listing the Presidents and their years of dedicated service, also announced the plan for collecting as much history as possible. The Presidential plaque was finished in June 1975 and hangs next to the Charter membership plaque in the "Goodyear Cottage", our Jekyll Island Arts Association, Inc. Civic Arts Center.

We have gathered the events of the past ten years 1966-1976 into a history of two volumes that we may safely guard them against the forgetfulness of time.

Mrs. Joseph D. Baird (signed Gloria E. Baird)
Mrs. Walter B. Yeager (signed Helen L. Yeager)

Origin

The Jekyll Island Art Association, Inc. had its founding meeting on Sunday evening November 27, 1966 at the home of Mrs. W.T. Carlisle, 10 Austin Lane, Jekyll Island, GA.

Twenty-four members gathered to discuss plans for an Art Association. The evening was full of enthusiasm. Mr. Dewey Scarboro presided over the meeting and explained the purpose of the Art Association, the development of the arts and appreciation.

Our first effort was to obtain the services of an art instructor. Mrs. Carlisle explained that the use of the "old Skeet House" had been given by the Jekyll Island Authority for our use as a Headquarters and a place to have painting classes. The electric bill would be taken care of by the Authority. Mrs. Carlisle said she had plans to meet with Mr. Bill Hendrix and Mr. and Mrs. Scarboro at the home of Mrs. Dade Kelley on the following Tuesday evening. Dates and arrangements with Bill Hendrix would be finalized for a class to begin immediately. Mrs. Carlisle also agreed to have her attorney draw up a charter.

Now the Jekyll Island Art Association was named, founded and officers elected all in one evening.

President-Mr. Dewey Scarboro
Vice President-Mrs. Joseph D. Baird
Treasurer-Mrs. William T. Carlisle
Secretary-Mrs. J.P. Millican
Building Chairman (House)-Mrs. Walter B. Yeager
Publicity Chairman-Mrs. Tallu Fish

It was further decided that the membership would be limited to Jekyll Island and visitors vacationing on the Island. Dues would be five dollars per person, ten dollars per couple. Keys to the building could be obtained from Mrs. Millican for thirty-five cents apiece.

The Art Classes began with eight members, later increased to twelve. You had to become a member of the Association in order to take lessons. Benches were purchased, a place for your easel and a place to sit. In recalling that first winter, Bill Stakely helped cut the grass and built the fires. This had to be substituted with an electric heater. Dewey Scarboro gave us a large electric coffee urn and some cups. A tourist passing, seeing the little cottage with a cozy fire and the aroma of coffee and food and with the painting class gathering would stop and in absolute amazement declare they had never seen anything like it. It was truly "old world". Then when

Bill Hendrix arrived in his plane and landed just across from the Skeet House at the airport, they left shaking their heads. Some of these tourists and visitors would stop by the Authority office in the shopping center, where the bank and post office are now located, and relate to Judge Hartley their adventure in hospitality. Some of these tourist visitors decided to come to Jekyll for the winter season and also to enter the Art Classes. These classes have continued in growth and popularity. Outgrowing the Skeet House location, the classes have moved to the Jekyll Island Hotel for warmth and space. Later in the Presbyterian Church for better light and more space. Bill Hendrix is a wonderful teacher and his knowledge of art history of all phases, ancient and modern is inexhaustible. He has the extraordinary gift of verbal communication and each lecture is fresh and never stereotyped, never dull. Twenty-five members are in the class at present and it will be larger when the winter visitors arrive. There are only three of the original class left still enjoying the classes. They are Bill Stakely, Claudess Walker and Helen Yeager.

We have to admit that an Art Association grew out of an Art Class. Acting as docents for and in the Association, we point with pride to the painting class. It has been self-supporting all the way. Sponsored by the Jekyll Island Arts Association, Inc., we are now proud possessors of easels and equipment given by the Association this year.

On January 12, 1967, a Thursday, at ten o'clock in the morning, President Dewey D. Scarboro presented Judge A.J. Hartley to the group. At this second meeting, Judge Hartley explained "this is the first organization on the Island to be given permission to use a building. The Skeet House could be used for an indefinite period of time. "Perhaps", Judge Hartley said, "until the restoration of the village was completed. He also added that should the time come that the Skeet House could not be used, he would help the Association to find another building. He generously offered his services anytime to our project. The Authority had given the house a fresh coat of paint. We had a headquarters which we had already outgrown. It was a beginning. Judge and Mrs. Hartley were given Honorary Memberships in the Association as a token appreciation for their interest and support.

ADDENDUM 3

FRIENDS OF HISTORIC JEKYLL ISLAND[583]

About 22 years ago, when the JIA decided to save the old "Millionaires Village", the Jekyll Island Museum was formed to preserve this vignette of American History. The need for a strong support group was immediately recognized and The New Jekyll Island Club, Inc. was organized and registered as a 501(c)3 organization in January 1985. At the same time, a group of investors came together and began renovation of the old Jekyll Island Club Hotel. The hotel name and the organization's name soon became a source of some confusion – so we began to call ourselves the Jekyll Island Museum Associates and changed our name to that officially in March 1990. By 1999, the organization's mission had grown, along with the JI Museum's, to encompass all of the historic sites on the island (such as the Horton House etc.). Consequently, on February 1, 1999 we became the Friends of Historic Jekyll Island, Inc. with a mission "to assist in the preservation and interpretation of Jekyll Island, its natural and historical heritage.

From its inception until today, our membership has been mainly Jekyll Islanders (full and part time residents)

---

[583] Source reference: "A Thumbnail Sketch of the Friends of Historic Jekyll Island," by Jean Poleszak, Spring 2006.

and some who simply want to support our endeavors. Our membership has always been open to everyone and now stands at approximately 350 persons.

What have we done during the past 20 years? Here is a list of projects and work in roughly chronological order:

-Helped with DuBignon Cottage restoration and formal opening.
-Helped with restoration of lights on S. Riverview in district.
-Coordinated volunteers for running museum tours for the Museum's first 12+ years.
-Funded first conservation survey of museum furniture.
-Funded staff attendance at State Historic Preservation Conference.
-Sponsored Museum Christmas tours of historic homes in district.
-Helped with Mistletoe refurbishing and reopening party.
-Obtained Fiore Sculpture collection.
-Opened Fiore Sculpture Gallery with cooperation and help of Museum.
-Gave $ to purchase a computer and to help train staff in computer use.
-Gave $ to purchase exhibit cases. (2 or 3 times over the years).
-Partnered with Coastal Museum in purchase of microfiche machine.
-Donated $ and much volunteer time to furnishing and refurbishing Rockefeller Cottage.
-Gave $ and labor for sprucing up of Cherokee Cottage – when it housed Museum offices.
-Gave $ for historic signage.
-Gave $ for faith Chapel projects – two pianos, study of stained-glass windows, restoration of Maitland-Armstrong window and, most recently, new seat and kneeling bench cushions.

-Have funded intern programs in the past and have done so again for the most recent years.
-Restored and furnished DuBignon kitchen.
-Obtained grant and helped fund study for preservation of Horton House.
-Funded restoration of fountain at Villa Marianna.
-Contributed $ to restoration of power house and conversion to GA Sea Turtle Center.
-Have given $ for many museum "incidentals".

Our activities are not "all work and no play". We have always had interesting monthly meetings for the membership and guests. We have sponsored book signings, jaunts to visit other historic places, and fund-raising activities such as "Victorian Days", Day of Croquet, Dinners at the Club, Silent Auctions, etc.

So far it's been a great ride!

ADDENDUM 4

JEKYLL ISLAND HOTELS-MOTELS CHRONOLOGICAL TIMELINE

Jekyll Estates (1957)

First beachfront motel built on Jekyll Island. The first twenty units were completed by June 1958. An additional sixteen units were completed by 1959. The motel was renovated in 1997 and renamed Beachview Club Resort.

Wanderer (1957)

The second motel constructed on the island consisted originally of ninety-six units when it opened in the summer of 1958. By the end of the year, eighty-four units were added.

Motel Properties Inc. purchased the motel in 1970 and renamed it the Comfort Inn Island Suites in 1987. It was renamed again in the early to mid-1990s the Oceanside Inn & Suites until it closed in 2011.

The original outside structure of the Wanderer was kept intact, while the interior was renovated in 2015 and renamed the Holiday Inn Resort.

Dolphin Motor Lodge (1958) (demolished in 2015)

While the original land lease was signed in 1956, construction did not begin until late 1958. The hotel and adjacent Dolphin Club lounge and restaurant opened in July 1959. The authority purchased the buildings in 1960 and leased the hotel, club, and restaurant until June 1966 when it permanently closed.

The original buildings, including the beach house, picnic shelter, and St. Andrews Auditorium were used by the 4-H center until demolition in 2015.

Seafarer Apartments (1959)

Originally built as a twenty-one-apartment complex, the Seafarer became a twenty-one-unit motel shortly after opening. Additional rooms were built in 1965 and again in 1971, bringing the total to seventy-one rooms. The name was changed to the Seafarer Inn & Suites and operated like a large family house until 1984. The complex was renovated in 1999 and renamed the Quality Inn & Suites.

Corsair Motel (1960)

Constructed as the first motel on the south end of the boardwalk, the motel featured 160 rooms. It became known as the Ladha Island Inn in 1980 when the hotel was purchased out of bankruptcy protection. In 1984, the hotel was renamed to the Jekyll Inn & Resort until it was called the Days Inn Jekyll in 1986.

The hotel was renovated extensively in 1999, and the number of rooms was reduced to 124. It has since been known as the Days Inn & Suites.

Sam Snead's Buccaneer Motor Lodge (1961) (demolished in 2007)

Located just south of the Corsair, the motel, sponsored for one year by Sam Snead, originally featured ninety-six units. In 1962, sponsorship ended, and the motel was simply known as the Buccaneer Motor Lodge. The number of rooms increased to 206 with the 1967 and 1969 expansions. It was renamed the Quality Inn Buccaneer in 1985 until another name change in 1990 to Clarion Resort Buccaneer. The hotel was last known as the Buccaneer Beach Resort and demolished in 2007.

Holiday Inn (1961) (demolished in 2005)

Built just south of the Buccaneer Motor Lodge and known for its state-of-Georgia-shaped swimming pool, the hotel had 106 rooms. In 1963, the hotel changed its name to Stuckey's Carriage Inn after state Rep. William Stuckey purchased the property. By 1970, the name changed again to Atlantic Carriage Inn.

After a lengthy title case in superior court, the hotel reopened in 1980 as the Ramada Inn. It was later operated as an independent Georgia Coast Inn. The hotel closed its doors permanently in 2003 and was demolished in 2005.

Sand Dollar Motel (1971) (demolished in 2015)

The motel included 263 rooms and was the largest motel constructed on the island. After several attempts to convert the motel into condominiums, it was operated as the Jekyll Hilton Inn from 1979 through 1987, and from 1992 to 1997 as the Best Western Jekyll Inn.

In 2008, the motel became known as the Jekyll Island Clarion Resort, also later referred to as the Jekyll Oceanfront Resort, until it permanently closed in 2011 and was demolished in 2015. The Cottages at Jekyll Island currently occupy the site.

Holiday Inn Beach Resort (1972) (demolished in 2006)

Opened in 1974 just south of the Atlantic Carriage Inn, the hotel featured 205 rooms. The hotel is the only one that was always known as a Holiday Inn franchise until the building was demolished in 2006.

By-the-Sea Hotel (1973)

Opened in 1974, the hotel could accommodate 176 guests in one- to three-bedroom units. It became a Sheraton By-the-Sea Hotel after bankruptcy filing in 1975 and was ultimately renamed Villas by the Sea in 1981. A conference center was added in 1986, and the hotel was converted into a condominium-hotel in 1989.

Hampton Inn & Suites (2010)

The first new hotel structure to be built on the island since 1974, it replaced the old and demolished Holiday Inn. The hotel has 138 guest rooms and was the only four-story hotel structure until construction of the Westin Hotel in 2015.

Westin Jekyll Island (2015)

The newest beachfront hotel features two hundred guest rooms. With its five-stories-high U-shaped configuration, it is the tallest hotel building on the island, matched only in height by the Jekyll Island Club Hotel's turret.

ADDENDUM 5

M. E. THOMPSON MEMORIAL BRIDGE TIMELINES

1986. Preliminary plans for a new high-rise bridge are discussed. Authority meeting, December 5, 1986.

- Use section of old bridge for fishing recreation area.
- Close section of Riverview Drive between Parkway and Old Village Boulevard.[584]
- Build a new collection station.
- Open Latham River area as part of the bridge construction project.

1987. Letter from Hal Rives, commissioner of Department of Transportation, to Downing Musgrove, member of State Transportation Board (June 19, 1987). The letter states that the numerical rating of the existing bridge is 29.8 and does not meet the Federal Highway Administration's requirement for funding. The current requirement is a rating below 10. The emphasis on a new bridge shifts from an immediate schedule to a schedule for the early 1990s.

1994. Contract for the new fixed-span bridge is awarded to Tidewater Construction Company (August 17, 1994). Preparations have started, and construction will take three years or less.

---

[584] Now known as Stable Road.

1995. Construction of the new bridge is in progress. The dimensions are 2,430 feet in length, 65 feet high. and a 110-foot wide navigational channel. The total cost is $10,107,000.[585]

1997. Completion of the new bridge (August 1997).

---

[585] Eighty percent of the cost is covered by federal taxes and 20 percent by state taxes (authority meeting, September 1994, addendum to the minutes).

BIBLIOGRAPHY

Primary Sources

Archive files of the Jekyll Island Museum. Jekyll Island.

Bagwell, Tyler E. *Jekyll Island. A State Park*. Charleston: Arcadia, 2001.

Business Week, 1954. Jekyll Island Museum Archives, Jekyll Island.

Davis, Jingle. *Island Passages: An Illustrated History of Jekyll Island, Georgia*. Athens: University of Georgia Press, 2016.

Georgia Department of Commerce Newsletter, 1956. Jekyll Island Museum Archives, Jekyll Island.

Fish, Tallu. *Once Upon an Island. The Story of Fabulous Jekyll*. Jekyll Island: Mrs. Tallu Fish, 1959.

Jekyll Island Authority Meeting Minutes, 1950–1986. Jekyll Island Museum Archives. Jekyll Island.

Jekyll Island Club. *Meet Me on Jekyll Island*. Nashville: Southwestern Publishing Group, 2012.

Lake Lanier Islands Development Authority. *Building a Georgia Treasure, Celebrating 50 Years*. Ramsey: Smith Printing Co., LLC, 2015.

McCash, June Hall. *The Jekyll Island Cottage Colony*. Athens: University of Georgia Press, 1998.

McCash, June Hall, and Brenden Martin. *The Jekyll Island Club Hotel*. Virginia Beach: Donning Company Publishers, 2012.

McCash, William Barton, and June Hall McCash. *The Jekyll Island Club: Southern Haven for America's Millionaires.* Athens: University of Georgia Press, 1998.

National Geographic, 1971. Nick Doms, private collection. Savannah, Georgia.

New York Times, 1955. Jekyll Island Museum Archives, Jekyll Island.

Novotny, Patrick, PhD. *This Georgia Rising: Education, Civil Rights, And The Politics Of Elections In Georgia In The 1940s.* Mercer University Press, 2007.

Tallu Fish Scrapbooks, 1954–1970. Jekyll Island Museum Archives. Jekyll Island.

The *Brunswick News,* 1946–1961. Jekyll Island Museum Archives, Jekyll Island and Brunswick-Glynn County Library, Brunswick.

The *Florida Times-Union,* 1946–1985. Jekyll Island Museum Archives, Jekyll Island.

The Scenic South, 1958. Jekyll Island Museum Archives, Jekyll Island.

Secondary Sources

Jekyll Island Authority. Online www.jekyllisland.com.

Bagwell, Tyler E. Online www.jekyllislandhistory.com.

Online www.explorejekyllisland.com Stratatomic Web Design, Greenville, South Carolina.

Online http://neptune3.galib.uga.edu/ssp/cgi-bin/legis-idx.pl Athens, University of Georgia.

Egan, David, and Mindy. Online http://www.savejekyllisland.org/JRed1.html. Initiative to Protect Jekyll Island.

Galis, Leon. Online http://likethedew.com/2016/02/22/clearing-the-air-over-jekyll-island/.

Jekyll Island Authority. Online http://greenlaw.org/pdf/JIMPdraft9-16.pdf.

Online http://www.georgiaarchives.org/ Morrow: University System of Georgia.

Online http://www.theatlantic.com/.

Online http://www.crdl.usg.edu/ Civil Rights Digital Library.

Online http://www.rixen-cableways.com/en/investors/history/. Rixen Cableways GmbH.

Online http://www.georgiaencyclopedia.org/. New Georgia Encyclopedia.

Online https://en.wikipedia.org/. Wikimedia Foundation, Inc.

Online http://www.golflink.com/golf-vacations/georgia/johnny-paulk.

Online http://www.Jacksonville.com/. *Florida Times-Union.*

ABOUT THE AUTHOR

Nick Doms grew up in Belgium, where he initially studied nursing and medicine. He moved to Amsterdam in 1985 to pursue an MBA in international finance, which ultimately led to his career on Wall Street.

He lived and worked in the USA, United Kingdom, Japan, Australia, and Hong Kong until 2001 when he retired and moved to Savannah, Georgia, where he currently lives with his wife, Teolita.

He is the author of four poetry books: *Inspirational for a Day* (2003); *Colors* (2005); *I am, Ik ben, Ich bin, Je suis* (2008); *and Symbiosis* (2008).

From Millionaires to Commoners is his first nonfiction historical publication.

ABOUT THE BOOK

The transformation of a private, secluded, and exclusive island into a state park with open and affordable access to all Georgians requires a well-thought-out plan and the meticulous implementation afterward. It also necessitates a group of people inspired by M. E. Thompson's mandate to offer the island's amenities at the lowest rates "reasonable and possible" for the "ordinary people" of Georgia.

The story of Jekyll Island State Park is marred with politics since the early beginning, despite Gov. Talmadge's decision to create a Jekyll Island Authority, "To create a non-political authority and to remove Jekyll Island from politics" (*Brunswick News*, February 17, 1950).

Since the Authority Act specifically mandated that Jekyll Island be self-sufficient, it is fair to assume that the motivation behind the development was to create the necessitated amount of revenue centers to support the low-cost facilities that had to be included. Right from the beginning, this duality of revenue generation versus public and free cost centers took precedence over any type of vision the board members might have had. That duality is best described as the perpetual Dr. Jekyll and Mr. Hyde—that is, the battle between the year-round resort and the state park that still exists today.

It is remarkable that given the strict mandate and the lack of expertise in 1946, Jekyll Island has developed into what we see today, all while maintaining its natural beauty and surroundings.

The use of the present tense while narrating aids in creating understanding and amplifies the multitude of difficulties the early authority faced. It also enforces their daily struggle with the multifaceted problems and decisions that had to be made mostly immediately and with little time to digest the consequences of their decisions.

The intention of this book is not to question the destiny of the island but merely expose, clarify, and narrate the road traveled so that we may see the road ahead more clearly.